Remembering John Hanson

Underground Railroad Free Press
2455 Ballenger Creek Pike
Adamstown, Maryland, 21710
Publisher@urrFreePress.com

REMEMBERING JOHN HANSON

Live appearances: Author@RememberingJohnHanson.com
Website: RememberingJohnHanson.com
Editing: Word Spectrum, WordSpectrum.com

Library of Congress Control Number: 2011961544
Library of Congress Cataloging-in-Publication Data

Michael, Peter H.
  Remembering John Hanson: A Biography of the First
  President of the Original United States Government

  Includes bibliographic references and index.
  1. John Hanson (1715-1721). 2. United States presidents.
3. United States—History—Revolutionary War. 4.United
States—Politics and government—1765-1783. 5. Articles of
Confederation. 6. Jane Hanson.

ISBN-13: 978-0-615-62107-4 (Hardcover)
ISBN-10: 0-615-62107-4 (Hardcover)
ISBN-13: 978-1-4679-5806-6 (Paperback)
ISBN-10: 1-4679-5806-9 (Paperback)
ISBN-13: 978-1-51346-882-7 (E-book)
—

The cover's John Hanson presidential portrait was painted by Charles Willson Peale, famed portraitist of early presidents and Revolutionary War leaders. Among Peale's first, Hanson's portrait set the style for his portraits of official subjects in bust pose with colorful classic backgrounds sitting at slight angle to the painter. Peale's John Hanson portrait hangs in the Independence Hall Portrait Collection in Philadelphia and is owned by the National Park Service which operates Independence Hall National Historical Park. Some years ago, the portrait collection was moved to the adjacent Second Bank of the United States building.

Advance Praise for Remembering John Hanson

The author's meticulous research and irrefutable arguments show that the "indispensable man" in 1781, when the United States of America first took its place among the nations of the world, was John Hanson. While the country was still celebrating the surrender of Gen. Cornwallis at Yorktown and the end of hostilities with the British, the United States in Congress Assembled met to organize the new government and elect its first president. Among all the luminaries recognized today as founders of our country, they chose John Hanson to be their first leader. This book tells why, and in so doing casts much-needed light on an undeservedly neglected moment at the beginnings of our nation's history.

William Van der Mei, author

Δ

This work represents the most comprehensive and — equally important — extensively documented exploration of the life and contributions of John Hanson. It provides the context and critical analysis to properly elevate Hanson to the pantheon of the fathers of our nation.

Aldan Weinberg, Professor of Journalism and Director of the Communications Arts Program, Hood College

Δ

You contribute greatly to our understanding of Hanson, his times, and why he became largely forgotten by the mid-nineteenth century. *Remembering John Hanson* is also clearly and engagingly written, with excellent illustrations.

Ralph Levering, Professor of History, Davidson College

Δ

I have found your information to confirm my arguments why John Hanson was the most significant first president of the United States. The story of John Hanson is much greater than previous authors have given credit to.

John Cummings, author on John Hanson

Δ

Some of the best information on Hanson I have ever seen.

Edward Edelen, Founder, The John Hanson Institute

Also by Peter H. Michael

All Peter Michael books may be ordered at Remembering-JohnHanson.com, Amazon.com or anywhere books are sold.

Palace of Yawns

Palace of Yawns is a fast-moving, remarkably adventurous journal of the year Peter Michael spent in Thailand fully engaged in the cultural and historical time and place that was Southeast Asia in 1975 while directing a key multinational United Nations project. Khmer Rouge, Bangkok diplomatic nightlife, tranquil Buddhist monks, Thai princesses, Soviet spies, cave temples, cobras, a Nobel Prize and more crowd these pages. In some passages, the reader will find it hard to believe that *Palace of Yawns* is nonfiction. Buy or learn more at Amazon.com.

Guide to Freedom: Rediscovering the Underground Railroad In One United States County

An expert compilation of research by the author and others of more than sixty rediscovered Underground Railroad safe-houses, routes and personages of Frederick County, Maryland, and nearby. This book uses a groundbreaking method for assessing the authenticity of Underground Railroad site claims. *Guide to Freedom* also provides detailed entries on several of the nation's most important Underground Railroad sites nearby including the original Uncle Tom's Cabin, and several highly charged accounts of Underground Railroad escapes including one through the author's farm. Buy or learn more at Amazon.com or urrguide.com.

An American Family of the Underground Railroad

A very readable and heavily documented history of the author's ancestors' involvement in the Underground Railroad and the family's fights for racial justice in the United States during the twentieth century. In a rare account, the book sheds light on one of the most courageous and now famous escapes of the Underground Railroad and its direct conjunction with the author's family then and today. Buy or learn more at Amazon.com or freedomrailroad.com.

Above all for my mother
Mary Agnes Hanson Michael
and also for my grandparents
Robert Winder Hanson II
and Mary Agnes Price Hanson
for their keeping the flame of John Hanson burning
and instilling in my brother and me the
importance of the nation's first president

Contents

Acknowledgements

I am grateful to a number of people for materials provided, research assistance, editing, reviews of drafts and encouragement as I wrote *Remembering John Hanson*.

I am particularly indebted to Professor Aldan Weinberg, attorney and novelist William Van der Mei and Hanson descendant Mary Jo Pundt for their incisive critiques of drafts of *Remembering John Hanson* and for their many useful suggestions made from their vantages as journalist, author and genealogist, respectively. Professor Weinberg has also been indispensable in publicizing the John Hanson Memorial Association's work in re-illuminating President John Hanson and in his faithful service as an officer and director of the Association. Ms. Pundt's Hanson family genealogy containing over 4,000 names which she has complied over many years, by far the best genealogy ever on the Hanson family, has been invaluable in the research for *Remembering John Hanson.* She descends from President John Hanson's grandfather, also named John Hanson, through the senior John Hanson's eldest son Robert. My long-time close friend, backpacking partner and novelist Bill Van der Mei has given me any amount of useful advice over many years not the least of which has been on *Remembering John Hanson*.

I am grateful to Professor Ralph Levering of Davidson College, a John Hanson scholar, who reviewed an early draft of *Remembering John Hanson* and offered useful suggestions and encouragement. As the reader will note, I have relied frequently on the scholarship and insights of Professor Levering's *John Hanson: Public Servant*, though brief, the best annotated work on John Hanson used in writing *Remembering John Hanson.*

I gratefully acknowledge Judge John Hanson Briscoe, Robert Hanson and John C. Hanson for their constant, thoughtful and much appreciated encouragement on this book and especially for their work as directors of the John Hanson Memorial Association. Judge Briscoe, a relative of President John Hanson through the president's sister Chloe, has done as much as anyone during and since his stint as Speaker of the Maryland House of Delegates in the 1970s to keep John Hanson's name alive and to rekindle the nation's memory of the president. For this, the nation and posterity owe John Briscoe a debt of gratitude. As much as anyone, Judge

Briscoe has steadily and incisively encouraged me in the writing of *Remembering John Hanson.*

I am much in the debt of Edward and Lexy Edelen, owners of Mulberry Grove, the first home of John and Jane Hanson, for their unflagging support as I wrote, and for opening Mulberry Grove for viewing and an overnight stay. Ed is also a member of the Board of Directors of the John Hanson Memorial Association. He and I continue to explore how best to coordinate the work of his planned John Hanson Institute and the John Hanson Memorial Association which I chair at the time of this writing. The strong mutual interest in John Hanson has made the Edelens and the Michaels colleagues and friends.

I thank the 2009-10 Frederick County, Maryland, delegation to the Maryland General Assembly, particularly Delegate Galen Clagett and Senator David Brinkley and their staff members for assistance in researching State funding for the John Hanson National Memorial, submitting a successful Maryland state bond bill for the Memorial, and their very enthusiastic encouragement of the John Hanson National Memorial project and this book. I am also grateful to the 2011-12 delegation for their unanimous interest in the John Hanson statue in National Statuary Hall of the United States Capitol. I am particularly grateful to Maryland Senator Ronald Young and former Delegates Sue Hecht and Richard Weldon for their enthusiastic support and encouragement.

I am especially indebted to former Frederick, Maryland, Mayor Paul Gordon and to Frances A. Randall, Chair of the Board of Directors of *The Frederick News-Post,* both ardent and prolific historians of Frederick County and Frederick where John Hanson rose to political prominence. The two patiently, often and with much astuteness illuminated for me a long list of important points on local history, much of which I might not have otherwise uncovered in my research. From these two friends, I have a bolstered appreciation of the indispensability of local historians.

My friend Fergus Bordewich, author on the Underground Railroad, the American Indian, the founding of the nation's capital, the Kansas-Nebraska Act, old Cathay and many other historical topics, provided astute recommendations on topical perspective, research and the current publishing environment, and otherwise just good conversation.

I am thankful to Bordewich, Weinberg, Knox College Professor of History Owen Muelder and Chad Baker, Director of

Museums at the Maryland School for the Deaf, for their thoughtful opinions on why the 1780s have been neglected by historians and writers on United States history.

Underground Railroad author Karolyn Smardz Frost, former Executive Director of Canada's Ontario Historical Society, provided intriguing and rare information on Josiah Henson, one of the most famous Underground Railroad freedom seekers, and on what she suspected as Henson's blood relationship to the Hanson family, a suspicion investigated in *Remembering John Hanson* and shown here to be all but certainly correct.

I thank Burton Kummerow, Director of the Maryland Historical Society, for his keen interest in all things Hanson, for the Society's forthcoming 2012 exhibit on John Hanson, and for his encouragement of this book. The staff and volunteers of the Maryland Historical Society's fine H. Furlong Baldwin Library, especially Marc Thomas, Iris Bierlein and Kathryn McDermott, were very knowledgeable and helpful as I made my way through their library's unmatched collection of Hansoniana. Heather Haggstrom, Collections Manager of the Maryland Historical Society, was most accommodating in opening to me the Society's rare unmatched collection of original oil portraits of Jane and John Hanson and many of their family members, and in researching the donors of the collection. The Society's extensive Hanson holdings are listed in one of the bibliographies here.

Especially accommodating and enthusiastic in researching John Hanson official and family records were Maryland State Archivist and Hanson writer Edward Papenfuse and Jennifer Hafner, Deputy Director for Research at the Maryland State Archives. Mary Clare Briscoe McNatt of the National Archives headquarters in Washington, DC, a relative of President Hanson through the president's sister Chloe, and Marie Washburn and Brigette Kamsler, Archivists at the Historical Society of Frederick County, Maryland, were very helpful and unfailingly cheerful in guiding me through their institutions' Hanson holdings. Ms. McNatt also arranged a private tour of a very infrequent showing of the original Articles of Confederation.

I most appreciate the wealth of information provided by Barbara Zipp and her sons Luke and Brandt on the treasure trove of information involved in the auction by their Crocker Farm auction house of John Hanson possessions and related items in September, 2011. Barbara Zipp's transcriptions of the nearly 150 Civil War letters between President

John Hanson's great-grandson John Hanson Thomas, Jr. and his wife have been most illuminating and useful to me in rounding out the picture of the Hanson family as it descended from the President.

Several people were key in my long search in rediscovering the lost burial sites of Jane and John Hanson. Jennifer Stabler, historian with the Maryland-National Capital Park and Planning Commission, was essential in locating and providing maps and archeological survey reports which were the keys in my rediscovery of John Hanson's burial site. Ms. Stabler also uncovered various archived documents which, when pieced together with other research, finally illuminated the astonishing account of what happened to the crypt where President Hanson had been interred in 1783 and to John Hanson's coffin and body. Mark Mittereder of the Peterson Companies, owner of the property where the John Hanson burial site lies, kindly opened the ancient Addison Cemetery near the John Hanson burial site for me to inspect.

Bruce Champion and C. Larry Bishop of the Frederick, Maryland chapter of the Sons of the American Revolution were very generous in sharing their research on Jane and John Hanson. Larry Bishop had done as much as anyone in trying to solve the mystery of Jane Hanson's burial place. Ronald Pearcey, Superintendent of Mount Olivet Cemetery in Frederick, was especially helpful in assisting Bishop and me in researching the very well kept burial records of his cemetery in our successful quest to locate the grave of Jane Hanson. Alyssia Gilbert of the Episcopal Churches of Frederick, Maryland, was also helpful in this quest.

Hannah Westall of Girton College, Cambridge University, and Annabel Peacock of the Bodleian Library, Oxford University, were very informative and quick to respond to my inquiries about their universities' student archives regarding John Hanson's time in England in the 1730s.

I am also grateful to the late Peter Craig, Fellow of the American Society of Genealogists, who provided much useful information on the contentious mystery of President John Hanson's ancestry. John Cummings has been generous in sharing results of his research on Hanson family ancestry.

I am most grateful to my wife Vicki Michael who for more than three years provided any amount of encouragement as I wrote and on more than one occasion waited for me to join her in doing one thing or another after hearing, "Just another few minutes; I'm almost finished with this paragraph." As a professional editor, she expertly edited, critiqued and proofread *Remembering John Hanson* for which I am most grateful.

My highest thanks go to my mother, Mary Agnes Hanson Michael, and to my maternal grandparents, Mary Agnes Price Hanson and Robert Winder "Rob" Hanson II, who are the main reasons for my deep interest in President John Hanson. I did not have the privilege of knowing my grandfather Rob Hanson who died eight years before I was born and who during his lifetime put together a nice collection of published and unpublished materials on John Hanson and his presidency that I inherited.

I well recall while growing up and in young adulthood my grandmother and mother speaking often and fondly of their John Hanson legacy. It is an understatement to say that they took pains to drill this into my brother and me. My grandmother Aggie Hanson, as she was called, who had married into the Hanson family, took special pride in Hanson family history and became quite a student and expositor of it herself. I should mention that my father, Pierce Baynard Michael, Sr., who also had married into the Hanson family, made it a point to absorb the detail of the history of his distinguished in-law family and help to ensure that his sons knew it. In retrospect, I treasure the diligent job that my parents and Hanson grandparents did in passing down an important national and family history. If they hadn't, it is very doubtful that *Remembering John Hanson*, the John Hanson National Memorial and the John Hanson Memorial Association would have been forthcoming. Following their fine examples, I am endeavoring to keep this flame burning with my children, grandchildren and you with *Remembering John Hanson.*

Any errors here are mine solely and not the responsibility of those acknowledged or others.

Peter Hanson Michael
Cooling Springs Farm
Adamstown, Maryland

December, 2011

Foreword: Indispensable Founder

Remembering John Hanson reintroduces the now nearly forgotten John Hanson, collects, amplifies and clarifies the historical record on him and his presidency, corrects some irritating modern myths about him and the nation's first government, the United States in Congress Assembled, resolves two long-standing mysteries about him and his wife Jane Hanson, and burnishes John Hanson's deserved high reputation as the indispensable Founding Father which he was in the dawn of the United States.

In part, *Remembering John Hanson* has been undertaken in support of the John Hanson National Memorial which seeks to better memorialize John Hanson through the programs of the John Hanson Memorial Association in his adopted hometown of Frederick, Maryland, where he came to national political prominence during the Revolutionary War and as President. The Memorial project and *Remembering John Hanson* also enthusiastically support Edward and Lexy Edelen's planned John Hanson Institute at Port Tobacco, Charles County, Maryland, near Mulberry Grove, John Hanson's first home now owned by Mr. and Mrs. Edelen.

Much of my motivation in writing *Remembering John Hanson* and in promoting the two projects stems from my being a Hanson family descendant steeped in Hansoniana by my mother and grandmother while I was growing up. Because they represented the last generations of surnamed Hansons in our line of the family, they made a point of schooling my brother and me in Hanson family history, on the key roles that John Hanson played in the Revolutionary War and birth of the United States, and especially on the Hanson presidency.

Writing of Charles County, Maryland, the seat of President John Hanson's branch of the Hanson family, Walter Hanson Stone Taylor, President Hanson's great-great-grandnephew, wrote in 1874, "From having been the most, they are now the least numerous of the old families still residing in the county."[1] This decline continued and the author's uncle, Robert Bennett Hanson who died in 1965 having had no children, was the last of the direct Hanson male line in his branch of the family, which is related to President John Hanson's line through the president's grandfather. To keep the name alive, the author's middle name is Hanson as is his son's first name. Lengthy research has not identified any living direct descendants of President Hanson who carry the family surname today, or any others, but possibly there could be some in a distant Hanson line.

The earliest writing which could be considered a biography of John Hanson is that by the president's great-grandson, Dr. John Hanson Thomas, Jr. in 1875. In 1898, Dr. Thomas's son, Douglas Hamilton Thomas, on assignment from the Maryland General Assembly, wrote the second John Hanson biography as the case for Hanson's inclusion in National Statuary Hall of the United States Capitol. The 1930s produced a spate of three John Hanson biographies, all obviously deeply researched but none annotated and only one with a short bibliography. In 1976, Ralph Levering authored a brief but well researched, written and annotated thirty-six-page monograph on John Hanson. Until *Remembering John Hanson*, these six publications have comprised the main body of John Hanson biography. A fuller accounting of these works may be found in the first bibliography here.

Remembering John Hanson collects the Hanson record which re-illuminates that he was an indispensable Founder in forging United States independence, raising money, materiel and militias to prosecute the Revolutionary War, solving the impasse over the western lands, brokering the Articles of Confederation, creating the first United States government, keeping the nation whole, and serving as the first president of this original government.

My sources in compiling this biography have relied mainly on the collection of published and unpublished Hansoniana which I inherited from my mother and her parents, my own expansion of this collection including a number of old hard-to-acquire publications on John Hanson, sources cited in this personal collection, the John Hanson collections in a number of libraries, especially those of the Maryland Historical Society, the Historical Society of Frederick County, Maryland, Southern Maryland College and the Maryland State Archives, Hanson's official presidential records at the National Archives, land records of Charles County and Frederick County, Maryland, an exceptionally complete Hanson family genealogy, the oral traditions concerning President Hanson handed down in several branches of the Hanson family and elsewhere, correspondence with John Hanson scholars, authors and genealogists, and carefully vetted Internet sources. The many other sources used less often than those mentioned here number over three hundred and are listed in the book's six bibliographies.

Regarding online sources, it is essential to warn the reader that much of what one finds on the Internet regarding President Hanson is erroneous, some of it wildly so. He was not the third (or fourth) but the first president. He was not the first Black president. He was not the grandson of an indentured servant. He does not appear on the back of the two-dollar bill. He was not a signer of the Declaration of Independence but of the Articles of Confederation. His wife Jane did not outlive all of their children. Not only is the Internet a superior means of propagating accurate information on virtually any topic, it is equally efficient at spreading inaccuracies which unfortunately is the case with much, perhaps even a majority, of the Internet's information available on John Hanson. This problem is serious enough to warrant a section of its own in *Remembering John Hanson* and a formal effort by the John Hanson Memorial Association to correct the John Hanson Internet record.

Sources which I have used more sparingly consist for the most part of the Maryland State Archives' extant official records of Hanson's time in the colonial Maryland legislature, the Maryland Committee of Correspondence and then the state's General Assembly after independence was declared. I have inspected all I could find of the little that remains of Hanson's personal records, much of which were lost by a historian in 1836 along with George Washington's diary from November 6, 1781, the day after John Hanson was inaugurated as president, to August 31, 1784.[2] The remnants of President Hanson's personal records, which include some of his once voluminous personal correspondence, reside almost entirely in the John Hanson Collection at the H. Furlong Baldwin Library of the Maryland Historical Society, and in much lesser volume in several collections of the Pennsylvania Historical Society and collections of other important historical figures of the era. Reliable sources which made good scholarly use of these collections have also been employed in preparing *Remembering John Hanson* and are cited here.

I have frequently quoted from or otherwise referenced John Hanson's fifty-four extant letters to his son-in-law Philip Thomas and to others. In each case of direct quotation, I have presented what Hanson wrote exactly as he wrote it, preserving his forms of English usage of the era including all differences from today's usages in punctuation, capitalization and spelling. Most of what John Hanson wrote before and during his presidency to Philip Thomas is woven into *Remembering John Hanson* in a number of places as appropriate, and comprises the best window on the personal John Hanson.

What I set out to produce is the best possible, most complete, accurate and appealing biography of John Hanson to date. While past biographers obviously poured heart, soul and talent into their Hanson biographies, there was no existing work on John Hanson which had collected all available references on him in one volume, annotated carefully, and provided a thorough bibliography of sources. With more than seventy years having gone by since their biographies other than Ralph Levering's short monograph in 1976, it seemed that time was running out on reviving the memory of John Hanson, hence *Remembering John Hanson.*

I very much hope that mine is not the last John Hanson biography but, if it is, I wanted it to be more rather than less detailed. Therefore, I have leaned rather heavily toward inclusion of information rather than omission to get as much as possible into the record for the benefit of readers, future John Hanson researchers, posterity and as complete a record as possible. This is why the endnotes and bibliographies make up so much of the book. At many junctures in writing, decisions had to be made on how much detail to include in the body of the book versus what to provide in endnotes instead. I have tried to strike a balance in this regard while at the same time leaning heavily toward inclusion of material one place or the other. This has resulted in an abundance of endnotes, some of which are lengthy, to keep tangential or finely detailed information out of the body of the book and provide a smoother passage for the reader. However, there is a good bit of important material placed in the endnotes, much of which will prove essential to the researcher. Readers are encouraged to refer to the endnotes.

Particularly because I am a Hanson family descendant related to the subject of this biography, I have taken special pains to stay away from any writing flavor which might in the slightest appear hagiographic. I have asked the reviewers of *Remembering John Hanson* to be especially watchful on this score and they report no transgressions into undue praise, avoidance of critical assessment or familial favors. I have not been reluctant to take John Hanson to task in instances in which he erred, especially on his being a slave holder. At the same time, I have found that it was not always easy to write with an objective hand given a subject who accomplished so much of importance and deserves far more recognition today than he has received. In this circumstance, I have made special effort to give John Hanson his fair, complete and accurate biographical due while at the same time steering clear of embellishment. *Remembering John Hanson* would have been easier to write if I were not related to John Hanson.

At least in Maryland, one still hears the historically factual boast that it was John Hanson rather than George Washington who was the nation's first president. One often hears this dismissed out of hand by those who have no real grasp of the national record on the matter including a few historians and others who ought to know better. In fact, as the historical record clearly demonstrates, both Hanson and Washington were first presidents, Hanson under our nation's original government, the United States in Congress Assembled, and then Washington under our second and present constitutional government, and this is just how Hanson, Washington and others of their fabulous time saw it. Further, the two presidents and their peers also understood that the two governments served only one nation and that Hanson, preceding Washington in office, therefore was in fact the nation's first president. Washington and other presidents well into the twentieth century affirmed this in their writings and utterances.

For the sacrifices of sons, treasure, health and his waning time which he bore during the Revolutionary War, for the indispensable leadership which he exhibited in getting a doubting Maryland to subscribe to the Declaration of Independence, for his solving of the western lands impasse to permit the very founding of the United States, for the admiration shown him by the Founding Fathers and other national heroes of his era who unanimously chose him as the nation's first president, and for the unparalleled new ground which he and his finely chosen cabinet so necessarily and adroitly broke in his presidential administration, John Hanson deserves far better than he has received from the nation which he served so extraordinarily well and selflessly at its birth.

We will see here his two nation-saving deeds and exactly why some of the greatest Americans who ever lived looked to John Hanson to be their nation's first president. We will also see why the nation he was pivotal in creating barely recalls him today. And here we will see solved all of the old Hanson mysteries but one, and new myths about John Hanson answered and put to rest.

My fond hope is that *Remembering John Hanson* does its

part in furthering President John Hanson's long overdue recognition and rekindles his nation's affection for him.

Prologue

The scene above is of the signing of the Articles of Confederation by the delegates to the Second Continental Congress on March 1, 1781. The artist is unknown. We see Maryland Delegate John Hanson, quill in hand and last to sign, with his signature ratifying the Articles of Confederation creating the nation's first government, the United States in Congress Assembled, of which he would be elected its and the nation's first president.

Timely Providence

When they laid him to rest, he was revered and sorely mourned by Washington, Adams, Jefferson, Franklin, Hancock and the other American icons of his day and by the entire new breed he had done so much to help bring into being, his countrymen now known the world over as Americans. Only the year before he had been their president and he was their new nation's first former president to die.

In the few years before, his fledgling nation teetered on the edge of history, its precarious condition no match for its soaring ideals. Its starving army was fighting the mightiest on Earth. Revolutionary patriots were tracked down and executed. The colonies' and then the states' funding of the Revolutionary War was voluntary, sporadic and sparse. Without a government, the United States were still plural, remaining sovereign states in nearly every respect, united in name only. The states' consultative body, the Second Continental Congress, was weak, impoverished, poorly attended and no substitute for a government. Only three years before, ratification of the Articles of Confederation to form the nation's first government was being held off in state after state for quarrelsome parochial interests, stalling nationhood in its tracks. No, in the years leading up to his presidency, the New World's grand republican democratic experiment faced the entirely plausible prospects of only a brief sickly life and collapse.

Even today, what followed seems miraculous. Not only were the more fortunate states persuaded to subordinate their substantial advantages for the sake of nationhood but, after the glowing propositions of the Declaration of Independence, the nation's first government was put forth in yet another ringing American document, the Articles of Confederation. But as the era's history played itself out, these crucial steps could take place only if fortune produced a transformational figure possessing the personal power to gather up and articulate the aspirations of his countrymen into a vision which would rise above dispute and to which all would subscribe.

Such a man, if he existed, would be the new nation's best, perhaps only, chance to bring forth its first breath. The brave, esteemed and sacrificing Washington, leader of the heroic rag-tag Continental Army and the one eventually to claim the mantle of father of his country, did not step for-

ward. The brilliant Jefferson, he of the incandescent prose
of the nation's founding declaration to the world, held back.
The polymath Franklin, perhaps brightest of them all, chose
sage mentorship as his place. Not Adams, nor Hancock, nor
Hamilton, nor Henry, nor any signer of the Declaration of
Independence, nor any other but one did the Founders
summon to take on the challenge.

To borrow from William Manchester's apt appraisal of Churchill as he formed his government after all seemed lost following Dunkirk, a most timely providence in the early 1780s
called forth an American who by personal example gave his
countrymen a heroic vision of what they and their nation
might become, who gathered the blazing light of his young
nation's aspirations into his prism and directed it to his and
his country's ends, who imprinted his will and vision on his
people and had them cherish it, who possessed the personal
power to bring his country to life after its bloody birth without diluting its visionary ideals.

Such a man, if he existed, would face a more than Churchil-
lian challenge. While Churchill inherited an appeasing but
functioning government, the new American leader would
have to fashion one from whole cloth, his country's first.
This man, if he existed, would need to possess such a compelling character as could kindle from the embers of his
countrymen's hopes the fire of a people transformed, a beacon of liberty and reason new to the world, charging them
with his vision and, from the world over, beckoning others to
its promise.

From Maryland, there was such a man and in 1780 the
stage was his. He had given up comfortable Tidewater
Maryland plantation life to attain colony-wide political power
in Frederick, a roiling frontier town where a raw electorate
resonated with his ideas of nationhood. He had led Maryland in opposing British rule and become a key Revolutionary War financier, militia raiser and arms agent. When his
state alone had demurred on declaring independence with
the other colonies, he, with sheer force of persuasion and at
the last minute, had moved Maryland into making the union
whole. He would lose two of his three sons to the war. But
more than any other gift to his country, he, when all others
had failed the challenge, persuaded the states with large
trans-Appalachian land grants to cede those lands to the
new nation permitting political parity among the states.
Only this nation-saving plan that became named for him
permitted the thirteen entirely independent nation-states to

then charter and form a unified nation and government.

Americans celebrate July 4, 1776, as Independence Day but in fact the consummation of nationhood was not attained until November 5, 1781, a day now all but forgotten in American history. The Declaration of Independence had spoken only of thirteen colonies which announced their respective independence as associated but independent nation-states. In fact, for another seven years they fought more as allies than as part of the same nation. Upon declaring independence, there was a war to be won, the western lands impasse to be resolved, a governing charter to be thrashed out, and a viable government yet to be launched. United nationhood was not to be chartered until the ratification of the Articles of Confederation on March 1, 1781, nor finally attained until the first government was organized on November 5, 1781, a now obscure nation-defining day in American history. Until that day, although the war's last major battle had been fought the month before, it was the long-time friend, mentor and self-effacing ally of George Washington who had cleared the political impasses that stood in the way of the new nation, completed the founding charter, and formed and led the first government.

In the eight months after ratification of the Articles of Confederation which created the framework for the first government, there was intense assessment of possible candidates to become the nation's first president that fall. On November 5, 1781, the delegates to the new government, the United States in Congress Assembled, including the American icons mentioned, the best of the best the new nation had to offer, knew acutely at that golden hour that they must choose the very best among them to lead the first government of the United States, he least likely to fail the challenge. In that all-important convening in Independence Hall of the new nation's best that morning, when the last star finally aligned for the actual birth of the United States, all eyes fell on Maryland's John Hanson who was elected unanimously.

Why has John Hanson become so thoroughly neglected by history? Of all of the key figures of the Revolutionary War era and the founding of the United States, none appears to have slipped further from the nation's memory. A century ago, Hanson was still well remembered, particularly in his native Maryland. In 1903, the Maryland General Assembly chose Hanson as one of two Marylanders to be honored with a statue in National Statuary Hall of the United States Capitol. In the 1930s there was an outpouring of three Hanson biographies. A John Hanson Society was active in Maryland until the 1980s, and at about that time highways, schools and even a savings and loan association were being named for Hanson. But even before then, the nation's memory of John Hanson had begun to ebb and we now see perhaps the majority of historians confused about the Hanson record, many of them altogether unaware of his contributions or who he was. This fading national memory has led Wikipedia, Snopes and several other amateur history websites to propagate a number of odd inaccuracies about President Hanson, the Hanson lineage, his public record, and the nation's first government, the United States in Congress Assembled.

History has let John Hanson's friend George Washington take on the claim of first president which Washington himself said he wasn't, the plain fact so routinely ignored in nearly all histories on their era. Long after the deaths of both of these Founding Fathers and of all who had first-hand knowledge of this turning point in the nation's history, Washington has been given the honor of remembrance as the first president. He wasn't and it takes nothing from his irreplaceable contribution to his country's birth to recognize this. Washington was the first President to hold the office under the Constitution that remains in effect, as amended, to this day. But the United States was a nation for eight years before his inauguration in 1789, operating under its original constitution, the Articles of Confederation of 1781. During the years of the first government, there were nine presidents of whom John Hanson was the first, and Hanson deserves to be remembered as such. The astounding confluence of blows to his nation's memory of him does not excuse the virtual abandonment of the man who was in fact the first president or that his indispensible accomplishments have increasingly been relegated to the dusty back shelves of American history.

When they laid him to rest in 1783 and the nation he had done so much to usher onto the world stage grieved the loss of its first president, little could his countrymen anticipate that even his burial place would become unknown, an astounding climax to a tragic historical obliteration of an indispensible and sterling American performance.

Here is the story of the most forgotten major figure in American history.

Part I

Mulberry Grove: Birth of an American Outlook

The Hanson Family's Arrival In America

In looking at the life of John Hanson, one cannot help but be struck by the several coincidences of history which have obscured his record. Aside from being the most forgotten major figure of his era or indeed probably in the nation's history, certainly as much sheer mystery and historical inaccuracy surround John Hanson as any of the Founders of the United States. For example, there is widespread modern confusion even among some historians over which of the four bodies of the Revolutionary War era was and wasn't a government and that the United States In Congress Assembled of which John Hanson was the first president was in fact a government and the nation's first. Adding to the confusion, a historian who in 1836 had borrowed much of the personal papers of John Hanson and some of George Washington's diaries to write a history on the collaboration between the two men never returned these two vital national collections, now lost. Most astonishingly, for most of the twentieth century and into the twenty-first, John Hanson's gravesite became uncertain. Obscuring John Hanson's record more, there is probably no other Founder of the nation about whom there is more misinformation on the Internet than John Hanson.

The earliest of the mysteries surrounding John Hanson is his ancestry. While his lineage is not essential to portraying Hanson's life and official record, it is necessary for the biographer to comment on how the Hanson family arrived in America since a modern dispute on this point occupies much of the contemporary conversation about John Hanson. Four possibilities have been put forth, two of them as serious competing claims, as to how the immigrant Hanson from whom President John Hanson descends arrived in America.

For more than a century, the account provided in 1876 in George Hanson's *Old Kent*[3], that President John Hanson's grandfather of the same name was one of four brothers who arrived in America in 1642, was accepted and unquestioned. In 1988, the genealogist George Russell claimed in a published article that George Hanson's work not only was incorrect but a deliberate hoax. Russell then mistakenly hypothesized that President John Hanson descended from one John Henson (*sic*), an indentured servant from Barbados who arrived in Maryland in 1661, several years after the first John Hanson shows up in colonial records.

A third possibility advanced by the historian and genealogist

Harry Newman in 1940 involves another John Hanson who arrived in the colony with five relatives later in the 1660s, a conjecture all but disproven here. A fourth conjecture put forth is Newman's hypothesis that the immigrant John Hanson could have been the son of Sir Robert Hanson, Lord Mayor of London, an intriguing possibility which has strong circumstantial support explored in an appendix here. The sorting out of the debate over which of these four possibilities reveals the president's ancestry — if indeed any of them does — and refutation of several modern myths regarding John Hanson's ancestry are presented at length in this appendix. The reader is invited to inspect this critical analysis of the four claims and the conclusion that none of them is yet conclusive as to John Hanson's ancestry. The only agreement among the four theories of ancestry is that President John Hanson descended from a namesake immigrant grandfather John Hanson.

In any case, the future President Hanson was born into a family with an already well established tradition of leadership. His grandfather, from whom he inherited his name, arrived in America already possessed of the qualities, and apparently the status, that made him a leader in his new land. The children of the next generation, including Judge Samuel Hanson, father of the future President, continued on in a tradition of highest influence and public service.

Planter Life and Mulberry Grove

Over the nearly four hundred years since its first English arrivals, the area along the sides of Maryland's Port Tobacco River where the Hansons would settle and establish a dynasty would become one of the first European settlements in the American colonies in the early seventeenth century, grow into an important colonial port and commercial center, then waste itself through soil exhaustion from the overplanting of tobacco in the eighteenth century, see itself eclipsed as its county's seat of government in the nineteenth, dwindle from bustling center to just a few buildings, then experience a mild historical revival in the twentieth century.

When Captain John Smith of the year-old colony at Jamestown, Virginia, sailed up the Port Tobacco River in 1608 during his exploration of the Chesapeake Bay and its tributaries, the journal and map which he compiled show him landing at a Native American village then located at the site of today's Port Tobacco, Maryland. He was met by local Native Americans who called their village, depending on which European transliterated its name, Pretafacco, Poto-paco, Potobac or Portobatoo, meaning, in each rendition, "between the hills." The first European to settle the area was the Jesuit priest Andrew White who had arrived among the first European settlers of the western shore of the Chesapeake Bay when they landed at nearby St. Clement's Island in 1634. Kent Island, the colony's first settlement, had been settled on the opposite shore of the bay in 1631. Father White lived amongst the Potobac Indians, complied a dictionary, grammar and catechism of their language, and became Maryland's first historian.

The second settler of the area was Job Chandler to whom in 1638 Governor Leonard Calvert granted 6,000 acres on both sides of the river. The following year, Chandler built Chandler's Hope above the eastern bank of the river directly adjacent to where the Hansons would settle in a few years. Chandler fashioned his new home after the one he had left in Lancashire, England, and named it in the hope of persuading Anne Thoroughgood of Lynnhaven, Virginia, to marry him and make real his new home's name. Job and Anne were married in 1650. Chandler's Hope is believed to be the oldest surviving frame structure in Maryland and perhaps on the eastern seaboard. It is still occupied as a home and has been featured on Charles County home tours. In 1921, the home was purchased and carefully restored by Henry DeMott.

In the early seventeenth century, the Native American village of Potobac morphed into the mostly English Port Tobacco and began living up to its adapted name. This makes Port Tobacco one of the oldest towns in the English-settled parts of the United States. When Job Chandler died in 1658, his eldest son William inherited the property and that year deeded sixty acres for a town site at first known as Chandler's Town and not long afterward as Port Tobacco. Charles County, Maryland, was chartered in 1658 and on April 13 of that year Port Tobacco was established as the county seat. The first Masonic Lodge in Maryland was founded there the following year. Old Christ Church in Port Tobacco was dedicated in 1692 following the founding of Christ Church at nearby Durham Parish in 1666. St. Ignatius Catholic Church and Convent, established near Port Tobacco in 1641 by Father Andrew White, are the oldest in the United States.

In 1656, the immigrant John Hanson, President John Hanson's grandfather, accompanied William Stone, Governor of colonial Maryland from 1649 until 1656, into the Potobac country and chose as his home site a picturesque spot on the east side of the river with a grand view of the lovely valley through which the river flows. The Governor settled two miles upstream on another hilltop looking down the river toward its confluence with the Potomac several miles away.

Colonial civil records and those of Mulberry Grove, the Hanson estate where the future president was born, show a land grant to the immigrant John Hanson in 1656 when he is thought to have been twenty-six years old, and within a short time after his arrival in the county, probably the same year.[4] Possession of such a large tract so quickly indicates that the immigrant arrived with wealth and influence. This John Hanson thus arrived in the part of Maryland which would become Charles County at least two years before the county was created in 1658. Twentieth-century historian and Hanson genealogist Harry Newman finds this John Hanson, by then Colonel Hanson, appearing in Charles County colonial civil records by 1672, fourteen years after the county was chartered.[5]

Maryland's first European settlers of the western shore of the Chesapeake Bay had set sail from Cowes, Isle of Wight, England, on November 22, 1633, aboard the *Ark* and *Dove*, made stops in the Madeiras, the Canary Islands, several Caribbean islands and at the Jamestown colony in Virginia, and on August 15, 1634, reached St. Clement's Island in the Potomac River, a few miles upstream from its confluence with the Chesapeake Bay. The island being only four hundred acres, the colonists shortly after left it and sailed twenty miles east and up the St. Mary's River to establish St. Mary's County and City, the first capital of the province of Maryland.

Contiguous to St. Mary's County, Charles County was proclaimed in 1658 by Josias Fendall, fourth colonial governor of Maryland, who had succeeded William Stone, to give legal status to the part of the colony where Fendall maintained his estate near Allen's Fresh on the west bank of the Wicomico River. In 1656, Fendall had been appointed Governor of the colony for putting down a rebellion at the Battle of the Severn, the first battle ever fought between American soldiers on American soil (and in which dum-dum bullets were introduced). As Governor, Fendall enforced a truce among feuding Puritans, Protestants and Catholics, and first organized district militias in the colony to keep peace and order. In 1660, Fendall led his own unsuccessful insurrection, Fendall's Rebellion, was removed from office and retired to his Charles County estate. He went on to a checkered career in Maryland, Virginia and England, accused of repeated contests of authority against the British. As an example of the long interconnectedness of the southern Maryland colonial gentry families, Governor Fendall was the great-grandfather of Sarah Fendall who married Thomas Contee, brother-in-law and business partner of the future president John Hanson.

The first John Hanson shows up in civil records in increasingly responsible capacities as guardian of a young child, bondsman, witness to wills and executor of estates. His service in the punitive expedition against the Nanticoke Indians of the colony's Eastern Shore region gained him the title of Colonel and an award of 830 pounds of tobacco — a common medium of exchange in Maryland at the time — by His Lordship's Assembly in 1678. The Assembly awarded Colonel Hanson another sixty pounds of tobacco in 1682 for Hanson's further public services to the colony.[6]

All four of the ancestry claims analyzed in an appendix here have this John Hanson as the president's grandfather, which, as we will see, has been proven conclusively, and as the family immigrant to America; but the claims disagree as to whom his parents were. It is not disproven that this earlier John Hanson's father was the immigrant Hanson having arrived perhaps in the 1630s when Maryland first began to be settled by Europeans, but this is very unlikely. The competing claims of ancestry do not rule out another generation in America before this first known John Hanson but there is no known American or European record upon which to settle this. It is assumed here that the president's grandfather was the immigrant progenitor of the Hansons in America, all but conclusively the case.

Whatever his original status upon arrival in Maryland, the immigrant John Hanson was a man of education and wealth. By the next generation, the Hanson family had without doubt firmly established itself in the very top rank of Maryland society when Gent. appears after the names of the first John Hanson's sons. Given his literacy and high social status evident from his appearances in Charles County records, the elder John Hanson either must have arrived in the colony with high social pedigree or enough status to allow him quick upward social mobility. His recorded civic roles as bondsman, executor and military officer show that he was literate, trusted by the Governor and established upper classes, and thus apparently that gentry status or something close to it was brought with him upon his arrival in the colony.

With multiple property acquisitions, the 1670s saw this presidential ancestor firmly established among the ranks of the colony's landed planters, the power-wielding elite of Maryland.[7] By 1678, he had gained his appointment as Colonel in the provincial militia by which time we see a man and his family established without doubt among the Maryland colonial elite. Colonel John Hanson, founder of an eight-generation American dynasty of prominent public servants, died in 1714 at the age of eighty-four. We see here that the grandfather John Hanson missed by a year knowing his namesake grandson, born in 1715[8], who was to become a president.

Colonel John and Mary Hanson had four sons and three daughters, the adult survivors of whom married well, joining the Hanson family with some of the most firmly established landed families of the southern Maryland peninsula, among them the Harrisons who would produce two presidents, the Briscoes who would produce a Speaker of the Maryland House of Delegates in the twentieth century, the McConchies with their line of respected clergymen, and signers of the Declaration of Independence, the Articles of Confederation and the Constitution.

The eldest of John and Mary Hanson's sons, Colonel Robert Hanson (1680-1748), married Benedicta Hoskins, granddaughter of Bennett Hoskins of Herefordshire, England, a Baronet and Member of Parliament. Robert Hanson represented Charles County in the colonial legislature from 1719 until 1740, and established a line of influential planter descendants. Colonel Robert Hanson is the uncle of President John Hanson and the fifth-great-grandfather of the author.

Little is known of John and Mary Hanson's second son, Benjamin, who died at the age of forty-two unmarried, nor of the third, John Hanson, Jr., possibly because he converted to Catholicism when marrying Elizabeth Hussey, a Port Tobacco tavern keeper's daughter of lower station than he.

The youngest of John and Mary Hanson's sons, Judge Samuel Hanson (1684-1740), was to father a president, significantly expand the family's lands, do very well financially as the leading tobacco broker in his part of the colony, and become an influential figure in the political and social life of Charles County and the colony.

When Colonel John Hanson died in 1714, his will indicated

that his eldest son Robert, named as executor, inherited his father's plantation and home. As further indication of the status of the Hanson family by only its second generation in America, Robert Hanson's son William (from whom the author descends) married Mary Stone, the great-granddaughter of Maryland colonial Governor William Stone.[9] William and Mary Stone Hanson were uncle and aunt of Thomas Stone, a signer of the Declaration of Independence.

Colonel John Hanson's other children including Samuel, then thirty, were also named in the will. As had his father, Samuel Hanson extended the family's land holdings. Between 1717 and 1736, Samuel made four land purchases totaling 1,036 acres, adding this much to the family's already extensive holdings. Samuel Hanson built the original Mulberry Grove home in 1700 and inherited his father's 1,000-acre Mulberry Grove estate upon his father's death in 1714. The name Mulberry Grove was given the estate when one of the Hanson generations — which isn't clear — attempted to found an American silk industry at the plantation after importing silk worms and planting the mulberry trees on which the worms feed. The newly named Mulberry Grove long outlived the silk worms which were not a success. Several gnarled old mulberry trees existed as late as 1951.[10]

At the age of thirty-two, Samuel Hanson was elected to serve the 1716-1717 term in the lower house of the colonial assembly but did not run for re-election when he gained the Proprietor's appointment as High Sheriff of Charles County in 1717. He served in this role until at least 1720 when he was appointed County Clerk in which position he served for twenty years until his death in 1740. Simultaneously, Samuel Hanson served as Charles County's Deputy Commissary in the Proprietor's Council, the approximate equivalent of a member of the State Senate today, from 1724 until 1733 or 1734, with an interruption to serve again in the Maryland House of Delegates from 1728 to 1731. In the midst of these appointments, Samuel Hanson was also appointed as Judge of Charles County, a lucrative life-time sinecure. In addition to adjudication, the last position entailed much of the chief administrative duties of a Maryland county.[11]

All of these positions were appointive at the pleasure of the then Proprietor of the colony, Caecilius Calvert, second Baron Baltimore, referred to by his colonial subjects as Lord Baltimore. Samuel Hanson's appointments indicate his high social rank in the colony and an intimate relation with its governing power. His sheriff, commissary, clerk and judge-ship positions were among the most lucrative in the colony and therefore among the choicest plums of patronage. Clearly, Samuel Hanson was the Proprietor's and the Governor's man in Charles County. His being able to obtain these positions one after another and even simultaneously is further confirming indication that Samuel's father arrived in the colony with high social *bona fides* which some writers have questioned.

Judge Samuel Hanson and his wife Elizabeth Story Hanson had five sons and seven daughters. Walter Hanson, eldest of the sons, at one time or another served in nearly all of the highest positions in Charles County including Judge, High Sheriff, Deputy Commissary and, during the Revolutionary War and well into his sixties, as an Army Captain. The couple's third son, Samuel Hanson, Jr., served in the colonial era as Charles County's Sheriff, Delegate, Justice and Judge, and in the revolutionary era chaired the Charles County Committee of Safety, the first government of the county as it broke away from British rule in 1775. Samuel, Jr. also served as Brigadier General during the Revolutionary War. Samuel and Elizabeth Hanson's fourth and fifth sons were both named William, the former dying at the age of four, the latter, named for his brother when he was born five years later. The second William operated a mercantile house in Talbot County on Maryland's Eastern Shore of the Chesapeake Bay.

Another indication that by the second generation of the family in America the Hanson family was moving in the top circles of the colony is the marriage of the last of Samuel and Elizabeth's children, Chloe Hanson, to Philip Briscoe of a prominent tobacco planter family still active in the twenty-first century in Maryland society and politics. Chloe and Philip's descendant, Judge John Hanson Briscoe, served as Speaker of the Maryland House of Delegates from 1973 to 1979, and during that period was the key player in conferring protection on Maryland's extensive wetlands for the first time. As of 2011, Judge Briscoe serves as a member of the board of directors of the John Hanson Memorial Association, and has long been among the most active individuals ever in keeping alive the name of President John Hanson.

On April 14 of 1715, Samuel and Elizabeth Hanson became the parents of their third son, the sixth of their twelve children, John, named for Samuel's father. This boy would become the first president of the United States. Under the old Julian calendar used when John Hanson was born, his birthday was April 3 but when eleven days were added in Britain's American colonies by their adoption of the Gregorian calendar in 1752, Hanson's birthday became fixed at April 14, the date used since. Some have argued that a leap year was wrongly figured into the interim between 1715 and 1752 making a true difference of only ten days in Hanson's birthday putting it at April 13. Virtually all modern references use the April 14 date. (However, the one-day error persisted when in 1973 the Maryland General Assembly in a near miss almost legislated the annually observed John Hanson Day in Maryland to be observed each April 13. The legislation named April 14 as Maryland John Hanson Day.)

One sometimes sees John Hanson's birth year as 1721. The weight of evidence points to 1715 and includes the Hanson family bible, nine of eleven John Hanson biographies, each John Hanson monument, and the consistent Hanson family oral tradition all using 1715. The strongest pieces of evidence for the earlier birth year are the family bible and Hanson's travelling to England in 1731-32 when he was sixteen if born in 1715 but only ten if born in 1721.

The two oldest pieces of evidence for 1721 as the birth year are a suspect Charles County, Maryland, civil record and John Hanson's earliest obituary published by the *Maryland Gazette* a few days after his death in 1783 stating that he died in his sixty-third year which would have put his birth year at 1721. What brings the civil record under suspicion is that it gives John Hanson's birthday as only forty-four days after his sister Jane's birthday in 1721. Given that John and Jane's father Samuel long served as Clerk of Charles County, one would think that Samuel would have seen to it that the county correctly recorded the birthdays of his children but, given the conundrum over John's and Jane's birthdays as recorded, no such check would appear to have taken place.

What keeps the 1721 conjecture from being put to rest is that, other than the family bible, there is no known original written evidence for 1715, and where the bible is today, after it was auctioned in 2011, is unknown. So when searching for documentation of John Hanson's birth year, one does come across the suspect obituary stating 1721, and later writings which picked up the wrong year from the obituary, but nothing definitive for 1715. This has misled some writers and even historians, especially in the age of the Internet, to dismiss 1715 and assume that 1721 must be correct. Regarding 1715, lack of primary evidence cannot by itself prove falsity of a claim. Regarding 1721, the Charles County civil record has an impossible birth date for John Hanson.

In a heavily researched series on the Hanson family published in the Baltimore *Sun* in 1906, the historian Emily Emerson Lantz confronted the birth year conundrum by examining the Charles County civil record and Hanson family records, determined that the former was incorrect and concluded that "1715 according to family records accepted as correct"[12] is demonstrably the accurate birth year. The fairest conclusion is that, absent the bible or anything else definitive, the weight of evidence strongly supports 1715. With this caveat, *Remembering John Hanson* uses 1715 as John Hanson's birth year based on the key evidence that the oldest record purporting 1721 — the civil record of the birthdays of Samuel Hanson's children — is clearly suspect while there exists no such factual challenge to 1715.

Though extant records are not entirely definitive, John Hanson was almost certainly born at Mulberry Grove along the Port Tobacco River in Charles County, Maryland. Newman's entry on John Hanson indicates Mulberry Grove as the birthplace but does not provide a source for this. Pundt's Hanson genealogy has John Hanson born at Mulberry Grove, also without source data. This genealogy and Newman both have the president's older brother, Judge Walter Hanson, born "Tuesday the eleventh day of March 1711 about 6 in ye morning at ye head of Portobacco Creek."[13] If the head of Port Tobacco Creek is reckoned to be where the creek in those days tapered quickly from broad navigable river to its narrow feeder creek, this is precisely where Mulberry Grove is situated.

A fainter possibility for the president's birthplace is that at the time of his birth his parents could have resided at Equality where Samuel Hanson was buried in 1740. Equality later passed into the hands of the Stone family, related in marriage multiple times to the Hansons. The Equality graveyard where Samuel and perhaps his wife Elizabeth are buried is located near the intersection of Mount Air Road and Crain Highway (US Route 301) in Charles County, Maryland, four miles from Mulberry Grove. The burial place of Samuel's father, the immigrant John Hanson, is not known to have been recorded, but given that he earlier owned Equality, he, too, may have been buried there.[14] His son Robert is also buried at Equality. This possibility, newly suggested here, is the only known conjecture as to the burial place of the immigrant John Hanson.

A third and also faint possibility for the president's birthplace is suggested by Samuel Hanson's not beginning to purchase property of his own until 1717, two years after John Hanson's birth, when Samuel received Hanson's Discovery of 150 acres and then Tyrall of 300 acres in 1719. It is known that Judge Samuel and Elizabeth Hanson resided at Littleworth, another of their Charles County plantations, at the time of his death in 1740, as Elizabeth inherited "the dwelling-plantation known as Littleworth."[15] It is possible that John Hanson could have been born there if that had been where his parents resided at the time of his birth.

Of the three possibilities for the president's birthplace — Mulberry Grove, Equality and Littleworth — the strong weight of evidence points to Mulberry Grove which is accepted here as where John Hanson was born. Finally, long firm oral tradition holds that John Hanson was born at Mulberry Grove.

The future president's father apparently knew that he was in declining health as Samuel's will is dated only four days before his death on October 26, 1740. Judge Samuel Hanson died at age fifty-six and was buried in the Stone family graveyard at Equality, where he was apparently visiting his daughter and son-in-law when he died. His wife Elizabeth inherited the Littleworth plantation with the couple's home and 203 acres of another property, Wilkinson's Throne. John Hanson, twenty-five at the time of his father's passing, received a bequest of two of Samuel's properties, Hereford where the Mulberry Grove home is located and the residue of Addition to Hereford.[16] The estate adjacent to Mulberry Grove to the north is today called Herefordshire recalling the property's ancient name and relation to England.

Jane Contee Hanson

Samuel Hanson missed by three years the marriage between his son John and Jane Contee of the high gentry Contee family of neighboring Prince George's County. The woman who was to become a new nation's first First Lady was born September 28, 1728, (September 17 on the old calendar) at Oaklands, her parents' Prince George's County, Maryland, estate. Jane Contee was the great-granddaughter of Dr. Peter Contee, the immigrant progenitor of the American Contees. Peter and Catherine Contee had emigrated with their children from Barnstable, Devonshire, England, about 1703, to Charles County where they lived for a time before settling in neighboring Prince George's County. The family arrived wealthy, rapidly acquired large tracts in Prince George's and Charles Counties, and from their arrival onward moved among the gentry of the colony. The 1740 will of Alexander Contee — Peter's son and Jane's father — shows a silver punch bowl, "much silver plate" and a "tea service with a muffineer and waiter all bearing the family arms and the Tower of London stamp from 1620."[17]   These items were passed down to Jane Contee Hanson and remained with her descendants until at least 1919 when her great-great-grandson Douglas Hamilton Thomas, who is known to have possessed them, died.

The Contees were French Huguenots who had emigrated to England sometime before 1643 to escape religious persecution after revocation of the Edict of Nantes. The de Contee family, the name they went by in France, were among the French nobility as far back as 1375, the English and then American Contees descending from the Viscount de Contee of Rochelle. The French immigrants to England were Dr. Peter Contee's parents, Adolphe and Grace de Contee. Adolphe de Contee gained appointment as High Sheriff of London and Middlesex in 1643. That an immigrant would step into such a high position so soon after arriving in his new country indicates wealth, influence and, in de Contee's case, noble blood. As we will see in an appendix here, Adolphe de Contee's shrievalty will provide a strong clue as to the possible European origin of the Hanson family.

The Contees would exert a degree of influence in the colony and then the state of Maryland nearly equal to that of the Hansons. Jane Contee Hanson's brothers and male cousins occupied a number of high elective and appointive positions, and were active in the Conventions of Maryland, which put the colony on the path to independence, and then in the Revolutionary War.

The year following John and Jane Hanson's marriage in 1743, John bought from her family the 603-acre Rozer's Refuge[18], a beautiful tract situated on a bluff overlooking the confluence of the Port Tobacco and Potomac rivers. The purchase was made on February 28, 1744, and on March 12, John conveyed part of the property to Jane at which time she "relinquished her third." This tract, part of the larger St. Thomas Manor, had been granted by Caecilius Calvert, the second Proprietor of Maryland, to Benjamin Rozer in 1672 and later purchased by the Contee family.

Jane Hanson would go on to preside over one of Maryland's great estates, raise a family of thirteen children, witness her husband's political ascent to the highest office in the land, and serve in the first presidential mansion as the nation's first First Lady. Her children and grandchildren would be elected to the United States Senate, the House of Representatives and the Maryland House of Delegates, and would serve as a college president, the Chancellor of Maryland, Electors of George Washington and in other distinguished capacities. They would be related or related by marriage to four presidents and to the longest-serving chief justice of the United States.

In huge contrast to these distinctions of her life and legacy, Jane Hanson also suffered deeply the particular vicissitudes of her era including infant mortality, war, reduced circumstances and long widowhood. She would move in midlife to the frontier, have her and her husband's fortune dissipated to war and independence, be a widow for nearly three decades, and suffer the death of twelve of her thirteen children during her own lifetime. However, Jane Hanson would spend her last years in the care of a remarkable widowered son-in-law and surrounded by four grandchildren to whom she would act as surrogate mother after their own mother, her daughter, had died young.

From the Toil of Others

Sometime in the 1750s while at Mulberry Grove, Jane and John Hanson sat for their portraits painted in oils by John Hesselius, one of the colonies' most acclaimed portraitists, and the teacher of Charles Willson Peale, who in 1782 would produce the nation's first presidential portrait, that of John Hanson. Hesselius's full-size likenesses of Jane and John Hanson, which today hang in the portrait gallery of the Maryland Historical Society, show Jane in a full-length, finely woven gown of gold brocade with cuffs and shawl collar of intricate lace, and John in what appears to be a heavy velvet gentleman's long coat and breeches in the buff color popular at the time. These costly luxurious garments, among the most fashionable and refined which one would have seen in the colonies in the 1750s, may have come from Philadelphia or New York but more likely from one of the European capitals. The fabrics certainly came from abroad. Sitting for one's portrait was a luxury within the grasp of only the wealthiest of colonial elites.

Ned Barnes was an enslaved African-American who in July 1781 and again in early 1782 fled his master in a desperate attempt to rejoin his wife and children after he and they had been forcibly separated when Barnes was permanently assigned by his enslaver to duty several days travel from his family. Barnes did not try to flee north along the nascent Underground Railroad where his chances for permanent freedom would have been best but, with a stolen horse, fled simply to be reunited with his family. On his first attempt at reunion, he was captured by a slave catcher and returned to his enslaver for the thirty-dollar reward which the enslaver had offered. On Barnes's second attempt, he was again captured and this time sold away to another enslaver. Though again within a day or two of traveling distance of his family, he was once more kept apart from them.

The enslaver who sold Ned Barnes in 1782 was the newly inaugurated President of the United States, John Hanson. The president's reward poster for Barnes is provided here.

The luxuries, privileges and comfortable lives enjoyed by the future president, his family and the privileged class to which they belonged were made possible in great measure through the enslavement and taking of land of other human beings. During his childhood, John Hanson saw first hand that the burgeoning family wealth yielded from his parents' tobacco fields was derived from stealing the toil of his family's enslaved labor force. Throughout his life, John Hanson not only witnessed slavery around him but, in fact, from early adulthood until his death was an enslaver himself. When his father Samuel died in 1740, the estate included twenty-two slaves.[19]

John Hanson continued the practice of slavery when he moved to Mulberry Grove in 1744 and later in Frederick after moving there in 1769. Baptismal records show at least eight people listed as the couple's Negroes[20] in Frederick just in the years from 1780 to 1785. Following the demeaning practice of slavery, the eight were listed only by their first names: John and Sarah and their son William, John and Nancy and their son John, and an unnamed father and his daughter Maria.[21] There were also Jennie, Chloe and Toney in the Hanson household for a total of at least eleven enslaved souls kept by John and Jane Hanson in Frederick. The record is not certain that these people were not free Blacks but nothing encountered in preparing *Remembering John Hanson* indicates that John Hanson employed free Blacks. The family's enslavement of African-Americans continued during John Hanson's presidency, by Jane beyond his death and by their descendants well into the nineteenth century until Maryland rewrote her constitution outlawing slavery on November 1, 1864. The enslaved people noted here and any other John Hanson slaves, by the comforts and time which their stolen lives afforded John and Jane Hanson, lent themselves in silence to the founding of the United States. Millions of them passed utterly anonymously through the nation's history in this way as uncounted but profoundly productive souls. It is gratifying to be able to identify these few and mention them. Perhaps they rest in Frederick's old Colored Cemetery.

Though there is little indication that John Hanson had many qualms about slavery, two incidents make it appear that at least he leaned away from its harsher aspects. After Hanson's slave George had twice run away and been recaptured in 1780, Hanson wrote to his son-in-law Philip Thomas, "It is better to part with him at allmost any price than exercise the Cruelty which would be necessary to oblige him to stay with you." But, of course, separating a family by selling a slave was a terrible cruelty in itself.

In January 1782 the then President John Hanson was notified by his Charles County cousin Hoskins Hanson via the president's son Alexander that William Farr, a slave catcher, had responded to a newspaper reward notice which the president had placed. Farr had caught Ned Barnes and written, "I have become Security for the reward, and Keep him 'till you send for him, or I can get an opportunity of continuing him to you without danger of his escaping." John Hanson's reward notice had appeared in *The Maryland Gazette* of July 12, 1781.[22] Barnes had known freedom for six months.

The president's letter asks Philip Thomas to fetch Barnes from Farr, reimburse the owner of a horse stolen by Barnes and, "When you get him home, employ him as you think proper, while his wife continues at home, I suppose there will be no danger of his making a second attempt to get off. You may let him Know, that his pardon depends on his future behaviour, that if he behaves well, and endeavours to make amends for his past Conduct, I will when I return home purchase his wife, if her master will sell at a reasonable price." Barnes, unaware that he might be reunited with his wife, escapes Hoskins Hanson but is again apprehended as he made his way toward his family. At this, John Hanson instructs Philip Thomas to sell Barnes for £200 but says he would accept £150. In the spring of 1782, the president sold Ned Barnes to Hoskins Hanson for £150.[23]

Another exploitation of slavery was the hiring out of an enslaved person with the enslaver collecting the slave's wages. In the summer of his presidency during a drought which had hurt his crop yields, John Hanson wrote to Philip Thomas regarding one of the president's slaves, "Please tell Toney to endeavor to Settle with all his Customers & receive payment before I return which I hope in God will be the middle of November at the furthest."

In the midst of the monstrous cruelty of slavery, enslavers varied considerably in their treatment of the enslaved, especially toward those who had attempted escape. There are well documented accounts of escapee punishments of five-hundred lashes, severing of an Achilles tendon to hobble an escapee, amputation, severing of body parts, branding, other mutilations and execution. One of the more common punishments was the dreaded "selling south" of a slave to the cotton plantations of the deep south where a day's toil was harder, life shorter and separation from one's family almost invariably eternal. John Hanson's choices of treatment of Ned Barnes and George, while bad enough, do not display a disposition toward these harshest of treatments. While this in no way excuses his enslaving people in the first place, it makes him less severe than some.

Among several of John Hanson's direct descendants, slavery, or at least support of it, continued through the Civil War and later. Dr. John Hanson Thomas, Jr. (1813-1881), John Hanson's great-grandson, a member of the Maryland General Assembly from 1861 to 1865 even while he was a prisoner of war, was arrested for advocating secession and imprisoned for six months in four Union forts. His son, Captain John Hanson Thomas III (1841-1905), President Hanson's great-great-grandson, served all four years of the Civil War for the Confederate Army, one year in the 1st Maryland Regiment and the final three as captain under General Loring. His brother, Lieutenant Raleigh Colston Thomas (1844-1886), served two years in the Confederate Army as an aide to General Lomax.

The auction of an estate of a Hanson-Thomas descendant in 2011 included large collections of letters home from these three during the Civil War.[24] Nearly one hundred fifty letters were written between Dr. Thomas and his wife Annie while he was a prisoner of war. In his letter of October 16, 1861, to Annie, written from Fortress Lafayette in Brooklyn, New

York, Dr. Thomas muses over what his presidential great-grandfather might have thought about the Civil War. Wrote Thomas, "Just fancy, John Hanson President of Congress in '81 & '82 after he had signed the Articles of Confederation on the part of Maryland — calm & dignified as his features indicate in his picture hanging over our sideboard — receiving & congratulating George Washington, when he returned from his glorious victory at Yorktown — just fancy that he could have imagined after all his sacrifices that men will be by any probability incarcerated in this country for opinions sake — that all liberty was overthrown & that tyranny with its armed heel crushed all opposition to its behests!!"[25]

It does not distinguish the Hanson family that its generations extending even late into the nineteenth century were opposed to freedom of their own countrymen. Hanson descendants today feel the profoundest shame over their ancestors having been involved in slavery.

With the exception of John Hanson's letters, conspicuous in researching this book is the almost complete absence of mention of slavery in the records drawn on from the time of the Hanson family's arrival in America in the mid-1600s all the way through to the John Hanson biographies of the twentieth century. While the colonies and then the new nation, especially Maryland's tobacco economy, were being built in great degree on the backs of enslaved people, this isn't mentioned often in the records of the time and barely at all in writings on John Hanson since. While the era's laws, court records, wills, other "property" documents involving slaves, private correspondence and diaries including the president's did occasionally mention individual slaves by name, slavery and its influences and effects in the seventeenth and eighteenth centuries are barely mentioned in nearly all of the sources examined for writing *Remembering John Hanson*.

Not mentioned whatsoever in any source used here is the Underground Railroad[26], the ubiquitous, illegal, clandestine moral network which spirited enslaved people to freedom in the northern states, Canada and elsewhere for 280 years.[27] This, too, was an intimate part of daily life in John Hanson's time. Every American — white, black, Native American — knew that slavery existed, that any enslaved person yearned to be free, that the bravest of them would attempt flight to seek their freedom, and that some free people of all races would, as a moral principle, aid freedom seekers. These facts were so ubiquitous that they comprised part of the fabric of daily life, the very consciousness of the time, and much of the inherited bedrock of American morality today. It is well known that the dangerous nature of Underground Railroad participation nearly always kept freedom seekers, safehouse operators and conductors as they came to be called from recording, and in many cases from even speaking about, their Underground Railroad work and that this has left a thinly documented record of the Underground Railroad which, however, is fortunately being bolstered today by increasingly revealed oral traditions.[28]

America Revealed: Josiah and Josias

Josiah Henson, one of the most famous Underground Railroad freedom seekers whose life was in significant part the basis of Harriet Beecher Stowe's 1852 landmark *Uncle Tom's Cabin,* was born enslaved at Port Tobacco probably in 1795 or 1796[29] when the area was in sharp decline. It appears that Josiah Henson is related to John Hanson.

After escaping slavery on the Underground Railroad in 1829, Henson settled in Canada, founded the town of Dawn, Ontario, established the first school for Underground Railroad freedom seekers, and became one of history's most prominent and articulate advocates for emancipation and human rights. At a time when a best-seller might sell ten thousand copies in the United States, Stowe's definitive exposé of slavery quickly sold a half million copies at home and within a few years as many abroad. *Uncle Tom's Cabin* has been translated into sixty languages, is still regarded as the most influential book ever written by an American, and has never been out of print since its original publication in 1852.

In his 1849 autobiography which heavily influenced Stowe's book, Henson's description of the mistreatment of his parents is as vivid as it gets in exposing the horrors of slavery. In the words of the son, "I was born, June 15, 1789, in Charles County, Maryland, on a farm belonging to Mr. Francis N[ewman], about a mile from Port Tobacco. My mother was the property of Dr. Josiah McP[herson], but was hired by Mr. N., to whom my father belonged. The only incident I can remember, which occurred while my mother continued on N.'s farm, was the appearance of my father one day, with his head bloody and his back lacerated. He was in a state of great excitement, and though it was all a mystery to me at the age of three or four years, it was explained at a later period, and I understood that he had been suffering the cruel penalty of the Maryland law for beating a white man. His right ear had been cut off close to his head, and he had received a hundred lashes on his back. He had beaten the overseer for a brutal assault on my mother, and this was his punishment. Furious at such treatment, my father became a different man, and was so morose, disobedient, and intractable, that Mr. N. determined to sell him. He accordingly parted with him, not long after, to his son, who lived in Alabama; and neither my mother nor I, ever heard of him again. He was naturally, as I understood afterwards from my mother and other persons, a man of amiable temper, and of considerable energy of character; but it is not strange that he should be essentially changed by such cruelty and injustice under the sanction of law."[30]

Dr. Josias Hanson McPherson's grandfather, Samuel Hanson of Robert, was the first cousin of President John Hanson. Their common ancestor was the immigrant John Hanson. Among four known marriages between the Hanson and McPherson families, all between 1754 and 1821, a daughter and a granddaughter of Samuel Hanson of Robert married McPhersons, Benedicta Hanson to Henry McPherson and Elizabeth Fendall Hanson to Thomas McPherson, respectively. The fifth of Benedicta and Henry's children was the Josias Hanson McPherson of interest here.

In his autobiography, Henson writes of his enslaver Josias Hanson McPherson, "*As the first negro child ever born to him*, I was his especial pet. He gave me his own Christian name, Josiah, and with that he also gave me my last name, Henson, after an uncle of his, who was an officer in the revolutionary war."[31] (Emphasis added) The uncle was Major Samuel Hanson (not Henson) McPherson.[32] That Josias Hanson McPherson would name his "first negro child" and "especial pet" Josiah Henson — or perhaps originally Josiah Hanson or Josias Hanson — gives rise to the suspicion that Josias Hanson McPherson fathered Josiah Henson, an all too frequent indignity inflicted on enslaved families by their enslavers.

That Henson describes himself as McPherson's first negro child could be literal and begs deeper conjecture. In his biography, Josiah Henson ascribes his father as his mother's husband sold south, but Henson also reveals that this man was kept on the plantation of his enslaver, Francis Newman, and that his mother was the property of Josias Hanson McPherson. Though for some period Henson's mother was hired out by McPherson to Newman after Josiah Henson's birth, McPherson would have had access to the mother whenever he wanted before (or after) the birth. This combination of circumstances raises the possibility, and perhaps the likelihood, that Josiah Henson was actually a McPherson related to the Hansons through Josias Hanson McPherson. Remaining unexplained is the one-letter difference in the spelling of the surnames Hanson and Henson. This might be attributed to Henson's London biographer John Lobb recording the name as he thought he heard his illiterate subject narrate it in the 1870s.[33] DNA comparison of a Henson descendant and a Hanson descendant would tell the story if Josiah Henson is indeed related to the Hansons. If President John Hanson and Josiah Henson were related, they were first cousins three time removed.[34] If so, then Josiah Henson and the author are related.

In 1805, Josiah Henson's mother was sold to Isaac Riley, a farmer in Montgomery County, Maryland. In the same auction, Josiah, then nine or ten years old, was sold to Adam Robb, a tavern keeper in Rockville near the Riley farm. After the boy fell ill, Josiah Henson was sold in either 1805 or 1806 by Robb to Riley and began living in the Riley household's slave cabin reunited with his mother. In an ironic twist of history, this cabin and the farm where it is located were later owned by John Hanson's grandson, United States Senator Alexander Contee Hanson, Jr., sometime before 1819 when the Senator died.[35] Riley's slaves were not included in the sale.

In 2006, the Riley farmhouse where Josiah Henson had been enslaved was rediscovered in Montgomery County, Maryland, and purchased as a public historic site by the Maryland-National Capital Park and Planning Commission. This, the actual site of Uncle Tom's Cabin, is now regarded by many as the single most spectacular rediscovery of the Underground Railroad.[36] The farmhouse's attached cabin, which for a time was believed to be the actual place of enslavement of Josiah Henson and therefore "the original Uncle Tom's Cabin" is now thought to have been the home's kitchen.

Josiah Henson died May 5, 1883, probably in his late eighties, deeply revered in the United States, Canada and elsewhere. In 1909 his great-grandnephew, Matthew Henson, who accompanied Admiral Robert Peary on his expedition to the North Pole, became the first person ever to set foot at the Pole as he scouted ahead of Peary and the exploration party.

The last half-century in the United States has seen long strides toward equality and mending the soreness of the national soul on past racial wrongs. The author's happy immediate family is triracial and comfortable in any part of the country.

By the time of John Hanson's presidency in 1781 and 1782, American opposition to slavery had begun to coalesce and be heard. The Mennonites in 1688 and the Quakers in 1754 had already publicly opposed slavery and banned it among their members. Other denominations including the Methodists and Virginia Baptists would formally oppose the institution beginning in the 1780s. Anti-slavery sentiment had run high among Swedish, German, Swiss and some other immigrant groups since their arrival in the American colonies. Though the rendering of aid to fugitive slaves had existed since the days of Spain's St. Augustine, Florida, colony in the sixteenth century, it first became organized only two hundred years later in the 1780s as abolitionists, safehouse operators and escorts of freedom seekers began finding one another and coordinating their work. In the years of the United States in Congress Assembled in the 1780s, legislation introduced by delegate Thomas Jefferson would come within one vote of abolishing slavery in new states and thus probably avoiding the Civil War (or perhaps accelerating it). The Constitution in 1788 would suffer the same failure, dodging the slavery pitfall, but did manage to outlaw the further importation of enslaved people after 1808.

In addition to enslaved African-Americans, there were two other groups of people savaged not just by colonial elites but by most other whites in the founding of the United States.

Except for the one brief mention of Colonel John Hanson's involvement in suppressing the Nanticoke Indians on Maryland's Eastern Shore, also entirely absent from sources used in researching *Remembering John Hanson* is any mention of Native Americans or of the thorough taking of their lands by the colonists. By the mid-eighteenth century, Maryland's Native Americans had either been driven from the colony entirely as with the Tuscaroras, felled by the introduction of Old World diseases to which they had no immunity, or reduced to small remnant groups pushed off into marginal out-of-the-way forest crannies that settlers were not interested in. The ravaged tribes of Charles County and nearby included the Patuxents, Piscataways, Mattawomans, Nanjemoys, Chopticans and the Potopacs from which Port Tobacco took its name. The Native American presence in Maryland today is barely vestigial: in the 2000 United States census, 907 residents of Charles County — well less than one percent of the county population — identified themselves as

Native American, and not one of the 564 federally recognized Native American tribes as of 2011 is in Maryland.

Also never mentioned from sources used in researching *Remembering John Hanson* except tangentially in one of the theories on the Hanson immigrant's origins are indentured servants, another group on whose backs colonial elites built their wealth. Indentured servitude was usually a contract — often involuntary on the part of the indentured person — between a person who was bound to provide his or her labor exclusively to another person in exchange typically for the latter's payment of ship's passage from Europe. Indentured servitude was time-bound and, upon the successful completion of the contract, the indentured person was set free. Though closely akin to slavery, it was not slavery in the strict permanent sense. Indentures were not similar to modern employment contracts which cannot force a person's labor. For most indentures, the labor of the indentured person was compelled. Much as slaves were, indentured servants were listed as property in wills and thus conveyed to heirs as new indenture holders.

From the settlement of Jamestown in 1607 until the Revolutionary War, the British government packed off thousands of souls to the colonies as unwilling indentured servants. Indentured servants did include some people who of their own volition had agreed to trade several years of their time, five typically, for passage and perhaps a stipend of land upon completion of their indenture, but, more often, indentured servitude was involuntary on the part of the servant. Many indentured servants sent to North America, perhaps a majority, were prisoners, vagrants, the marginally mentally ill, paupers, prostitutes or other impressed women, miscreants and, saddest of all, kidnapped children.[37] "The indentured servant was in effect, little different from a transported felon: both were slaves in every sense, and ranked as part of their master's estate to be bought and sold at will."[38]

The Hanson family was not exempt from exploiting the labor of the indentured. In one instance, Colonel Robert Hanson, the president's uncle, brought James Macintosh and Hugh Macdougall into the colony from Liverpool when the ship *Good Speed* landed the two at Annapolis on October 18, 1716. The ship brought in fifty-two other involuntary Scottish rebel prisoners that day. Forty-nine were sold, one managed to run away, one was unsold and one arrived dead.[39]

It is no wonder that when many of these from the margins of

society had finally worked off their indentures, they could only fall back into the desperate straits in which they had struggled in Britain. As the Jesuit priest Father Joseph Mosley of Maryland had to say even at the height of the colony's prosperity, what awaited indentured servants when they had gained their freedom was that Maryland "has been a fine poor man's country, but now it is well peopled, the lands are all secured and the harvest for such is now over. The Lands are mostly worked by the landlords' negroes, and, of consequence, white servants after their bondage is out, are strolling about the country without bread."[40] Upon working off an indenture, the indentured servant often went overnight from employed to unemployed, from housed to homeless. While the owner of the servant had been obliged to provide food and shelter during the indenture, even if no better than what was provided to the permanently enslaved, these modest comforts, too, were lost upon freedom. Working off one's indenture often led to the same homelessness, unemployment, destitution, vagrancy and fathomless future that emancipated slaves encountered upon their suddenly attaining freedom in the 1860s.

In the period covered by *Remembering John Hanson*, most African-Americans were enslaved; Native Americans had suffered near extermination and had had their lands usurped; indentured servitude was a widespread and officially sanctioned scandal; women, Catholics and the poor were disenfranchised; and the particular narrow minority comprising white, wealthy, landed, tax-current, British Protestant men held virtually all power. One needs to keep in mind that it was in this context that the United States was born, that many if not most of the signers of the Declaration of Independence, Articles of Confederation and Constitution were practitioners and beneficiaries of these exploitations themselves, and that John Hanson, despite his accomplishments and virtues, was squarely amidst this milieu.

A New Breed Called American

The seventh of Judge Samuel and Elizabeth Story Hanson's eleven children was the future president who grew up at his parents' comfortable plantation in Charles County. Early in life, John Hanson began deeply absorbing the family traditions of public service, the importance of international relations as he witnessed his father's trans-Atlantic tobacco trade at Port Tobacco, and was molded by the emerging ethos of the colonies into something more than just a British expatriate. John Hanson was a second-generation American and a century removed from his European roots. The son of parents who had themselves been born and reared in America, and surrounded by contemporaries of similar New World pedigree, John Hanson could not have failed to share the burgeoning identity of this new generation which began proudly calling itself American. Though British subjects, most of this generation had little personal experience with Britain or its everyday life, and did what was only natural in reckoning themselves as a new breed, fond of but by then distinct from their distant British relations. Now different from those fellow subjects of the British crown who remained on the sceptered isle an ocean away from the American experience, John Hanson became increasingly aware that, though he was a British subject, he was to his thinking first a new breed called American.

The record of the future president in early life is thin. It is clear that he grew up amidst the privileged tidewater Maryland colonial plantation elite. The young John Hanson claimed a grandfather who had been a colonel and a father who was the county's sheriff, representative of the county in the colonial government in Annapolis, judge and therefore one of Charles County's most prominent citizens, if not the single most important politically. The future president's uncle Robert Hanson was a colonel, and virtually all of the future president's aunts, uncles and cousins moved in the same privileged stratum as did he.

By no later than 1730, John Hanson's father, Judge Samuel Hanson, had become what would appear to be the major tobacco broker of Charles County, operating his brokerage at the port of Port Tobacco adjacent to Mulberry Grove where the president was growing up. Port Tobacco and Annapolis were the major ports of the colony in 1730, with Baltimore still a bare village established only the year before, and the founding of Georgetown and its port still twenty-nine years in the future.

There are two known surviving journals of John Hanson, one dating from 1730 to 1737, the other from 1776 to 1779. The earlier journal, begun by the future president when he was fifteen, has as its first entry his accounting for that year of his father's brokerage for shipments of seventy-three hogsheads of tobacco from the same number of local client accounts by name from Port Tobacco to Reed & Gray of London, Samuel Hanson's broker-agent there. In this ledger, the future president goes on to record his father's annual brokered shipments through 1737 when the number of Samuel's accounts had risen to one hundred twenty-one. Few names in this ledger are of prominent Charles County families and none of the individual accounts is large indicating a clientele of small farmer-growers as opposed to the large wealthy local plantations which probably arranged for shipment of their tobacco themselves. In this ledger in the president's hand, we see the teenage John being trained young by his father in the family business recording weights, values, the Hanson commissions, the Reed & Gray commissions, and precise accounting references to *liber* and *folio* of individual accounts. In this journal, the teen proficiently uses the European accounting conventions of double-entry bookkeeping, originated in the Italian trade fairs of the thirteenth century, with its matched debits and credits. For the rest of his life, John Hanson was to put to good use this early accounting apprenticeship and his easy facility with mathematics.

Aside from his occupation as a political figure, John Hanson pursued two lines of work during his career. He was a planter, first of tobacco and then probably of other soil-restoring crops during his years at Mulberry Grove, and a planter again with the more than five hundred acres which he owned or leased after moving to Frederick. Simultaneously, and apparently as his primary occupation, John Hanson worked as a merchant with his father's tobacco brokerage and his own store in Port Tobacco, and then with the store which he and his brother-in-law, Thomas Contee, owned in Frederick after the Hanson family moved there in 1769. The Maryland State Archives officially lists John Hanson's occupation as merchant.

It is clear from his work as an adult that John Hanson was well educated. His letters show not just literacy but a honed persuasiveness with English and special ability to convey his thoughts and arguments appealingly. Hanson's specialization in finance in his assignments with Maryland's colonial assembly, his later work as one of the chief financiers of the Revolutionary War, and his sure-handed oversight in the creation of the nation's first central bank when he was president show an especially skilled numeracy for his era and an adroit facility with mathematics, accounting and finance. This might have run in the family: in addition to John's father's accounting skill which he taught the son, the will of John Hanson's uncle, Robert Hanson, gives "28 Acres; also my instruments and mathematick books" to Robert's son William.

In his 1876 history of the Hanson family, George Hanson relates that it was passed down that the young John Hanson had been sent to England to study at Oxford University. Hanson biographer J. Bruce Kremer states that the young John Hanson had gone "to England for a few years to school."[41] Emily Emerson Lantz is most specific in stating that, "According to a family manuscript, John Hanson . . . was educated for the church and had taken passage on board of a vessel for England to obtain orders. He was shipwrecked and deterred from a second attempt." [42]

If the future president was a student in England he most likely would have been there about 1730 to 1735 in his late teens as was the custom of his era. The earlier of John Hanson's journals, rediscovered in 2009 by the author uncatalogued at the Maryland Historical Society library, shows that he did make a trip to England, though it would have allowed him to study there for only the time which today would be reckoned as one semester.

The sixteen-year-old's journal includes his daily logs from "Cape Henry [Virginia] Forward England" aboard the *Caleb & John*, Thomas Reed Master, from March 10 to April 7, 1731, when "making land" and again from August 23 to 30 of that year, arriving in England on the latter date. The long layup between April and August could have been the result of the shipwreck which Lantz mentions or other repair necessary in port. That the last leg took only a week would indicate that the ship had put in somewhere near England, perhaps the mid-Atlantic Azores, about a week's sail away.

John Hanson records his return trip, "A Journal in the *Vine* Tho. Reed Master From England Forward Maryland *Cum Sans Deo*," from February 22 to April 18, 1732, this eight-week trip apparently nonstop. Showing his analytical bent, the teen's meticulous meteorological entries during his two ocean voyages include wind speed and direction, weather, latitude, longitude and time of his observations every two hours around the clock.[43, 44]

The timing of his stay in Britain would coincide with a university fall semester. The archives of both Oxford University and Cambridge University do not show a John Hanson from the North American colonies having matriculated at that time. However, the records do not account for course auditors or it is possible that the young John attended some other university or a seminary if he was bent on clergyhood.[45] If John Hanson did attend university during this time as was passed down in George Hanson's line of the family and asserted by Bruce Kremer, it remains to be determined why he stayed only one semester.

George Hanson reports that the future president had studied and was especially fond of the Roman stoic philosopher and statesman Lucius Annaeus Seneca. Seneca's philosophies were a fixture in British university curricula in 1731 when John Hanson might have studied during his sojourn to Britain. A clue to the friendship and similar later outlook of John Hanson and George Washington is that Washington, too, was guided by his self-study of Seneca whose teachings Washington mentioned in his professional life. As Washington biographer John Ferling has noted regarding Washington's education, "*Seneca's Morals* emphasized that success in part hinged on the virtues of sacrifice, tenacity, courage, restraint and the control of one's emotions,"[46] hallmarks of the makeup of both Hanson and Washington.

John Hanson has also been characterized as a student and thoughtful practitioner of the philosophy of juridicalism of Saint Anselm of Canterbury, the eleventh-century English Christian philosopher and theologian.

Whether Hanson was educated abroad, in his community or tutored at home, the wide practice among colonial elites in his time, or some combination of these, what is clear is that he was an adept pupil who became well educated, especially in practical disciplines, and proved especially competent in putting his formal learning and his family's tutoring him in commerce into skilled use.

As the young John Hanson came to maturity in the 1730s, he was living through a period when the people of Britain's thirteen American seaboard colonies were beginning to loosen their ties to the mother country. That did not, however, mean that John Hanson and his fellow Tidewater aristocrats were yet comfortable in following their political inclinations; on the contrary, they still owed much of their status and position to the local agents of the British crown, the successive Proprietors of Maryland, the several Lords Baltimore, and their appointee governors of the colony.

The Seeds of Revolt

To the Proprietor and Maryland's stiff gentry system of social stratification, the first John Hanson owed his colonelcy, Judge Samuel Hanson his high appointments, and the future president his Charles County sheriff's appointment, among the colony's most lucrative sinecures in the seventeenth and eighteenth centuries. That three generations of

Hansons enjoyed these highest county appointments is affirmation of their loyalty to the British Crown and its Maryland Proprietors, as only resolved British loyalists gained these appointments. Sheriffs and judges administered Maryland's counties and were outranked in the colony only by the Proprietor himself and his appointed governor and secretary. To begin tracing the evolution of John Hanson from a member of this high gentry well rewarded for his British loyalties, to his revolutionary roles risking all of what his family had gained to oppose British rule, it is necessary to understand the unique nature of British and particularly Proprietary rule in Maryland.

Because Britain's North American colonies were founded by charters granted to separate private companies or individuals rather than being established by the British government itself, the administration of different colonies varied significantly and at the whim of the colonies' proprietors, and lent no uniformity to aid the British government as it tried to impose its sovereignty over the colonies. As this system of non-uniform proprietorship administration evolved, Crown and Parliament found that the only two means they had of exerting control were through the colonies' governors and by the disallowance of laws passed by colonial legislatures. The inevitable result was a growing friction between colonist and ruler.

After Virginia, Massachusetts and New Hampshire, the colony of Maryland in 1634 was the fourth to be chartered when Great Britain's King Charles I granted a land patent comprising the upper half of the Chesapeake Bay from the Potomac River to the Delaware River, and from the Atlantic seaboard to a longitude 250 miles to west, to Sir George Calvert, first Baron Baltimore, as a reward for Calvert's services and close friendship to the King, and previously to the King's father. Because George Calvert died when the grant was in the making, it was awarded to his son Caecilius Calvert who became the second Baron Baltimore upon his father's death. Unlike the royal edicts which established the other North American colonies, the grant which created Maryland was fashioned in a spirit archaic even at the time. The Maryland colony was owned as personal property by Caecilius Calvert, ownership of the colony was hereditary to be passed down to generations of Caecilius's heirs, and the colonial title of the successive Barons Baltimore was Proprietor. The term carried the literal meaning that it does today: owner.

As long as the laws which the Proprietor laid down for the

colony were not in conflict with those of Britain and the Proprietor did not enact laws or levy taxes without the ostensible consent of the freemen of the province or their deputies, Maryland's Proprietors could govern their colony however they chose to, and sell and control all of the colony's lands as they saw fit. In high deference, Maryland's colonists referred to the Proprietors as His Lordship or Lord Baltimore. The medieval features of the Calverts' charter in effect made their colony a demi-monarchy run at their whim which put significant limitations on Maryland's political development even as the first John Hanson and other colonists began arriving to settle the colony in the mid-1600s. The antiquated provisions of the Calverts' Maryland charter were in contrast to those of any other of Britain's North American colonies and made Maryland the least of the colonies in the rights of its citizens, including its gentry, to have meaningful say in governance and even in certain important aspects of their daily lives. Exacerbating what was to become festering resentment over these restrictions was that the Proprietors were not resident in Maryland but ruled from afar in Britain through their appointed resident governors whose loyalties lay strictly with the Proprietor rather than with his governed subjects. Thus Maryland had been established essentially as a feudal fiefdom and it was the anachronistic flaws in its founding charter which one hundred forty years later led to the particular kind of rebellion which would arise against Proprietor rule in Maryland.

The only provision for popular expression afforded by the Calverts' charter was that the House of Delegates, the lower house of the colony's bicameral Assembly, would, to a limited extent, be popularly elected. (Members of the Proprietor's Council, the upper house, were appointed by the province's governor with the approval of the Proprietor and, right up to the demise of Proprietor rule in 1775, were firm loyalists of the Proprietor and of the mother country.) To be qualified to vote for a candidate for a county's delegation to the House of Delegates, a Maryland resident needed to possess at least fifty acres of land held in freehold without mortgage or lien or to possess £40 sterling of visible estate, and to have been resident in Maryland for at least three years. One also needed to be a British citizen, male, twenty-one years of age, current in taxes, unindentured and, after 1718, non-Catholic. Though not explicitly codified, in practice voters were also white.

Based on the work of David Skaggs, a reasonable estimate of how these multiple denials of the franchise — especially to women, those with small land holdings, the unlanded and the poor — reduced voting eligibility is that only about twenty to twenty-five percent of otherwise eligible males were qualified to vote by owning fifty acres of land or £40 visible estate, but this estimate includes the disenfranchised Catholics after 1718.[47] Accounting for the colony's slaves and Native Americans who together comprised nearly a quarter of the province's population, the disenfranchised Catholics who comprised another seven percent, and its adult women, a best estimate of the true proportion of adults with voting rights sinks to about one in twenty adult Marylanders. The exclusion of small farmers is worthy of special note because they were the colony's most typical and numerous residents. This Proprietor-established regime was more restrictive than voting qualifications in any of the other twelve colonies. For example, Virginia's freehold qualification of twenty-five acres approximately doubled the proportion of landowners there who qualified to vote compared to Maryland.

This stringency was quite by design. Not only the Proprietor and his hip-pocket governor and Council but also the elected House of Delegates, ostensibly representative but drawn virtually exclusively from the gentry, deliberately used the colony's voter eligibility laws to confine voting to a privileged elite who had the most cause to favor maintaining the status quo and not jostling the interests of the Proprietor. In practice, rarely was anyone not of the high gentry elected or appointed to public office in Maryland until a decade or two before the Revolution. If small landholders were left beyond the fringe of the electorate, the opposite was just as true: it was a wealthy aristocracy of mainly the owners of large Tidewater plantations which undemocratically ruled the province. Tightening the control of this squirearchy were the frequent marriages among these few score families.

To secure the allegiance of the gentry, the Proprietor and Governor held out plum political appointments, most of them lucrative, to the key opinion leaders in each of the Maryland counties. The six appointive positions in each of the colony's counties were a county's Justice, Sheriff, Deputy Commissary, Deputy Surveyor, County Clerk and Farmer of the Quitrents. A county's Deputy Commissary and Deputy Surveyor were not deputies to anyone in their county but only to the Proprietor appointees of Commissary General and Surveyor General in Annapolis, the provincial capital. The aim of successive Maryland Proprietors in securing the acquiescence of the gentry through these appointments was probably never made clearer than by Frederick Calvert, sixth Baron Baltimore, in his letter of March 17, 1760, when he was more than candid in issuing his dictum to Governor Horatio Sharpe to curry the favor of the Maryland gentry "by throwing out a Sop in a proper manner to these Noisy animals." By this time, we see an absentee landlord utterly disdainful of and out of touch with his subjects, and within fifteen years of province-wide revolt.

From its first generation in America, the Hanson family was part and parcel of the mutual reliance between Proprietor and gentry, a relationship which was intimate and advantageous for the family in the earlier decades of the province, strained and then broken at the end. The first John Hanson had been recognized by the Proprietor with his colonelcy. His son Samuel had enjoyed successively and even simultaneously the choicest county appointments of Sheriff, Deputy Commissary, Clerk and Judge. Samuel's eldest sibling Robert enjoyed the perquisites of his own colonelcy. Samuel's son, the president to be, benefitted from his Charles County appointments as Sheriff and Deputy Commissary, and would gain appointment as Deputy Surveyor of Frederick County. Samuel's son Walter, the president's brother, became Judge of Charles County. The extent of the Hansons' early influence in Charles County and the colony, and the closeness of the family to the proprietors and governors of the colony show plainly in John Hanson's shrievalty and position as Deputy Commissary and Walter Hanson's judgeship which the two brothers virtually inherited from their father Samuel. With two generations of the Hansons by the 1750s occupying the four most important and lucrative public positions in Charles County right up to the period of rebellion, one can say that the Hansons would appear to be the single most influential family in Charles County and one of the most so in the colony. They could only have enjoyed such status as a result of the patronage of the province's rulers.

During the 143 years of Calvert rule[48] from the chartering of the colony until the onset of the Revolution, a nativist American and Marylander identity was taking root and growing, stoked by fervent discussion among the great tobacco plantations along the Chesapeake and its tributaries, and in the drawing rooms of Annapolis. The small handful of Maryland families comprising the province's squirearchy was engaged in lively evolving discussion which entailed an increasingly cherished indigenous sentiment, rising resentment against the imperiousness of the Proprietor, and growing openness of opposition to the Proprietor's oppressive control over the daily lives of Marylanders. It should be noted that the notion of democracy which the Maryland gentry were beginning to promote little resembled any modern definition of it, their thinking far from universal suffrage or even broad male suffrage. What they meant by democracy in the colony was an increase in the prerogatives and voice of their own narrow elite at the expense of both a dictatorial Proprietor and ordinary people. The Revolution would gain the gentry their voice but at first only marginally extend the voting franchise in Maryland, even in the name of democracy.

Among these Tidewater tobacco families was one of the leading families of Charles County, if not its foremost family in the eighteenth century, the Hansons. The twentieth-century Charles County historian Harry Newman has reckoned only the Edelen and Dent families as possibly approaching the influence of the Hansons in Charles County in the seventeenth and eighteenth centuries.[49] The Briscoes should also be included in this very short list. As with the majority of the province's gentry, but more so on Maryland's western shore of the Chesapeake Bay than the eastern, the Hansons over the generations since settling in the colony found their allegiance to the Proprietor first in doubt, then in open but still polite opposition, then impossible to maintain. In this flow of change, the Hansons and Marylanders of all social stations felt a gathering yearning for a stronger voice in the province's affairs at first regarding taxation, but later on all political matters. The break between Proprietor and subject occurred in the third and fourth generations of the Hanson family with the future president, his children and a notable son-in-law. By then, the seeds of democracy which had been sown in the colony's grossly anti-democratic feudal period and which had taken firm root by Samuel Hanson's time were to bear the full fruit of revolt by the hand of Samuel's son.

The Future President Enters Politics

The earliest reliable civil record of John Hanson, grandson of his immigrant namesake, is his marriage to Jane Contee in early 1743 when he was twenty-eight and she was fifteen. Other civil records of the 1740s show Hanson serving as bondsman, court witness and executor of estates, and we thus see the John Hanson of his twenties being groomed in increasingly responsible civic roles.

John and Jane Hanson began their family with the birth of

their first child Heloise in 1743, followed in early 1744 by twins Anne and Mary who died soon after birth, and then their daughter Catherine on November 16, 1744. That these births occurred over no longer than a twenty-four-month period makes it appear that the twins were born prematurely. Jane and John would produce a total of thirteen children by 1772, three years after the family moved to Frederick. Only three would live beyond the age of twenty-five, only four would bear grandchildren to Jane and John, and Jane would end up outliving all but the youngest of the couple's children.

From his base in Port Tobacco, the Charles County seat, John Hanson in his thirties became involved in county and then provincial politics. In 1750, at the age of thirty-five and following in his father's footsteps, John Hanson was appointed by Governor Horatio Sharpe as Sheriff of Charles County beginning a thirty-three-year political career that would continue until his death. In 1757, the future president was elected to Maryland's colonial House of Delegates and got his first direct official taste of the colony's political life in the capital at Annapolis. In early 1758, foreshadowing one of his Revolutionary War roles and career-long specialization in finance, John Hanson was appointed to two Assembly finance committees putting to use the finance and accounting skills which he had been applying since he began keeping the account books for his father's tobacco brokerage twenty years before.

It is not clear why his service was not continuous, but during his Mulberry Grove years, John Hanson served off and on in the House of Delegates from 1757 until 1768. He made a clear mark in colonial politics during this period and would return to the House during his Frederick years. With his first election to the House of Delegates, Hanson joined the Country Party, also called the Popular Party, which sought more colonial independence and rights, and stood in opposition to the Court Party, also called the Proprietor Party, which swore allegiance to the Maryland Proprietor and resisted popular expansion of rights. Hanson's choice of party reveals his political sympathies by his early forties and of the budding of his public positions on the incipient colonial independence movement.

During Hanson's stint representing Charles County in the House of Delegates, the political lines were becoming more clearly drawn between the Country Party and the Court Party. Up to mid-century, the lower house contained

roughly equal representation of the two parties with sentiments divided between those of the Court Party, who still felt
allegiance to and a fond patriotism toward Britain and the
Maryland Proprietor, versus others of the newer Country
Party who might still hold love for the mother country but
chafed for a greater say in the affairs of their province. The
name of the parvenu Country Party is indicative of the sentiments of the delegates attracted to it: this is Country not in
the sense of countryside but of nation. The Country Party
represented the growing slice of the ruling gentry now thinking of the colonies as a country, their country, and of themselves as its citizens, as Americans.

The middle decades of the century saw a pronounced shift
in the province's sentiments in the direction of more independence from the Proprietor as election after election left
the House of Delegates controlled by growing majorities of
the Country Party. Partly this occurred as a result of county
electorates favoring Country Party candidates but also from
some nativist-minded Court Party delegates changing their
views and switching their party affiliation. By 1767, Charles
County Delegate John Hanson was a member of a House of
Delegates which had no Court Party representatives at all.
Only the upper house of the Maryland Assembly, the Proprietor's Council, offered a place for the Court Party and
then only by Proprietor appointment. By 1767, the province's political lines had hardened into a visibly drawn philosophical contest which many rightly suspected would only
get hotter.

A signal event in the evolution of Hanson's growing predis-
position toward more colonial autonomy was the Stamp Act
enacted by the British Parliament on March 22, 1765, to
take effect that November, newly taxing every colonist in
Britain's North American colonies on most paper forms they
used including even playing cards. Britain had just concluded the expensive French and Indian War and sought to
allay possible future colonial military costs by a tax on the
colonists. Following closely the Proclamation of 1763 prohibiting further English settlement beyond the first ridges of
the Appalachians, the 1764 Sugar Act raising British revenues with an import duty on the colonies, and the Currency
Act of 1764 prohibiting issuance of currency by the colonies,
the timing of the Stamp Act served to finally catalyze the
colonies' sentiments into active resistance.

Up to the time of these measures of the 1760s, taxes in the
colonies had been used for the most part for the legitimate

purpose of regulating colonial commerce and had not been widely opposed by the colonies. However, in the new Stamp Act the colonists saw a blunt means of the British Parliament to extract money from the colonies without any consultation with the colonial legislatures, a precedent that engendered immediate and strong opposition by the colonies and at least the lower houses of their provincial assemblies. By this time, the general belief among the colonists regarding taxation had come to be that any tax on any of the thirteen colonies needed to be approved by that colony's legislature, that is, by the colonists themselves, and not imposed unilaterally from afar by the British Parliament. This amounted to a clear position by the people of the colonies of self-government with regard to taxation.

With Patrick Henry leading the way, the Virginia House of Burgesses, the provincial assembly, volubly opposed the Stamp Act passing four resolutions to this effect. In heavy-handed reaction, the resolutions were not enacted by Virginia Governor Francis Fauquier — appointed by and loyal to the British — who instead dissolved the House of Burgesses in his opposition to the resolutions.

On September 23, 1765, the Maryland Assembly met to discuss the Stamp Act, a resurrection of the body after it had been forbidden by the Proprietor and governor to meet in 1764. In preparation for a meeting of the all-colonies Stamp Act Congress called by the colonial assemblies, the Maryland Assembly chose Charles County Delegate John Hanson as one of seven Marylanders to draft instructions for the Maryland delegates to the Stamp Act Congress. Another of the seven was Hanson's colleague from Anne Arundel County, Maryland, Thomas Johnson, the future first governor of the state of Maryland, who, like Hanson, would relocate to Frederick County on the province's western frontier before long.[50] The Stamp Act Congress met in New York City's Federal Hall in October 1765. Despite the Congress's remonstrances to the British, the Stamp Act took effect on November 1 as scheduled.

Some legislative bodies at the provincial and county levels in the colonies did, in their official capacities, eventually oppose the Stamp Act. The very first to do so was at the county level when the twelve judges of the Court of Frederick County, Maryland, on November 15, 1765, declared unilaterally that all individuals, businesses and other entities in the county did not have to pay the Stamp Tax there. This defiance proved successful and immediately put the thereto-fore obscure Maryland frontier county squarely onto the American political map. Further cementing the county's new rebellious reputation was the hanging in effigy of the British tax collector by a stalwart group of Frederick citizens, the Frederick Sons of Liberty, who on November 23 held a mock funeral of the Stamp Act replete with coffin on which had been inscribed, "The Stamp Act expired of a mortal stab received from the genius of liberty in Frederick County Court 23rd November 1765, Aged 22 days." The riotous celebration in Fredericktowne was led by the already legendary frontiersman, Colonel Thomas Cresap, leader of the Sons of Liberty, military associate of George Washington in the French and Indian War, and fellow investor in Washington's land development Ohio Company.

Another of the earliest official defiances of the Stamp Act came from Port Tobacco in the person of the future president's brother, Judge Walter Hanson, Charles County Commissioner of the Prerogative Court of Maryland. "Court days were always big days in any county, but what a day it must have been at Port Tobacco when Judge Walter Hanson came riding down from Harwood to hold his court and tell the sheriff to serves his papers 'on any old kind of paper' and to the devil with waiting for a supply of stamps."[51] Witnessing first hand his elder brother's willing disobedience put John Hanson amidst the earliest, boldest resistance to the Stamp Act.

Riots against the Stamp Act ensued in the colonies soon after it took effect. At one point, the British governor of Georgia had to defend himself at gunpoint at the governor's mansion from a mob demanding repeal of the Act. After the Stamp Act Congress, John Hanson found himself increasingly strident in his advocacy for greater colonial independence and, as a result, rising in political stature in the Maryland House of Delegates and the province. Agitation brought on by Hanson and others throughout the colonies caused Parliament to repeal the abhorred Stamp Act on March 18, 1766, only to replace it on June 29 of that year by the even more draconian Townshend Revenue Act creating import taxes on all glass, paint, lead, oil, paper and tea imports, even British, into the North American colonies.

Again riots and widespread defiance erupted but the Act remained in effect for four years before colonial pressure again led to repeal except of the tax on tea imports. During this four-year period, John Hanson grew increasingly put off by British superciliousness toward the American colonies and began throwing himself into resistance. In June of 1769, he was one of forty-three Maryland signers of the Non-Importation Resolution that called on the colonies to prohibit any British ship from putting into American ports for trade purposes. That summer and fall until he moved to Frederick, Hanson oversaw the inspection of British ships putting in at Port Tobacco. We now see the future president in his first overt action against British rule.

On July 26, 1775, three months after the outbreak of the Revolutionary War, Hanson would become a charter member of the Association of Maryland Freemen, a Who's Who of the Maryland elite, whose vow was that, " . . . said colonies be immediately put into a state of defence, and now supports, at the joint expence, an army to restrain the further violence, and repel the future attacks of a disappointed and exasperated enemy."[52]   With this bold step, John Hanson would give his name to the call for armed resistance against the British government explicitly labeled as an enemy. As this occurred, the colonies' remaining frayed strands slowing full detachment from Great Britain were a waning sentimental allegiance to the British crown, at least to the institution if not to the monarch George III himself, and to outright advocacy of American nationhood.

Late in 1769, a few months after being a signatory to the Non-Importation Resolution, John Hanson, late in life to be contemplating such a move, looked beyond his comfortable Mulberry Grove to the developing frontier of his colony to best position himself to oppose the British in the fight to come.

Part II

Greener Political Pastures: Hanson on the Frontier

Opportunity Heads West

As a few adventurous souls at the dawn of the eighteenth century began exploring Maryland westward of the counties huddled along the shores of the Chesapeake, they encountered the large inviting unsettled residual area of the province in which no counties had yet been chartered and none would be until 1748. In what was to become Frederick County, the westward traveler first encountered thirty-five miles of beautiful rolling piedmont rising slowly from the Chesapeake to the Linganore Hills looking down upon the broad Monocacy Valley drained by the Potomac's largest tributary, the Monocacy River. Through the center of this plain of rich alluvial soil ten to fifteen miles wide east to west, and running north-south the full fifty miles from Virginia to Pennsylvania, ran the important aboriginal Susquehanna Path trade route adopted by European settlers as they began trickling into the valley in the 1730s attracted by the excellent growing conditions, natural beauty and low land prices.

Continuing west, the traveler encountered Catoctin Mountain, the long narrow ridge that is the easternmost of the Appalachians in Maryland, and then the alternating series of valleys and long mountain ridges characteristic of the continent's major eastern range, the world's second-oldest mountain range.[53] From Catoctin Mountain, the most intrepid of early travelers, such as early Maryland frontiersman Thomas Cresap, crossed the Antietam Valley and Catoctin Creek, summited South Mountain, crossed the Cumberland Valley and Conococheague (CO-no-co-cheeg) Creek, and continued the valley-mountain-valley excursion with its striking scenery until descending the Appalachians' western slopes at the Ohio River and crossing into the Ohio Valley not far beyond Maryland's western extremity.

What was to become Frederick County was first explored and mapped by the Bernese nobleman Franz Ludwig Michel[54] (mee-KEL as German-speaking Swiss pronounce it) in 1707. Michel was a naturalist and explorer who spent his time after arriving in Williamsburg, Virginia, in 1702 collecting plant and animal specimens which he took back to Europe. In his return visit beginning in 1707, Michel explored what were then the frontier regions of Virginia, Maryland and southern Pennsylvania in the hope of finding investment opportunities, which he did. While in this region, he sketched maps and drawings of what he saw, most of which made its way into an account later published in Bern by his brother Hans Ludwig Michel.[55]   Franz Ludwig Michel's explorations in 1707 took him up the Maryland side of the Potomac River at least as far as the Monocacy Valley and probably a valley or two further into the Appalachians. The map he made of the area details the features of the Monocacy Valley including Sugarloaf Mountain and the point of rocks jutting into the Potomac where the northern and southern Indian tribes met to trade (Potomac means great trading place in the Tuscarora language), and shows Catoctin and Conococheague Creeks further west more or less where they ought to be. For a brief period, Michel served as William Penn's Commissioner of Mines in the Pennsylvania colony.

Michel liked what he saw in the colonies, returned to Bern, recruited Baron Christoph von Graffenried, Georg Ritter and Petter Isoth as investors, travelled to London, and petitioned the British Crown for permission to establish two Maryland colonies, one at the point of rocks mentioned where the town of Point of Rocks, Maryland, at the foot of Catoctin Mountain, exists today, the other downstream on the Potomac at Great Falls near where Washington, DC, would be founded ninety years later. The petition was declined but Michel and his partners were allowed to establish a colony in the Carolinas and did so naming it New Bern after their hometown. New Bern, North Carolina, today is a pretty town of about 28,000. New Bern was not the financial success which the investors had envisioned and Franz Ludwig Michel returned to Switzerland in 1713 to live out the rest of his life in Bern.[56] He produced four sons all of whom in the 1750s would emigrate from Bern to Frederick County and become either merchants in the county seat of Fredericktowne or large landowners. Their arrival was in the second decade of the county's existence which puts the four amongst the county's earliest settlers.

The third of the sons, Andreas Michel, who would anglicize his name to Andrew Michael, bought two lots on the northwest corner of All Saints Street and Carroll Street in Frederick upon his arrival in 1762, and built a handsome two-story stone home where he and his family lived until 1768. That year, Michel sold his Frederick home which went through several owners until July 1776 (note the month) when John Hanson bought the property. This rustic old building is owned today by an engineering company. In 2010, the building burned leaving only the original stone shell standing. The owner is rebuilding using as much of the original materials and layout as possible.

In 1768, Andrew Michael and his family settled a large tract which they named Cooling Springs two miles from Point of Rocks where his father had wanted to establish a colony sixty years before.[57] Cooling Springs grew by additions to 447 acres before Andrew died a United States citizen in 1800. Over seven succeeding generations, Cooling Springs Farm has remained in the Michael family and is now owned by the author and his wife. Cooling Springs was a working farm until the late twentieth century and is now a residence and historic Underground Railroad site open to the public.[58]

After returning home to Switzerland, Franz Ludwig Michel published an illustrated enthusiastic account of his Maryland explorations, and he and his sons spread the word in Switzerland, Alsace-Loraine and elsewhere in Europe about the appeal of western Maryland. Even before the four brothers' arrivals in Frederick County, German-speaking Swiss and Germans had begun arriving and settling the Monocacy Valley and eventually further west. Michel's fond recounting in Europe of his explorations of western Maryland helped to uncork a tidal wave of non-English settlement into the region which in a single generation would have a profound effect on the colony by tilting it politically. Most of Franz Ludwig Michel's writings, drawings and maps may be found in the Biblioteka Bern. Michel's 1707 map of the area which would become Frederick County, which he used in his application to found a New World colony, is held by the Public Records Office in London. For the researcher, these and other sources are provided in the last of the bibliographies here.

Δ

As early as 1723, the Maryland Proprietor began selling large tracts of what was to become Frederick County to major English investors. In March of 1732, wanting to attract settlers to the western area of the province, he issued a proclamation declaring special land prices and taxes for those, including immigrants, willing to settle the western reaches of Maryland. At concessionary terms, families were offered two hundred acres, singles one hundred. Immigrant settlers were taxed and the security of their land was insured as if they were British subjects which led to a growing land rush by Swiss, German, Scottish, Irish and other immigrants.

In the 1730s and 1740s, large tracts of the finest parts of the Monocacy and the Antietam valleys were sold or granted by the Proprietor. Among these were Monocacy Manor, an

8,983-acre tract acquired by Daniel Dulaney the elder; an adjacent tract where the county seat of Fredericktowne went up bought by Patrick Dulaney; Leonard Calvert's and Thomas Johnson's Catoctin Furnace purchase; and the largest of the sales, Charles Carroll's 10,000-acre Carrollton Manor along the Potomac where Franz Ludwig Michel had wanted to found his colony.

Even before there were any European settlements in western Maryland, parties of Germans passed through it from Lancaster County, Pennsylvania, seeking home sites in what would be called the German Settlement of northern Virginia directly across the Potomac River from the future Frederick County. The main road between the two areas was the old Indian trail, the Susquehanna Path, which crossed the present Pennsylvania counties of York and Adams to the Monocacy River where it passed into Maryland, ran down the Monocacy Valley, traversed Crampton's Gap and crossed the Potomac into Virginia at several fords. Significant portions of the new settlers were German Palatines and other German-speaking migrants spreading south from Pennsylvania along this route through Maryland into Virginia's German Settlement.

The first European settlement in Frederick County was the village of Monocacy, settled by English and German migrants no later than 1729 and situated near the present village of Creagerstown, Frederick County. Here about 1732, western Maryland's first place of worship known as the Log Church was built by German Lutheran settlers. Before long, Creagerstown boasted several taverns used by travelers on the new Monocacy Road, a joint project of the colonies of Pennsylvania and Maryland. The road followed the Susquehanna Path from Wright's Ferry in Pennsylvania through the future Frederick County to the fords of the Potomac across from the German Settlement.

By the 1740s, the swell of population in the Proprietor's western lands had reached the level requiring surer administration leading to the platting and incorporation of Fredericktowne in 1745 and the chartering of Frederick County in 1748. Fredericktowne was designated as the county seat. After being created, Frederick County received the usual Proprietor's appointments of Judge, Sheriff, County Clerk, Deputy Commissary and Deputy Surveyor.

The rush of settlers to Frederick County was slowed by the French and Indian War begun in 1755 which visited violence on virtually all of the county in and beyond the Monocacy

Valley until 1763 when the war drew to a close. Many of the villages of western Frederick County were attacked, with the Scottish and Irish immigrants who had settled furthest west bearing the worst of it. Frederick Countians were killed, tortured and burned out during the Seven Years War as it was also called. The village of Monocacy was sacked until just the old Log Church and a few other buildings remained.

Four who delayed their planned settling in Frederick County because of the war were Christoph, Wilhelm, Andreas and Nicholas Michel, sons of Franz Ludwig Michel. The four brothers disembarked at the port of Philadelphia around 1757, the known year of Andreas's arrival. Andreas, and most likely his brothers as well, spent until 1762 in the heavily German Lancaster County, Pennsylvania, before completing their journey after the war had subsided to a safe enough level to Frederick County which their father had explored.

When the French and Indian War ended in 1763, the tide of immigrants arriving in Frederick County resumed more strongly than ever, with German and German-speaking Swiss arrivals now outnumbering all others. The inflow was accelerated in the 1760s by the new shorter route from the Maryland port of Annapolis directly across the province, supplanting the more cumbersome journey of landing at Philadelphia and making one's way overland through Pennsylvania and then down into Maryland and Frederick County.

Δ

When it officially defied the Stamp Act in 1765, Frederick County had been settled by Europeans for barely a generation and had been organized as a county for only seventeen years. The longest operating church in western Maryland, Frederick's Evangelical Lutheran Church, thriving today, was founded in 1738 as the first trickle of Swiss and German immigrants began arriving.   The county seat of Fredericktowne, as it was then known, platted by Daniel Dulaney the elder and first settled in 1745, still numbered fewer than one thousand occupants by the time of the Stamp Act. Dulaney's ambition to create a transportation and trading hub along the Susquehanna Path was realized as settlers began arriving in the 1730s in search of the rich inexpensive farmland of the county's lower piedmont and the Monocacy, Antietam and Cumberland valleys.

Frederick County comprised fully the western third of the

colony until it was divided in 1776. By 1763, virtually all of the remaining unpatented land in the colony was in Frederick County whose immigrants brought with them industriousness, trades, modest grubstakes in many cases, and, for the most part, lack of any affinity to Britain or the Maryland Proprietor. The flavor of life in Frederick County at the time of the Stamp Act was strongly influenced by the independent nature and individual reliance of these pioneering people who had chosen to make their way in a new land and hew their livelihood from what was then still virgin wilderness. In large measure, it was the sensibilities of these adventurous pioneering immigrants that emboldened their county to become the first to officially defy the Stamp Act. With their emerging identity as Americans, the colonists felt a buoyant optimism, perhaps none more so than the industrious non-English-speaking newcomers who were largely unburdened by a tradition of royal subservience to the British crown and who were filling up Maryland's expansive frontier in Frederick County. One heard German spoken on the streets of Frederick County communities until late into the 1800s and in homes later than that. Much of the influence of these early German and Swiss settlers including family names, food, architecture, religion and customs survives in the county today. Frederick County's dual German-British heritage is also much evident in the three counties further west that were formed from Frederick County in the eighteenth and nineteenth centuries.

As the newcomers poured in, the county as early as 1755 — after only seven years in existence — had become Maryland's most populous and was again in a 1765 count. In both of these years, the county lagged only the city of Baltimore in size and then only by a few hundred people.[59] In the decade before the advent of the Revolutionary War in 1775, Frederick County grew by 117 percent, a rate not remotely approached by any other county in the province, and had become larger even than Baltimore. Due almost exclusively to the growth of Frederick County, the balance of the colony's population had shifted from the eastern to the western shore of the Chesapeake. By 1755, the western shore had twelve percent more people than did the Eastern Shore[60], and by 1775, sixty-two percent more. This relatively faster growth led to a concomitant shift in representation in the provincial House of Delegates toward the counties west of the Chesapeake though this change lagged the weight of the population shift to a degree.

Frederick County's population predominance would continue well into the nineteenth century. As Lewis and Clark were outfitting their continental expedition at the Frederick Barracks in 1803, Frederick with a population of 4,000 was the largest town until reaching Pittsburgh, and four times the size of St. Louis, the jumping-off point for Lewis and Clark.

Another kind of shift was also taking place. From the time of first European settlement after being chartered in 1634, the colony's power center was heavily skewed toward the owners of its oldest and largest tobacco plantations lined up along the shores of the Chesapeake and the broad rivers of both of its shores. Enslaved African-Americans comprised a third or more of the population of the Eastern Shore counties with their tobacco plantations and wood manufactories turning out shingles and barrel staves. The proportion of the population enslaved in the southern Maryland tobacco counties along the western shore of the Chesapeake was similar. Twenty-five percent of the province's population as a whole was African-American, nearly all enslaved. In sharp contrast during John Hanson's lifetime, only one percent of Frederick County's population was enslaved as the flood of non-slave-owning German and British immigrants arriving there occupied the territory with their grain and livestock farms, virtually shutting out tobacco plantations before they were able to get that far west. Furthermore, because of their backgrounds, their Lutheran beliefs and the fact that some of the Frederick County immigrants had arrived as indentured servants, Frederick County's German and Swiss immigrants were largely opposed to slavery with very few of them ending up practicing it themselves. Because the most rapidly growing part of the colony had so few slaves, the numerical impact was that the proportion of slaves in the colony as a whole dropped as Frederick County grew. By 1810, Maryland would have more free Blacks than any other state, a condition which would last through the Civil War.

By 1769 when John Hanson secured his Proprietor's appointment as Deputy Surveyor of Frederick County, the county existed in stark contrast to the rest of the province: huge versus all of the much smaller older counties, rapidly growing versus nearly stable in population, new versus old in outlook, experimental versus settled in traditions, anti-slavery versus pro-slavery, affordable versus hard to afford, multiethnic versus essentially monocultural, and very fertile versus the increasing soil degradation from tobacco cultivation elsewhere. In short, the vast western third of the colony comprising Frederick County was the part of the colony of maximum financial and social opportunity not only for the average person but also for any member of the established gentry elsewhere in the colony looking for new prospects. Because of its attractiveness, growth, open-mindedness and financial surge, Frederick County was also rapidly becoming the land of political opportunity in Maryland.

Among a number of Marylanders who found greener political pastures in Frederick County as the Revolution approached were three who picked up from their comfortable Southern Maryland existences, moved to Frederick County, and walked into the pages of history. The self-made Thomas Johnson who came to Frederick County from Anne Arundel County would become Maryland's first governor after independence and then a United States Supreme Court Justice. Thomas Sim Lee who removed to Frederick County from Prince George's County would succeed Johnson as the state's second governor. And Charles County's John Hanson who would also adopt Frederick County would become the nation's first president and the only Marylander ever to occupy the nation's highest office.

Why Hanson Moved to Frederick

Son of a judge and grandson of a successful immigrant planter and colonel, John Hanson grew up very comfortably in southern Maryland amidst the ruling patrician plantation class of the colony, enjoying the privileges which accrued to well-positioned British loyalists. Hanson's Mulberry Grove plantation and home sustained John and his family in the highest level of comfort which one could find in the province. The family was deeply ensconced at Mulberry Grove where the children were being schooled and often saw their many Charles County cousins. Deep into this comfortable midlife at Mulberry Grove, Hanson's aspirations for colonial independence quickened further. At this juncture in the 1760s, he began to press his views on his riverine neighbor George Washington and others. "The Washingtons at Mount Vernon on the Virginia side of the Potomac and the Hansons at Port Tobacco on the Maryland side, were friends and neighbors."[61] "In life they were neighbors, for Washington lived just across the Potomac River from Maryland; and the Washingtons and Hansons were intimate friends of many years' standing. In Washington's records of visitors to Mount Vernon, the name of Hanson occurs frequently."[62]

Aside from their budding restlessness for a more autonomously American way of life, John Hanson and George Washington had much else in common which must have made the two especially receptive to one another, and the close friends and allies which they became to one another. Both were the grandsons of immigrants. Both maintained their families' fortunes as Tidewater planters at splendid riverside estates, Hanson on Maryland's Port Tobacco River, Washington on Virginia's Rappahanock and then the Potomac between the two states. Both were, as Washington Irving put it, "home-bred school boys" drilled mainly in the practical mercantile and legal disciplines but also in some measure in the arts, classics and European languages. Their biographers note their journals meticulously kept in special accuracy and neat hand. Both were especially numerate leading them into important appointments as surveyors. Hanson and Washington also had the benefit of tutelage by accomplished and admired older brothers, Judge Walter Hanson and Lawrence and Augustine Washington. And both men were life-long enslavers who in large measure attained their comforts and high accomplishments in life by extracting the stolen toil of other human beings.

Far more alike than not, Hanson and Washington did have at least two noticeable differences, one perhaps unimportant, the other definitive of the relative posterity in which the two have been held.

While Hanson enjoyed growing up in an intact family in one location, Washington was fatherless for much of his childhood and put out to his brothers' homes to be raised. Hanson was born at his family's Mulberry Grove estate where he lived his first fifty-four years, knew his father until age twenty-five when Judge Samuel Hanson died, and his mother Elizabeth until he was fifty-one. When Washington's father Augustine died when the boy was eleven, his mother first sent him to live with his brother Augustine, Jr. at Bridges Creek where George had been born, and then with his brother Lawrence at his Mount Vernon estate which George would inherit. Not quite an orphan, the boy nevertheless grew up amid comfort, care and excellent guidance from his older brothers and extended family.

A difference which existed in vivid contrast between the two men was that of their self-presentation to the public and posterity. Washington was an assiduous life-long diarist and deft shaper of his public persona while Hanson seemed to have no particular affinity for the limelight, or perhaps even a distaste for it. As explored later in *Remembering John Hanson*, this difference has had a defining course on how history has remembered the two.[63]

Previous biographers have not been able to explain why Hanson decided to uproot himself from contented life at Mulberry Grove and relocate to what was then the frontier. The oral tradition passed down in the author's family and other evidence gathered make his reason clear: that after Frederick County's official defiance of the Stamp Act in 1765 displayed the county's temperament and the county had attained its weight as demographic powerhouse, John Hanson moved to Frederick for the clear-cut prospect of greener political pastures.

As one of the gentry of Southern Maryland — the longest settled and most British part of the colony — Hanson had been expected to be loyal to the British crown, the benefactor of Maryland's old privileged class to which Hanson belonged. It was in the interest of this class to maintain the loyalties to the crown and the Proprietor on which their own fortunes rested and who felt threatened by the rising talk of American independence. Hanson and a small but growing number of his aristocratic friends were exceptions and, in fact, comprised the early intellectual budding of nationhood. Mount Vernon's logs record Hanson as having made periodic visits to Washington's home. In turn, Washington would call at Mulberry Grove to visit John Hanson or Washington's physician over nearly fifty years, Dr. James Craik, who lived along the Port Tobacco River within a mile of Mulberry Grove.[64] "George Washington, the young soldier and planter, already with a reputation made on the western frontier, came often by way of Port Tobacco in preference to another road, and visited with Craik, and Jenifer, and Hanson, and Dr. Gustavus Brown of Rose Hill, and Thomas Stone, one of Maryland's Signers of the Declaration of Independence, who was building Habre de Venture, the one of the Stone family mansions still standing on the Port Tobacco hills."[65] Hanson and Washington corresponded and conferred in person before the Revolutionary War, discussing British colonial abuses and prospective nationhood for the colonies.[66]

As his sentiments evolved, Hanson felt increasingly distanced from his own class, indeed from many of his own relatives and friends, because of the widening divergence between his and their views on independence. After 1765 when its court became the American colonies' first official entity to defy the Stamp Act, Hanson saw Frederick County as fertile territory for his nation-building ideas and visited to test the waters. As Hanson scholar Ralph Levering has noted, " . . . western Marylanders, who had less need to fear divisive social and economic conflict, had been strongly anti-British for several years . . ."[67]

Liking what he saw of the county's disposition on independence, Hanson in the fall of 1769 gained the Proprietor's appointment as Deputy Surveyor of Frederick County, a position which today would seem to be inadequate for the now senior statesman but one that was actually one of the Maryland colony's best compensated and most prized offices. We recall that each county had one Deputy Surveyor who reported directly to the colony's Surveyor General in Annapolis. That John Hanson was able to gain this appointment indicates that, despite his views on Proprietor rule which were well known by this time, he was still trusted enough by the colonial Governor to receive the plum appointment essentially for the asking. The appointment gave Hanson a good toehold into Frederick County political life, let him get to know the sprawling county and its power brokers, and incidentally allowed him rapidly to make well informed property investments in the county seat which by this time had contracted its name into Fredericktowne from Frederick Towne. Hanson began purchasing buildings and lots in the town. John Hanson was reappointed as Deputy Surveyor of Frederick County by the Proprietor in 1771 and 1773, and by the new Maryland General Assembly in 1777 after Independence.[68] There is at least one surviving record of John Hanson acting in his role as the county's Deputy Surveyor when on April 14, 1774, he surveyed and platted the village of Accident, Maryland, in what was then the westernmost extremity of Frederick County in today's Garrett County, Maryland.[69]

John Hanson resigned as Sheriff of Charles County when he moved to Frederick County in late 1769, and secured the Proprietor's appointment as Sheriff of Frederick County in 1771 in addition to his continuing role as the county's Deputy Surveyor. By then, we see Hanson firmly ensconced as a Frederick County power broker, well positioned to lead the County in the coming years when it would form its extralegal government in opposition to British rule. The probable reason why the Proprietor would grant these appointments to John Hanson was that he thought Hanson would act as an experienced, even if not entirely sympathetic, bulwark against anti-British sentiment in Frederick County.

Most indicative of the deliberateness of John Hanson's intentions in moving to Frederick is that even before his appointment as Frederick County Deputy Surveyor and the move from Mulberry Grove, he had already made a calculated decision to shift his entire life focus from one place to the other and began investing in Frederick County and divesting in Charles County. On March 17, 1769, six months before his appointment, he sold one hundred acres of Davis's Thought in Charles County to James Allen, a Charles County planter, and that November 25, shortly after his appointment, sold 547 of the 603 acres of the Rozer's Refuge tract where he and his family lived to his brother, William Hanson.[70] This tract includes the Mulberry Grove home and cemetery. The remaining fifty-six acres not sold were apparently Jane Hanson's and retained by her. Her brother Peter Contee lived at Mulberry Grove until his death in 1779 and is buried in the Mulberry Grove cemetery. William Hanson did not own the Mulberry Grove property long, selling it to Thomas Contee, another of Jane Hanson's brothers, on December 21, 1771. John Hanson's decisive action in making the move shows his commitment to leaving behind a conventionally successful life for the prospect of achieving something greater in the new lands of the West.

It is not clear exactly when Hanson moved his family from Mulberry Grove to Frederick, but the move is unlikely to have occurred before his appointment as Deputy Surveyor in fall of 1769 nor later than the known date of the family's occupancy of their Frederick home on Patrick Street by late 1773. It is known that by 1772 he owned a store in Frederick though it might have been tended by its co-owner, Hanson's brother-in-law, Thomas Contee, or by a hired hand. Another possibility is that, though the Mulberry Grove home had been sold to Thomas in 1771, Jane and John Hanson could have continued to live there by arrangement until a move not later than 1773. Harry Newman's well documented *Charles County Gentry* written in 1940 has John Hanson moving to Frederick in 1773, but cites no source for this.[71]

It is also known that when the Hanson's daughter, Jane Contee Hanson the younger, married Dr. Philip Thomas in February 1773, the marriage took place in Charles County. If Jane and John Hanson were living in Frederick by that time, having the marriage in Charles County might have been for the convenience of Dr. Thomas's family who resided across the Chesapeake on Maryland's eastern Shore. As the Hanson and Thomas families did not move into their newly built adjoining homes in Frederick until fall of 1773, the choice of Charles County for the wedding might also have been to provide a nicer venue for the wedding than whatever temporary quarters the bride's parents were occupying in Frederick if that is where they were living at the time.

Perhaps the strongest clue to the timing of the family's move to Frederick County is that John Hanson's appointments as Deputy Surveyor and Sheriff there would appear to have required residence in the county from 1769, though this is not certain. At any rate, the life-changing decision had been made to relocate to Frederick County and the move occurred sometime during the forty-six-month period between November 1769 when most of Mulberry Grove was sold and autumn of 1773 by which time it is known that the Hansons were living in their permanent residence on Patrick Street in Frederick. On the strength of the likely residence requirement of John Hanson's official appointments, it is assumed here that the move occurred in late 1769 though this is not proven.

Having left his long off-and-on service representing Charles County in the Maryland House of Delegates by 1768, these next few years might have afforded Hanson something of a hiatus from political life. It could seem that John Hanson took the Frederick County Deputy Surveyor position mainly to prospect for good property investments in a growing part of the colony or to temporize politically while he considered his options, but the sale of Mulberry Grove belies this. It is also plausible that at the age of fifty-three in 1768, considered well advanced in age at that time, Hanson might have left politics and begun exploring western opportunities as a deliberate full-time return to private life. In fact, in large measure because of the colonial prosperity of the time, the period from his Frederick County appointment in 1769 until 1773 was one of relative calm in the colonies. This period was, however, punctuated on March 5, 1770, by the Boston Massacre.

A contributing factor to the sale of Mulberry Grove and the move to Frederick could have been the silting in of the Port Tobacco River and its port, and the consequent demise of international trade which Mulberry Grove depended on there. Over time in the seventeenth and eighteenth centuries, the river, not deep to begin with, became shallower and less navigable as silt was carried down from increasing cultivation upstream. Eventually, ocean-going ships could no longer reach the wharf and a new one was constructed about a half mile downstream from the original one during John Hanson's time at Mulberry Grove. Later in the century, this too had become silted in, finally halting any commerce involving deep-draft ships. This in turn led to the rapid commercial recession of Port Tobacco. One of the town's main casualties was the family's wharf-side tobacco brokerage that John Hanson had learned at his father's side which could no longer operate from Port Tobacco.

By the time of the Hanson family's sale of Mulberry Grove and move to Frederick, the Maryland tobacco economy had been in decline for a generation from soil exhaustion, overplanting, the resulting poor quality of tobacco and concomitant lower prices it fetched on the world market. As early as 1731, Maryland Governor Samuel Ogle declared that he was, "heartily concerned for the calamitous Condition the Country is in, occasioned by the Decay of its Trade and the Lowness of its Staple."[72]

By 1797, the English traveler Isaac Weld wrote that, "Port Tobacco contains about eighty houses; most of which are of wood, and very poor. There is a large English Episcopalian church on the border of the town, built of stone, which formerly was an ornament to the place, but is now entirely out of repair; the windows are all broken, and the road is carried through the church-yard, over the graves, the paling that surrounded it having been torn down. From Port Tobacco to Hooe's Ferry, on the Patowmac River, the country is flat and sandy, and wears a most dreary aspect. Nothing is to be seen here for miles together but extensive plains, that have been worn out by the culture of tobacco, overgrown with yellow sedge, and interspersed with groves of pine and cedar trees, the dark green color of which forms a curious contrast with the yellow sedge. In the midst of these plains are the remains of several good houses, which shew that the country was once very different to what it is now. These were the houses, most probably, of the people who originally settled in Maryland with Lord Baltimore, but which have now been suffered to go to decay, as the land around them is worn out, and the people find it more to their interest to remove to another part of their country, and clear a piece of rich land, than to attempt to reclaim these exhausted plains. In consequence of this, the country in many of the lower parts of Maryland appears as if it had been deserted by one half of its inhabitants."[73]

Soil exhaustion at Mulberry Grove was probably not a factor in the family's move to Frederick as there is evidence that John Hanson had shifted to rotated crops some time before. Hanson may have adopted the practice at the suggestion of

Washington who had begun experimenting with crop rotation. But by 1797, the traveler Weld might have been describing Mulberry Grove as one of the decayed estates he saw.

By the 1890s, Port Tobacco had declined to the point at which the newer Charles County town of La Plata, with its rail head and better road to Washington, vied to become the county seat. On August 3, 1892, after all of the county records had been mysteriously removed, the old court house at Port Tobacco burned. Port Tobacco's decline continued until 1895 when Charles County dethroned it as the county seat, moving the government to La Plata. Today, Port Tobacco is a ghost of its former self consisting only of the courthouse, restored by a citizens' group in 1973 and now used as a museum, a stabilized but unused one-room school house, two dilapidated barns, four or five very old homes and the cemetery, without gravestones, of the Episcopal Church which is long gone. In 1904, twelve years after the Port Tobacco courthouse burned, the town's Episcopal church was dismantled stone by stone and rebuilt in La Plata.

In the author's opinion, the most plausible scenario as seen through the lens of his later actions is that John Hanson moved to Frederick and re-entered politics there so as to most advantageously position himself politically for what he saw as the coming split with Great Britain and a stronger role in the colonies' growing aspirations for independence. Hanson knew that continued service as a legislator in either Charles County or Frederick County would have limited his effectiveness because he would have been operating from within the British colonial power structure where his ideas of more colonial autonomy would continue to be thwarted. Based on John Hanson's and the colony's tenor at the time, the author believes that greener political pastures were the reason for his leaving the independent-minded but still British-supervised colonial House of Delegates in 1768 and moving to Frederick the following year.

Most crucially, Hanson also would have understood that to maximize his effectiveness, he needed to occupy an executive as opposed to a legislative role. That left it to Hanson to identify the executive position in the colony which offered the most personal power and the best vantage from which to exercise his political will and aspirations for independence in the colony. By 1769 when Hanson made his move to Frederick County, all of the southern Maryland counties, all of the Eastern Shore counties but Wicomico, and all of the counties on the western shore of the Chesapeake Bay but Howard had been formed. Eleven of these sixteen counties had been chartered in the seventeenth century. All are much smaller than Frederick County geographically and, though many had growing anti-British sentiments, all of these counties still had large strong elements of British loyalty. Easily the most fertile new political territory for John Hanson was that which occupied the huge western reach of the colony, Frederick County which had been organized barely two decades before Hanson began visiting there.

One must speculate that John Hanson's calculus of Frederick County took into account several other realities. In taking the continent-wide lead in officially defying the Stamp Act in 1765, Frederick County demonstrated that it was the part of the Maryland colony most ready to oppose further British impositions. In addition, the hardy German, Swiss and Scots-Irish immigrants flooding into Frederick County hadn't much inclination for taking orders from the colony's British governor or others of the loyalist ruling hierarchy. After 1769 when Hanson began to reconnoiter the county as its Deputy Surveyor, he seems to have concluded that his political chances were good there and, through his discussions with local power brokers, it would appear that he struck a deal to lead the county politically in the event of a breakaway from British rule. Most important if a politician were seeking a vantage point of maximum power is that, even before Hanson's move to Frederick County, the young county had become the province's most populous and forward looking. Finally, it seems highly unlikely that Hanson would have uprooted his family from its comforts at Mulberry Grove and made the move to Frederick County just for further land investment opportunities which he could almost as easily have transacted from Mulberry Grove.

Rather, the most plausible motivation for his move was the opportunity for John Hanson to command the most potent political base in the colony. With a warm reception in Frederick County to his ideas of independence, John Hanson would certainly have been tempted to move if his intention at this point in his life was to launch a higher political career within the best political base from which to put his talents to work for independence. In fact, in exchanging his non-executive position as a Charles County legislator for his chief executive position running the colony's largest, most populous, fastest growing and most rebellious county, John Hanson vastly increased his political power and influence and became no longer just another strident but powerless voice in the colony for less British control, but a force to be reckoned with colony wide. The probable demise of his family's tobacco brokerage because of the closing of the port at Port Tobacco and the further possibility of exhausted soil of the farms of John Hanson's brokerage clients from planting tobacco too long could well have been additional motivations for the move to Frederick.

John Hanson also had the advantage that, from the enactment of the Maryland Constitution in early 1777 until the conclusion of his presidency in late 1782, Maryland's first two governors were Frederick Countians and close to Hanson. Like Hanson, Thomas Johnson and Thomas Sim Lee had moved to Frederick County from southern Maryland. In 1774, Johnson and his brothers founded the Catoctin Furnace, a Frederick County forge which did well for the brothers and produced much of the state's munitions which John Hanson arranged for during the Revolutionary War. Lee established a large prosperous plantation, worked however by his two hundred slaves, in the county's Catoctin Valley.

Johnson and Lee both led long distinguished political careers which put them in positions one after another in which they could advance Hanson's political goals and vice versa.

John Hanson and Thomas Johnson had worked together as members of the colonial House of Delegates as far back as the 1760s. Thomas Johnson served two terms as Maryland's first governor from statehood until 1779 to be succeeded by Lee who served three terms, the constitutionally prescribed limit, from 1779 until 1782, overlapping John Hanson's presidency in the last year. Johnson had earlier served as a Maryland delegate to the Second Continental Congress. On Hanson's recommendation and George Washington's nomination, Johnson commanded the Maryland militia with the rank of Brigadier General during the Revolutionary War.

Thomas Sim Lee served as a Maryland Representative to the United States in Congress Assembled in the 1782-1783 term, filling John Hanson's seat there after Hanson had retired as president. Lee also served as a Maryland delegate to the Constitutional Convention in 1787, as a presidential elector with John Hanson's son and son-in-law in 1792 casting his vote for George Washington, and two more terms as the governor of Maryland from 1792 to 1794.[74] At seventeen and thirty years Hanson's junior respectively, Johnson and Lee were something of protégés of the older man. It would not have been by coincidence that the three rose to state and then national political prominence from the same county at the same time after all had decided to move there in quick succession. One suspects a likelihood that the three had had discussions while still residing in southern Maryland about Frederick County and its political opportunities, and that their more or less simultaneous moves were coordinated.

While other Frederick Countians also attained measures of significant political influence, the sextet of John Hanson, Alexander Contee Hanson, Sr., Alexander Contee Hanson, Jr., Philip Thomas, Thomas Johnson and Thomas Sim Lee kept the county's sway at the forefront in Maryland for a half century from 1769 when John Hanson began his political assent from his new Frederick County base until 1819 when his grandson, United States Senator Alexander Contee Hanson, Jr., died in office. One of the six occupied the highest office in the land, four of the six served as presidential electors, two occupied the governor's mansion, one served in the United States Senate, one sat on the nation's highest court, and collectively they made critical contributions virtually continuously to the development of their nation for a half century. There could not have been many counties in the colonies and then the early United States which could have claimed such impact at the time. Frederick County has never seen such a simultaneous constellation of political talent since.

Given the older, more traditional, predominantly British background of all of the other Maryland counties, it is likely that no other county leader in Maryland commanded as much political muscle as did Hanson after his move to Frederick and his election as the county's first chief executive. His move from his many comforts at Mulberry Grove has long puzzled John Hanson biographers and writers, but looking at the move in the context of Hanson's aims, the political potency of Frederick County and his paler political prospects in the more British-leaning parts of the colony, the move makes sense as the product of a deliberate and well-calibrated political calculus by the future president: John Hanson sought, found and ended up controlling the strongest political base there was from which to press his plans for independence and nationhood. This scenario squares congruently with the oral tradition passed down in the author's line of the Hanson family that John Hanson moved to Frederick for greener political pastures.

In the fall of 1769 at the age of fifty-four, late in life for his era, John Hanson gave up his easy plantation life at Mulberry Grove with its grand long views from the bluff overlooking the Potomac and Port Tobacco rivers and moved his wife and children to Frederick as revolutionary ferment rose in the colonies and the Revolutionary War approached. The couple had lived at Mulberry Grove for twenty-five years beginning the year after they married. John Hanson would make his home in Frederick for fourteen years, Jane for forty-three, longer than she had spent on the banks of the Port Tobacco River. It is fortuitous that virtually all of the owners of Mulberry Grove since John and Jane Hanson have taken pride in the fact that the country's first First Couple had lived there. These owners did as much through the years as any to keep alive the memory of John Hanson and his presidency, a national benefit which continues today with the present owners, Edward and Lexy Edelen.

As John Hanson stepped into his position as Frederick County's Deputy Surveyor in 1769, another newcomer who would make his mark came onto the scene in Frederick. The young Dr. Philip Thomas took up his medical practice in Frederick as the county's first physician on August 1, 1769, after his recent graduation from medical college in Philadelphia.[75] In a town of only about 1,700 at the time, the county's only doctor and the recently appointed patrician Deputy Surveyor from Charles County would not have taken long to meet one another and discuss politics. The younger man would become the beloved son-in-law, confidant and indispensable aide to the elder man. Sometime after John Hanson and Philip Thomas got to know each other in Frederick, Dr. Thomas was introduced to the Hansons' daughter Jane. It is not beyond probability that John Hanson played Cupid in an introduction. Philip Thomas and Jane Hanson the younger were married on February 18, 1773, in Charles County. Both were twenty-five, she five days shy of her twenty-sixth birthday. As both the president and Jane the elder were to learn in different ways, they could not have asked for more in a son-in-law.

Earlier in 1773, Benjamin Franklin had proposed that representatives of the thirteen colonies meet to discuss the deteriorating relations with Britain and the prospects of more colonial autonomy. On September 23 the vocal Massachusetts activist Samuel Adams formally called for what he termed a continental congress to be formed to discuss Britain's continuing imposition of taxes on the colonies. This call for an all-colonies congress would have influenced the crystallization of John Hanson's political repositioning. As the family was completing its fourth year in Frederick, the French and Indian War which had rent Frederick County was barely a decade in the past and the Boston Tea Party lay only weeks ahead that December.

After his move, the Frederick County electorate resonated with Hanson's ideas of nationhood and not only elected him to every county, colonial and state office he ever sought but continued to elect him to represent the county in the new State Assembly after independence even when he was away in Philadelphia serving as president. Frederick County first elected John Hanson as its chief executive in 1774, continued electing him time and again, and, beginning with John Hanson's first election in the county, elected or appointed his son and son-in-law to some of the county's most important positions. If the Hansons had adopted Frederick County, the County with equal ardor had adopted the Hansons.

Life on the Frontier

Four of Jane and John Hanson's thirteen children were surviving at the time of the move and one was yet unborn assuming that the move took place in fall 1769 between the time of John Hanson's Deputy Surveyor appointment and the sale of Mulberry Grove that year. At that time, Jane and John Hanson's daughter Jane was twenty-two and their sons Alexander, Peter and Samuel were twenty, nineteen and fourteen, respectively. The couple's youngest child, Elizabeth Arianna Adolphus Hanson, was born in 1772 presumably in Frederick. Within a few years, all three sons were away serving in the Continental Army as the Revolutionary War got underway leaving just the two daughters at home.

The family established its new home in Frederick and John and Jane Hanson, their children and Philip Thomas quickly became engaged in the top tier of the social and political fabric of the county or quite possibly established a stratum above what had existed before. Drawing on his knowledge acquired as Deputy Surveyor, Hanson bought several Frederick properties and at least one Frederick County farm as investments. By 1772, John Hanson and his brother-in-law, Thomas Contee (ca. 1729-1811) owned a store and warehouse in Frederick Towne. Between 1769 and 1779, Hanson purchased 223 acres in Frederick County, took two fourteen-year leases on another 255 acres in the county, owned the two Frederick Towne lots where his and Dr. Thomas's homes were built, owned the large stone building previously owned by Andrew Michael (Andreas Michel) on the northwest corner of Carroll and All Saints Streets in Frederick, and owned a lot in Georgetown, Frederick County, now in Washington, DC.[76] At one time, John Hanson also owned the property across from his home where 143 West Patrick Street now stands.[77]

In 1773, John Hanson bought two lots for £315 and £100 from Adam Coon near the southwest corner of Court and Patrick Streets in Frederick.[78] That year, two adjoining homes, one for John and Jane Hanson, the other for Philip and Jane Thomas, were constructed on these lots. It is not clear where the Hansons and Thomases lived from the Hansons' presumed arrival in Frederick in 1769 until their homes were completed in 1773. Next to this site today is the John Hanson National Memorial completed in May 2011. The Hanson home had a useful natural spring in its basement. "Numerous springs near the base of the limestone hill made the location attractive for early settlement. Among these is the Town Spring, or Riehl's Spring, near the Barbara Fritchie and Jacob Engelbrecht house sites, and the spring which was in the cellar of the John Hanson house."[79]

From photographs and the size of the surviving basement, the home appears to have been about the same size as Hanson's large Mulberry Grove home. Jacob Ramsburg, who operated an insurance agency in John Hanson House as its last occupant, reports that the floor plans of the Hanson and Thomas homes were mirror images of one another. Together, the two homes comprised a unified façade eight bays across which, from West Patrick Street where they fronted, appeared as a large single dwelling. The surviving basements of the two homes adjoin as did the homes themselves. An 1858 entry by an assiduous Frederick diarist records the addition of another story and a new roof to the home: "Mr. Jacob Byerly (Daguerreotypist) is about raising his two story dwelling, another story (3). The house is the old 'John Hanson Thomas' house, between James M. Harding and George Markell's Houses on West Patrick Street. They commenced tearing down the roof this morning. Charles W. Haller, carpenter."[80] The John Hanson Thomas here is Philip Thomas's grandson, Dr. John Hanson Thomas, Jr., John and Jane Hanson's great-grandson.

One occasionally hears in Frederick today the erroneous doubt that the Hansons might have resided at some other place in Frederick than at the Patrick Street home after the home was completed. However, the precise references to the Patrick Street location, the spring and John Hanson Thomas's ownership of one of the homes there belie this. In addition, the Hanson home on Patrick Street occupied the nicest location and is the most likely for his use as a home of any property which Hanson owned in Frederick, and firm oral tradition holds that the Patrick Street property is where John and Jane Hanson resided. In addition, the National Historic Trust certified the Patrick Street home as where John and Jane Hanson resided in Frederick in the Trust's certification of the home for the National Register of Historic Places. The homes remained in the Hanson-Thomas family for three generations until 1836 when they were sold by John Hanson Thomas Sr.'s widow Mary to Joseph Talbott.[81]

John Hanson House stood until 1981 by which time it was being used as the offices of the Frederick Underwriters insurance agency and needed restoration. Despite the strenuous objections of local newspapers, the Mayor of Frederick, the Frederick County Chamber of Commerce, civic leader Ann Lebherz, other local preservationists and historians, John Hanson House was not restored but demolished to make room for the Frederick County Public Defender's office which stands there today. One hears that John Hanson House actually collapsed but Ronald Young, Mayor of Frederick at the time who tried to preserve John Hanson House, states that the County "accidentally" knocked it down. The demolition of John Hanson House was, in fact, the annihilation of the home of the nation's first president, an extremely grievous and entirely avoidable national tragedy.

The basements, front façade, front steps and their handrails are all that remain of the homes. While the front façade was built with the bricks from the old homes, and does retain the eight-bay appearance with six-over-six windows, the interior configuration is different from the original.

Until the John Hanson National Memorial arose, a small plaque on the Patrick Street side of the Public Defender's building commemorating the Hanson home site was the only remaining memorial in Frederick to its adopted native son who played such a central role in national independence and forming the nation's first government. Led by ardent John Hanson champion Bruce Champion, the Frederick County chapter of the Sons of the American Revolution on April 16, 2011, placed a larger more comprehensive plaque commemorating John Hanson House on the east wall of the building. Another plaque dedicated in June, 1938, to John Hanson in the old Frederick County Courthouse, now the Frederick City Hall, is on an interior wall of the new Frederick County Courthouse. As mentioned, the John Hanson National Memorial, shown later here, was erected in 2011 beside the site of John Hanson House.

The only other extant physical reminders of John Hanson in Frederick County today are the hamlet of Hansonville and Hansonville Road.

Δ

Especially numerate and already having served on two legislative finance committees, John Hanson's personal accounting during the Frederick period of his life would be expected to be detailed and careful, and it is. His accounts ledger for the years 1776 to 1779 survives in the John Hanson Collection of the Maryland Historical Society and provides a revealing window into the daily goings-on of Hanson and his family in Frederick, and of Hanson's indispensable financial roles in the Revolutionary War. John Hanson would have kept similar ledgers for other periods but this is one of only two known to have survived. The other which he kept in his teens and early twenties has been previously described. In his later account book, Hanson proficiently used the accounting convention of debits and credits detailing uses and sources of funds, kept his household, business and Revolutionary War accounts separate, and, after advancing significant sums to the Second Continental Congress and the State of Maryland, had his accounts audited and attested to as to their accuracy.

The personal accounts in Frederick which John Hanson recorded in his ledger show what for the era were the more expensive purchases of his household including a horse for £60, a saddle, linens, coffee and tea bought in bulk, and payments to hired help, nearly always local African-Americans, presumably therefore free Blacks. One purchase gives an idea of how new Frederick and Frederick County were when the Hanson family moved there. On May 4, 1777, Hanson purchased three pairs of size-nine shoes from cobbler Jacob Schley, son of John Thomas Schley who had built the very first house in Frederick in 1745 upon his arrival from Germany. Shoes during this era were handmade by skilled cobblers and gentleman's shoes were expensive.

Only thirty-three years before the size-nines, Frederick had not existed.

With the sole exception of Jacob Schley, it is notable that Hanson's Frederick ledger shows no discernible purchases from the burgeoning local German and German-speaking Swiss population of tradesmen and farmers. It is possible that John Hanson looked upon his German-speaking constituents and neighbors with some degree of antipathy. In his letter of October 10, 1780, from Philadelphia to Philip Thomas, Hanson says, "As to the election, I care not how it has been determined and shall never be anxious of representing a people who are altogether influenced by two or three ignorant Dutchmen and while this is the case in our country, I apprehend we shall be miserably represented." The term Dutchmen was the local English vernacular for Germans.

On November 5, 1777, Hanson's account book records the retirement of two mortgages from Daniel Delaney and William Tasker, two of the original land patenters of the Frederick region of the county. A number of entries, particularly in 1776 and 1777 even as Hanson began funding the Revolutionary War from his own pocket, were donations to the local poor house. Jane Hanson had her own household account from which groceries, provisions, firewood, clothing and other household necessities were purchased. Her husband's letters show that her account was funded at least in part from the sale of meats and vegetables raised by the family servants in Frederick. In his letter to Philip Thomas of May 8, 1782, from Philadelphia during his presidency, the president writes, "Your mother [meaning Thomas's mother-in-law Jane Hanson] requests you to tell Toney to raise her all the money he can from his and Moll's chickens &c. You will be pleased to sell the Hemp if the price is not lowered. Chloe too is to sell all she can out of the garden. The old Lady says she is in great want of money." Jane Hanson was fifty-four at the time, considered old for her era. Toney and Chloe were two of the Hanson family's enslaved servants.

The future president's ledger also records under plantation accounts some of his revenues and expenses for the unsold portion of Mulberry Grove, transacted mainly through his Charles County brother William Hanson as his agent. Throughout John Hanson's time in Frederick, Mulberry Grove continued to yield part of the income from which John and his family met their and the Revolution's expenses. Given the substantial sums discussed later here which John

Hanson advanced on behalf of prosecuting the Revolutionary War, it is apparent that the unsold remnant of his Mulberry Grove plantation remained profitable to some degree throughout Hanson's life. One of the president's letters to Philip Thomas mentions John Hanson's grain which would have been grown at Mulberry Grove and at his new farm in Frederick County. In any case, it appears to be the remnant of Mulberry Grove, fueled by the labor of the enslaved, which in some part provided John Hanson the wherewithal for his role in financing the Revolutionary War. As this was true of a number of major supporters of the war, the financial role of the African-American in winning independence, though utterly silenced, is seen as central.

Mulberry Grove's extraction of wealth at the expense of slaves is explicit in John Hanson's 1776-1779 ledger. From May 5 through 21, 1778, William Hanson purchases several slaves and rents others on behalf of his brother John. Derivative of this is that during the period of this ledger John Hanson's son Alexander Contee Hanson, Sr. received much if not most of his living expenses from what appears to be an allowance from his father because Alexander, like his father, was having great difficulty getting paid what the State of Maryland owed him for services performed and advances which he had made on the State's behalf. There is no entry in this ledger regarding the other surviving son of this time, Dr. Samuel Hanson, receiving anything from his father. During most of the period of the ledger, both Alexander and Samuel Hanson were serving in the Continental Army in the field, Alexander as *aide-de-camp* to General Washington and Samuel as an Army physician. As was the custom for physician education at the time, Dr. Samuel Hanson had learned the practice of medicine under the one-on-one tutelage of another physician, in this case his brother-in-law, Dr. Philip Thomas. Lieutenant Peter Hanson, John and Jane Hanson's youngest son, had already perished from his wounds at the Battle of Fort Washington by the time of the second ledger.

Foresight Proven: Annapolis Again

If John Hanson's motivation in moving to Frederick was political, it paid off in its entirety as Frederick County voters elected him time and again from his first drafting into public office there in 1774 to the end of his life. The Frederick County electorate would even go as far to elect Hanson to an office which he did not seek. The county's electorate, mostly still rough-hewn frontiersmen and new European immigrants, resonated with Hanson's political vision and quickly elected the well-established public servant, though a new-comer, to represent Frederick County first in the highest ex-ecutive position of what had become the colony's largest county, and after independence to represent the county in the colonial and then state legislature in Annapolis while he continued to hold the chief executive position of the county. From Frederick, Hanson raised the two earliest Revolution-ary War militias, became a prime Revolutionary War finan-cier, put forth the proposal for nationhood adopted by the Maryland colonial legislature, kept Maryland in the union as it was formed with the Declaration of Independence, and was launched into national politics. "Between 1774 and 1782, the Frederick voters elected Hanson to every office he sought. In fact, they continued to elect him to the Assembly in Annapolis while he was serving in Congress in Philadel-phia in the 1780s."[82]

A crystallizing event for John Hanson and his forthcoming second political career in Frederick County was the Boston Tea Party. In 1770, when the British government of Lord North removed the import duties which had been imposed on the colonies by the Townshend Acts, it kept one duty on tea for the dubious purpose of propping up the East India Company and its global reach so important to the British Empire. Not only was tea still taxed but the East India Company was given a new monopoly on its importation into the colonies and a government subsidy to encourage de-mand for it. Further, tea was no longer to be sold by the colonies' hundreds of merchants who had been benefitting from carrying it, but only by a new cadre of East India Com-pany agents. If this was not bad enough, the precedent of the tea monopoly made it clear that Britain could replicate it with similar protection for other commodities at the expense of the colonies, in Americans' minds a blunt hazard to their freedom. Led by Massachusetts firebrand Samuel Adams and to the undisguised delight of Bostonians, the East India Company's first shipment of tea to the colonies — all three ships, 90,000 pounds and 342 chests of it — was tossed into Boston Harbor on the evening of December 17, 1773, by Bostonians masquerading as Native Americans.

On June 14, 1774, Frederick County formed its Committee of Observation, the county's shadow governing body which would before long supplant British administration in the county. The meeting at which the Committee was formed was held in a tavern in Williamsburgh, Maryland, which later was to be renamed Rockville and become the seat of the future Montgomery County. On June 20, 1774, the Committee of Observation met in Frederick to hold its first elections, and Hanson was elected as its founding Chairman, the first of many offices to which the county was to elect him. In this position, Hanson functioned as head of the county's emerging shadow government. One of the first actions taken by the Committee was to renounce proprietary rule in the county and establish the Committee as a provisional government. At this juncture we see John Hanson formally switching his allegiance from British to indigenous loyalty. He was now an openly proclaimed rebel soon to have a price on his head. His lucrative British appointments as Sheriff and Deputy Surveyor had been exchanged for his uncompensated position as Chairman of a breakaway county government. From well-connected to outlaw, well-compensated to unpaid, secure to the threat of the noose, John Hanson had now put himself, his family and his fortune all on the line for the sake of a new nation and its self-determination.

In the same meeting in which he was elected Chairman, John Hanson, his son Alexander Contee Hanson, Sr., and John Hanson's son-in-law Dr. Philip Thomas, were appointed by the Frederick County Committee of Observation as the county's delegates to the newly convened General Congress at Annapolis, a new colony-wide consultative body standing openly in opposition to the Proprietor's provincial government. After his earlier service in the colonial Assembly as representative from Charles County, Hanson's second arrival in Annapolis representing Frederick County, essentially as an insurgent, came as the colonies had begun organizing in earnest to decide what to do about the increasingly troublesome yoke of British rule. We will see that John Hanson and Frederick County propelled one another into the very forefront of colonial and then national politics.

Δ

By the time of the Hanson family's arrival in Frederick, Jane and John Hanson had had twelve of their thirteen children. Their thirteenth and last, Elizabeth, arrived in 1772 after the move. Infant and childhood mortality was an ever-present curse in their time, and by 1773, the couple had already lost eight of their children at Mulberry Grove, the twenty-two-year-old Catherine only two years before the move, and were to lose three more during the Revolutionary War. By the time he died in 1783, President John Hanson had lost eleven of his thirteen children, only Alexander and the eleven-year-old Elizabeth surviving.   When she died in 1812, Jane Hanson had outlived all but Elizabeth.   This is a couple who suffered untold heartache from the vicissitudes of early mortality, disease and war taking all but one of their large brood during their lifetimes.   As detailed later, the early loss of so many of President John Hanson's children contributed much to the dying out of his line of the Hanson family within a few generations.

Part III

The Unifier

The Rising Tide

By spring 1772, John Hanson had begun concretely discussing the tide toward independence with Washington in their visits to each other's homes. "[T]here is a significant entry in Washington's diary for the spring of 1772. He was at his home in Mount Vernon, awaiting the arrival of important visitors with whom he intended to discuss the future outlook of the colonies; and among those who were to be his guests that day was a man far older than he, and both socially and in point of wealth one of the widely known figures in the colonies. Washington tells in his diary of the visit of John Hanson."[83] Given the year, this visit to Mount Vernon was more likely made from Frederick rather than the closer Mulberry Grove. From Boston's churches, to New York's finance houses, to Philadelphia's drawing rooms, to the Maryland Tidewater Tobacco Coast, to southern cotton and cane plantations, many other colonial leaders were having the same discussions and beginning to propose formal moves to assess the colonies' sentiments toward independence. In 1773, Benjamin Franklin, already American sage and elder statesman at sixty-seven, called for a meeting of representatives of the colonies to discuss problems with the British and more colonial autonomy. On September 23 of that year, Samuel Adams of Massachusetts called for what he termed a continental congress to be convened to discuss British taxation of the colonies.

While in Charles County in the 1750s and 1760s John Hanson's prime civic role had been his service in the Maryland House of Delegates. His public emphasis in the 1770s in Frederick put House of Delegates service into an active but secondary role while he concentrated on the sprawling county's contributions toward national needs of pushing for independence and then prosecuting the war. In gauging the collective breadth of these roles which he was taking on, it is necessary to keep in mind Frederick County's extensiveness, rapid growth, rebellious nature and burgeoning influence at that time. The huge county would only later be organized into the Frederick, Montgomery, Carroll, Washington, Allegany and Garrett Counties of today. In the decade leading up to national independence, Frederick County, the most rapidly growing part of the colony, more than doubled its population to 14,000. Frederick, the county seat with 1,700 people was for a while the largest town in the colony before Baltimore surpassed it.[84] This vast, swelling, independent-minded frontier county had become a force in colonial politics with its political leader having to be reckoned with in

Annapolis and beyond. From 1774 until his election as the nation's first president in 1781, the undisputed leader of Frederick County was John Hanson.

After the Boston Tea Party the previous December, Britain raised the stakes by enacting the Coercive Acts in spring of 1774, shutting down the Port of Boston and in effect placing Massachusetts under martial law, further inflaming the sentiments of the colonies. Among reactions of the colonists, the Committee of Fifty-One, a group of opinion leaders in New York City, called for a meeting of the colonies to form a coordinated response to the British.

That they did. Each colony established a Committee of Correspondence or Committee of Observation to begin formally coordinating communication among the colonies. Many counties within the colonies, including Frederick County, Maryland, set up committees of the same names for similar coordination purposes reporting to their colony-wide committees. Representatives from the Maryland counties began meeting in conventions held in Annapolis, the first of which was held from June 22 to 25, 1774. The nine Conventions of Maryland would be held off and on through November 1776 when the Ninth Convention of Maryland authored the first Maryland State Constitution five months after United States independence had been declared. The Maryland Council of Safety met between the Maryland Conventions to ensure continuity of effort and a colony-wide coordinating presence. Similar bodies in the other colonies, all of which were extra-legal as far as the British were concerned, sprang up and began acting as shadow governments in open opposition to the British. By September of 1774, this earliest organization of the thirteen colonies was to take the next logical step when the colonies' Committees of Correspondence convened the First Continental Congress, the earliest formally organized unified voice of the colonies and the first consultative body among them.

In Maryland, the Proprietorship found itself powerless to act without the backing and physical presence of the British military which would not be sent for another year, and because of the utter disdain in which the Maryland Proprietors had come to be held even by some of the colony's staunchest British loyalists. Frederick Calvert, sixth Baron Baltimore, had nominally served as Maryland Proprietor until his death in 1771 and can be credited with much of the unrest in Maryland that contributed to the anti-imperial attitudes that led to American Independence. Frederick's disastrous personal relationships became so sordid as to hold him up to ridicule in Maryland and Britain, and persuade him to leave Britain for a super-tramp existence on the European continent. In 1753 he had married Lady Diana Egerton, daughter of the Duke of Bridgewater, but usually lived apart from her. Upon her death, he then lived with Hester Whalen of Ireland with whom he had an illegitimate son and daughter. In 1768, he was acquitted of charges by Sarah Woodcock in London of abduction and rape. By 1770, Frederick had fathered twins by yet another woman and then a daughter by yet one more. Frederick fled Constantinople when a scandal erupted because of his having procured his own private harem producing even more illegitimate children.

On September 4, 1771, Frederick died in Naples but the many problems which his debauchery had spawned still much affected his Maryland colony. Before his death, Frederick had made his illegitimate son Henry Harford his heir as Maryland Proprietor and instructed Maryland Governor Robert Eden to declare the province for Henry upon Frederick's death. Harford was born April 5, 1758, and attended Eton and then Exeter College at Oxford University where he obtained a degree in 1779. Henry had inherited Maryland from his father in 1771 but, being only thirteen years old, his authority over his colonial dominion was exercised by his uncle, standing in as Maryland's provincial secretary, until Henry reached the age of majority in 1779. Henry ran unsuccessfully for Parliament in 1781. The province did recognize the bastard Henry as heir and Proprietor but barely and with much derision. Because of his loyalty to the crown, Henry lost all of his extensive Maryland holdings during the Revolutionary War, but, having great wealth in England, was able to maintain the lavish life of a country gentleman. A Maryland county, still so called, was named for Henry Harford.

In the eyes of Americans, the British kings of the eighteenth century were not much better. During John Hanson's lifetime, he lived first under the rule of George I of the House of Hanover who could neither read nor write the language of his subjects, and then the imperious George III who treated his American colonies as an extractive industry.

After the setting of the stage of the Revolution in 1774 and Maryland Governor Eden's departure in 1775 abandoning the colony to the revolutionaries, the Loyalist cause and the stabilizing force that the astute Eden had until then been able to exert against the drift toward revolution were lost.

As we shall see, the Maryland colonists, once they had thrown off proprietary authority, were reluctant to join the remaining colonies against the King of England, and Maryland became the last colony to agree to independence and then with only hours to spare after a final exhorting push from John Hanson.[85]

Despite their diffidence toward independence, Maryland's political leaders were first in the colonies to fashion a response when Massachusetts appealed to her twelve sister colonies in June 1774 for support against British punitive actions. Wasting no time, the Maryland Committee of Correspondence the day following receipt of the Massachusetts appeal requested county leaders across the state and Virginia's House of Burgesses to cease trade with Britain and join a new all-colonies association to enforce the embargo until Britain repealed the Coercive Acts. Soon after this call for colonial coordination, the colonies put out the word to their counties which began dealing with the issues of British dominance and invoking wide popular discussion through the then-forming county and provincial Committees of Correspondence up and down the Atlantic seaboard. Such fervor, or insurrection as the British viewed it, found no more fertile ground than with the upstart farmers and tradesmen of Frederick County, Maryland.

To act on these requests, county meetings ensued in all three subdivisions of Frederick County, four other Maryland counties and Baltimore. In Frederick County's first central meeting convened on June 20, 1774, interested citizens met at the old courthouse in Frederick where Frederick City Hall now stands and elected the patrician newcomer John Hanson to his first elective position in Frederick County to preside over the newly formed Frederick County Committee of Correspondence. These committees of correspondence first operated, in effect, as shadow governments opposing parallel British-controlled colonial bodies which had governed until that time, and then, as they attracted local loyalty and its concomitant authority, rapidly evolved into actual county and provincial governments. In contrast to British rule in the colonies and as precursor, authority flowed upward from these new local governments to the emerging provincial governments, thence to the First and Second Continental Congresses and their later successor, the United States in Congress Assembled. As the national bodies could not function without the support of the provincial and later the state Committees of Correspondence, the state bodies likewise could not operate without the consent and support of the county bodies which in turn existed only through local popular support. Hanson writer Ralph Levering has described this grassroots period in which authority flowed upward as the most democratic in United States history.

The Hanson-led Frederick County meeting urged the most strident positions and recommendations put forth by any of the Maryland counties, quickly recommending a halt to all commerce with Britain, compelling the reopening the Port of Boston, and demanding that "every other act repressive to American liberty, be repealed." While the Frederick body's positions necessarily closely reflected the sentiments of a particularly independent-minded frontier electorate, John Hanson exercised a strong hand in promoting the meeting's open rebelliousness toward Great Britain and in shaping the defiant wording of the meeting's resolutions. We now see a man forsaking his life-long allegiance to Britain, not just willing to run the gauntlet of British condemnation but to risk all by leading the efforts in his adopted territory in the active undermining of what he now resignedly regarded as illegitimate foreign authority. Perhaps it was in this meeting when John Hanson put aside any remaining doubts of himself being a British subject and in his own mind fully became an American.

It was in this meeting that the Frederick County Committee of Correspondence elected John Hanson, his son Alexander Contee Hanson, Sr., and John Hanson's son-in-law Dr. Philip Thomas, to represent Frederick County at the colony-wide First Convention of Maryland in Annapolis to select Maryland's delegates to the forthcoming Continental Congress. It is remarkable and not fully explained that the county would elect three relative newcomers from the same family to represent it in the First Convention of Maryland. The most likely explanation is that the opinion leaders in Frederick saw in the three a level of sophistication and colony-wide influence not possessed by many, if any, others in their county.

In the First Convention of Maryland and its successors, John Hanson gained wide notice in Maryland and began making his mark beyond its borders for his clear articulation of nationhood, his early leadership in executing war logistics, and particularly for his diplomatic skill in bridging differences of opinion among the delegates and their evolving and often disparate views on independence. There were to be nine Conventions of Maryland held intermittently from June 22, 1774, when the First Convention convened, through November 11, 1776, when the Ninth Convention adjourned after Independence and on the eve of Maryland government under its first state constitution. The Conventions replaced the Proprietor's provincial Assembly of Maryland which ceased to operate on April 19, 1774. Despite this, the Proprietor's Governor, Robert Eden, continued to hold office, and the province was still considered by both British and Americans to be British as were the twelve other colonies.

John Hanson was to be at the forefront when Maryland declared its independence. The most critical of the conventions was the Fifth Convention of Maryland held from July 26 through August 14, 1775, which dealt conclusively with the outbreak of war and how Maryland should respond to it. Firm of mind on its opening day, the convention delegates passed and signed the Declaration of Freemen of Maryland proclaiming Maryland's political independence but not yet a complete severing from Britain. This was a year before the all-colonies Declaration of Independence, so what the Declaration of Freemen of Maryland had actually proposed was creation of Maryland as an independent sovereign nation-state with continued fealty toward Britain but not subject to its authority. "In 1775, the Maryland Convention issued its declaration of independence, known as the 'Association of Freemen of Maryland.' This meant the downfall of the proprietary government and the assumption of power by the provisional government of the people themselves. Matthew Tilghman was the president of this convention, and John Hanson one of its most distinguished and forceful members."[86] To be sure, Maryland remained more closely than ever in association with the twelve other colonies but was now associated with them as a new nation unto itself.

At this watershed juncture, Maryland had declared only an independence of sorts from Britain. In Maryland, as in varying degrees in the other colonies, what the Americans sought were friendly relations and a peaceful reconciliation with the mother country accompanied by American self-governance, much akin to the relationship that most British Commonwealth nations have with Britain today. The prime movers for American self-governance still hoped to retain their long fond ties with Britain and avoid a rupture with her.

Over the next few months, all of the other twelve colonies would shed their own colonial status, begin to convert their committees of correspondence into indigenous governments and become independent entities. In less than a year, through their mutual Declaration of Independence, the thirteen newly independent nation-states would formally band together not yet fully as a nation but as an association of like-minded independencies with an outlook toward a possible formal union later.

To begin to appreciate the critical contributions that John Hanson made in the formation of the United States and in leading its first government, an understanding of the context of the two colonial consultative bodies, the brief odd hiatus which followed, and the succeeding two United States governments of the eighteenth century is necessary. These five bodies, in the order in which they were created, were the First and Second Continental Congresses, a briefly held interim body which existed for 249 days in 1781, the United States in Congress Assembled which was the nation's original government, and the second and present Constitutional government. We begin by looking at the earliest substantial all-colonies gathering in opposition to British rule, the First Continental Congress which existed for fifty-two days in 1774, and which comprised the initial step toward the formation of the nation and its later government.

The First Continental Congress

By 1774 as Committees of Correspondence were being formed in the colonies and their counties, and the tide rose among them for some degree of greater independence from Britain, there was yet to occur any continent-wide gathering of these extra-legal bodies. It was Maryland which took the lead in urging such a meeting which would come to be called the First Continental Congress.

On May 31 in Baltimore, leaders of the burgeoning town met and recommended "a general congress of deputies, from all the counties" of Maryland. Ninety-two delegates responding from around the colony met in Annapolis in the First Convention of Maryland. Eight more conventions would follow through late 1776 when the Ninth Convention of Maryland would author the State of Maryland's first constitution. An early action of the First Convention was to write to the Virginia Committee of Correspondence " . . . to propose that the general congress be held at the city of Philadelphia, the twentieth of September next. . . . The limits of our province and the number of its inhabitants, compared with yours, afforded an opportunity of collecting our general sense, before the sentiments of your colony could be regularly ascertained, and therefore, as this province had the first opportunity, it has taken the liberty of making the first proposition"[87]

On May 16, 1774, John Murray, Third Earl of Dunmore, the last colonial governor of Virginia, had dissolved the colony's legislature, the House of Burgesses, for the House's mounting opposition to British treatment of the colony. On May 31, the very same day on which the Baltimoreans had met, eighty-nine of the now former burgesses first convened as the newly formed Virginia Committee of Correspondence at Williamsburg's Raleigh Tavern[88] where they continued their discussions, formed an association to boycott British imports, and proposed a gathering of like-minded men from all of the colonies later that year "to deliberate on those general measures which the united interests of America may from time to time require."

As the two colonies called for it literally on the same day, one may debate as to whether Maryland or Virginia took the continent-wide lead in calling for the First Continental Congress. Though the two colonies conceived the idea independently and simultaneously, it was Maryland which issued the call. John Hanson had just taken his place in this earliest formal coalescing of the colonies when he was elected head of the Frederick County Committee of Correspondence that June 20 and, with his son and son-in-law, to represent Frederick County in the First Maryland Convention two days later.

That summer, Virginia Committee of Correspondence member Thomas Jefferson articulated the sense of the colonies' budding extra-legal movement in his "A Summary View of the Rights of British-America" published by Williamsburg printer Clementina Rind. On August 1, Virginia chose her delegates to attend the proposed congress. Jefferson's sensibility that the colonies, though seeking more independence, were "British-America" reflected the colonies' continuing sentimental if not political allegiance to Britain.

There must have been high excitement and hopeful if unclear promise of the future when the fifty-six delegates to what they would name the First Continental Congress met at Carpenters Hall in Philadelphia on September 5, 1774. The three accomplishments of the briefly held Congress were articulation of the colonies' grievances, creation of a Continental Association, and provision for convening a more expansive congress the following year. All of the colonial Committees of Correspondence but New York's approved the convening of the First Continental Congress and New York did not register any opposition. The First Continental Congress amounted to the official all-colonies opening act of united rebellion against the British, achieved its three major accomplishments and lasted for fifty-two days, dissolving itself on October 26, 1774.

Virginia's Peyton Randolph was elected president of the First Continental Congress when it convened but was replaced by Henry Middleton of South Carolina who chaired the last four days of the Congress when Randolph was called back to Virginia. Maryland was represented at the Congress by Samuel Chase, Thomas Johnson and Matthew Tilghman. The minutes of the First Continental Congress were recorded by Pennsylvania's Charles Thomson who was not a delegate but an appointee with the title of Secretary. The extraordinary and under-sung Thomson would prove to be the only continuous official American presence from this time, through the Second Continental Congress, the first government in the 1780s, and into the Washington administration of the second government.

In response to the Intolerable Acts, the Continental Association, formed on October 20, 1774, by the First Continental Congress, was a compact among the colonies to boycott British imports beginning December 1, 1774, and cease exports to Britain after September 10, 1775, allowing colonial exporters time to adjust to the loss of their most important market. The successful embargo cut British imports almost entirely in 1775 and was a proximate cause of the Revolutionary War. The First Continental Congress called for the Committees of Observation in each colony to enforce the trade restrictions of the new Continental Association. This charge to the Committees strengthened their role as shadow governments in the colonies, now not only existing in parallel with the colonies' British administrations but in unmistakable opposition.

The "Declaration and Resolves of the First Continental Congress," adopted on October 14, 1774, listed colonial objections to the Intolerable Acts, detailed the colonies' grievances and put forth a colonial bill of rights. One also sees the Declaration and Resolves referred to variously as the "Declaration of Colonial Rights," the "Declaration of Rights" or the "Declaration of Rights and Grievances," an example of modern confusion with the terminology of the 1770s and 1780s. We will see more of this kind of nomenclature problem further on. The Declaration spelled out the Congress's plans to petition the king, lobby the people of Great Britain and British America, and boycott British trade until the colonies' grievances were redressed.

Though there had been previous complaints put forth to Britain by some of the colonies, the Declaration and Resolves constituted a united and much more tangible manifestation of the growing animus among the colonies against British rule, and came to be an immediate precursor to the Declaration of Independence two years later. As much as it was a petition against British policies, the Declaration and Resolves served equally as a unifying pact among the colonies themselves to recognize common problems and lay out a common course of action. It is notable that the Declaration and Resolves refers to the colonies collectively as America and to their people as American, rather than British, subjects. This was the formal beginning of collective declaration of the identity long felt by many, many of whom by this time were the grandchildren and great-grandchildren of immigrants to America, and had been raised with a primarily indigenous American character as opposed to the British outlook of their forebears.

The last major action of the First Continental Congress was the call for a Second Continental Congress to convene in 1775. In addition to the thirteen colonies invited to the First Continental Congress, several Canadian colonies and the two Spanish Florida colonies[89] were invited to attend the Second Continental Congress but didn't.

Adjourning just the month after it had been convened, the First Continental Congress clearly was not a national government. Not until the following May did the Second Continental Congress convene and in the interim it was the colonies' Committees of Correspondence, and in Maryland also the Conventions of Maryland and the Council of Safety, which acted fitfully in coordinating the colonies' mutual affairs. Quickly after the Congress adjourned on October 26, 1774, meetings began being held in Maryland's counties bolstering county Committees of Correspondence, putting forth resolutions and generally finding their voices in support of the Congress's actions. The Second Convention of Maryland was held from November 21 to 25 and the Third from December 8 to 12, 1774. The Third Convention of Maryland requested financial support from the counties in proportion to county population. Being the largest, Frederick County was requisitioned for £1,333, the least populous, Caroline County on the Eastern Shore, for £358.

In Maryland that fall, several incidents of resistance to British control erupted at the hands of more radical leaders of

the Democrat faction of the Country party and their follow-
ers among Annapolis townspeople who were ready to react
to British authority with force. In the month before the First
Continental Congress had met, angered citizens of Georgetown, then in the sprawling Frederick County, forced the
British ship *Mary Jane* to flee the port of Georgetown without unloading. That November, Georgetown merchant John
Parks was forced to burn his inventory of British tea in the
street which still wasn't enough to prevent a mob from then
ransacking his home. At about the same time, two British
tax collectors were tarred and feathered near Baltimore.

The most brazen challenge to the British in any of the colonies that year was the burning of the *Peggy Stewart* shortly
after its arrival in Annapolis harbor on October 19, 1774,
while the First Continental Congress was still in session.
When it was discovered that the ship's owner, Annapolis
merchant Anthony Stewart, had lied about the consignment
of British tea he had aboard, Stewart was forced to burn his
£396 worth of tea on deck which, not according to the mob's
plan, took the entire vessel valued at £1,500 down in the
blaze. The previous December, Bostonians had dumped tea
into their harbor; now Marylanders had not only destroyed
another entire shipment of British tea but this time the ship
that carried it. As historian Arthur Schlesinger put it, "Annapolis had out-Bostoned Boston."[90] Maryland's fierce challenges, of course, did not go unnoticed in London where the
burning of the *Peggy Stewart* was recognized for what it was,
the single most blatant affront to British authority so far in
the lead-up to the Revolutionary War.

Robert Eden, the last Proprietor's governor of Maryland, was
not the aloof feared autocrat that were many of his predecessors, Maryland Proprietors and governors of the other
provinces. The deft Eden foresaw the eclipse of British rule
in the American colonies and, adapting to its inevitability,
may be credited with effecting what under the circumstances of rebellion could be called a graceful transition.
Upon his return to Maryland from Britain two months after
the burning of the *Peggy Stewart*, Eden wrote back to London, "The spirit of resistance to the Tea Act, or any mode of
internal taxation, is as strong and universal here as ever. I
firmly believe that they will undergo any hardship sooner
than acknowledge a right in the British Parliament in that
particular, and will persevere in their non-importation and
non-exportation experiments, in spite of every inconvenience
that they must consequently be exposed to, and the total
loss of their trade."[91] Eden's assessment of Maryland's mood

proved to be on the mark. Again in the vanguard and confirming Eden's foresight, Frederick County, by then under the authority of John Hanson for six months, ordered John Parks of Hagerstown to burn his imported tea and forbade him to trade with others in the county. In a few months, Eden would forsake his governorship and depart for Britain.

During the interim between the First and Second Continental Congresses when it was charged to implement at the county level the Articles of Association drafted by the First Continental Congress, the Frederick County Committee of Observation on November 18, 1774, re-elected John Hanson its Chairman and charged him with execution of the Articles in the county. On January 25, 1775, the Frederick County Committee of Correspondence reconvened and with Hanson presiding began concretely supporting colonial resistance by, among other measures, forming and financing militias and raising £1,200 in the county which was sent to Boston to support the welfare of that city's people after the British had blockaded the port of Boston. Hanson raised another £1,333 in Frederick County for the purchase and manufacture of war materiel, fulfilling the new Maryland Committee of Correspondence requisition of the county. While it was Hanson who led Frederick County's early and active reaction to the British, what has not been stated elsewhere as clearly as it could be is that this was possible only because Hanson's adopted county closely resonated with the recommendations made to it by its adopted son who in turn had attuned himself to his new frontier electorate. This was a good match.

For the British, the First Continental Congress and its Articles of Association brought to a head the threat of most of Britain's North American colonies attempting to break away from Britain politically. Responding, the decision was made by the British Parliament to resist such efforts by force and compel the colonies at gunpoint to continue to submit to British rule. This decision by Britain was first acted out in its most insubordinate of colonies, Massachusetts, in the opening battles of the Revolutionary War at Lexington and Concord. On April 19, 1775, British General Thomas Gage, by then in effect the Governor of Massachusetts, marched to Concord to confiscate arms being stockpiled by colonists. Met on the way at Lexington by a recently raised rebel militia, Gage pushed on through the first shots of the Revolution and was able to take the armory at Concord only to have his troops severely ambushed nearly the entire way back to Boston. The Revolutionary War was on.

Three weeks later, the colonies, now closer to regarding themselves as independent states — united but still with a small "u" — convened again in the Second Continental Congress. As in the First Continental Congress, those sent by the colonies to the Second were often designated with the title Ambassador, indicative of the separateness by which the colonies thought of themselves, common enemy or not.

The Second Continental Congress

While the First Continental Congress measured its life in days, the Second Continental Congress served for more than six years and took on far greater roles. The Second Continental Congress first met only nineteen days after the American Revolutionary War had begun, raised provincial armies, advised on war strategy, coordinated the colonies' war effort, moved the colonies toward independence, authored and adopted the Declaration of Independence fourteen months after first convening, chartered the first government through the Articles of Confederation, established weak but lasting treasury and postal functions, conferred with foreign nations, made treaties, recruited French assistance in the Revolutionary War, and acted as a *de facto* national coordinating body until 1781, though with no empowered executive, little funding and without much authority except as sporadically conferred on it by the colonies and then states when they did so at all. Depending on how one interprets a sometimes vague record, the Second Continental Congress ceased to exist either on March 1, 1781, when it replaced itself with a briefly held interim body by ratification of the Articles of Confederation pending inauguration of the nation's first government, or on November 5, 1781, when the first government, the United States in Congress Assembled prescribed by the Articles, came to life.

When the Second Continental Congress first met on May 10, 1775, it was, in effect, a reconvening of the First Continental Congress. Many of the same fifty-six delegates who attended the first meeting were in attendance at the second, and the delegates straight away appointed the First Continental Congress's first president, Peyton Randolph, and secretary, Charles Thomson, into these positions in the Second Continental Congress. The Second Continental Congress benefitted from the participation of several notable new delegates including Benjamin Franklin of Pennsylvania, John Hancock of Massachusetts and the thirty-two-year-old Thomas Jefferson who replaced Randolph in the Virginia delegation when Randolph was again summoned back to

Virginia to preside over its House of Burgesses.

With Randolph's resignation, John Hancock was then elected presiding officer on May 24, 1775. Hancock would remain in this position for two and a half years, serving longer than any national leader until George Washington would in the 1790s. Hancock would be honored with an even more prestigious role when he was elected as head of state of the United States as the fifth president of the first government, the United States in Congress Assembled, in 1785. (However, due to a temporary health setback, Hancock did not serve as president of that body, with David Ramsay and Nathaniel Gorham serving in Hancock's place during his one-year term.)

Although the Second Continental Congress's constituent colonies had granted no explicit legal authority to it to govern, the Congress, of necessity, took on a few of the functions of national coordination such as foreign relations, more or less harmonizing provincial militias, financing the war by borrowing abroad, and printing and disbursing currency, Continentals as the bills were known. With no means to levy taxes, the Second Continental Congress had to rely on money, supplies and troops from the individual colonies and then states, and from domestic and foreign pleadings to operate and conduct the war. Not all of the colonies were forthcoming, leading to one of the first Revolutionary War fundraising efforts directed by John Hanson who went on during this period to lend his financial and organizational skills heavily toward the prosecution of the war. "The level of coordination that was achieved in the early years of the Revolution can be credited to Hanson and hundreds of other conscientious leaders throughout the colonies."[92]

While the Second Continental Congress did conduct the important war business of the time, its creation of the Articles of Confederation in 1781 to bring about the United States in Congress Assembled was the Second Continental Congress's explicit recognition that it was not a government. Later here, we will draw comparisons between the relatively few powers and charges of the Second Continental Congress versus the much stronger authorities explicitly granted by the Articles of Confederation to the United States in Congress Assembled, the nation's original government. To keep perspective and give due credit, the Second Continental Congress did accomplish the vaulting strides of boycotting British trade, engaging the mightiest nation on Earth in war, mustering a new Continental Army, issuing a national currency, and authoring the Declaration of Independence, all within the Congress's first fourteen months and without vigorous backing of a few of the colonies, soon to become states.

Call to Arms: Militias, Munitions and Money

During the earliest days of the Second Continental Congress, the Revolutionary War exploded with military engagements in battle after battle in Massachusetts and then elsewhere. After the battles of Lexington and Concord on April 19, 1775, the month before the Second Continental Congress convened, the war spread rapidly on nearly a daily basis. April 20 saw the British lay siege to the city of Boston, by May 25 British Generals John Burgoyne and William Howe had arrived in Boston with firm orders to put down the colonial rebellion, and on June 17 the Battle of Bunker Hill took place (though mostly at Breed's Hill). It was in the midst of this on May 23 when Peyton Randolph resigned the presidency of the Second Continental Congress and was succeeded by John Hancock.

On June 15, Maryland delegate Thomas Johnson of Frederick, the future first governor of his state, nominated George Washington to become commander in chief of the continental forces. The appointment was unanimous by the Congress and Washington was in place in Massachusetts by July 2, taking command of the new Continental Army the following day at Cambridge. Washington would command continuously for eight and a half years in inaugurating this enduring national military role, longer than any American military commander since. One of the first orders of business for Washington was appointment of his commanding generals and central staff reporting directly to him. Among his *aides-de-camp*, Washington chose Alexander Contee Hanson, eldest son of Washington's close confidant John Hanson.

Despite the unfolding of hostilities, the Second Continental Congress still held out hope that a peaceful independent relationship between the colonies and Britain could be forged. To this end, the Congress in July 1775 extended the Olive Branch Petition affirming American loyalty to Britain and King George III who in August summarily rejected the entreaty and issued the Proclamation of Rebellion formally ordering the military subjugation of the colonies. In his proclamation, George was explicit that leaders of the rebellion were to be tracked down and executed. There was no turning back the Revolutionary War now.

As the colonies received word of the unfolding war, the Maryland Committee of Correspondence called on John Hanson to bolster the colonies' war effort in a number of critically important ways.

To facilitate the mustering of militias and implementation of Frederick County's war financing, the county's Committee of Correspondence on June 21 had elected Hanson to the position of Treasurer of Frederick County in addition to his position as Chairman of its Committee of Correspondence, now regarded as the county government. On Hanson's recommendation, the county's Committee of Correspondence authorized the raising of militias from the county, the first militias organized for the war effort in Maryland and what were to become the first military units outside New England to reach Massachusetts and Washington's gathering Continental Army. On the spot, the meeting appointed the commanding officers for two companies of trained riflemen, set salaries according to rank, and authored enlistment contracts. Hanson put out the call, organized the two companies and by July 18 had them, more than two hundred strong, marching their way to Massachusetts 550 miles away, one company headed by Michael Cresap, son of Frederick County frontiersman Thomas Cresap, the other by Thomas Price.

Hanson's appointments of these two company captains is in keeping with his life-long astute judgment of character which would serve him so well when choosing the nation's first cabinet. In particular, Michael Cresap was a near legend on Maryland's outer western frontier in the Appalachians for his Indian fighting, sharpshooting and backwoods skills. Hanson's announcement of Cresap's appointment was a magnet bringing some of Maryland's best riflemen out of the forests a hundred or more miles deep from Frederick. "He was sending them to the aid of his young friend and neighbor of Charles County days, George Washington of Mt. Vernon, Virginia, who was now the General."[93] The Maryland companies' formation in Frederick had created a prideful sensation there with one Fredericktonian writing to Philadelphia that, "I have had the happiness of seeing Captain Michael Cresap marching at the head of a formidable company of upwards of one hundred and thirty men from the mountains and back woods, painted like Indians, armed with tomahawks and rifles, dressed in hunting shirts and moccasins."[94]

Twenty-two days later, the two units reached General Washington in Cambridge, Massachusetts, and by August 13 were putting their fearsome sharpshooting prowess to work against the Redcoats. In the summer of 1775, a resident of Roxbury, Massachusetts, described the dexterity of these Maryland frontiersmen thus: "They are now stationed on our lines, and their shot have frequently proved fatal to the British officers and soldiers, who expose themselves to view, even at more than double the distance of common musket shot."[95] While it was Hanson's two Frederick County companies which famously first reached Massachusetts, Virginia deserves credit for being not far behind. Virginia soldiers, under the command of Captain Daniel Morgan, had rendezvoused with the two Frederick County companies in Frederick commencing a good-natured rivalry as to which could reach Massachusetts first.

As the first units outside of New England to arrive in support of the organizing Continental Army, Hanson's rifle companies brought quick notice to him not only as ardent supporter of the American cause but now as an operator who could be relied on to get important things done well and fast. In large part because of Hanson's organizing acumen, Maryland by the end of the war had provided nearly fourteen thousand troops to the Continental Army, a full eighteen percent of the state's adult male population. As others have observed, Maryland during the Revolutionary War never lagged in her support and throughout, given her population, did much more than her share relative to most of the other states toward the struggle for independence and the eventual winning of the war.

John Hanson's earliest of all Maryland contributions to the war effort established a distinguished standard for the state. "That Marylanders, when they felt free to act, were not lax in carrying out their military obligations in a matter of common defense is shown by their unsurpassed, if not unique, response to the call for troops and service on all fronts throughout the whole period of the American Revolution. The record of Massachusetts, for instance whose citizens so promptly sprang to the defense of colonial freedom, when their own firesides were immediately menaced, bears no comparison to the contribution of Maryland when it came to fighting on all fronts for the Confederation."[96] Recognizing Hanson as one of the war's most reliable leaders, Second Continental Congress President John Hancock appointed him as a member of a committee of two to raise $300,000 for the Continental Army's operations. The dependable Hanson would perform time and again in this manner on behalf of the war effort through the end of his presidency in 1782 and beyond.

By summer of 1775, we see the mounting bustle of earliest Revolutionary War organization as the Maryland and Frederick County Committees of Correspondence met simultaneously between June 22 and 25 in Annapolis and Frederick. During these days, Hanson began organizing Maryland's purchase and manufacture of arms, gun locks, gunpowder, musket balls and other army materiel, much of it in Frederick County from the Catoctin Furnace forge of his long-time House of Delegates friend and fellow southern Maryland transplant Thomas Johnson. In these days of late June 1775, John Hanson also persuaded the fledgling Frederick County government to pledge all adult men in the county as prospective conscripts to the war effort.

From July 26 until August 14, Hanson was in Annapolis as one of Frederick County's eight delegates to the Fifth Convention of Maryland which became the most important of Maryland's nine conventions. Known across the colony from his previous House of Delegates service when he lived in Charles County and now from his recent organization of the first aid to Massachusetts, Hanson was among the most senior and respected delegates at the Fifth Convention. On July 26, 1775, the day it convened, the one hundred forty-one delegates of the Fifth Convention declared the Convention to be the government of Maryland existing now in parallel to British officialdom which, in a stroke, had now been rendered impotent because of the clear majority will of Marylanders to have control over their province's affairs. This was not yet a complete break from British control as sentiment still ran high in Maryland, including within the Fifth Convention, for continued fealty toward the mother country but with far greater say in and control over the affairs of the province by its inhabitants. The Fifth Convention of Maryland issued the *Association of Freemen of Maryland*, a manifesto in which they vowed among other pledges to "repel force by force," and to "promote and support the present opposition." The Fifth Convention also established provincial leadership and continuity of control between the Conventions by electing an executive Committee of Safety comprising eight delegates each from the eastern and western shores of Maryland.

Much of the impetus for the Fifth Convention's decisiveness came from John Hanson, his spreading reputation for boldness and competent execution, and his growing aura which put him among the key voices of the Convention. By being among those at the forefront in forming Maryland's response to the war, Hanson had bolstered his place among the vanguard of Maryland's war effort and move for independence. Responding to the call of Hanson and the Convention's other opinion leaders, the Fifth Convention on July 26 gave formal support to the proposals of the Association of the Freemen of Maryland and put the colony along with Massachusetts at the forefront of armed opposition to the British and the escalating move toward independence among the colonies. In forming Maryland's logistical response to the war, the Convention chose John Hanson to chair a committee on the manufacture and purchase of arms for Maryland. It was Hanson who must now arm Maryland. Further along in this logistical role, John Hanson would be drafted the following year to find additional ways of financing the Revolutionary War. "After the Declaration of Independence, Hanson, at the request of Congress, rivaled Robert Morris by raising $300,000 within 90 days to help finance the war."[97]

John Hanson's mounting roles in the Revolutionary War soon went beyond his political leadership and organizing of funding, militias and war materiel. Early on in the war effort, he found little choice but to use his own fortune and income from his Mulberry Grove and Frederick County farms and investments to finance military payrolls, the manufacture and purchase of war materiel, and other of the war effort's expenses to sustain it and the ability to fight. In his ledger covering the thirty-nine-month period from March 20, 1776, through June 16, 1779, Hanson records seven very large personal expenditures ostensibly in the form of advances to the new State of Maryland totaling 22,868 pounds, ten shillings, three pence (£22,868-10s-3d in that currency's notation). In the first of these advances on June 22, 1776, he pays for guards, boarding of prisoners, officers' servants, wares and other expenses. Guard pay varied between £6 and £15 per nine weeks of service. From July to October of that year, he spent £425-1s-4d purchasing guns and blankets for the Continental Army, many of the blankets bought one at a time from individuals. During the winter of 1776-1777, John Hanson spent £259-8s-3d of his own money purchasing guns for the state's Committee on Safety, and fed part of the Army with his £6,765-15s of purchases of Army provisions, mainly beef, whiskey and bread (noted in his hand in that order). By far, Hanson's largest outlay on behalf of the war effort during the period covered by this ledger was the £14,454-8s-9d disbursed to officers, mostly colonels, in July of 1777 to meet their militias' payrolls. Further demands on Hanson's fortune came in quick succession, for example, his expenditures from July 30 to September 2, 1777, of £300-1s-1d "on account of Torey prisoners" to keep their guards from quitting for lack of pay from the state. John Hanson was rapidly drawing down his and his family's fortune.

The difficulty which the colonies, the Second Continental Congress and then the nation's first government had in meeting their financial obligations and paying creditors including John Hanson stemmed from the obstacles they encountered in being able to levy and collect taxes. In the worst case, the nation's first government in the 1780s had no authority at all to tax and therefore didn't. It and the preceding Second Continental Congress had to go hat in hand to the states beseeching them for funding which often was either tardy or not forthcoming at all. In a futile attempt at solvency, the Second Continental Congress within weeks after war broke out in 1775 began printing money, Continentals as they came to be called, which quickly eroded in value and were soon shunned in transactions. Complicating commerce, the settling of debts and most other financial matters, the states began issuing their own currencies the year after independence. John Hanson experienced what many did, that his state's dollars could not be spent in other states, a difficulty which he experienced in Pennsylvania even when later serving as president. By August 1779, inflation of currency was so rapid that Hanson and other members of the Maryland House of Delegates installed wage and price controls in the state, reversing a ban on such controls which they had legislated only months before in April of that year. In December of 1779, the House of Delegates saw fit to raise the governor's salary from the £2,500 set the previous December to £25,000, a nine-hundred-percent annual inflation rate. Most draconian was a bill passed by the Maryland House of Delegates in March of 1779 which permitted the State to seize wheat, flour and bread from citizens for use by the military as long as families were left with enough for themselves, no way to popularize a war or new state government.

Except for his account books mentioned for the 1730-1737 and 1776-1779 periods, other account books including those which John Hanson presumably kept for the period from 1779 until his death in 1783 are missing. Without the rest of John Hanson's ledgers, it would be difficult if not impossible to know how much he eventually advanced to the

United States and Maryland governments in prosecuting the Revolutionary War, or how much he was or wasn't reimbursed. What is known is that neither he nor his estate was ever fully repaid and that by the time he became president his sacrifices had changed his own financial situation from comfortable to worrisome for him and his family. In his letter of March 10, 1782, to Philip Thomas, John Hanson, by then President Hanson, wrote, "I shall in a little time be in great want of money. If you can get me 100 pounds, it will make me easy. I should be under no difficulties if the State would remit me but half of what is due me."[98] One estimate is that the states collectively remitted to the Second Continental Congress and then the United States in Congress Assembled only about ten percent of what had ever been levied on them.

Owing to a variety of economic, accounting and currency factors, it is difficult to precisely translate expenditures from the 1770s and 1780s into today's pound or dollar values. An estimate of current value of John Hanson's expenditures from his own pocket on behalf of the Revolutionary War effort just during the thirty-nine months covered by his 1776-1779 ledger approximates seven million dollars today. His correspondence with Philip Thomas shows that Hanson continued to spend down his assets on behalf of the nation from the ending of this ledger's period in June of 1779 through the end of his presidency in November 1782, another forty-one months. *Pro rata* based on the known (and probably exact) expenditures shown during the period of his ledger, John Hanson would have later spent on behalf of the nation another seven to eight million of today's dollars for an imprecise estimate of a total of fourteen to fifteen million in 2012 dollars of his own money to support the war and nation, most of it never reimbursed.

In contrast, he spent about £400 per year, about $75,000 in 2012 dollars, on his household expenditures. It is interesting to see that one of the nation's wealthiest men spent only as much in current dollars as it takes to run many upper-middle-class households today. However, part of the explanation for what seems to be the unexpectedly modest expenditure to operate Jane and John Hanson's gentry household is the unaccounted value of the slave labor which the couple used to provide many of the household's goods and services.

Many of the nation's wealthiest families pledged their fortunes to independence during the Revolutionary War with some losing everything they had including their homes, businesses and farms burned or confiscated by the British. Their sacrifices, in many cases total, are a tribute to these families. John and Jane Hanson and their family strained under their own sacrifices but came through the Revolutionary War and his presidency, though greatly diminished financially, still comfortable, and with their Frederick County farms and the remnant of their fields at Mulberry Grove intact and able at least partially to replenish their accounts. But the Hansons were luckier than many, with more than a few leading patriots during the Revolutionary War losing everything they had to British vengeance.

Independence: Hanson Keeps the Nation Whole

With his re-election as head of Frederick County government on September 12, 1775, and his appointment in January 1776 by the Maryland Council of Safety to expand his raising of war funds from his large county to the province as a whole, John Hanson stepped up his work supporting the war. Throughout these efforts, Hanson continued to encounter the prime weaknesses of the colonists' quest for independence and later in their first government: the near fatal difficulty the Second Continental Congress and later the United States in Congress Assembled had in raising money to support the colonies' and later the post-war central government's operations.

Nevertheless, Maryland's first brigade of soldiers was raised with Frederick County's Thomas Johnson commanding with the rank of Brigadier General.[99] It is probably no coincidence that this appointment was given to the county in which Hanson, the colony's top militia organizer and war financier, resided, but Johnson's appointment was certainly based largely on his own merit and not as any kind of political sop. Thomas Johnson, a self-made man born bright to a small-farm family in Maryland's Anne Arundel County, studied law, married his law tutor's daughter, served in the colonial House of Delegates, and founded his large successful Catoctin Furnace iron works in Frederick County which led him to move there. His brigadiership ended in February 1777 when, with John Hanson's backing, he was elected as Maryland's first governor after statehood. Upon election, Johnson sponsored the appointment of John Hanson's son, Alexander Contee Hanson, Sr., as the first judge of the General Court of Maryland, the new state's highest court. In the 1790s, Johnson was appointed by George Washington as an Associate Justice of the United States Supreme Court and later turned down an appointment as Secretary of State. Through most of the 1790s, Thomas Johnson headed the three-member Board of Commissioners of the Federal City which was charged with choosing a site and name for the new national capital and getting the capital city up and running. Thomas Johnson's niece, Louisa Catherine, would become First Lady in 1825 after marrying John Quincy Adams.

During John Hanson's time heading Frederick County government from 1774 until the first Maryland State Constitution took effect in February of 1777 and he began concentrating more on his state government roles, he was faced with numerous tests of resolve in establishing fundamental means of operation of the fledgling county government. The most difficult of these was establishing reliable local revenue sources to fund both local official operations and the County's support of the war. The province's Committee of Correspondence and Council of Safety, and later the state government after independence, were so starved for funds that they labored through continual difficulty in funding their own prescribed war plans. Complicating the funding of county government was the difficulty of collecting taxes by a new unproven collection authority on which many people were not yet willing to place their bets.

As troublesome as funding itself, Frederick County also was forced to deal with all of the political dislocations and public disorder attendant to the contest of authority between established British rule and the new claims of legitimacy put forth by the rebels who were still struggling to organize. To convince the Frederick County populace of the legitimacy of the new authorities and give people some measure of assurance in abiding by them, Hanson and the Frederick County Committee of Correspondence in October 1775 decreed that continued use of much of British colonial law was not inconsistent with defiance of the British. In fact, when later devising their state constitutions and first setting up their systems of laws, all thirteen of the new states would borrow heavily from both British codified and common law.

As jurisdictions in all thirteen colonies were forced to do, Hanson and the Frederick County Committee of Correspondence had to sort out who was loyal to the rebellion and who wasn't, and put in place means for dealing with dissenters to the new order. For this purpose, the Fifth Convention of Maryland had gained the counties' consent for them to gather lists of those of its residents agreeing to swear allegiance to the Convention's *Association of the Freemen of Maryland* declaration. The counties set about doing this by recruiting Associators as they came to be known, and identifying others as fence-sitters or as outrightly opposed Non-Associators as they were labeled. Hanson and the Frederick County insurgent government were generally lenient with those who did not immediately pledge as Associators, taking the largely successful approach of persuasion over time. However, those advocating or taking overt action against the rebellion were dealt with firmly by fines, warnings, banishment from specific locales, having to post bonds, jail, confiscation of property or, in the most severe cases, execution. Any of these exigencies could occur close to home: in the president's letter of August 10, 1782, to Philip Thomas, John Hanson opines that Philip Thomas's British loyalist neighbor will meet the hangman's noose.

The height of punitive necessity in the county came in 1775 with John Hanson's detection and thwarting of an encroaching British spy ring and a planned military operation against Frederick County instigated by Lord Dunmore, Virginia's British governor until he had fled the colony to Canada earlier that year. Dunmore and others had laid a plan to ally with the Native American tribes of Ohio and Kentucky to attack Maryland's western frontier and move eastward town by sacked town. By May 1775 as Hanson's suspicions became aroused, he wrote to Peyton Randolph, President of the newly convened Second Continental Congress, alerting the Congress to the plot and urging reinforcement of the Frederick Barracks with additional troops and arms. Hanson's worries were well founded. On November 17, a party of four led by British Lieutenant Colonel John Connelly were arrested in their beds by thirty-six Frederick County riflemen at the home of Dr. Snavely along Conococheague Creek near Hagerstown. The four were caught red-handed with Dunmore's detailed written plan involving an ultimate goal of seizing Alexandria, Virginia, followed by the entire colony of Virginia, and reinstalling Dunmore as governor. Among the four was Dr. John F. D. Smith, formerly of Port Tobacco and therefore probably known to John Hanson.

The day after Dunmore's agents fell into Hanson's trap near Hagerstown, at the time within the old borders of Frederick County, they were brought before Hanson in Frederick, indicted and remanded to John Hancock, who had succeeded Randolph as president of the Second Continental Congress a few days before. Hanson's cracking the plot, seizing its operatives, quashing Dunmore's North American designs, and embarrassing the British caused a sensation in the colonies.[100]

Hanson's trumping the British was only one among a swirl of defiant acts and a growing number of military successes by the colonies at the end of 1775 and going into 1776. During that December alone, Virginia and North Carolina patriots routed loyalist troops and burned Norfolk. Colonel William Thomson with his fifteen hundred rangers and militia captured British loyalists at Great Canebrake, South Carolina. Just within the first ninety days of 1776, Thomas Paine's *Common Sense* was published, patriots drove British loyalists from Moore's Creek Bridge, North Carolina, the Continental fleet captured New Providence Island in the Bahamas, and the British were finally driven out of Boston, retreating with their navy to Halifax, Canada, a major turn in the war for both sides. This series of victories, one on the heels of another, the British evacuation of Boston in particular, showed that the colonies could indeed succeed in battle on their own soil, lent confidence to the Second Continental Congress, boosted popular support, and quickened the rising talk of a final break with Britain.

As sentiment in the Second Continental Congress moved closer to declaring independence from Great Britain, many delegates to the Congress lacked the authority from the Committees of Correspondence in their colonies to endorse such an action but, with the exception of New York which did not oppose independence, consent was gained colony by colony, concluding at the last hour with a doubting Maryland. On June 7, 1776, Virginia delegate Richard Henry Lee and Massachusetts delegate John Adams brought matters to a head in the Congress when Lee presented his formal resolution for independence and nationhood to the Congress and Adams seconded it. On June 11, a committee comprising Adams, Thomas Jefferson, Benjamin Franklin, Robert Livingston and Roger Sherman was assigned to produce for the Congress's consideration the draft of an independence declaration along the lines of what had been proposed in Thomas Paine's *Common Sense* a few months earlier. The committee assigned Jefferson, possessed of "the Reputation of a masterly Pen" in Adams's words, the task of drafting the declaration. [101]

On May 4, Rhode Island, the most standalone of the colonies which time and again would be politically out of step with her twelve sisters through the rest of the century, actually had already declared full independence from Britain. The

Declaration of Independence would then in effect be a re-prise of Rhode Island's action by the other colonies.

It would not be easy for the pro-independence colonies to persuade Maryland, Pennsylvania, South Carolina and New York to agree to independence, and all knew that anything less than unanimity could well prove to be a grave weakness to the prospects of nationhood. Arguments against severing ties to Britain were most strongly urged by Pennsylvania's John Dickinson, South Carolina's Edward Rutledge and the four-member New York delegation. Maryland's four delegates were tepid, did not participate vigorously in debate, and, at any rate, lacked authorization from their colony whose leaders still had serious misgivings about joining into union with the other colonies. Led by the scholarly and well-spoken Dickinson, the delegates in opposition held out hope that relations with what they still regarded as their mother country could be reconciled, and doubted that a fledgling nation without even a government or means of funding itself could prevail against the mightiest military on earth. As Thomas Jefferson described them, these four doubting colonies "were not yet matured for falling from the parent stem."

John Dickinson, an outstanding but now somewhat over-looked figure of the revolutionary period, had begun public service in 1764 as a member of the Pennsylvania Assembly which the following year appointed him as its delegate to the Stamp Act Congress. There he first made his mark as an especially compelling writer when chosen to draft the *Resolutions of the Stamp Act Congress.* He went on to serve as a Pennsylvania delegate to the First and Second Continental Congresses from 1774 to 1776 and again in 1779. Dickinson is unusual in that he represented two colonies and then states off and on over a period of several decades. Born in Maryland, he was elected to the Delaware Assembly in 1780 but then returned to Pennsylvania where he served as governor from 1782 until 1785. Dickinson then served as a Delaware delegate in the Constitutional Convention in 1787, after which, as the pseudonymous Fabius, he volubly promoted the new constitution in nine essays. In 1792, he helped to write a new Delaware constitution.

At the end of debate on the Declaration of Independence and still prepared to withhold the Pennsylvania delegation's consent, Dickinson was persuaded by his fellow Pennsylvania delegate Benjamin Franklin to demur on the Declaration. By abstaining, Dickinson opened the door to his colony's assent to the Declaration. If he had voted, he would have done so as a Pennsylvania delegate. He later signed both the Articles of Confederation and the Constitution as a Delaware delegate.

Dickinson's erudition, diplomatic temperament and clarity of expression were called upon at two critical moments in the nation's formation when he was appointed to head committees which drafted both government charters: the Articles of Confederation and the Constitution. To be clear, it was Dickinson ahead of all others who was chosen to lead in drafting the only two governing charters his nation was ever to know. With the exceptions of Benjamin Franklin and perhaps John Hancock and Alexander Hamilton, American history seems to have made it a virtual rule that only those of the revolutionary era who later became presidents of the second government would be enshrined as Founding Fathers and remembered as such by succeeding generations of Americans. As this kind of omission from the American pantheon is certainly the case with John Hanson, so it is with John Dickinson. Dickinson died February 14, 1808, and is buried in the Quaker cemetery in Wilmington, Delaware. His main lasting remembrance today is Pennsylvania's Dickinson College, a memorialization of which few Americans are still aware.

The pro-independence voices in the Second Continental Congress were led by a delegate at least the equal of Dickinson in scholarship and steadfastness to his own point of view. Not the orator nor diplomat that was Dickinson, Massachusetts' John Adams brought forth his arguments for independence with the skilled marshalling of facts and resolute insistence on logic which had made him one of the most respected and feared lawyers in the colonies. Son of a cobbler and a mother who could not read, the Harvard-educated Adams had served Massachusetts as a delegate in both continental congresses where he quickly rose in influence. What he lacked in tact, Adams made up for in argument, tenacity and political astuteness. Understanding that his side could not carry the debate on independence without bringing in the oldest, largest, most populous colony, Virginia, it was the shrewd Adams who vocally backed the nomination by Maryland delegate Thomas Johnson of the southern colony's George Washington to command the new Continental Army after Lexington and Concord, thus in a stroke insuring a stronger measure of unity in the Congress. Adams then persuaded Virginia's assuaging Richard Henry Lee to make the motion instead of himself in Congress to declare independence. Adams, unlike Lee a lightning rod for opposing views, seconded the motion.

Having the good fortune to continue his political career into the second government, John Adams went on to compile one of the best known and most studied records of any American political figure. The first vice president and second president of the government under the Constitution, Adams lived long enough to see his child elected as the sixth president of the Constitutional government and fifteenth overall. In late June of 1826, anticipating the fiftieth anniversary of the passage of the Declaration of Independence and aptly distilling a lifetime of prescient political philosophy, Adams wrote in warning to his countrymen, "My best wishes, in the joys, and festivities, and the solemn services of that day on which will be completed the fiftieth year from its birth, of the independence of the United States: a memorable epoch in the annals of the human race, destined in future history to form the brightest or the blackest page, according to the use or the abuse of those political institutions by which they shall, in time to come, be shaped by the human mind."[102] A few days later, he witnessed that fiftieth anniversary on which day both he and his vice president and successor as president, Thomas Jefferson, died in one of the most astounding transits of history that any nation ever experienced.[103] Adams's famous last words were, "Jefferson survives," but Adams had survived Jefferson by a few hours. Both of the Adams presidents rest in the crypt of the United First Parish Church in Quincy, Massachusetts, their hometown.

Aside from their brilliance, learning, leadership and force of personality, one other trait they had in common, which, however, put them in the minority among their fellow delegates, was that the Quaker Dickinson and the Unitarian Adams and their families never enslaved other human beings.

As the independence debate in the Congress came to a head in late June of 1776, Maryland remained saddled with her doubts, causing great concern in the Congress that a declaration might not be unanimous, with Maryland ending up as a geographical wedge interposed between two discontiguous groups of the other states, and squarely between the disparate northern and southern blocs of states.

Maryland's reluctance had two sources. There was serious disinclination by the conservatism of the traditional landed gentry now running the colony who, once they had shed Proprietor rule, were guarded with the new structure they had installed which favored them and their vested interests, and were not at all sure that Maryland's joining an only lightly defined confederation would be to their own or their class's good. Second, the Maryland Conventions had developed a strong ethic of taking their cues not so much from the other colonies or the Second Continental Congress but from enfranchised opinion leaders province-wide. Not until the Fifth Convention of Maryland had put forth to these elites of the province the proposition of joining a continent-wide independence decision and received their affirmative consensus on the matter was the Convention willing to consider independence and, even then, opposition remained among many of the Maryland Convention's delegates. In 1775, an earlier Maryland Convention had actually issued unambiguous instructions to its delegates to the Second Continental Congress to disavow in frankest terms any invitation to join other colonies in a call for independence.

As the clock wound down and each of the other colonies but New York had indicated its assent to union or was swinging toward it, an annoyed John Adams on June 14 wrote to Maryland Delegate Samuel Chase, "Maryland now stands alone. I presume she will soon join company; if not, she must be left alone."[104] Exasperated with Maryland and New York, the Second Continental Congress by July 2, 1776, was forced to consider forming a union of only eleven of the colonies which would have resulted geographically in an unadjoined three-piece nation, if any nation at all. The pro-unification delegates and especially Adams knew that this kind of checkerboard arrangement would drastically lessen the prospects of the new nation, and they held fast in their arguments that unification would have to be unanimous or at least without dissent.

With this rising tide elsewhere favoring formal declaration of independence, Hanson once more took the lead in Maryland as he had in raising militias and war funding, this time making his voice heard beyond the borders of his colony. "Hanson was mortified in seeing the Maryland representatives tied down to those unwise and timid instructions and resolved to exert himself at once for their repeal. For this purpose he roused the people of Frederick (his adopted county) to assemble in public meeting on June 17, 1776, and they resolved that they would support the union of the colonies with their lives and fortunes."[105]

To give his proposal full weight, Hanson had persuaded the Freemen of Frederick that he put forth the resolution over their name to the Eighth Convention of Maryland. The group agreed and the recommendation was presented by Hanson at the colony-wide Convention which convened on

June 21 in Annapolis. Over the next week, John Hanson weighed in. "The Frederick resolution was, to a large extent, the basis of the resolution adopted by the Convention of Maryland on June 28, and on July 4, 1776, the Maryland Delegates in Congress voted with the other colonies for independence."[106] Hanson had persuaded the Convention delegates to rescind the 1775 instructions opposing independence and replace them with the polar opposite, a feat which the Convention only days before had thought impossible.

Hanson's arguments, winning over the Convention and finally moving the colony into the independence column ". . . took the first decided action on the part of the colony looking to an armed contest with Great Britain."[107] John Hanson concluded his remonstrance with words which have lasted: "These resolutions ought to be passed and it is high time," which his biographers have reckoned as the Convention's final and convincing argument on the debate. As soon as Hanson had begun shifting the weight of the Convention, Congress delegate Samuel Chase in his return letter of June 21 to John Adams urged Adams to "be assured that Frederick speaks the sense of many counties." On June 28, the Convention ratified the independence position which Hanson had put forth and sent it off to its delegates at the Second Continental Congress.

Robert Eden, the last British colonial governor of Maryland, had seen the change of power coming when the previous year in wishful thinking he had written, "All power is getting fast into the Hands of the very lowest of the People. Those who first encouraged the Opposition to Government, and set these on the licentious Behaviour will probably be amongst the first to repent thereof."[108] Eden had gotten it backwards. Maryland and Robert Eden may be credited with what is generally reckoned as the most orderly and moderate transition from British to American rule of any of the colonies. In the face of the Hanson-authored independence proposal and the certain adoption of it, the Maryland Council of Safety courteously informed Governor Eden that there was no further role for him to fill. Robert Eden departed for England on the warship *Fowey* on June 23. Seven years later after the signing of the Treaty of Paris, Sir Robert Eden, by then a Baron but homesick for the land where he had spent most of his adult life, would return to Maryland and resettle there. He was to enjoy being reunited for only a year, dying in 1784. He is buried in Annapolis. Robert Eden was the ancestor of twentieth century British Prime

Minister Anthony Eden.

It was Hanson and the politically rambunctious Frederick County who had taken the lead in Maryland in urging independence since "many of Maryland's leaders, and such parts of the province as the Eastern Shore, were highly reluctant to take this final step."[109] By June 24, most of the Eastern Shore counties and all of those west of the Chesapeake had come around and endorsed the Hanson proposal for national independence. While John Hanson was only one of the earliest movers for independence in the colonies, he was among the most strident Maryland proponents of it, if not the most so, and his leadership was crucial in getting Maryland to cast aside her doubts about joining the union.

At this crossroads, we see John Hanson at the forefront of the independence movement in Maryland and playing the critical role in Maryland in assuring unanimity of the colonies for independence. His success came just in time. It would be hard to overstate the importance of Hanson's accomplishment at this key juncture in United States history. Four years later, he would reprise his rescue of the union. Hanson's convincing arguments and his manner of putting them forth, bolstered by the public support he had marshaled, were able to carry the day and convince his fellow delegates of the wisdom of a stronger unsplintered alliance of all of the colonies in declaring unified nationhood.

Perhaps as strident in urging independence in the Eighth Convention of Maryland was Anne Arundel County Delegate Charles Carroll of Carrolton, so called to distinguish him from his father, Charles Carroll of Annapolis. On the strength of his role, the Convention on July 4 appointed Carroll as a delegate to the Second Continental Congress where he took his seat on July 18 and on August 2 became a Signer of the Declaration of Independence. In this Signer role which later came to be revered and capitalized, Charles Carroll, by a few days' margin, happened to be in the right place at the right time. In 1903, Hanson and Carroll would be chosen by the Maryland General Assembly to have their statues represent the state in National Statuary Hall of the United States Capitol. At the age of ninety-five in 1832, Charles Carroll was the last Signer of the Declaration of Independence from any state to die.

As the Eighth Convention was ratifying Hanson's recommendation that Maryland join in declaring the all-colonies independence, also on June 28 Thomas Jefferson's draft of the Declaration of Independence had been presented to the

Congress whose independence proponents could only hope that positive word would somehow still arrive from Maryland. It finally would. By the evening of Monday, July 1, Congress president John Hancock saw that he did not have unanimity yet, with the Pennsylvania and South Carolina delegates not ready to vote for the Lee resolution, New York still lacking its Committee of Correspondence's permission to endorse independence, the two Delaware delegates split, and, for all the Congress knew, Maryland still in opposition. Hancock adjourned the Congress to give the Pennsylvania, South Carolina and Delaware delegations the evening to try to reach consensus, and ready to declare independence with Maryland left out.

On July 2, 1776, with John Dickinson and Robert Morris agreeing to abstain, the remaining Pennsylvania delegation led by Benjamin Franklin voted for independence. Pennsylvania was in.

South Carolina's Arthur Middleton, son of Henry Middleton, his colony's delegation head, broke with his absent and ailing father, bringing South Carolina in.

In one of the most heroic and important single votes the nation would ever see, Delaware's Caesar Rodney, weak from facial cancer, rode eighty miles through a night rain, arriving at the Congress just in time to break the Delaware delegation's deadlock by casting his vote in favor of independence. In Delaware's three-member delegation, Rodney was joined in voting for ratification by Thomas McKean who would become the last Second Continental Congress president before the nation's first government would be launched in 1781. Rodney and McKean had brought Delaware in.

With the New York delegation openly sympathetic to independence but abstaining for fear of what the Declaration of Independence might provoke the one hundred fifty British war ships in New York harbor to do, New York was in by not opposing independence making the vote eleven for with one abstention and Maryland not voting or abstaining.

Now only Maryland remained out of the proposed union. Maryland's consent reached her delegates at the Second Continental Congress late that day, July 2, 1776, when they cast Maryland's vote for independence, making unanimous among the thirteen colonies, now states, the adoption of the Lee resolution. With New York formally not opposing the resolution, no state had.

To recapitulate, four men with their astute political acumen and sheer courage brought around their colonies to allow the Declaration of Independence to pass without dissent. Three of these — Franklin, the younger Middleton and Rodney — were delegates of the Second Continental Congress who were there to cast their votes for the Declaration. The fourth, a frontier county delegate to a colonial assembly, was called up by destiny to make the quest whole. Still indispensible in his key Revolutionary War roles of war materiel production, militia raising and funding, John Hanson would not make his appearance at the Congress for another four years. When he did, it was to put forth yet another Hanson Plan just as crucial which once again would be the key in holding the hopeful union together as one. His two nation-saving strokes would make him his country's first president. There may have been others in other colonies who had similar influence in persuading their assemblies to vote for independence but, if so, they had not had to fashion a pivot of national destiny at the eleventh hour as Hanson had.

What the Congress voted to accept on July 2 was independence itself. It did so with several changes in wording to Jefferson's draft of the Declaration of Independence agreed in discussion leading up to the vote that day. The Congress did not meet July 3. On Thursday, July 4, 1776, Jefferson reported back to the Congress with a reworked Declaration incorporating the few wording changes, which, with one exception, were minor and which had already been agreed upon two days before. As a quick *pro forma* matter with little discussion, the Congress voted on the final version on July 4, 1776, accepting it unanimously before adjourning. One of the wording changes between July 2 and 4 was the very title of the document, *The Unanimous Declaration of the Thirteen United States of America.* It had not been unanimous or thirteen until Maryland's word had reached the Congress late on July 2.

The one major change which did radically alter the future of the nation was the deletion of Jefferson's wording opposing slavery. Jefferson, bitter over this particular change, wrote, "The clause too, reprobating the enslaving the inhabitants of Africa, was struck out in compliance to South Carolina and Georgia, who had never attempted to restrain the importation of slaves, and who on the contrary still wished to continue it. Our Northern brethren also I believe felt a little tender under these censures; for tho' their people have very few slaves themselves yet they had been pretty considerable carriers of them to others."[110] As we shall see, eight years later as a delegate to the first government, Jefferson would try again to abolish slavery and very nearly succeed.

From Jefferson's handwritten, hemp-paper draft, the Declaration which was printed and distributed to the colonies, General Washington and others was produced late into the evening of July 4 by John Dunlap, a twenty-nine-year-old Irish immigrant printer, with Benjamin Franklin, the colonies' most famous printer, and Thomas Jefferson, the Declaration's author, essentially looking over Dunlap's shoulder. These copies are called the Dunlap Broadsides, twenty-seven of which are known to survive today. They contained only the names of Second Continental Congress President John Hancock, Congress Secretary Charles Thomson and Dunlap. The next day, these copies were sent out to the Committees of Correspondence in the colonies for ratification.

By a few hours on the morning of July 5, the Dunlap Broadsides were actually second into print behind that day's issue of the *Pennsylvanischer Staatsbote*, a Philadelphia German-language newspaper. On July 4, Second Continental Congress President John Hancock had ordered that the Declaration be translated for the benefit of Pennsylvania's large German population, from then until well into the twentieth century, the nation's largest ethnic group. *Pennsylvanischer Staatsbote* publisher Heinrich Miller, who had previously worked in Benjamin Franklin's publishing house until 1762, right away put his assistants, Carl Cist and the nineteen-year-old Swiss-born Melchior Steiner, to work on the translation and printing. Working through the night, the three got their paper out early on the fifth, getting the world scoop on the story of the Declaration of Independence.[111]

Signatures to the actual governing copy which one sees at the National Archives were gathered over the next few weeks. Maryland was next to last to sign when Charles Carroll of Carrollton[112], Samuel Chase, William Paca and John Hanson's Port Tobacco neighbor and relative by marriage, Thomas Stone, added their signatures. It is a modern myth that John Hanson was a signer of the Declaration of Independence. The last signature was added on August 2, 1776, thereby ratifying the Declaration of Independence by the colonies themselves including New York, and bringing the Declaration and all that it meant into effect on that date. It was actually on this August date when the United States came into being in name and spirit though it would require five more years of war and hard political struggle to form the nation's first government, thus achieve nationhood in fact, and make the United States more than just an alliance of independent legal entities.

On July 3, John Adams had written to his wife Abigail that, "On July 2, 1776 the Association known as United Colonies of America officially became the United States of America."[113] Writing to Abigail in a second letter the same day, John exults, "But the Day is past. The Second Day of July 1776, will be the most memorable Epocha, in the History of America."[114] It is clear that it is this date, July 2, 1776, that Adams thought would be celebrated in history as the American birthday. So did the rest of the Congress.

It is instructive to contrast what transpired on the three dates mentioned. On July 2, 1776, the Second Continental Congress passed the Declaration of Independence; on July 4 it perfunctorily approved a small number of wording changes already agreed upon; and on August 2, the Declaration first attained legal effect. Yet none of these dates completed the formation of the nation which would not occur until November 5, 1781, when the United States was finally able to launch a government. Of the three 1776 dates, clearly July 4 was the least consequential but that happened to be the date when the Declaration of Independence was first read to the Philadelphia public causing immediate celebration and which has been observed since as the American birthday. It was also the day before the first printed notice of the new Declaration — in a German-language newspaper. Such is the lost and found of history. The author happens to be writing this, entirely coincidentally, on July 4, 2010.

In Frederick, John Hanson must have taken special contentment that ratification of the Declaration of Independence had been unanimous, that there were all thirteen rather than twelve of the states in the new union, that Maryland was not an odd-man-out geographical wedge between two discontiguous groups of states, and especially that it had been he as much as any who had ensured national wholeness.

The first printed version of the Declaration of Independence with the signatures was not published until the following January after victories in the battles of Trenton and Princeton gave the Congress enough faith in its new army's military strength to make the names of the Signers safely public. Late in 1776, fearing that the British would take Philadelphia, the Congress moved to Baltimore and there on January 18, 1777, the Congress ordered the signed Declaration put into print. Congress Secretary Charles Thomson that day recorded that an "authenticated copy of the Declaration of Independency, with the names of the members of Congress subscribing the same, be sent to each of the United States, and that they be desired to have the same put upon record." The honor of publication went to Baltimore's Mary Katherine Goddard, publisher of *The Maryland Journal* and postmistress of the Baltimore Post Office.[115] The nine known Goddard Broadsides make it even rarer today than the Dunlap Broadsides.

The new appellation "United States" for years to come was literal with each of the thirteen new states almost entirely independent of the others and united more in common sentiment than politically. This independent-mindedness of the states would first prominently rear its head in 1781 with the creation of a weak national governing charter, again in 1789 in the nation's second charter, the Constitution which incorporated what came to be known as states' rights, most seriously with the Civil War, and well into the twentieth century in southern states' ruse of a states' rights façade to oppose the Civil Rights Movement. It was not until the Civil War that the country, following President Lincoln's lead, began referring to the United States in the singular, "the United States *is*" rather than the "United States are" which had been said up to that time.

Δ

This American war for independence was a revolution which in its most key aspect was the polar opposite of the other major national revolution of its time and many since. While the French Revolution thirteen years later and the Russian Revolution more than a century into the future were largely driven from the bottom up by disaffected commoners, the American Revolution was for the most part led by elites. It was the American colonies' wealthy, well-educated gentry who drove the revolt against British rule and first manned the ramparts (or caused them to be manned). To be sure, they were quickly followed by many an American commoner, but it was the old bewigged and powdered landed aristocracy which forced the break. With few exceptions, not until the dismantling of European colonial empires after World War II would the world again see elites leading many national revolutions.

The actual political change wrought by the Declaration of Independence was that each colony became a sovereign nation-state more or less fondly associated with each other in sentiment, geography and cause, but not yet in legal union nor with a central government. Indicative that the new association's member states related to one another at arm's length, some would continue to refer to their delegates to the Second Continental Congress as ambassadors. On June 14, 1777, the new nation would adopt the Stars and Stripes as its single flag, an early step toward tangible unity, but, as contrasting example, Maryland in the winter of 1778 would independently ratify the treaty with France *in association with* the other states.

John Adams, then forty, had seen the future perhaps as clearly as any in his July 5, 1776, letter to Abigail, to whom he wrote, "You will think me transported with Enthusiasm but I am not. I am well aware of the Toil and Blood and Treasure it will cost Us to maintain this Declaration, and support and defend these States. Yet through all of the Gloom I can see the Rays of ravishing Light and Glory. I can see that the End is more than worth all the Means. And that Posterity will triumph in that Days Transaction, even although We should rue it, which I trust in God We shall not."[116]

Adams had foreseen the future clearly. When British Minister Lord North, in the equivalent position of a modern prime minister, was informed of the signing of the treaty between the United States and France in 1778, he and his government repealed the Intolerable Acts, issued a full pardon to what he and his government still regarded as the thirteen British colonies, and urged that his government grant essentially everything for which the colonies had petitioned before the Declaration of Independence. The Americans thus had at hand all they had sought but, in their minds now, the pains of war had created too great a gulf of estrangement and made the British capitulation too late. And as fragile and tentative as it was, the new nation's taste of its own freedom was too pleasant to be anything now but permanent in the former colonists' minds. The United States now insisted on independence with no strings attached and desired no longer to be a part of the British Empire. In the face of the Americans' refusal of peace under continued British rule, Britain elected to pursue the war rather than explore options for comity with independence. Britain remained the mightiest nation and military on Earth, and the outcome of the Revolutionary War as of 1778 was still anyone's guess, with the hinge of the Revolutionary War at Yorktown a long three years and more hence.

In October of 1776, John Hanson, Thomas Contee and two others were elected Commissioners by the Maryland Convention and dispatched on a two-month journey to meet with the Second Continental Congress in Philadelphia and General Washington at his camp near New York regarding the enlistment of Maryland soldiers. Thomas Contee (1729-1811) was John Hanson's brother-in-law, Prince Georges County tobacco merchant, militia man and delegate to the Maryland Conventions. The diary which Contee kept during the mission contains personal details of encounters with Hanson, Washington and Congress President John Hancock as well as a sad first-hand account of the British invasion and capture of New Brunswick, New Jersey. The diary, long thought lost, surfaced in the 2011 auction of the estate of Mathias Oppersdorff, Jr., a fifth-great-grandson of the president.[117]

Δ

A significant shift in the makeup of those exerting influence in Maryland was reflected in the makeup of the Ninth Convention of Maryland, the last before government under the state's forthcoming constitution. The major accomplishment of this Convention, which met from August 14 to November 11, 1776, was its authoring of the first Constitution of Maryland. Where the previous eight Conventions and the Maryland Assembly both before and after independence had been drawn almost exclusively from the Maryland gentry and heavily from Maryland's old Tobacco Coast families, the Ninth Convention for the first time dipped well into the colony's middle class. By this time, the Court Party loyal to the Proprietor had been relegated to history but some who had served the party in the Assembly's upper House — the colonial Proprietor's Council — had changed parties and begun to coalesce as a conservative faction within the Country Party in the Conventions, the county Committees of Correspondence and elsewhere in Maryland politics. At the same time, the voting franchise had been extended to all freeholders, no longer just to those possessing fifty or more acres of land. This put a number of middle-class Marylanders including fourteen merchants, thirteen lawyers, twelve farmers, six physicians, six manufacturers, four millers, a dentist and a clerk among the delegates to the Ninth Convention.[118] Their presence wrought a state constitution which ensured decent chances of election of middle-class candidates to both houses of the new state legislature, the Maryland General Assembly.

The gravitation at the same time of both the more conservative elements from the old Court Party and the more democratic and, as it turned out, more radical elements from the ranks of the middle class into the Country Party produced a polarization which resulted in the two factions taking classic conservative and progressive positions on many issues. The two groups became referred to as Whigs[119] and Democrats, respectively. This bifurcation was set in place when in early 1777 many of these same Ninth Convention delegates were elected to one house or the other in the new state General Assembly. In both the final Convention and the new legislature, it was the conservatives, many of whom were old colonial gentry, who were in the majority and usually able to push their agendas despite the inroads of the more democratic middle-class voices.

On September 17, 1776, the Ninth Convention ordered the draft of the proposed Maryland Constitution printed and distributed to the counties for consideration by the citizenry, or at least that small slice of it that was enfranchised. The Convention adjourned that day, reconvened on October 2, received the consent of the counties, and formally adopted the Constitution six days later followed by a Maryland Declaration of Rights adopted on November 3. It is interesting to note how closely the Constitutional Convention and the adoption of the United States Constitution a decade later would follow the process established when Maryland wrote, sought public approval for, and adopted her constitution.

One result of the particular complexion of the Ninth Convention is that it produced the most conservative of the thirteen new state constitutions being written at the time. The new Maryland constitution hoarded central control, ceding relatively little autonomy to the counties. It provided for only one elected county official, the sheriff, who was required to have a minimum £1,000 visible estate, and was to be chosen by the Governor from the two top vote-getters. White male freeholders but not others could vote. The governor was not elected popularly but by an electoral college. There was little in the way of checks, balances or separation of powers. The major advance of the Maryland Constitution was that religious, racial and national origin restrictions were relaxed though the racial liberalization was to prove brief. However, while Catholics had their voting rights restored, the Constitution disenfranchised non-Christians altogether, an exclusion in which even the Proprietors had not engaged. All in all, the first Maryland constitution was actually "far more restrictive and less democratic than the proprietary charter."[120] To correct the shortcomings of the first Constitution, the Maryland General Assembly would rewrite the charter in 1801 and again on November 1, 1864, when it abolished slavery in Maryland.

The last of Maryland's nine conventions adjourned on November 11. The state's first General Assembly under the new Maryland Constitution convened on February 10, 1777, and elected Frederick's Thomas Johnson as the first governor of Maryland four days later. Johnson defeated Samuel Chase, the only other candidate, by a vote of forty to nine. Among the Assembly's five-member Executive Council was John Contee, John Hanson's brother-in-law.

John Hanson, elected by Frederick County to every office he ever sought there, could not have been elected by the county's unique electorate as anything but a Democrat. Hanson, his progressive electorate and the Frederick County delegates to the Ninth Convention took the positions of the forward-looking Democrats but saw many of their aspirations for the new state Constitution shunted aside as it was being written by the Convention. This might have been one element in Hanson's decision later in 1777 to sidestep more political service within Maryland and in 1779 begin what he could not have known would be his meteoric rise on the national stage while serving as a Maryland delegate to the Second Continental Congress. But if he thought that he was avoiding the headaches of governing under a flawed governing charter in the Maryland Constitution, he was perhaps yet to fully assess the Articles of Confederation which had been drafted by September 1777.

What the future president possessed was not only the prized asset of being able to see issues from the dual perspectives of a yearning progressive frontier electorate *and* of the old gentry planter society, but also of being able to mix comfortably with both groups, gain their respective confidences and serve as a skilled go-between. It was this bridge-building skill, honed when the patrician Hanson successfully adjusted to a middle-class, multiethnic, largely immigrant electorate new to him, that would before long come to the fore as he found himself the point man in resolving the nation-breaking western lands impasse.

The War Brought Home

Toward the end of its session, the Ninth Convention of Maryland dispatched John Hanson and three others to the Second Continental Congress and to General Washington, who was then fighting in New York and New Jersey, to coordinate first-hand Maryland's contributions to the war effort. It is conspicuous that the Convention could have assigned this vital mission to any of its delegates, or to any other Marylander, and chose Hanson. On October 9, 1776, Hanson, Thomas Contee, Benjamin Rumsey and James Lloyd Chamberlaine received their orders from the Convention and on the seventeenth set out from Annapolis for the Congress in Philadelphia. By fourteen years, Hanson was the eldest of the group.

Thomas Contee, younger brother of Hanson's wife Jane, was a Prince George's County delegate to the Convention. This is the same Thomas Contee who had been, or perhaps still was, co-owner with John Hanson of their store in Frederick. By 1776, Thomas had apparently moved back to Prince George's County as in his diary of the commission's trip he notes, "Prince Geroge's County, Wednesday, 16 Oct., 1776-Set out from home; reached Annapolis and attended the Convention, 5 o'clock; got no answer that evening; next morning waited on the Convention and got their resolves."[121] Thomas Contee served as Secretary of the commission, keeping a daily record in a diary which covers only the dates of the trip. As this record was passed down in the Hanson and then Thomas families until it was auctioned in 2011, it is surmised that Thomas Contee wrote the diary as the commission's official record to be kept by John Hanson.

The Ninth Convention's charge to the Hanson commission was to respond to the Congress's resolution of September 19 ostensibly requiring each state to raise specified quotas of battalions to form a unified army for the new United States. As all would see, the "requirements" put forth by the Congress to the states would prove to be only partially fulfilled pleas. Maryland's quota was eight battalions. In its October 9 response to the Congress to be delivered by the Hanson delegation, the Ninth Convention had affirmed, "That this State, desirous of exerting the most strenuous efforts to support the liberties and independence of the United States, will therefor use its utmost endeavours to raise the eight Battalions required." As the Ninth Convention was not at all certain that Maryland could muster as many as eight battalions, the Hanson delegation's role was to convey this to the Congress and its president, John Hancock, and discuss what might be possible. After three days' travel in their carriages, the party reached Philadelphia on October 20, remaining there in consultation with the Congress until November 24. The conclusion of the mission was the understanding with the Congress that Maryland would do the best she could in military recruitment.

That day, with the delegation's business with the Congress as completed as it was going to get, Hanson departed Philadelphia, leading his delegation north to fulfill its second charge from the Ninth Convention, to confer with General Washington and inspect Maryland troops already in the field. What Hanson witnessed was dismaying.

The Ninth Convention's second charge to Hanson and the commission was, " . . . to consult with, and take advice from, his Excellency General Washington, respecting the appointment or promotion of Officers in General Smallwood's Regiment, and the appointment to be made in the Batallion to be formed of the Independent Companies and Flying-Camp of this State." By November 28, Hanson and his fellow commissioners received word of Washington's defeats at Fort Washington in New York and Fort Lee across the Hudson River in New Jersey days before. John Hanson knew that his son, Lieutenant Peter Hanson, was stationed at Fort Washington. On the twenty-ninth, the four commissioners witnessed Washington and his army retreat on their way to New Brunswick, New Jersey. Later that day, Hanson and the commissioners met briefly with Washington who was too preoccupied with the British in pursuit of his army to afford much time to the commissioners. The four dealt with Washington's aides and generals that day and reconnoitered with Hanson's son Alexander serving high in Washington's retinue.

The following day, the commissioners caught up with the two Maryland brigades whose enlistments, coincidentally, expired that day. Neither commander was able to persuade enough men to stay to maintain either brigade which devolved into much smaller units the following day. Of this, Thomas Contee recorded in his diary that, "The same day, in the evening, I went with Colo. Ramsey to headquarters, and informed the General that our flying camp would not be prevailed on to stay, for which he expressed his sorry (sic) and expatiated on the inconvenience of short enlistments."[122] Maryland's soldiers were not the only state's whose enlistments would expire at this time. New Jersey's did as her soldiers, too, melted away and headed for home.

On December 1, now much in the advantage, the British bombarded Washington's army garrisoned in New Brunswick, forcing it to abandon the town. Thomas Contee recorded the day. "The enemy fired six to our one. We left our carriages at our lodgings, went there to order our servants to go away with them. The cannonading soon ceased. When we got our horses we intended to go to the bridge and the town to see what was going on, but we had not got half way before we met our army retreating to Trenton, upon which we rode on to overtake our carriages. Never did I see such a scene of distress — women and children crying, not knowing what to do with themselves."[123]

After drafting Maryland's first state constitution, the Ninth Convention of Maryland had adjourned on November 11 leaving the state in the hands of the Committee on Safety, the small executive stopgap body which had been authorized to maintain an official state presence between the Maryland Conventions. Upon its return, the Hanson commission reported the desperate state of affairs to the Committee and all realized the gross misdirection of having sent a commission whose charge was officer promotions when the army in which they served was on the run and being depleted by the day. There is every indication that John Hanson's first-hand witnessing of both the condition of the army and the anemic vision of his own state toward his mission further galvanized him into the outstanding Revolutionary War organizing performance for which he would be praised since.

After reporting on his sixty-five-day mission to the Committee on Safety in Annapolis, John Hanson made it back home to Frederick on December 19 almost certainly still not knowing the fate of his son Peter.

Fort Washington, at Harlem Heights near the northwestern tip of Manhattan in present-day Harlem, was a fortification which General Washington elected to defend for the dubious proposition of holding the city of New York against the much stronger British Army and a British frigate which had its guns trained on the fort from the Hudson River. Generals Lee and Greene had tried unsuccessfully to dissuade Washington from investing precious Continental Army manpower and materiel in trying to hold the city and its environs which they correctly saw could not be successfully defended. But Washington vaingloriously clung to the hope that the nation's largest city could be held and sought the laurels that would be his in being able to do so. As the British trained their sights on New York and Washington vacillated indecisively, his generals finally convinced him to save his army by retreating to New Jersey. This he did, retreating to Fort Lee across the Hudson River, but leaving a significant part of his army behind, ordered to hold Fort Washington.

Left there were a considerable amount of war materiel which ended up in British hands and 2,600 doomed soldiers of the Continental Army. The four-day battle of Fort Washington, begun on November 16, 1776, was savage, costly, hopeless and decisive. This occurred in the last days of the Hanson commission's time in Philadelphia before its four delegates left for New Jersey. John Hanson may have learned of the capture of Fort Washington as he was leaving Philadelphia but more likely not until he encountered Peter's brother Alexander at New Brunswick. It is unlikely that either father or brother new of Peter's fate at that point or even if he was still alive.

At the time of Peter Hanson's capture, his elder brother, Alexander Contee Hanson, Sr. was serving General Washington. "He was the confidential friend of Washington and for several months while acting as Washington's private secretary was a member of Washington's home circle."[124] Alexander would have been aware of Peter's peril as soon as Washington ordered Fort Washington held. From his vantage point across the Hudson with Washington, Alexander would have known of his brother's plight as soon as the fort was overrun by the British, perhaps within Alexander's sight.

Lieutenant Peter Hanson had been commissioned as Second Lieutenant in the First Maryland Battalion of the Flying Camp only that July. He had been promoted to First Lieutenant of Stephenson's Maryland Rifle Battalion on September 17, and was wounded and taken prisoner at Fort Washington on November 16, dying of his wounds sometime the following month as a prisoner of war. Peter Contee Hanson left behind his young widow Mary and infant son named for him. She and Jane and John Hanson would have learned of Peter's loss within a few days of Christmas 1776.

Conflicting sources have Peter Hanson's age when he died at eighteen, twenty-five (or twenty-six) and thirty. George Hanson has Peter Hanson's birth date as December 9, 1758, and age at death therefore at eighteen.[125] This date would be impossible if accepting as correct the birth date of Peter's son, Peter Hanson, Jr., on March 27, 1768. Aside from making Peter a ten-year-old father, the 1758 birth year would also have made him a seventeen-year-old lieutenant, possible in the Revolutionary War but improbable. Pundt's Hanson family genealogy has Peter's birth date as December 9, 1746, and his age at death as thirty. However, this birth date is also impossible as Peter's sister Jane is reliably known to have been born February 23, 1747. The author's family records, which show no source for Peter's date of birth, have him born on December 9, 1751, making him twenty-five or twenty-six depending on which date in December of 1776 he died. There is nothing known which would rule out this birth year and though its source is lost and research has not been able to verify it, it is accepted here at least provisionally that Peter Hanson was twenty-five or twenty-six when he died.

Among the captured were the fort's commander, Brigadier General James McCubbin Lingan who in 1812 would die defending John Hanson's grandson. Also captured were Major (later General) Otho Holland Williams of Frederick, and Private John Adlum who would become the continent's first vintner. Williams and Adlum were released in prisoner exchanges later in the war. General Lingan was held as a prisoner of war aboard a British ship for three and a half years until released in a prisoner exchange. After the Revolutionary War, James Lingan attained appointment as Collector of the Port of Georgetown, Maryland, later to be folded into the District of Columbia. General Lingan would die days following the outbreak of the War of 1812 after a mob attacked the offices of *The Federal Republican*, the Baltimore newspaper operated by John Hanson's grandson, United States Senator Alexander Contee Hanson, Jr. A fuller account of the episode is provided later here in the last chapter when discussing Senator Hanson. John Adlum planted his vineyard in Washington, DC, in the neighborhood today known as the Vineyard. His first wine was made from the native Catawba grape, a varietal still made today.

Washington was criticized at the time and has not received much sympathy since by historians for his blunder in thinking it possible to contest the British at New York and not evacuating the ill-fated American soldiers at Fort Washington with the rest of his army. There is some debate over to whom to assign the blame for the losses of Forts Washington and Lee. Washington biographer John Ferling describes the losses and Washington's culpability along the lines presented here. Historian Matthew Andrews asserts that Washington was reluctantly complying with the order of the Second Continental Congress in defending Fort Washington. The two accounts are entirely at odds on whose decision it was not to abandon the fort. Other long-accepted accounts generally ascribe the loss to Washington.[126]

Now holding Fort Washington, the British were not finished

and crossed the Hudson in pursuit of Washington and his debilitated army. Within seventy-two hours of his arrival at Fort Lee, Washington had to abandon it, too, leaving behind 30 cannon, 8,000 cannon shot, 4,000 cannonballs, 2,800 muskets, 400,000 cartridges, 500 shovels, 300 tents and 1,000 barrels of flour, all then put to use against him by the British.[127]   Then on December 1 came the taking of New Brunswick. The British had decisively routed Washington's army three times in two weeks.   In an almost miraculous turn of fortunes for the American cause the following month, Washington was able to defeat the British in his surprise attack at the Battle of Trenton, New Jersey, on the day after Christmas, and again at the Battle of Princeton, New Jersey, on January 3, 1777. These victories occasioned Congress's promotions of five officers to the rank of major general including Thomas Mifflin and Arthur St. Clair both of whom would go on to be elected presidents of the United States under the first government.

Losing their first of two sons in the war must have been difficult enough for Jane and John Hanson but especially bitter when they realized that the loss resulted from Washington's indecisiveness and entirely avoidable lurch in strategy. But, if this put a strain on the long-time friendship between Hanson and Washington or their cooperation in prosecuting the war, it is not evident in the surviving record showing their ongoing constructive collaboration and clearly continued affection for one another.

Nor did the avoidable loss of Peter seem to affect the relationship between Alexander Contee Hanson and George Washington. Alexander would twice serve as a presidential elector casting his vote for Washington, the first time over his own cousin who was seeking the office. Alexander would turn down President Washington's offer to sit on the first United States Supreme Court in order to become Chancellor of Maryland which position he would take up on October 3, 1789, five months after Washington's first election.

Δ

Amidst his demanding mid-1770s Frederick County roles as chairman of the county's Committee of Correspondence and as county Treasurer, John Hanson continued serving in his appointment as Frederick County's Deputy Surveyor, a position which had been held over from Proprietor rule after independence. He resigned as Deputy Surveyor in 1777 before being appointed the following year to the new Maryland State Court of Appeals, the state's highest court. For a period sometime after 1771, John Hanson had also served as Sheriff of Frederick County. The multiplicity of his essentially simultaneous occupations in nearly all of the county's highest offices combined with the top-level influence of his son and son-in-law in the county and in Annapolis attests to the power which John Hanson had accrued unto himself in Maryland's largest, most populous county and in the state itself. Until the election of his Frederick County protégé Thomas Johnson as the state's first governor in 1777, John Hanson arguably held the most powerful executive position in Maryland from 1774 until then. Given the deliberate paucity of executive powers delegated to governors in Maryland's first constitution, Hanson might well be said to have continued to hold the most powerful if not the highest executive position in the state even after statehood.

From the time of independence until 1779 when John Hanson agreed to be a Maryland delegate to the Continental Congress, he busied himself with the production of war materiel, raising militias from Maryland and devising various means including continued reaches into his own purse for the new nation to finance its war. As a national leader in these endeavors, Hanson was extremely busy keeping each of these fronts moving. Some have wondered why John Hanson did not make his way earlier than 1778 into his statewide role again serving in the House of Delegates or than 1779 into his national role as a Maryland delegate to the Second Continental Congress, but an inspection of his record in the rapidly unfolding events of the late 1770s makes it apparent that he made a deliberate decision to devote his energies to the logistics rather than the politics of prosecuting the war — executing rather than formulating. In this, he chose the more difficult assignments and ones where his particular talents were more indispensable as the imperative for political union among the states became as important as winning the war itself. During the three years until 1778, John Hanson positioned himself where he saw that his nation could make best use of him. When his nation's heaviest need for him would shift to the political arena, he was to redirect his efforts, again putting himself at the nation's disposal where his talents could be applied where they would then do the most good, and, in fact, where they were to prove crucial.

Letters Home

Indispensable to John Hanson's ability to serve on the national stage effectively was a man who would appear to be the most valuable son-in-law any United States president ever had. Jane and John Hanson's fifth child, Jane Contee Hanson, her mother's namesake and Janey to her parents, had married Dr. Philip Thomas of the Eastern Shore who in 1769 had arrived in Frederick County as its first physician. During the Revolutionary War and his presidency when John Hanson spent much time away from home in Annapolis and then Philadelphia, it was Dr. Thomas who became the closely trusted confidant of the president and managed the president's business and political affairs in Frederick for him. These duties devolved upon Dr. Thomas as all three of John Hanson's surviving sons were away in the Revolutionary War.

The Thomas home directly adjoined the president's on what is today the second block of West Patrick Street in Frederick. After Jane Hanson the elder became a widow in 1783, she lived the rest of her life in the care of and next door to her son-in-law who himself had been widowered in 1781. Mother-in-law and son-in-law lived adjacent to one another until her death in 1812. It appears but is not conclusive from available records that living with Philip Thomas in Frederick for an unknown period was his mother, Elizabeth Bellicum Thomas. Also living in Philip Thomas's household were his and Jane Hanson Thomas's four children, James, Catherine, Rebecca and John Hanson Thomas, aged six through two when Jane Thomas died. In her letter to her father Philip Thomas of March 5, 1782, as a young child while staying with President and Jane Hanson in Philadelphia to attend school, Catherine "Kitty" Thomas mentions her and her siblings' Frederick "Mammy" Jennie, almost certainly a slave though possibly a free Black.[128] After the president's death in November of 1783, Philip Thomas became the patriarch of a family comprising one or two elderly widows, four young children, Jennie, other household help and himself, a widower. Certainly the one or two grandmothers and Jennie would have had much to do with raising the four youngsters. One imagines three close-knit generations both rent and bound together by their losses.

Dr. Philip Thomas attained significant stature in his own right. After graduating from medical college in Philadelphia and becoming Frederick County's first physician in 1769, he founded and served as the first president of the Medical and Chirurgical[129] Faculty of the State of Maryland, predecessor of today's Maryland State Medical Society. He was elected Chairman of the Committee of Safety of Frederick County. For a time, Philip Thomas served as a Frederick County

Magistrate until resigning this post in October of 1781 a few months after his wife's death to give him more time for his duties as a single parent. He represented Frederick County in the Maryland colonial Assembly and remained active in Maryland politics during the period of the United States in Congress Assembled. During the Revolutionary War, Philip Thomas was appointed Captain of the Fourth Battalion of the Maryland Militia on November 29, 1775, and Captain of the Thirty-fourth Battalion on March 7, 1776. Later in 1776, he had risen to the rank of Colonel which he retained for the rest of his life. Philip Thomas's military duty was apparently served locally in Frederick County.

On February 4, 1789, Dr. Thomas and his brother-in-law, Alexander Contee Hanson, Sr., each cast a Maryland presidential elector vote in favor of George Washington and their votes for vice president for Robert Hanson Harrison of Charles County, Alexander's second cousin and President John Hanson's nephew. All four other Maryland electors also voted for Washington and Harrison.

Beginning April 11, 1793, Dr. Thomas made part of his home available for a private school, one of Frederick's first.[130] Soon afterward, he founded and was president of Frederick County's first public school which he got the Maryland General Assembly to charter in its November 1796 session, and which opened October 2, 1797. Dr. Thomas also was the founder and publisher of the *Frederick Town Herald* in 1802.[131]

Philip Thomas was a widower for thirty-four years — more than half of his life — from June 1781 when Janey died at the age of thirty-four until his death April 25, 1815, at the age of sixty-seven. Dr. Thomas's portrait, shown here, reveals a somber perhaps sad man at an age after he became a widower. Reading the sparse history on this man, one concludes that his chosen role in life was that of giver and comforter, one who chose medicine as his profession in the first place, selflessly attended to the affairs of his father-in-law president, and looked after his widowed mother-in-law, living beside her for the last twenty-nine years of her life. Having founded Frederick County's first medical practice, its first public school, a private school, his state's medical society and a newspaper, Philip Thomas may also be reckoned as a highly successful entrepreneur. As with John Hanson, Philip Thomas much deserves his historical due.

John Hanson's fifty-two extant letters to Philip Thomas during Hanson's time away in Philadelphia with the Second

Continental Congress and then during his presidency of the United States in Congress Assembled offer the best glimpse of the personal John Hanson of any of the meager remaining sources on his private life. These letters are preserved in the John Hanson Collection in the H. Furlong Baldwin Library of the Maryland Historical Society.

When John Hanson was appointed to serve as a Maryland delegate to the Second Continental Congress in December 1779, it necessitated his being away from home for months at a time. Though he was able to spend short periods at home in Frederick, he was not to return home permanently until the expiration of his presidential term in November of 1782. During these thirty-five months spent mostly away, Hanson relied on two people to manage his business affairs for him. They were his brother William who managed his and Jane's remaining stake in Mulberry Grove and John Hanson's other Charles County interests, and Philip Thomas who looked after Hanson's affairs in Frederick.

John Hanson must have written regularly to the two but the only known letters from him to either of them which survive today are the fifty-two to Philip Thomas during this period. The reason for their survival is that they were passed down and long treasured in the Thomas family. Hanson's letter of August 10, 1782, still has its original red wax seal intact with John Hanson's imprimatur stamped into it. These letters, John Hanson's two extant ledgers and a small memorandum book, the entirety of the known personal record on him, do the most today to reveal the private John Hanson. To his biographers, these are a national treasure.

The series begins with a letter from John Hanson to Dr. Thomas on June 21, 1780, and concludes with Hanson's letter to Thomas on June 18, 1783, eight months after concluding his presidency and five months before the president's death. The series thus begins when John Hanson began his service as a Maryland delegate to the Second Continental Congress in Philadelphia, encompasses Hanson's presidency from November 1781 to November 1782, and concludes eight months later when the former president was visiting Annapolis. All of the letters were sent from Philadelphia where Hanson was attending the Second Continental Congress and then the United States in Congress Assembled except for the last from Annapolis after President Hanson's term had expired. Important figures of Hanson's era spent much time with quill in hand corresponding, filling diaries and committing their business and affairs to pos-

terity in longhand. Hanson was no exception. Just his letters to Philip Thomas during his presidency averaged a fre-
quency of every nine days. As did his contemporary statesmen, Hanson often took late hours to correspond as when
he notes in one letter to his son-in-law that he is writing at
"9 Oclock at night" and in another at "10 oClock at night."
The president was not always fastidious in his spelling.

Some of these letters were sent by post such as it existed in
that era but many were carried by individuals heading more
or less in the right direction toward Frederick and Dr. Thomas. Transit times varied but were usually within two
weeks. For example, John Hanson notes in his letter to
Philip Thomas of September 19, 1780, that he received that
day two Thomas letters dated September 3 and 9, so transit
times were ten and sixteen days for those two missives. The
salutation of all of the letters is "Dear Doct.". Given gaps in
subjects, questions and known events from letter to letter, it
appears that the series could be incomplete but this is not
certain. Some gaps in dates, for example that between Hanson's letters to Dr. Thomas of April 10 and October 2, 1781,
are probably at least partly accounted for by Hanson's being
back in Frederick. Many of the letters were sent to Dr.
Thomas along with Philadelphia newspapers and a few, but
very few, were only a short paragraph amounting in effect to
cover letters for the newspapers. In the remainder of *Remembering John Hanson,* we will continue to rely on these
invaluable letters to round out the lives of both men, illuminate events as they transpired during the Revolutionary War
and the ratification of the Articles of Confederation, expand
on the official record of John Hanson's presidency and further reveal the personal John Hanson.

Part IV

Onto the National Stage

The Articles of Confederation

While in its ringing tones the Declaration of Independence proclaimed to the world the radical democratic republican experiment called the United States, the Declaration had made no provision for how the new nation was to govern itself. Even as they declared independence, the delegates to the Second Continental Congress understood that a national government must be formed to administer the new nation and prosecute the war, but deciding how the nation should be governed would prove a far tougher proposition than had agreeing to declare its independence. "There were no examples, no precedents available to Americans of a people constructing its own government and establishing the fundamental principles under which it would be governed."[132] It had taken fifty-six days from Richard Henry Lee's motion for independence made to the Second Continental Congress until the states' ratification of Independence. It would take a thousand and two days for the states to form a government by ratifying the Articles of Confederation.

Furthermore, despite the Declaration of Independence, nationhood itself could not be fulfilled until a government was formed. Not until the ratification of the Articles of Confederation on March 1, 1781, did the United States of America take the next step of authorizing its first government, and not until November 5 of that year with the election and seating of the first government would the United States finally come into existence as the unified political entity envisioned, distinct from the thirteen sovereign nation-states that created it. Until then, little more united these thirteen sovereign entities than their resolve to fight their way together to independence from Britain. While they cooperated with each other as allies, and permitted their representatives in the Second Continental Congress to join with those of other states in actions such as war and diplomacy normally taken under the auspices of a central government, the new states retained the absolute right to withdraw their cooperation at any time, to any extent, for any reason. Only by the Articles of Confederation would they agree to form their "perpetual union" and cede to the nation's new central government a portion of their precious sovereignty.

To reiterate, it is essential to keep in mind that, while March 1, 1781, accomplished the chartering of political union among the states by their ratification of the Articles of Confederation, it was not until November 5, 1781, that the states would actually consummate their nationhood with the launching of the first government, putting the final touch on nationhood.

Even as the Declaration of Independence was being proposed, the Second Continental Congress was debating how to construct the nation's first government when on June 7, 1776, the Congress entertained a motion for a national governing charter. In addition to his resolution for independence that day, Virginia Delegate Richard Henry Lee had moved that "a plan of confederation be prepared and transmitted to the respective Colonies for their consideration and approbation." On June 11, the Second Continental Congress began debate on how to construct the nation's first government when it took up Lee's motion to fashion a national governing charter.

The following day, one delegate from each colony was chosen to sit on a committee "to prepare and digest the form of confederation." John Hanson's nephew and former Charles County neighbor, Thomas Stone, was Maryland's representative on the committee. Pennsylvania's John Dickinson was appointed to head the committee, his learned knowledge of government institutions gaining him the appointment. On July 12, 1776, following the passage by the Congress of the Declaration of Independence (but before the states had ratified it), the Dickinson committee proposed an outline of a new governmental charter and was then further charged by the Congress with drafting what came to be called the Articles of Confederation. We recall that it was the cautious Dickinson who had most strongly opposed the Declaration of Independence and abstained from voting on it on grounds that a collection of colonies lacking a government or treasury could not hope to prevail in a war of independence against a much greater military power. He would prove too nearly correct in his assessment. But the Congress felt that despite his doubts, Dickinson, learned and astute on the classical history, theory and machinery of government, was the best choice to lead the drafting of the new document which would authorize a government.

The committee had its hands full not only with crafting a national governing charter onto an entirely blank slate but in confronting the thorniest impediments to unification of the newly declared states including multiple ongoing boundary disputes, conflicting laws and decisions by colonial courts, differing tariff and commercial practices, disjointed state-to-state roads and other infrastructure, differing trade restrictions imposed by states and much more. But easily the most difficult obstacles to forming a government and unifying what were still thirteen sovereign nation-states were to be slavery and the western lands impasse. Making the task far more difficult was that the Congress was forced to conduct the drafting of the original government charter amidst a peripatetic existence as it was forced by British incursions to relocate the capital several times over the next years and conduct its business on the run.

Dickinson and his committee used as a template for their work the sketch of a plan for a permanent union of the states submitted to the Congress the previous July by Benjamin Franklin. Although Franklin's plan had been rejected, it formed the successful basis of the Dickinson committee's work in drafting the Articles of Confederation. Due to Dickinson's off and on attendance at the Congress to fulfill other duties in the war effort, the Congress's Secretary, the ever-reliable Charles Thomson, had a strong hand not only in keeping discussion of the proposed Articles moving but in the Articles' actual wording. The scholarly and well-read Dickinson would be called on again in 1786 to head a committee charged with drafting the Constitution but in that effort would see his contributions lie in the shadow of James Madison and Alexander Hamilton who with their own skilled crafting of thought and words had the major influence in bringing forth nation-moving appeal once again.

Beginning on July 22, 1776, the draft of the Articles was discussed by the Congress for each of the next twenty days but then military concerns, poor delegate attendance and having to relocate the Congress from Philadelphia to Baltimore interrupted debate on the Articles. At one point a motion was made to consider the Articles every day in session but on September 2 this was rejected and Congress continued its regimen of two days per week. During the hiatus of discussion on the Articles, the Congress had moved back from Baltimore to Philadelphia but, with the growing possibility of British occupation there, it was again forced to relocate. On September 19, 1776, the Congress left Philadelphia and on the twenty-eighth reconvened in Lancaster, Pennsylvania, for one day before moving further west to the courthouse in the safer York, Pennsylvania. On October 8, Congress began daily discussion of the Articles which continued through November. On November 10, a committee of Richard Henry Lee, James Duane and Richard Law was appointed to review the Dickinson committee's draft of the Articles and recommend any changes, few of which found their way into the final version to be presented to the Congress.

In addition to actually chartering the nation's first government, the Articles of Confederation provided for essential features of the nation and the new government. These included naming the new nation as the United States of America; naming the new government separately as the United States in Congress Assembled; establishing that central government be (ostensibly) funded by the states; reserving foreign relations, national coinage and declarations of war exclusively to the central government; providing for national adjudication of disputes between the states; and decreeing fixed election procedures, qualifications and terms office for the president and the representatives of the states to the government. None of these features had been formally prescribed in the operation of the First or Second Continental Congresses nor in the Declaration of Independence.

It was at this juncture when the Congress was to vote on the Dickinson committee's draft that Maryland first brought to the fore in the Congress her position on the conundrum of the western lands as they were called. In October, the Ninth Convention of Maryland, the last to be held, was absorbed in writing the Constitution of Maryland which would take effect early in the new year, but spent considerable energy considering what the Maryland Convention foresaw as a nation-denying break between two groups of states. Forming Maryland's position vis a vis the seven states with large western land grants, the Ninth Convention in October 1776 wrote:

"Resolved, unanimously, That it is the opinion of this convention, that the very extensive claim of the State of Virginia to the back lands hath no foundation in justice; and that if the same or any like claim is admitted, the freedom of the smaller States and the liberties of America may be thereby greatly endangered; this convention being firmly persuaded, that if the dominion over those lands should be established by the blood and treasure of the United States, such lands ought to be considered as a common stock, to be parceled out at proper times into convenient, free and independent governments."

Maryland had put the other states and the Second Continental Congress on notice. Discussion of the Articles at the Second Continental Congress was then tabled until April 8, 1777, when the Congress decided to resume discussion two days per week.

On April 18, 1777, the newly instituted Maryland General

Assembly went further by formally instructing Maryland's delegates to the Congress that they were not authorized to sign the Articles of Confederation on behalf of Maryland unless provision were made for the full cession of the western lands to the forthcoming central government. To this effect, the Maryland delegation proposed an addition to the Articles of Confederation but, at first, only Maryland voted for the proposed change in the Congress. At this juncture, the Maryland General Assembly instructed its Congressional delegation to vote in favor of Articles of Confederation wording to be sent out to the states for ratification in the form proposed by the Congress, but to put the Congress on notice that Maryland would not agree to its own ratification of the Articles unless the western lands problem were resolved to Maryland's satisfaction. Now in spring of 1777, the gauntlet had been thrown down. It would be four very long years before what would be called the Hanson Plan could unravel the impasse.

The issue was between two groups of states, the seven with extended western land grants including three with nearly indefinite western boundaries, versus the six others including Maryland bound solely to the Atlantic coast with their original western boundaries. The hemmed-in states without these western lands feared the greater opportunity for population growth of those with western lands resulting in the eventual swamping of the former in national electoral power. After a protracted dispute between the two blocs over a forty-month period, all of the states would come around to seeing the peril of chartering a government which would incorporate such a serious disparity that would only fester into a worse division among them.

At the time, the western lands were divided into two large regions, the Northwest Territory[133] and the Southwest Territory together extending, with three exceptions, from the collective western boundaries of the original thirteen states to the Mississippi River which until 1803 was the eastern boundary of France's Louisiana Territory; and from the Great Lakes to within a few miles of the Gulf of Mexico. The Southwest Territory eventually became the states of Kentucky, Tennessee, Alabama and Mississippi. The Northwest Territory eventually became the states of Ohio, Indiana, Illinois, Michigan, Wisconsin and that part of Minnesota east of the Mississippi River. The extensive lands of these two western domains had been granted by various British monarchs during colonial times to seven of the thirteen colonies, with Virginia's, Connecticut's and Georgia's western lands as granted actually having their western boundaries fixed by their grants at the Pacific Ocean, the three exceptions just mentioned.[134]

The western land grant to Virginia by King James in 1609 is abundantly illuminating of the problem which held up ratification of the Articles. The grant's geographical definition of Virginia's western lands was, "All those lands, countries and territories situate, lying and being in that part of America called Virginia, from the point of land called Point or Cape Comfort, all along the sea-coast to the southward two hundred miles; and all that space and circuit of land lying from the sea-coast of the precinct aforesaid, up into the land throughout, from sea to sea, west and northwest; and also all the islands lying within one hundred miles along the coasts of both seas of the precinct aforesaid."[135]

This grant comprised a two-hundred-mile-wide stripe from Virginia's outer banks in the Atlantic to California's Farallon Islands in the Pacific, and included all or parts of eighteen future states and approximately nineteen percent of the total land area of the eventual forty-eight contiguous states. If Virginia retained this swath today, its state population would approximate one hundred fifteen million people, more than three times the size of the largest state population, California's, as of the time of this writing. Likewise, Georgia's coast-to-coast swath, running straight through today's populous sunbelt, would have contained nearly the same population. There was also Connecticut's narrower continent-wide stripe. If present state boundaries were as the old land grants provided, these three states would have about 175 of the 435 voting seats in the United States House of Representatives. Virginia alone would have eighty seats, half again as many as any state today has.

John Hanson and the Maryland General Assembly clearly saw that these huge prospective states would wield an ever-increasing and inordinate electoral power which would sooner rather than later bury the interests of the smaller states and lead to a serious rift between the two groups. In turn, that situation would probably have fatally jeopardized continued union among the states. Hanson saw the western lands problem for the nation-breaking threat that it was.

Further complicating the situation was the discontiguity of some of the western land grants from the colonies to which they had been granted. For example, the states of New York and Pennsylvania lay between Connecticut and her western

land grant. New York and Canada lay between Massachusetts and hers. See the map here for the western lands as
they were in the 1770s (less the three continent-wide depic-
tions).

After more than a year of what must have been the headiest
of debate, the Congress on November 15, 1777, passed the
Articles of Confederation and Perpetual Union, usually referred to as simply the Articles of Confederation, signed by
delegates of all of the states including Maryland. In contrast
to the exalted prose of the new nation's audacious founding
document, its Declaration of Independence, and later the
Constitution, the Articles of Confederation were freighted
with a much more prescriptive and procedural tenor. Perhaps this stodginess lessened the initial appeal of the Articles of Confederation to the states and in some part led to
the long period required for their ratification.

The last revision of the Articles of Confederation as passed
by the Congress and sent to the states was recorded in *The
Journal of the Continental Congress* the day it was passed.
Three hundred copies of the Articles, printed as twenty-six-
page leaflets, were delivered to Congress President Henry
Laurens on November 28 for distribution to the states.
Laurens had succeeded John Hancock on the first of that
month after Hancock's two and half years as president, the
longest that anyone would serve in either the First or Second Continental Congress or in the first government.

The Articles at last were ready for consideration by the
states. Congress asked the states for their ratification of the
Articles by March 10, 1778, in time for a scheduled final
printing by June 26, but underestimated the depth of discussion that was to take place in the state legislatures on
the very same issues that had confounded the Congress in
drafting the Articles, especially with what proved to be by far
the thorniest conflict, the western lands, but also slavery.
The Articles would not be approved for another three years
with Maryland in the key role the last to give assent.

As they reviewed the Articles of Confederation as submitted
to them, several states wanted changes. Meeting in joint
session on December 14, 1777, the Maryland General Assembly instructed its delegates to the Congress to seek three
changes to the Articles. These sought "that no State shall be
burthened with the maintenance of poor persons who shall
remove from another State" in Article I; that states should be
taxed by the central government on the basis of aggregate

property value rather than population in Article VIII; and, in a new article, that the western lands be ceded to the central government for its sole disposition. The unambiguity of the latter instruction to its delegates put the matter of the western lands front and center with the Congress and the twelve other state legislatures:

> "*Resolved,* That the Delegates to Congress, from this State, be instructed to remonstrate to the Honorable Congress, that this State esteem it essentially necessary for rendering the Union lasting, that the United States, in Congress assembled, have full power to ascertain and fix the western limits of those States that claim to the Mississippi or South Sea. That this State consider themselves jointly entitled to a right in common with the other members of the Union to that extensive tract of country which lies to the westward of the frontiers of the United States, the property of which was not vested in, or granted to, individuals at the commencement of the present war."

Note here that the Maryland House is using the new term United States in Congress Assembled recently proposed by the Second Continental Congress as the intended name of the government to be. By taking its early, strident, unmistakably articulated position on the western lands, it was Maryland which thrust the issue to the forefront of the debate on the nature not only of the government proposed by the Articles of Confederation but of the nation itself. At first, Maryland was the only state to take a position on ceding the western lands to the central government and initially was roundly ostracized for it by delegates from the other states. The version of the Articles of Confederation which the Congress had sent out to the states for ratification omitted the Maryland western lands amendment as Maryland alone had voted for it in the Congress.

Dickinson's Second Continental Congress drafting committee had found the western lands conundrum so intractable that it had sidestepped the issue entirely in drafting the Articles of Confederation, leaving it to be thrashed out by the states as their legislatures debated the Articles and whether or not to ratify them. As soon as the Articles were put forth to the legislatures, the document ran headlong into this major obstacle. It would be a long forty months before the division of interests between the seven states with western lands versus the interests of the six other states without such territories could be resolved, the states could agree on and ratify the Articles, and the nation's first government could be chartered.

While the entire Maryland delegation to the Congress and a few delegates of other states spearheaded the drive to re-solve the western lands impasse, it isn't disputed that John Hanson, once he arrived at the Second Continental Con-gress, played the central role there in settling this conun-drum which came perilously close to derailing the Articles of Confederation and nationhood as we know it.

As for the tinder-dry threat of slavery, reluctant agreement was easier that this issue was so intractable that not the Ar-ticles, the Congress nor the states would do more at this juncture than agree to shelve discussion in order to give the Articles of Confederation some chance of passage. This na-tion-defining moral issue would render its seismic shocks into the next three centuries.

Hanson Resolves the Western Lands Impasse

On August 14, 1776, the Ninth Convention of Maryland, meeting on its opening day at Annapolis for its main pur-pose of composing a Maryland Constitution and Bill of Rights, took up as its first item of business the western lands question. It would take the Convention ten weeks until October 30 to thrash out and adopt exactly what it wanted its delegates to present to the Second Continental Congress. "At this session, a powerful influence was exerted by John Hanson, and his able assistants. Through his efforts, the following resolution counteracting the Virginia Declaration, was adopted." [136] Restatement does not belabor its import:

> Resolved, unanimously, that it is the opinion of this Convention the very extensive claim of the State of Virginia to the back lands hath no foundation in jus-tice, and that if the same or any like claim is admit-ted, the freedom of the smaller states and the liber-ties of America may thereby become greatly endan-gered; this Convention being fairly persuaded that if the dominion over these lands should be established by the blood and treasure of the of the United States, such lands ought to be considered as a common stock, to be parceled out at proper times into con-venient, free and independent governments.

Maryland's position had been laid squarely before the Con-gress and to the twelve other state legislatures. The Mary-land delegates at the Congress proposed their state's amendments to the draft of the Articles of Confederation.

The Ninth Convention of Maryland concluded on November 11, 1776, after writing the Constitution of Maryland, chartering the state's government which would take effect shortly after the first of the coming year. It's legislative branch would be called the Maryland General Assembly. "John Hanson was the leading figure in the early sessions of the Maryland Assembly, and his selection to head the Maryland delegation in Congress at Philadelphia during the latter part of the war came as the natural result of his leadership. . . . Previous delegates had achieved material results — but it was the appearance of John Hanson on the floor of Congress which brought matters to a climax, and resulted in a complete victory for the principle that all undeveloped lands should belong to the nation."[137]

By late 1779, with the Maryland government nearly three years old and gaining capability in administering its part in the Revolutionary War, John Hanson could redirect his energies from his state to the pressing political needs at the national level, just as he had shifted his gaze from county to state two years before. Based on his key work as war financier, recruiter and logistician, but now more so on his compelling articulation in the Maryland General Assembly of the need to solve the western lands problem, the Assembly on December 22, 1779, appointed Hanson to represent Maryland as a voting delegate in the 1780 session of the Second Continental Congress. On the same day, he had been reelected by Frederick County to the Maryland House of Delegates but declined the honor to be able to concentrate on his new role. On June 14, 1780, John Hanson first took his seat in the Congress and now operated on the national stage. He arrived with a well secured reputation from his war roles but now more so as the nation's single most articulate voice on solving the western lands conundrum. In a short eight months, at a supremely critical juncture in the formation of the United States, he would again keep the nation whole as he had once before on the eve of the signing of the Declaration of Independence.

On December 16, 1777, Virginia had become the first state to ratify the original version of the Articles of Confederation which did not deal with the western lands. Virginia was the strongest proponent of granted states retaining control of their western lands and was only too glad to ratify the unamended Articles. By the 20th of June 1778 when delegates were asked to announce the instructions from their states on the Articles, the legislatures of New Hampshire, New York, Virginia and North Carolina had already ratified the

Articles without asking for amendments. Some of the other legislatures sought various amendments, but none dealing with the western lands except Maryland. All of the states but New Jersey, Delaware and Maryland had instructed their delegates to ratify the Articles whether or not the amendments proposed by them were eventually incorporated. The Articles of Confederation were signed by the delegates of New Hampshire, Massachusetts, Rhode Island, Connecticut, New York, Pennsylvania, Virginia and South Carolina on July 9. North Carolina ratified on July 21, Georgia on July 24, New Jersey on November 26 and Delaware not until six months later on May 5, 1779. Twelve states had ratified.

And there the Articles sat for the next twenty-two months.

Only Maryland's assent was now needed to complete the confederation, with the holdout state now being roundly criticized over lack of resolution to the western lands issue which by this time had become starkly recognized as a full-blown nation-breaking impasse. Worsening the situation was that, the longer this impasse lasted, the more emboldened the British became by the prospect of its breakaway colonies not being able to coalesce well enough to form a government.

Seeing the prospect of united nationhood among the thirteen states slipping away over the western lands split, John Hanson, in the bridge-building manner which his family and all of his biographers have noted, urged on the Maryland General Assembly a change in course from the correct but cool principled attitude up until then put forth to the Second Continental Congress to an approach of reasoned persuasion. Taking Hanson's lead, on December 15, 1778, after lengthy debate, the Assembly passed a new set of instructions to its delegates at the Congress. On the same day with Hanson's lead, the Assembly adopted the Declaration of Maryland as it came to be known, an artfully reasoned appeal for the necessity of cession of the western lands for long-term national unity and stability. A week later, the Assembly appointed Hanson to speak for it as a delegate to the Second Continental Congress.

The Declaration of Maryland stood fast that Maryland would withhold her ratification of the Articles of Confederation unless the new national government were to have sole authority over the western lands and the creation of new states from them. The wording of the Declaration of Maryland was in large part the change of course urged by Hanson from principled but rigid opinion to persuasive appeal of Maryland's position to the other states and the Congress to try to bring them around to Maryland's recognition of the urgency of the issue. Some in the Maryland General Assembly argued for giving up on cession, but, "In the Maryland legislature at this time, John Hanson was considered the most aggressive and outspoken member in opposition to a settlement of the land question, on the basis proposed in the Articles of Confederation."[138] While not the only voice for pressing the issue in the Assembly, it was by all accounts John Hanson who led in moving Maryland away from her perceived confrontational posture into a stance of positive petition based on fairness to the states without western lands and the long-term practical interests of all of the states and the new nation.

As it was being considered in the Maryland General Assembly, John Hanson's design for solving the western lands obstacle took on the name Hanson Plan. The term apparently came into everyday colloquial use in the Assembly as his design was being debated and has been handed down since. Even before John Hanson arrived at the Second Continental Congress in 1780, the term had made its way to Philadelphia where the Congress had begun referring to the Hanson Plan. When Virginia had bluntly pushed back at the Declaration of Maryland by opening land sales offices in Virginia's western lands, the Walpole Company, a private entity which already had claims in Virginia's western lands, sued Virginia to stop its conflicting land sales. "Soon afterwards the committee of Congress brought in a report upholding the legal claim of the American stockholders in the Walpole Company: and, more generally speaking, the undiplomatic attitude of Virginia as compared to the diplomacy and reason of Maryland had transferred many supporters to the Hanson plan."[139] While there is no apparent official labeling using the name Hanson Plan, the name has continued in use down to the present.

As the Declaration of Maryland was put forth to the Congress and out to states, the delegates of the Maryland General Assembly understood that their best chance of the Declaration's adoption by the Congress would come from the personal presence of the man who had persuaded his Maryland Assembly colleagues, and so the Assembly appointed John Hanson as one of its five delegates and sent him off to the Congress. Of the five, only he and Daniel Carroll ever attended or served. It then became time for the persuasive Hanson to do his work in the Congress itself.

Upon Hanson's arrival in Philadelphia, the Second Continental Congress seized on his financial acumen, keeping
him in the thick of the Congress's and nation's financial affairs. In quick succession, John Hanson was appointed to
the Board of Admiralty and committees dealing with setting
official salaries, supplying the French army fighting along-
side the Continental Army, the purchase of war materiel
from France, bills of exchange and, most important, the setting of amounts to be remitted by the states to the Second
Continental Congress to fund it and the war. John Hanson
would continue serving on the government's key Committee
on Public Credit even during his term as President.

In Philadelphia, fully absorbed in trying to coax resolution of
the western lands impasse, Hanson of necessity kept his
fingers on the pulse of the Maryland General Assembly, now
in its fourth year. Though the body led the nation in delib-
eration over the western lands, it did so amidst its own
share of spotty attendance and unwholesome distraction. "In
1780, Hanson expressed doubt about the patriotic resolve of
some of his fellow legislators, warning that 'the sordid interest and private views of individuals' threatened the war effort."[140]

George Washington had become worn down with the same
doubts. The month before Hanson took his seat at the Second Continental Congress, Washington lamented to Pennsylvania Governor Joseph Reed of his concern that the Congress had for three years been unable to charter a government and effectively prosecute the war. Said Washington in
imploring Reed to forward Pennsylvania's financial requisition to the Congress, "Nothing could be more necessary than
the aid given by your state towards supplying us with provision. I assure you, every Idea you can form of our distresses,
will fall short of the reality. There is such a combination of
circumstances to exhaust the patience of the soldiery that it
begins at length to be worn out and we see in every line of
the army, the most serious features of mutiny and sedition.
All our departments, all our operations are at a stand, and
unless a system very different from that which has for a long
time prevailed, be immediately adopted throughout the
states our affairs must soon become desperate beyond the
possibility of recovery. If you were on the spot my Dear Sir, if
you could see what difficulties surround us on every side,
how unable we are to administer to the most ordinary calls
of the service, you would be convinced that these expressions are not too strong, and that we have every thing to
dread. Indeed I have almost ceased to hope. The country in

general is in such a state of insensibility and indifference to its interests, that I dare not flatter myself with any change for the better."[141]

Within nine months, Washington was to see his old ally Hanson sever the Congress's Gordian knot, charter a government and prepared to launch it.

Hanson's challenge at the Congress had been aided in early 1780 by New York having agreed in principle, but not yet legislation, to cede her western lands to the forthcoming national government. It was slow going at first for Hanson in gathering support from the six other states with western lands to cede theirs to the national government-to-be, but, one by one during the eight months after his arrival at the Congress, the remaining three states with western lands in the Northwest Territory all acceded to Hanson's reasoning and persistence, and the three with Southwest Territory lands began to swing around in their thinking and agreed in principle to cession. At this point, Hanson and others were all too aware that the long hiatus in getting the states to align their thinking on the western lands had encouraged Britain to hope for a failure of the states to unite and to keep pressing ahead with the war.

In September of 1780, on Hanson's recommendation, the Congress's committee charged with dealing with the western lands hurdle recommended the Congress to resolve, "That copies of the several papers referred to be transmitted, with a copy of the report, to the legislatures of the several states, and that it be earnestly recommended to those states, who have claims in the western country, to pass such laws and give their delegates in Congress such powers as may effectually remove the only obstacle to a final ratification of the Articles of Confederation, and that the legislature of Maryland be earnestly requested to authorize their delegates in Congress to subscribe the said Articles."

On October 10, the Congress formally adopted the Hanson Plan and transmitted it to the thirteen state legislatures for adoption. Massachusetts and Connecticut then agreed to give up their western lands, Virginia finally had, and on February 2, 1781, New York's assembly voted to do so, thus putting the entire Northwest Territory at the disposal of the national government-to-be. It was primarily the Northwest Territory which was the crux of the debate regarding the western lands but the disposition of slavery in the Southwest Territory was already an issue of particular import to the southern states, an impediment to their ceding their lands just yet, and antecedent of an emerging major chapter in United States history. Though the three states with western lands in the Southwest Territory had not yet reached the same formal decisions to cede, their sincere assurances that they would do so were enough to deem the Hanson Plan a success and the western lands impasse as resolved.

Victory in hand, John Hanson then informed the Maryland General Assembly that it could safely ratify the Articles of Confederation and on January 29, 1781, the Assembly authorized him and Daniel Carroll to subscribe Maryland to and ratify the Articles on the basis of the agreements in hand of the four states with lands in the Northwest Territory, and the representations of the three with Southwest Territory lands that they, too, would give up their western lands. On February 3, 1781, the Maryland General Assembly elected John Hanson a second time as Maryland delegate to the Second Continental Congress.

On February 24, 1781, in a Saturday session, the Second Continental Congress set noon on the following Thursday as the time for final ratification of the Articles of Confederation and announcement to the world that the Articles would bring a government of the United States into being the following November as scheduled in the Articles. On March 1 in Independence Hall, Daniel Carroll and then lastly and dramatically John Hanson famously ascribed the final signatures to the Articles of Confederation bringing them to life and setting in motion the birth of the first national government that November. By their hand at that moment, the ratified Articles of Confederation, all thirteen feet, five inches of it in a single stitched vellum scroll, set the stage for the nation's first government to come into being 249 days later on the first Monday of November as the Articles prescribed.

Even considering his election later that year as the nation's first president, the many accomplishments of his presidential administration, and all that he had done for the nation during the Revolutionary War, it seems accurate now to reckon John Hanson's finest hour as the success of the Hanson Plan permitting what had been only the hope of the Declaration of Independence to become reality in a contiguous, politically-united country with a single central government. As the final paragraph of the Articles of Confederation reads, "The aforesaid articles of confederation were finally ratified on the first day of March 1781; the state of Maryland having, by their Members in Congress, on that day acceded thereto, and completed the same."

Once before on the eve of independence Hanson had held the nation together by persuading Maryland not to hold herself outside of the union, a nation-saving stroke. Now, to the notice of all, he had been the indispensable man once again in keeping the nation as one. This latter accomplishment immediately earned him the title Father of the Western Domain. His two dazzling nation-saving feats would cause his being drafted as the nation's first president.

With what his biographers have uniformly called his sheer determination, logical reasoning and long measure of hallmark personal diplomacy, Hanson had used Maryland's interposing geographic position between northern and southern states as a wedge to coax resolution of the differences among the states over the western lands, a dispute which, had it not been resolved, would have prevented formation of a nation with contiguous states, and quite probably have resulted in the states or groups of them in lesser unions attempting separate Balkanized nationhoods. The impact of Hanson's success on the geography of the United States as we know it today would be hard to overstate. "In its final analysis, the question of whether there would actually be a union or not hinged on a solution of the western land problem."[142]

The record of the role which Maryland Delegate Daniel Carroll played in the Congress coaxing the twelve other states toward agreeing to the requirement for cession is not as clear as Hanson's. It is known that Carroll, too, very actively supported the Declaration of Maryland and did put forth his own energies of persuasion in the Congress. But it is John Hanson to whom historians virtually uniformly have given credit for taking the lead in Maryland and then the Congress in remonstrating against the dangers of two classes of states, the frail union that such a division would have produced, and failure to get the western lands blockage resolved. Likewise, other delegates, as their states began to come around, joined Hanson's and Maryland's arguments. But it is John Hanson who is mentioned above all others as the outstanding voice in the Second Continental Congress in getting the western lands impasse settled, and clearing the way for ratification of the Articles of Confederation, formation of the first government and, thus at last, consummation of nationhood. Every one of his biographers goes further: had it not been for Hanson alone, full union would have failed.

To recapitulate John Hanson's nation-preserving success, practically no progress was made in the Congress on the western lands problem in the three years from 1777 when the draft Articles of Confederation were put forward to the states until Hanson's arrival at the Congress in June 1780, and then the hurdle was cleared within eight months after his arrival, leading to his presidency after another eight months. It is not an exaggeration to say that while Washington was saving the nation on the battlefield, Hanson had first saved it politically.

While the four states with western lands in the old Northwest Territory agreed by 1781 to cede their western lands and permit the new nation to create new states from them, the western lands of both the Northwest Territory and the Southwest Territory were not actually given up and formally ceded to the nation until after the Articles of Confederation were signed and the United States in Congress Assembled had come into being later that year. But all seven states with western lands kept their promises made to John Hanson and ceded their western lands to the new nation, Georgia the last in 1802.

March 1, 1781, a date now all but forgotten in United States history, was immediately celebrated throughout the states with parades, cannonades, decorations, oratory, effusive editorials and official congratulations from the emissaries of foreign powers. The expression of the *Maryland Gazette* on March 22 was typical: "Thus will the *first of March*, 1781, be a day memorable to the annals of America, for the final ratification of the Confederation and perpetual Union of the Thirteen States of America – a union, begun by necessity, cemented by oppression, and now finally consolidated into a confederacy of these new and rising states . . .."[143] (Emphasis in the original) Five years after declaring independence but with nothing more than the weak consultative Second Continental Congress to tenuously bind it together in the interim, the nation rejoiced in relief at finally being on the verge of attaining actual nationhood with agreement among what until then had been thirteen independent nation-states to join in "perpetual union" and form a central government. As a matter of historical fact, March 1, 1781, was the date in her history when the United States finally resolved to single nationhood, and November 5, 1781, was to be the date when the new unified nation and its original government actually came into being.

On March 2, Samuel Huntington, the continuing president

of the Second Continental Congress and now a caretaker in the interim pending the government's first election, announced in a circular letter to the thirteen state legislatures the ratification of the Articles.   Huntington rejoiced that, "We are happy to congratulate our constituents on this important Event desired by our Friends but dreaded by our Enemies."[144]   Huntington informed General Washington of the ratification by letter on March 5.

In the elation of 1781, the new nation understood that it was Maryland which had made unification possible and that it was Maryland's John Hanson who more than anyone else in the nation had delivered it.   Perhaps the most eloquent exposition of Hanson's accomplishment was not written until another 120 years had passed.   During the late 1890s when the Maryland General Assembly was trying to decide which two Marylanders it should honor with statues in National Statuary Hall, many names from the colony's earliest times through some famed nineteenth century governors were put forward.   Discussion in the Assembly over which two Marylanders should be chosen was protracted and spirited.   Even after John Hanson and Daniel Carroll were chosen by the Assembly in 1898, attempts were made to change the selections.   In responding to such a suggestion which had been published in *The Baltimore Sun*, the state's largest newspaper, Ella Loraine Dorsey wrote the following. Dorsey was a prominent author of children's books, the great-great-grandniece of President Hanson, and a relative of Priscilla Dorsey Hanson, the wife of John Hanson's grandson, United States Senator Alexander Contee Hanson, Jr.[145]

> "The crowning fame of John Hanson's public life is that he and Daniel Carroll had the honor and glory of representing Maryland in the fight she made for the Western Domain.   The contention of the State was that 'what was rescued from the common enemy by the common effort, ought of right, be common property, to enure forever for the common benefit of all the States.'   And she held this position through good and evil repute, through reproaches, threats and arguments until the other twelve wheeled in line and assented, and the generation of the world became the heirs of our magnificent land, for the general government was made its sole possessor, and John Hanson and Daniel Carroll signed for Maryland.   They became, in a word, two of the <u>founders of the United States</u>; for, had the federation been left

with its outlying territories, filled with clashing overlapping boundaries, the seeds of war would have
been sown and grown in every one, and the mind
shrinks aghast at what might have been our condition except for the stubborn courage of Maryland
and the ability of her two representatives to convert
the minority of one to the majority of thirteen, to
transform a mere compact into a mighty federation,
and colonies decimated by War into the parents of a
great sisterhood of states, — the ideal Republic of the
world."[146] (Emphasis in the original.)

The National Park Service lists six known copies of the Articles of Confederation extant today held by the Independence
National Historical Park in Philadelphia, the New Hampshire
Historical Society and two copies each by the National Archives and Library of Congress. However, this list omits the
copy held by Harvard University at its Dumbarton Oaks facility in Washington, DC, and inspected by the author. The
Articles of Confederation as ratified by the states is provided
as an appendix here.

The 249-Day Inter-regnum Before the First Government

Between the Articles' authorization of the government on
March 1, 1781, and seating the new government on November 5, the nation still had no government because it was yet
to be formed as required by the Articles. By the same token,
full nationhood would not actually be consummated until
November 5 when the election would take place and the government seated.

With the ratification of the Articles on March 1, 1781, we
encounter the frequent confusion which exists today and
likely puzzled people at the time over the transition from the
Second Continental Congress to the United States in Congress Assembled. However, we see in this transition two key
elements which clearly demarcated the two bodies: the Articles' explicit creation of the first government, and the end of
the Second Continental Congress. But sorely complicating
history's ability to track the transition — from consultative
body to first government — is the 249-day lull which existed
between March 1, 1781, when the Articles became ratified
and *authorized* the first government, and November 5 of that
year when the Articles *created* the first government.

Although the ratification of the Articles on March 1 finally
brought forth a unified nation, that nation still lacked any
government to make it whole until eight months later, the

last step to nationhood yet to be consummated under the election provisions set forth in Articles V and IX of the Articles. Establishing the method that continues today in only slightly modified form, the Articles called for the seating of the successive Congresses and election of presidents of the new government to occur on the first Monday of November each year which for the first election in 1781 fell on November 5. (In a nod to farmers' needs to be at markets on Mondays, Congress in 1845 altered the timing of presidential and congressional elections to occur on the first Tuesday after the first Monday of November, a practice continued today.)

The confusion wrought by this 249-day interim between chartering and creating the government begs elucidation here in its own right, and to dispel the modern misconception that the presidents who served during this interim period did so under the aegis of the first government which they didn't.

The Deliberately Attenuated National Presence from March 1 to November 5, 1781

Thus, March 2, 1781, the day after ratification of the Articles of Confederation, brings us to the moment in the series of the United States' two consultative bodies and succeeding two governments that marks the height of modern confusion regarding the order of these bodies, their names and especially their powers. The origin of this particular confusion is clear: in the 249 days from March 1 through November 4, 1781, with the Second Continental Congress having legislated itself out of existence, and the United States in Congress Assembled not yet convened, an interim body existed but barely, by agreement had many of its functions held in abeyance awaiting the birth of the forthcoming government, and operated as not much more than historical placeholder.

In sorting out the roles of the Second Continental Congress, the interim body and the United States in Congress Assembled, part of what one reads today, which to an unsuspecting public could appear authoritative, turns out to be patently incorrect, as misinformation from odd quarters has been sown on the Internet. The best guide in establishing an accurate delineation of the Second Continental Congress, the interim body and the United States in Congress Assembled, and the transitions from one to another, is the wording of the Articles of Confederation itself which provided that a new body entitled the United States in Congress Assembled, set up and explicitly recognized in the Articles as the nation's first government, *would form with its first election in November 1781* and not until then.

Even a cursory reading of the minutes and presidents' letters during the brief existence of the interim body and then those of the succeeding Hanson administration clearly shows that the interim body was just that, treading water with the explicit understandings that it would curtail its activities and cease to exist upon transition to the new government on November 5.   Technically, the interim body could perhaps claim to be the first breath of the United States in Congress Assembled since Article III of the Articles of Confederation "hereby" brought the union, but not the government, into being upon the signing of the Articles. But this stretch is only nominal at best as, upon ratification of the Articles on March 1, the Congress immediately began deferring nearly all authority and most actions it could have taken pending the November election, and its delegates mostly dispersed until then.   If the interim body seems thinly defined, this is because it was and deliberately so.

The prime reason for correctly placing the interim body in accurate historical context is the modern misinformation, sown only in recent years but metastasized effectively by the Internet, that the two presidents (or three depending by which folly one chooses to count) of the interim body served as presidents of the United States in Congress Assembled and therefore preceded John Hanson as presidents of the first government. For example, as of 2011, several websites show Samuel Huntington, the interim body's first president, as the nation's first president on the basis that he was the first American to serve with the title of president after ratification of the Articles. However, there was no government at the time when Huntington served of which Huntington could have been president, nor his two successors in the interim period, since the Articles of Confederation explicitly provided for the government to come into being in November 1781 by which time all three had completed their service. Samuel Huntington and Thomas McKean became presidents of a nongovernment — a committee of the whole at best — and Samuel Johnston, though elected during the interim period, never served as president of the interim body, either Continental Congress or either government.

Though thinly attended, deliberately restricted in authority and action, acknowledged only as placeholder in its own time, and by far the weakest of any body in the series of the 1770s and 1780s, the interim body could still claim to be a congress, essentially, if not nominally, the closing chapter of the Second Continental Congress. The interim body did exist after the Articles of Confederation had been ratified and dissolved itself before the Articles effected the original government, but the interim body clearly was not envisioned as part of the government which succeeded it, nor came close to functioning at the level of anything which preceded or succeeded it, and thus does not begin to rise to the status of the annual sessions of the United States in Congress Assembled which followed it.

During the 249-day hiatus, some of those who had served as delegates to the Second Continental Congress nominally continued in office so that the new nation would continue to have some official domestic and international presence until the United States in Congress Assembled was triggered into being that November. The unambiguous understanding was that the interim presidents would, whenever possible, defer important business to the forthcoming government and preside during the 249-day gap only to maintain a temporizing presence. In these last 249 days, the interim body was sparsely attended, became a bare cipher in United States history, and had three unwilling presidents, all of whom would cut short their service, including one who, not wanting to preside over a phantom body, actually refused to serve when elected.

The interim congress — if it could even be called a congress — found it difficult to find delegates to remain in Philadelphia or willing to preside over it. The interim body's first president was Samuel Huntington who continued in office from his Second Continental Congress presidency. During his 130 days presiding after the Articles' ratification, Huntington wrote letter after letter to state legislatures imploring them remit their then overdue subscriptions of financial support and to ask their delegates to return to the Congress so that it could again attain a quorum for business but the states were largely unwilling to deal with the interim body. On April 9, we find Huntington writing to Delaware delegate Thomas Rodney beseeching him to return to his seat in Congress so that the Congress may keep its quorum of nine states present. In the same letter, he notes the imminent departure from the Congress of Delaware's other delegate: "Chief Justice McKean sets out on this day on the circuit to be absent some time . . ".[147] The absent McKean would succeed Huntington as president of the interim body and need to be persuaded to cancel another absence which would have left the office of president of the interim body vacant.

A week after his letter to Rodney, Huntington pleads with Connecticut Governor Jonathon Trumbull to cause his state to pay its long overdue requisition to the Congress, saying that if states ignore Congress's acts, "otherwise the whole will be abortive," and that, "The Delegates in Congress, who are frequently retiring not to return again, can have no separate interest from their Constituents to prejudice their Minds in Favour of the Act requested . . .".[148] The following day Huntington writes to Massachusetts Governor John Hancock asking for Massachusetts' requisition. The same day, he writes to Maryland Governor Thomas Sim Lee and to the governors of New York, New Hampshire and Rhode Island noting the absence of their delegates or, in Maryland's case, the presence of only one. In fact, *all* of Samuel Huntington's lengthy official correspondence of April 20 deals imploringly with delegate absences and states' failures to fund the Congress. Huntington's successor, Thomas McKean, would continually struggle with the same apathy and temporizing as the states awaited the first election that November 5.

The three men who were named as the interim body's presiding officers during its brief eight-month existence all resigned with one of them outright refusing to serve.

The first of these, Samuel Huntington of Connecticut, stayed put in office from his presidency of the Second Continental Congress from before the signing of the Articles of Confederation, and was never elected as president of either the interim body or the United States in Congress Assembled. Huntington had been elected president of the Second Continental Congress on September 28, 1779, and served through the ratification of the Articles until July 9, 1781, the second longest serving president after John Hancock of either the First or Second Continental Congresses. As with all presidents of both Continental Congresses, Huntington was elected to an indefinite term with no statutory or customary expiration date, the condition which his presidency carried into its remainder after ratification of the Articles of Confederation.

The self-taught Samuel Huntington, never having had the benefit of a school or even a tutor, became a classic American success story, making himself into one of the greatest self-made men among the Founders and being acknowledged in his own era as one of its foremost legal minds. Huntington served in the Connecticut General Assembly, as a delegate to the Second Continental Congress for five terms, and to the United States in Congress Assembled during the 1783-1784 term. He later served as Chief Justice, Lieutenant Governor and Governor of Connecticut. Samuel Huntington is yet another under-recognized Revolutionary War patriot who sacrificed time, treasure and more to usher the United States into being.

On July 9, 1781, Huntington resigned his presidency of the interim body, for the record citing poor health but actually, as he had related to his colleagues, not wanting to continue presiding over a gutted assembly.

Upon Huntington's resignation, North Carolina's Samuel Johnston was elected the same day *in absentia* as the interim body's president but, when learning of his election the following day, refused to serve, reprising Huntington's grounds of not wanting to preside over a body with no mandate other than as interim vestige.

With Johnston's refusal to serve, Pennsylvania's Thomas McKean was then chosen but with the explicit understanding which he stated upon his election that he would stand down in September to resume his duties as Chief Justice of Pennsylvania's Supreme Court.

As a thirty-one-year-old county judge in 1765, Thomas McKean first made his mark by defying the Stamp Act, refusing to use the British-imposed stamps in the court's work. In his half century public career, it was Thomas McKean who proposed the one-vote-per-state practice used throughout the early period, helped draft the Articles of Confederation, drafted the constitution of Delaware, served as the second Governor of Delaware and then as Chief Justice of Pennsylvania. He was a Signer of the Declaration of Independence and the Articles of Confederation, and led the Pennsylvania Ratification Convention in urging adoption of the Constitution declaring it "the best the world has yet seen." In 1799 at age sixty-five, elected Governor of Pennsylvania, McKean's practice of appointing only fellow Republicans to office made him the father of the America political spoils system, tainting an otherwise glowing career. His three terms as Governor completed one of the longest public service careers of any Founding Father. McKean's likeness bears a striking resemblance to that of George Washington.

During his 118 days as figurehead president, McKean, too, had to be dissuaded from resigning. On October 23, McKean actually did resign offering his reason on the record that he, as Chief Justice of Pennsylvania courts, needed to get back to his state to preside: "Sir, I must beg you to remind Congress, that when they did me the honor of electing me president, and before I assumed the chair, I informed them, that, as chief justice of Pennsylvania, I should be under the necessity of attending the supreme court of the state, in the latter end of September, or the farthest, in October.   The court will be held today.   I must, therefore, request, that they will be pleased to proceed to the choice of another president."

Though Thomas McKean had been fair and clear in his terms which the interim body had accepted in electing him, his willingness to leave the interim body — and his nation — in the lurch, even for only thirteen days, is indicative that the interim body did not remotely approach being a government. During the seven-year existence of the government which was born that November, there were no resignations, attempted resignations or demurrals among the presidents, and the single incomplete presidential term was due to illness.

McKean's insisting on his state duties before his national responsibilities is as much indication as anything of how the few remaining members of the interim body viewed its placeholder status leading up to the inauguration of the first government. At this juncture, McKean also cited the futility of presiding over a body with stripped authority existing under a death sentence, the same complaint which had deterred Huntington and Johnston. The day after his resignation, McKean was persuaded by New Jersey Delegate Dr. John Witherspoon to continue serving "upon special request" for the next thirteen days until the first government was sworn in.   John Hanson's first official letter after his election as president, written on Saturday, November 10, to Thomas McKean, was a particularly gracious commendation thanking McKean for his service, acknowledging the undesirability of presiding through the demoted status of the interim body in its last days, and lauding McKean for his "exemplary patience."   This letter also marks the new government's first use in correspondence of its name, the United States in Congress Assembled.[149]

A few unvetted Internet sources make the mistake that Huntington and McKean (and sometimes Johnston) were United States in Congress Assembled presidents solely on the supposition of their having served in the last days of the Second Continental Congress after the ratification of the Ar-

ticles of Confederation. These sources then list John Hanson as the third (or fourth) president. The obvious error of
historical fact here is that when Huntington and McKean
served there was no government yet in existence, and that
Johnston did not serve at all.

John Hanson's Claims as First President

Thus, both the facts and opinions of the time are squarely
on the side of John Hanson as having been the first president of the original United States government. So is modern
expert opinion.

Edward Papenfuse, Maryland State Archivist, chief executive
officer of the Maryland State Archives, esteemed historian of
the Revolutionary War era, and writer on John Hanson, has
stated the case as well as any: "Those who argue against
Hanson's having the honor of being the first official president in congress assembled, ignore both the official record
and the context of the times. Until the battle of Yorktown [in
October 1781] there was uncertainty with regard to the very
existence of the nation itself, let alone the validity of the
authority of Congress in constitutional terms. Yorktown
brought legitimacy to the government in the eyes of the
world, and Hanson became the first duly elected president of
the legitimized United States in Congress Assembled, that in
turn, through its representatives in Paris, negotiated the
terms of peace. He deserves recognition for that 'first' and
that is why his statue is one of two representing Maryland in
the U.S. Capitol, and on the dais of the Maryland State Senate."[150]

All of John Hanson's biographers, each an assiduous reader
of the historical record on Hanson, recognize Hanson to
have been the nation's first president. In his 1932 John
Hanson biography, Seymour Smith wrote, "The first session
of Congress elected under the provisions of the Articles of
Confederation opened at Independence Hall in Philadelphia
on November 5, 1781, — the first Monday in November. . . .
The election of John Hanson of Maryland as President was
the first act of Congress of the United States, on its first day
of existence. Between the signing of the Articles and this
first Monday in November *no government was actually in existence*, though Congress continued to transact business
simply because there was a great deal of pressing business
to transact. During those few months there was a provisional president called Thomas McKean, the most prominent
jurist in the Pennsylvania courts, who was elected with the
definite understanding that he was to retire *with the forma-*

tion of the first government on November 5. The job of provisional President was at best a thankless one — it is recorded that Samuel Johnston was first offered it on July 9, and declined it in haste. It carried no reward with it except that of hard and honest work, and McKean who did his work admirably, had to be persuaded not to resign before the new government came into being."[151] (Emphasis added.)

In his 1939 Hanson biography, Jacob Nelson wrote, "The first election of a president, after the ratification of the Articles of Confederation, took place November 5, 1781, when John Hanson was chosen 'President of the United States in Congress Assembled'."[152]

Conclusive that the United States in Congress Assembled did not commence until John Hanson was elected are the many fundamental matters of state and of organizing a government which could have been transacted during the 249-day interim after the Articles of Confederation were ratified but which were intentionally postponed. Some of these were the ordering of the first census, authorization and launching of the nation's first central bank, authorization for the first United States Mint, establishment of the nation's first uniform system of coinage, authorization of the first foreign loan to the United States, the nation's first state dinner for foreign dignitaries, creation of a national Army and Navy, seating of the first Cabinet, the first correspondence to and from an American head of state, provision of a presidential mansion, and creation of the Great Seal of the United States to name only a few.

Perhaps the most definitive confirmation of John Hanson's being the first president, certainly the most official confirmation, is the long-held official position of the United States government itself that he was. In the January 31, 1903, joint session of the United States Senate and House of Representatives in which the Congress accepted the statue of John Hanson from the State of Maryland into National Statuary Hall, the Congressional Record reads that, "The confederation of the States was now complete, and on November 5, 1781, John Hanson was elected the first president of the Congress of the Confederation," and that, "He was the first 'President of the United States in Congress Assembled,' and his hand guided the fortunes of the new nation in the year which brought the final success of American arms, after a long period of vicissitude and changeful fortune."[153]

John Hanson was also abundantly recognized by his peers of the time and presidents of the second government as the first president of the United States. George Washington, who had reported to Hanson as Washington's Commander in Chief, referred to Hanson as the first president. Thomas Jefferson, realizing as Secretary of State that Washington at the beginning of his first term was not fully empowered to exercise the powers of the office of president without the Great Seal of the United States, introduced a resolution that, "President Washington accepts every condition, law, rule and authority, under the Great Seal and the first President of the United States, John Hanson." President Madison wrote praisingly of John Hanson as the first president. Abraham Lincoln would later say that Hanson should be honored equally with Washington as first presidents. On into the twentieth century, Calvin Coolidge would refer to Hanson as the nation's first president when he said on May 29, 1926, at the dedication of the John Erickson Memorial in West Potomac Park in Washington, "The title of President of the United States in Congress Assembled was held by John Hanson of Maryland in 1781, and he became the first president under the Articles of Confederation." In 1948, Harry Truman would refer to John Hanson as the first president.[154]

The federal government's affirmation of John Hanson as the first president continues. On November 5, 1981, the two-hundredth anniversary of John Hanson's inauguration, the federal government honored Hanson once more with the issuance of a postage stamp bearing his likeness. The first issue of the stamp occurred that day at a ceremony at the main United States Post Office in Frederick, Maryland, attended by federal and international dignitaries. For the occasion, the government had first-issue envelopes printed affixed with the stamp and, by an Act of Congress, with "John Hanson, First President under the Articles of Confederation, 1781-1782." For the same anniversary, the United States Capitol Historical Society had a medal struck with the inscription, "Honoring John Hanson, First President of Congress Under the Articles of Confederation, 1781-1782."

Not only the executive and legislative branches of the federal government but the United States Supreme Court as well has affirmed that John Hanson was the first president of government. In its landmark Marbury vs. Madison case of 1803, the decision of which hinged on the required use by presidents of the Great Seal of the United States in making appointments, the Supreme Court recognized John Hanson as the nation's first president. Explicit in this distinction is that, even though they may have had the title, those who had served as presidents of the three pre-government bodies before the introduction of the Great Seal of the United States had not presided over a government. The Supreme Court drew the line at John Hanson as the first president to preside over a government and first to use the seal.

Cementing John Hanson's claim as president of the original government is how the nation, all of the major players of his time, and posterity have viewed who was the first president of the *second* government after the interim between when the Constitution became ratified and when George Washington was inaugurated. This transition, too, had its odd placeholder inter-regnum as there was a 318-day gap between June 21, 1788, when the Constitution became ratified[155] and April 30, 1789, when Washington was inaugurated as president and the second government came into being. From June 21 until November 2, 1788, when his term expired, Cyrus Griffin, the last president of the United States in Congress Assembled, held the office and presided over the government of the United States. That he continued in office from the first government after the second government had been ratified but not yet installed matches exactly the situation in the previous interim between the Second Continental Congress and the United States in Congress Assembled: the new government had achieved ratification but had not yet come into operation with an election. The reason why one never hears the contention that somehow Cyrus Griffin was the first president under the Constitution is not just based on posterity or affection for the better known Washington, but factually that the second government had not yet begun operating through its first election when Griffin served. The same exact situation had existed eight years before during the interim presidencies of Samuel Huntington, Thomas McKean and, if he is to be counted at all, Samuel Johnston. (It is interesting to note, unlike during the first interim, that between November 3, 1788, and April 29, 1789, the nation had no president.)

Above all other proof, the main and indisputable historical circumstance undergirding the fact that John Hanson was the nation's first president remains that when Samuel Huntington and Thomas McKean served, no government was yet in existence. As Hanson biographer Seymour Smith has put it, "As first head of the American government John Hanson's position cannot be successfully disputed; sustaining proofs are too complete."[156]

The situation today isn't that John Hanson has less than a

solid historical claim on the nation's first presidency, but only that most historians have allowed themselves to forget that he does.

The Tangled Governmental Nomenclature of the 1780s

The seven annual sessions of the United States in Congress Assembled sometimes came to be referred to as congresses of the confederation, this tag coming from the United States in Congress Assembled being governed by the Articles of Confederation.   However, the Articles of Confederation, which established the new government and which, with abundant clarity, named it the United States in Congress Assembled, makes no mention of or any provision for even one "Congress of the Confederation" but this unofficial pseudonym stuck and passed into common usage early on. Even the National Archives today sometimes uses the term in describing the seven sessions of the United States in Congress Assembled. Because the term "congresses of the confederation" grew up as informal pseudonym, it only adds to the surfeit of confusion in modern nomenclature to apply the term to the interim body as well, a usage which, though infrequent, one does see.

From this confusion, one occasionally sees an incorrect delineation of these sessions to erroneously include the 249-day interim body of 1781 and its two or three presidents. In the incorrect version, the 249-day interim body is counted as the first of the congresses, the second ostensibly as the actual first term of the United States in Congress Assembled from November 1781 until November 1782, the third from then until November 1783, and so on. Just as the presidents of the interim body were not of the United States in Congress Assembled, neither was the sole vestigial session of the interim body which ceased to exist when the United States in Congress Assembled sprang into existence on November 5, 1781.

A further distinction of nomenclature to keep in mind regarding the original government is that it and its nation had different names, the United States in Congress Assembled and the United States of America, respectively. The second government under the Constitution did away with this unnecessary and meddlesome distinction, naming both the United States of America.

Yorktown and Victory

During 1781 the nation was still hard at war and, though the timing would be fortuitous, the signers of the Articles of

Confederation that March could not know that the decisive battle of the war would occur that October just days before the new government which they had created would come to life. John Hanson and some others did foresee the Battle of Yorktown looming, if not that it would be the beginning of the end of hostilities. The February 28, 1781, letter which Philip Thomas received from the man whose signature the next day would complete the ratification of the Articles of Confederation recounts the recent favorable military movements of the American, British and French armies and navies. As Hanson wrote, "Our affairs to the south brighten fast," and cautions Thomas that his letter's comments on Yorktown, Cornwallis, Lafayette, General Greene and others are military secrets.

Learning that Cornwallis had Britain's depleted southern army camped at Yorktown, Virginia, George Washington and his French ally, the Count de Rochambeau marched to Yorktown and trapped Cornwallis and his forces who were awaiting reinforcements by sea which did not arrive in time. Some modern Revolutionary War historians are of the opinion that it was not so much Washington, who through much of the war had had difficulty formulating strategy and tactics, as the more experienced Rochambeau who laid and executed the plan which attained victory at Yorktown. The French fleet commanded by Admiral Comte de Grasse blocked aid from reaching Cornwallis by sea while Washington's Continental Army and Rochambeau's French contingent shelled the British for weeks on end. There is the episode of the brave Thomas Nelson, a signer of the Declaration of Independence, urging Washington to fire on his own home, Nelson House, where Cornwallis had set up his Yorktown headquarters.

Cornwallis surrendered on October 19, 1781, precisely six and a half years since the war's first shot was fired at Lexington, halting Britain's southern campaign and effectively marking the end of major fighting in the Revolutionary War. While it was left to President Hanson in coming months to order peace negotiations and the mopping up remnant British units still fighting in some states, the Battle of Yorktown, the last significant fight of the Revolutionary War, is generally marked as the end of British effort in prosecuting the war and as the hour of victory for the United States. Soon after the news of defeat reached London, the British government fell from power and was succeeded by one amenable to peace negotiations.

It was Maryland Lieutenant Colonel Tench Tilghman who delivered the news to the interim congress in Philadelphia. Tilghman went on horseback from Yorktown to Annapolis, boated across the Chesapeake to Rock Hall, and completed his trip by horse relay to Philadelphia, arriving after midnight on October 24. He awakened interim president Thomas McKean with the news of Cornwallis's capture and surrender, and had a night watchman cry out the stunning news around Philadelphia. The following day when the Congress learned of the great victory, it adjourned for a service of thanksgiving at the city's Dutch Lutheran Church.

The timing of this decisive victory, just seventeen days before the nation's first government came into being, was sublimely providential and must have lifted an enormous load from President Hanson and the new government as they took office, giving them much more flexibility in launching the new nation, getting its first government up and running, and focusing on the nation's internal needs.

Nation Born: The United States in Congress Assembled

As prescribed in the Articles of Confederation, the original government of the United States of America took office on the first Monday of November 1781 — November 5 of that year. The new government's first act was its election of John Hanson as its president. "Hanson, in fact, did serve the first full term as President of Congress under the Articles of Confederation and is the only Marylander ever to serve in the highest office of the United States."[157] "He was recognized at home and abroad as the President of the United States of America, now officially a new member in the family of nations."[158] Charles Thomson, now serving as Secretary of the United States in Congress Assembled, as he had for the First and Second Continental Congresses and the interim body, certified President Hanson's election by the recorded declaration distributed to the state legislatures and others, and shown here.

Just as John Hanson is a forgotten figure who put forth much in the founding of the nation, so is Pennsylvania's undersung Charles Thomson, the Irish orphan immigrant patriot who had staked all he had for independence and served continuously as Secretary of both Continental Congresses, the phantom body, the United States in Congress Assembled and for a few months in the Washington administration, a period of over fifteen years in this capacity. On the original copy of the Declaration of Independence sent for printing, now lost, there were only two official signatures,

John Hancock's as president of the Second Continental Congress, and Charles Thomson's as Secretary. It was Thomson during the Hanson administration who designed the Great Seal of the United States still used today. After nineteen years in preparation, Thomson in 1808 published the first English translation from the Greek of the oldest version of the Old Testament of the Bible, and later that year published his translation of the New Testament. Charles Thomson died at the age of ninety-four in 1824.

At the launching of the first government, the United States had had two differently named national bodies and an odd interim body within a period of 249 days in 1781. A nation with hardly a print press at the time must have simply lost track of these rapid changes during a very exciting transition in the midst of war. To recapitulate, the Second Continental Congress exercised its authorities until March 1 of 1781, the nearly phantom interim nongovernmental body existed from the following day until November 4, and the United States in Congress Assembled came into being on November 5. It is important to note that these three bodies succeeded one another serially and that no two of them ever existed at the same time.

Here we encounter yet another instance of confusion as to names of the nation's governing and consultative bodies, as one occasionally sees the seven annual congresses of the United States in Congress Assembled from 1781 to 1789 referred to as "the Continental Congresses," a misnomer to be sure as the new body deliberately took on a name distinct from those of its predecessors, the First and Second Continental Congresses, which had passed out of existence.

What definitively reveals the differences in the roles and powers of the Second Continental Congress, the interim body, and the United States in Congress Assembled, and the temporal transitions from one to another of these bodies, are the Articles of Confederation themselves which established the United States in Congress Assembled by name and *do not mention the Second Continental Congress, Continental Congresses in the plural, the interim body or a Congress of the Confederation at all.* The Articles of Confederation specified only a United States in Congress Assembled, comprised the nation's first governmental charter and were the nation's first and sole legitimizing governing imprimatur until replaced by the Constitution in 1789.

The United States in Congress Assembled lasted for seven years, a record for any of the national bodies up to that time. It deliberately replaced itself by convening the Constitutional Convention to improve upon national governance, adopted the Constitution of the United States, and in 1788 effected the transition to the nation's second form of government under the Constitution.

Which Was the Nation's First Government?

A national government is a group of persons holding the political executive offices responsible for direction and supervision of public affairs of a nation.[159]   Clearly the level of authorization over direction and supervision of public affairs conferred by the states on the United States in Congress Assembled was vastly greater than that which the states had ever entrusted to the Second Continental Congress, much less to the interim body. In the comparison below of the authorities possessed by the three bodies, one sees demonstrated that while the United States in Congress Assembled was explicitly set up as a government, weak though it was, the Second Continental Congress and the interim body never had governing authority nor was either ever intended to function as more than a consultative body among thirteen independent nation-states.

Historians of the Revolutionary War period are usually, but not universally, explicit in their recognition of the United States in Congress Assembled as the nation's original government and its authorizing document, the Articles of Confederation, as the first United States Constitution. Historian Frank Garver demarcates the transition well. Speaking of the Second Continental Congress, Garver writes, "Its chief weakness lay in its revolutionary character, in its lack of any constitutional basis, of any legal sanction. To remedy this defect the Second Continental Congress adopted the Articles of Confederation in 1777 and referred them to the states for ratification. After the acceptance of the Articles by the last state, and after all of the necessary steps to put them into operation had been taken, they became the first written constitution of the United States, sometime in I781." [160]

Second Congress and Interim Body Not Created to Govern

While the Second Continental Congress and the interim body had to gain the consent of the colonies and then the states to act on nearly all measures, the United States in Congress Assembled was explicitly granted far broader authority unto itself by all thirteen states when they ratified the Articles of Confederation. The United States in Congress Assembled was the first body in the nation's history to rise to this level. In short, neither the Second Continental Congress nor the interim body could govern for lack of authority to do so, but the United States in Congress Assembled did govern because it had been explicitly granted governing authority in an agreement binding on all of the states.

The loosely gathered nature of the Second Continental Congress is well characterized by Matthew Andrews, often regarded as the definitive writer on the history of Maryland. "[T]he very term 'congress' was not at that time a word applied to a legislative body; the former colonies were careful not to call this continental assemblage a 'parliament'; they did not want a 'parliament' which signified control; they wanted a league of commonwealths, with a 'congress' acting as a clearinghouse, an advisory body, or at best, an agent or medium, with certain very limited specified powers any of which could be curtailed or withdrawn at the will of any one of the allied powers. The history of Maryland, as an 'associated' commonwealth' shows more clearly, perhaps, than that of any other state the nature of the Confederation, and how the people regard[ed] the relation between the state governments and the central organization."[161]

United States in Congress Assembled Comes After Independence

The timing of the two bodies' creation also shows that the first was not a national government while the later body was. The Second Continental Congress was called for by the fifty-two-day-long First Continental Congress which in 1774 sought deeper consultation among the then colonies two years before independence was declared. When created in 1775, the Second Continental Congress was neither envisioned as a government nor ever given powers by the colonies and then the states to act as such, though of necessity and on a limited basis it had to take on limited prerogatives and authority of a national government in the prosecution of the Revolutionary War.

In contrast, the United States in Congress Assembled was created only *after* the Declaration of Independence had called for the creation of a nation and a central government became necessary. The Second Continental Congress, immediately after independence had been declared, authorized the Articles of Confederation explicitly for the purpose of creating a government.

Second Continental Congress Dissolves Itself

If the Second Continental Congress had seen itself as sufficient as a government for the new nation and authorized by the states as the central government, it would have continued itself, but it didn't; it dissolved itself instead in order to create a new, stronger body, a government with powers and authorities that the Second Continental Congress never had. Likewise, the interim body, essentially the epilogue of the Second Continental Congress, never had any intention of continuing itself.

The View of the Public

And finally, the national press at the time reported the creation of the United States in Congress Assembled explicitly as the birth of the nation's first government.   For example, shortly after the adoption of the Articles by the states, *The Maryland Gazette* wrote, "Thus will the *first of March, 1781*, be a day memorable in the annals of America, for the final ratification of the Confederation and Perpetual Union of the Thirteen States of America — a union, begun by necessity, cemented by oppression, and now finally consolidated into a confederacy of these new and rising states . . .."[162] (Emphasis in the original)

From the timing and reasons for their respective creation, that two dissolved themselves to create the third, and public regard of the United States in Congress Assembled as the first government, we may conclude without ambiguity, as the people then and especially authors since have, that the United States in Congress Assembled was the first of two forms of government that the United States has had, the second being our current form of Constitutional government which did not come into being until 1789.

Relative Powers of the Second Continental Congress and the United States in Congress Assembled

Of the five successive forms of organization the United States had — the First Continental Congress, the Second, the briefly convened interim body, the United States in Congress Assembled or the present Constitutional government — clearly for the reasons following it was not the first, third or fifth of these which was the first government.

The First Continental Congress	It had few powers, was clearly only a consultative body, was not regarded as anything close to a government in its time or since, lasted only fifty-two days and dissolved itself.
The interim body	It had the feeblest powers of any of the five bodies, was never mentioned much less le-

gitimized as a government in the Articles of Confederation or anywhere else, was not regarded as anything but a temporizing body in its time or since, lasted only 249 days, and dissolved itself.

Government under the Constitution	National governance after winning nationhood in 1781 clearly took place throughout the 1780s before government under the Constitution began in 1789.

Ruling out these three bodies, the question then is, was the Second Continental Congress or was the United States in Congress Assembled the first government? Arguments can be made for both, or that neither was. At this point, let us put to rest the contention that the Second Continental Congress was a government and that the less often heard argument that the United States in Congress Assembled wasn't.

As in the following comparisons, while the Second Continental Congress of necessity in some ways functioned as a supreme national body in the eyes of the world, the United States in Congress Assembled was granted far broader powers, both domestically and in foreign affairs, and was in the minds of national leaders, the states, the American people and foreign powers of the era the first body established for the express purpose of full central governance. Again, the key indication that the United States in Congress Assembled was the nation's first government is that the Second Continental Congress dissolved itself to create the United States in Congress Assembled. If the Second Continental Congress had regarded itself as a government, it would not have been necessary for it to have created another body.

Following is a comparison of the powers and roles of the two bodies. A key advance of the United States in Congress Assembled was the role of the nation's top official, the President of the United States.

Strength of Governing Authority	Second Continental Congress	United States In Congress Assembled
Created in the era of:	British colonies	United States of America
Regarded itself as national government	No	Yes, explicitly
Role in independence	Declared and won it	Enforced and lived it
Authorizing document	First Congress resolution	Articles of Confederation

Authorized in writing to govern nation	No	Yes
States consent to cede essential powers	Very few	Substantially more

Presidential Powers and Perquisites

President authorized as Head of State	No	Yes, explicitly
President seen abroad as Head of State	Very limited	Yes, explicitly
President can issue executive orders	No	Yes (e.g., Thanksgiving)
Presidential residence provided	No	Yes
Presidential household staff provided	No	Yes
Presidential portraits provided	No	Yes
President hosts state dinners	No	Yes and did

Federal Government Organization

Had federal government departments	Ad hoc	Formally chartered
Had a President's Cabinet	No	Yes
Had national postal service	Ad hoc	Formally chartered
Had a national census	No	Yes
Had a national seal	No	Yes

Federal Government Powers

Fixed method of presidential succession	No, ad hoc	Yes, formally prescribed
Fixed presidential and congressional terms	No	Yes
Fixed annual sessions	No	Yes
Had authority to legislate for nation	No	Yes and did
Had authority to adjudicate for nation	No	Yes and did
Final word on disputes between states	No	Yes and exercised it
Regulated post offices	Advisory only	Yes
Regulated weights and measures	No	Yes

Authority Over National Defense

Relationship with Army	Autonomous army	Part of government
National Navy	Autonomous navy	Part of government
Standardized military uniforms	No	Yes

Federal Finance

National government funding	Much by individuals	By states (weakly)
Had a central bank	No	Yes and created it
Regulated the value of coinage	No	Sole authority to issue[163]
Federal construction projects	No	Yes

Foreign Relations

Status abroad	Consultations	Formally recognized
Had national Consular Service	No	Yes
Exchanges of ambassadors	A few emissaries only	Yes
Exclusive right to make foreign treaties	No but states did	Yes
States can have direct foreign relations	Yes	Prohibited
States can declare war	Yes	Prohibited

National Life and Customs

Press views as central government	No	Yes
Recognized a First Lady	No	Yes though not officially
Thanksgiving Day	Observed once	Fixed by Hanson decree
Fourth of July celebrations	Informal	Fixed by Hanson decree

Images and Maps

The John Hanson National
Memorial in Frederick

Hanson's statue in the
United States Capitol

John Hanson in middle age
by John Hesselius

Jane Contee Hanson
by John Hesselius

Dr. Philip Thomas,
son in law of President Hanson

Alexander Contee Hanson, Sr.
Chancellor of Maryland

United States Senator
Alexander Contee Hanson, Jr.

Elizabeth Arianna Adolphus
Hanson Floweree

Mulberry Grove where the
Hansons lived until 1769

The Frederick homes of the
Hansons and Thomases, 1981

The York, Pennsylvania, courthouse where the Articles of
Confederation were signed

The presidential mansion
provided to John and Jane
Hanson in Philadelphia

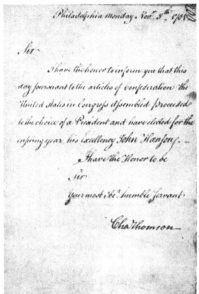

The announcement of John Hanson's election as President

The 200th anniversary medal of Hanson's election as president

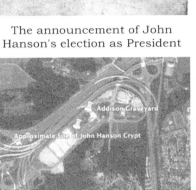

Site of the crypt where John Hanson was interred

The mass grave in Frederick, where Jane Hanson is buried

Map of the western lands chartered to seven of the colonies by the
British Crown (Transcontinental swaths of Connecticut, Georgia
and Virginia not shown)

THIRTY HARD DOLLARS REWARD.
Frederick town, July 2, 1781.

RAN away from the subscriber, living in Fre-
derick-town Maryland, on the first instant,
a negro man named NED BARNES, a likely
sensible fellow, a shoemaker, about 35 years of
age, about 5 feet 6 or 8 inches high; he carried
with him a good deal of valuable cloathing, among
which are a new light blue cloth coat and waistcoat,
a pair of leather breeches, a pair of boots, a pair of
neat shoes with silver buckles; it is probable he
may have a pass and intends to join the British
troops; it is suspected he went off on a likely roan
horse. The above reward will be paid to any person bringing home or securing him in any gaol;
it is requested he may be searched and the money
about him secured.   3 W
                     JOHN HANSON.

John Hanson's reward poster for Ned Barnes

Part V

The Hanson Administration

Best of the Best: America's Icons Elect John Hanson

By October 1781, the United States had evolved through each step but one to fully establish itself as a nation. Five years previously, the thirteen colonies had declared their independence, more formally associated, and named themselves collectively as the United States. In 1777 they had drafted the Articles of Confederation which called for a new government and prescribed how it would operate. Four years later, the success of the Hanson Plan had assured unified nationhood by resolving the western lands impasse. Earlier in 1781, the thirteen states had ratified the Articles of Confederation authorizing the first government. In October 1781, by its final major victory on the battlefield, the United States had virtually assured its safety and thus its independence. All that remained to attain full nationhood was the final step: implementation of the Articles of Confederation by finally launching the nation's first government. On November 5, 1781 — the first Monday of November as prescribed in the Articles — the new government sprang into being and the now full-fledged nation of the United States of America finally took her place among the family of nations on the world stage.

As its first action that day, the new government elected John Hanson as the nation's first president. The minutes of the meeting do not indicate that his election was unanimous though long oral tradition holds that it was, which is entirely plausible given that there were no other candidates. With his election, John Hanson became the first person in the nation's history formally designated as head of state of the United States and recognized at home and abroad as such. His prescribed title was President of the United States in Congress Assembled, the same title to be worn by his eight successors.[164]

With independence now won and the war all but concluded on the battlefield if not yet by treaty, there were innumerable questions of governance still to be settled, disparate state outlooks to harmonize, the mending from war of the new nation, and much, much more to do. The Hanson administration had enormous challenges laid before it which it must meet very thoughtfully to ensure a successful launch for this new venture in democracy and indeed the continuation of the still fragile association among the thirteen independent-minded states. When the Hanson administration began work, the new nation was as much as ever still grand experiment. While the eight other presidents of the United

States in Congress Assembled and all forty-four under the Constitution through 2012 inherited a functioning government upon taking office, the nation's first president and his colleagues inherited but a blank slate and had to create, without precedent, the entire structure, trappings and performance of a national government anew.

Who should lead the nation at this most critical juncture? To whom should the delegates to the new United States in Congress Assembled look as the one among them least likely to fail in successfully delivering the new government unto the nation and world?   What criteria should guide their choice?

The delegates had a dazzling array, a luxurious choice of brilliant Founding Fathers from among whom to choose their first president, some of the most competent Americans the country has ever produced: the heroic Washington himself who had just delivered military victory[165], the intellectually dazzling Jefferson who had penned a nation-founding canon such as the world had never seen, John Hancock who had served as president of the Second Continental Congress longer than any other and would be elected as a later president of the new government, the brilliant and rising John Adams of Massachusetts, Peyton Randolph who had served as president of both the First and Second Continental Congresses, Samuel Huntington who had served as president of both the Second Continental Congress and the interim body, Thomas McKean who was the outgoing and last president of the interim body, and Benjamin Franklin, counselor to them all, to name but a few.

In the eight months after the ratification of the Articles of Confederation and leading up to the inauguration of the first government, critical assessments and intense discussion among the delegates on the strengths and weaknesses of all of these possible candidates and of others took place as the delegates prepared to make the pivotal choice of their and their nation's first president. On the morning of November 5, 1781, the delegates to the United States in Congress Assembled including the American icons just mentioned — the best the new nation had to offer — understood that they were required at that golden hour to choose the very best among them to lead the first government of the United States. In that all-important convening of the new nation's best in Independence Hall that morning, when the last star finally aligned for the completion of national birth, all looked to Maryland's John Hanson, the best of the best in the eyes of some of the most astute Americans the nation has ever produced.

As history has amply shown, the nation's choices of president, whether by elites in the earlier decades of the republic or by something a step closer to popular election now, have not always been so careful, with weak and even harmful figures such as Tyler, Buchanan, Hayes, Harding, Nixon and Bush the younger being sent to the nation's highest office. In contrast and ever so fortunately, fate has repeatedly favored the nation with her best presidents at her most perilous junctures: Washington at the founding of the second government, Lincoln when the nation was cleaved apart, and the second Roosevelt when the nation's economy and very wellbeing crumpled. Looking back at the condition of the fledgling nation of 1781, it is not difficult to make the case that the first time fate delivered the nation an especially able president just when most needed was at the moment when the United States was a newborn, launching its original government and facing the imperative of electing a first president who could not afford to miss.

Just what was it that prompted the delegates to the new government to examine the prodigious array of individual talent among them and look to John Hanson as their first president over others many of whom since have entered the pantheon of American greats? Why did every one of the icons among the delegates including Franklin, Adams, Jefferson and Hancock regard Hanson as the best among them, the very best of the best? [166]

The conclusion which one comes to today, as the delegates must have then, is that John Hanson was tapped for two reasons: his nation-saving triumphs making both the Declaration of Independence and the Articles of Confederation unanimous and thus the nation whole, and the personal traits which he had brought to bear in delivering these two indispensable blessings to his country.

What the Second Continental Congress delegates saw in Hanson before his arrival as a Maryland delegate to the Congress in June of 1780 was an already considerable accumulation of key work on independence and prosecuting the war. Before joining the Second Continental Congress, John Hanson had been elected in his state to every office he had ever sought, become the first in the Maryland Committee of Correspondence to pledge to use force to resist the British, raised militias, organized the manufacture of war materiel, become one of the nation's key war financiers, saved the day in getting Maryland to subscribe to the Declaration of Independence, gotten his state to propose the Hanson Plan for solving the impasse over the western lands, and already sacrificed one son and much of his family wealth to the cause of independence. Even before his arrival as delegate to the Second Continental Congress, John Hanson had made his mark in the minds of many other delegates and on the fledgling nation.

After his arrival at the Congress, Hanson's effect on guiding the new nation became visible first-hand to the Congress's delegates, especially Hanson's solving of the nation-breaking conundrum over the western lands. It would be difficult to overestimate the negative consequences if this impasse had not been settled. Had John Hanson not been able to resolve the western lands impasse by getting the seven states with large Midwest tracts to cede those lands to the new government for disposal into additional states, the outcome very likely would have been multiple independent nations which would have been united only loosely at best or not at all, and which would have been forced to go their own ways after establishing individual nationhood. There might have been lesser unions among, for example, the New England states or the Carolinas which would have resulted in an American map today more resembling the fragmented and contentious territory of the former Yugoslavia. These incipient American nations would have shared a common heritage and history up to this point but their separate establishment of nationhood would have meant no United States. If they remained separate, they might well have been drawn into disputes among themselves that could be resolved only by arms, fostering enmity among them. As all of the Second Continental Congress delegates had seen first hand when they peered into this abyss, united nationhood hung in the balance as Hanson, where no other had succeeded over four years, arrived at the Second Continental Congress and within eight months bridged the gap between states with and without western lands.

John Hanson was able to resolve this impasse, put aside the single most difficult challenge facing the nation, and rise in the estimation of his fellow delegates. By September of 1780, three months after his arrival at the Congress, a committee of the Congress endorsed the Hanson Plan as the Congress's delegates chose to call it. The following month the Congress formally adopted the plan and put it forth to the thirteen states for their consideration. The Congress's delegates had witnessed and been highly grateful for the solution to the western lands impasse which John Hanson had been able to render when others couldn't. And as the delegates knew, only five months before his election as president, John Hanson had lost not only another son in the war but also his eldest daughter in a two-week span.

In addition to his war record and his two pivotal nation-saving deeds, the delegates saw something else in John Hanson: the particular way in which he had gone about marshalling the support of his colleagues and using his unmatched persuasive ability in convincing states with sharply disparate interests to subordinate themselves for the sake of national unity. John Hanson's biographers and family uniformly describe him as a modest man who conveyed an unerring sense of devotion to the new nation and its unity. These descriptions all speak of Hanson's diplomacy, natural ability in working constructively with others, organizational brilliance, and, most of all, his leadership acumen. Two centuries following, United States Senator Charles Mc. Mathias, himself a prominent Frederick political product, would say of Hanson, "John Hanson, confronted with problems common to his day and ours, handled those problems in a manner uncommon to his day and ours. Such is the stuff of leadership. Events pass; people pass. Leadership endures."[167]

Hanson biographer Jacob Nelson gathers the passed-down persona of John Hanson to reveal him as " . . . a man of unusual traits with a character that was above reproach. He was loved and revered by the great majority of people who knew him or had learned of his accomplishments. He can be described as a kindly man who entertained no ill will toward anyone . . . endowed with an air of simplicity, and a presence that was both captivating and uplifting. He was a leader among men and was fearless in fighting for their rights. He was by nature solemn, deliberate and reflecting, but he would also at times laugh heartily and would enjoy moments of good entertainment."[168]

On the day in 1903 when the Congress of the United States accepted the statue of John Hanson into National Statuary Hall, Maryland Representative Charles Schirm portrayed John Hanson as, " . . . one of those modest, unassuming great men who seek no glory for themselves, but find their highest reward in the good that accrues from their efforts to the great body of people. He was essentially a thinker, a contriver, an unraveler of knotty points, a man to whom the people looked when other leaders said, 'What shall we do now?'. In those days, when there was a great diversity of opinion among men of equal ability and patriotism, John Hanson proved himself a master of bringing to the front the central idea and enlisting the support of all men who in their adherence to the chief thought lost sight of minor differences."[169]

The delegates must have perceived that morning that, aside from his signal accomplishments, John Hanson's devotion, constructive instincts and temperament were together a most timely providence to the new government and nation. As much as for any of his qualities, his fellow delegates saw him as Hanson the Unifier.

Finally, at the age of sixty-six, older than nearly all of his fellow representatives in Congress, John Hanson was already an elder statesman of the new nation. Hanson was the third oldest person ever to serve in the nation's highest office, younger only than his distant relative William Henry Harrison who was sixty-eight when inaugurated, dying only a month afterward, and Ronald Reagan who was sixty-nine upon taking office. To put into perspective Hanson's seniority on becoming president, we observe that, while Reagan was still about five years younger than the male life expectancy of his era when taking office, Hanson was thirty to thirty-five years beyond his.

There is the implicit suggestion from Hanson's letters to his son-in-law Philip Thomas that the first delegates to the United States in Congress Assembled apparently had decided on John Hanson at least several weeks before his election on November 5 and perhaps as early as the previous spring when he was the last signer of the Articles of Confederation. In those days, letters often served as their own envelope by folding the written side inward, applying a wax seal to the resulting outside seam and addressing the back of the sheet which had in effect become the face of the envelope. On the obverse of John Hanson's letter of October 16, 1781, twenty days before his election, there appears for the first time among his letters the return address "His Excellency J. Hanson" and the same notation on his letter of October 23. (The sitting president of the interim body, Thomas McKean, continued to be referred to by the lesser title "the honorable" as had all of his predecessors.) These notations are clearly in a different hand than Hanson's. Unlike any of his previous letters to Philip Thomas, these two are franked with the notation "Free. John Hanson." Until this time, Hanson had paid his own postage as presumably did the other delegates to the Congress. (In the letter of October 23, Hanson elatedly tells Philip Thomas of his learning that week of Cornwallis's surrender at Yorktown.)

At least by the month previous to his election, Second Continental Congress staff, perhaps its Secretary Charles Thomson, had begun recognizing Hanson with a title customarily reserved for heads of state, and Hanson had been extended free postal franking privileges reserved for highest elected officials.   These two changes would have come about only from a decision already made and awaiting the election on the first Monday of the following month. At the time of these letters, Thomas McKean was serving as the titular head of the interim body but for some time Hanson was apparently already being regarded as President in Waiting.

And so, on November 5, 1781, respecting Hanson's now long record in winning the war, his critically important contribution to the unanimity of independence even before his election to the Second Continental Congress, in great relief over his having solved the western lands impasse with the Hanson Plan after his joining the Congress, and in admiration of his singularly effective leadership acumen, the delegates of the United States in Congress Assembled, including some of the greatest Americans who ever lived, unanimously elected their colleague John Hanson as the nation's first president, the highest position in the land. With his election, nationhood was thus fulfilled and begun.

Charles Thomson, appointed that day as Secretary of the Congress, sent the following circular announcement to the thirteen state legislatures, General Washington and foreign dignitaries.

"Sir

I have the honor to inform you that this day pursuant to the Articles of Confederation the United States in Congress Assembled preceded to the choice of a President and have elected for the coming year his Excellency John Hanson.

I have the honor to be

Sir

Your most &c. humble servant

Charles Thomson"[170]

An image of the original announcement is provided here.

To appreciate that the interim body did not regard its presidents as presiding over a government, one only needs to contrast with the notice of John Hanson's election the official minutes of Samuel Johnston's and Thomas McKean's elections by the interim body on July 9 and 10, 1781. For Johnston we see only, "According to the order of the day the house proceeded to the election of a President and the ballots being taken the Honorable Samuel Johnston was elected." For McKean, the minutes show, "Mr. Johnston having declined to accept the office of president and offered such reasons as were satisfactory, the house proceeded to a farther election and the ballots being taken the Honorable Thomas McKean was elected."[171] While announcement of Hanson's election was sent out widely by circular letter on the day of his election, there is no record of such notice being disseminated for Johnston's or McKean's elections.

How much John Hanson was revered by his colleagues is seen from their action when Hanson took ill midway through his presidency. In March of 1782, President Hanson, just turning sixty-seven and occupying the most difficult job in the land, suffered an incapacitating illness, probably influenza as later described, and was unable to work for a week or more. There was no provision in the Articles of Confederation for the election of any other officer of the United States or for the assumption of the duties of the president, and therefore there was no one who held any statutory authority to serve in a president's place in the event of illness or for any other reason. Charles Thomson, the only other member of Congress with an officer's title, was apparently not considered to serve in place of the president.

In deciding how to handle the complicated precedent of a president's incapacitation, Congress rejected suggestions to name a temporary president or to elect a vice president. The Congress passed a motion, "That whenever the President shall be prevented by sickness or otherwise, from attending the house, one of the members present shall be chosen by ballot to act as chairman for the purpose of keeping order only, but that all official papers shall nevertheless be signed and authenticated by the President as heretofore." The delegates then chose Hanson's fellow Maryland delegate and friend Daniel Carroll to chair the Congress's meetings with the title of chairman until Hanson's return, and to call upon the president at the executive mansion to sign official papers. Upon President Hanson's resumption of duties, the office of chairman was wisely kept throughout the life of the United States in Congress Assembled and was the antecedent of the office of Vice President of the United States when the Constitutional Convention fashioned the structure of the second government.

Though it would have been known to Frederick County voters that John Hanson would stand for election as the nation's president on November 5, on the same day they re-elected him to the House of Delegates of the Maryland General Assembly, a re-election which he had not sought. Suspecting as much, the president on the day following his dual elections wrote to the Speaker of the Maryland House of Delegates resigning his seat there, and to Philip Thomas urging him to persuade Thomas Johnson, Hanson's ally and the former first governor of Maryland, to run for Hanson's vacated House of Delegates seat, and for Thomas to campaign for Johnson. In the same state election, the new president's older brother Samuel had been elected to the House of Delegates from Charles County.

Who Was the Nation's First President?

John Hanson's election as president of the United States in Congress Assembled leads us to the old and controversial question of who then was the nation's first president, John Hanson or George Washington. One may be amused by this question. In fact, they both were first presidents of different governments but not of a different nation: the simple chronology is that in 1781 Hanson became the first president under the nation's original government, the United States in Congress Assembled, and in 1789 Washington became the first president under the second and present government under the Constitution.

It is worth noting that, while the United States has had two governments, these served only one continuous nation-state, the United States of America which has existed through both governments since November 5, 1781. A nation-state is a political entity not answerable to any superior political entity, as there is none, and that has full power to determine its form of government. If a nation-state changes its form of government from time to time as it sees fit, it does not cease to be the same state. The five French Republics are an example: in France's case, the same continuous state has existed with four major overhauls in its form of government since the French Revolution of 1789. France's Fifth Republic came into being in 1958.

When the United States in Congress Assembled decided to replace itself with a new stronger government through the

Constitutional Convention in 1787, it was the government but not the nation-state which was replaced. The magnitude of the change of government from the United States in Congress Assembled to the government of the Constitution did not bring about a change of state. Indeed, many of the same men who had fought and won the Revolutionary War and then forged a government with the Articles of Confederation were present at the Constitutional Convention, and, in fact, the same man, John Dickinson, was charged with heading committees to draft both documents. With the exception of John Hanson, four years in his grave by 1787, the key figures as the nation transitioned from its first government to its second remained much the same. The nation-state — the United States of America — survived the change in government, the clear intent of the Constitutional Convention and of the Constitution which it wrought. The Constitution famously begins with the words, "We the people of the United States of America . . . ." It thus assumes the continued existence of the nation consummated in 1781, and the power of its citizens to adopt a new and improved constitution to "form a more perfect Union." The people did not say they were dissolving their old union or that a new one would replace it. Rather, their elected delegates intended to improve the mechanisms of governance, not form a new nation.

From July 4, 1776, until November 5, 1781, the thirteen former colonies were free and independent states, as they had demanded in the Declaration of Independence and fought a war to achieve, but the United States, by design, did not yet fully qualify as a nation. By ratifying the Articles of Confederation in 1781, these sovereign states ceded a portion of their sovereignty to a newly created entity, the nation of the United States of America. The constitution for this new nation, the fundamental law governing its powers and the manner of their exercise, was the Articles of Confederation.

As its presidents and delegates would soon enough learn, the government constituted by the Articles proved too weak to cope with the exigencies faced by the new nation. A full history of the Constitution is beyond the scope of this book, but we will examine later here the need to provide the United States government with certain powers, absent in the Articles of Confederation, which it needed to function effectively.

While both governments had to have had their first president and did, the nation, of which there has been only one, could have had just one first president, he who first served, President John Hanson. Submitting that President Hanson's colleague George Washington, long enshrined as Father of His Country, was not the nation's first president is not well received in some quarters. Nevertheless, John Hanson and eight others were in fact elected to the nation's highest office before Washington. George Washington was indeed the first president of the second, stronger, lasting government but not of the country.

Some have argued that the Presidents under the Articles of Confederation were not the nation's chief executive officers in the same sense as those who have held that office under the Constitution. One argument used to this effect is that the earlier presidents were selected by their peers in Congress rather than by the states. Another argument put forth is that, though by specific act of Congress they held the highest office in the land and outranked all other officials including the Commander of the Army, the presidents of the first government had no explicit authority to command the armed forces. With the approval of Congress, the earlier presidents did have authority to appoint the cabinet and other subordinate officers of government and to name judges as modern Presidents do. Their one-year terms of office, with re-election then forbidden for a period of three years, gave them little time to accumulate individual power or make their marks on history. But even a cursory look at their powers and perquisites as earlier delineated here shows that the presidents of the United States in Congress Assembled were unambiguously the nation's chief executive officers. As further indication, when President John Hanson was incapacitated by illness for a period of weeks in the spring of 1782, Congress named a "chairman" to preside in the interim, this term implying a clear distinction between one who merely wields the gavel over meetings versus one who is invested with executive authority.

That Hanson was president in the fullest sense is amply demonstrated by the facts that he did head the sole branch of government at the time, was elected by the highest elected body in the land to do so, thus occupied the prescribed highest office in the land, and was the first United States head of state recognized at home or abroad. To be sure, his powers as executive were fewer than those of presidents under the later Constitution, but indisputably he was the new nation's first chief executive. It is upon these clear historical facts that the United States government, public officials, historians, authors,[172] the Hanson family and others have affirmed for 230 years that John Hanson was indeed the nation's first president.

Washington, Jefferson, Lincoln, Coolidge, Truman, various United States Senators and Representatives as recently as 2010, and the United States Supreme Court all understood and declared Hanson as the nation's first president. So did the press of the time. Upon the president's passing, the *Pennsylvania Gazette* wrote, "On Saturday the 15th ult. Departed this life, in Prince George (*sic*) County, Maryland, the Honorable John Hanson, Esquire; late president of the United States in Congress Assembled."[173] (The *Gazette* had wrongly picked up John Hanson's incorrect date of death of November 15 from a Baltimore paper.)

Beginning in the early nineteenth century, historians recognized John Hanson as the first president. For example, American historians Richard Hildreth (1807-65) and John Bach McMaster (1852-1932) referred to John Hanson as the first president in their well-regarded histories of the United States, generally accepted as standards from the mid-nineteenth century well into the twentieth.

The ardent abolitionist Hildreth's *opus magnum* was his six-volume *History of the United States of America* published from 1849 to 1853. Hildreth was among the first American historians to write history as factually as possible, "warts and all," rather than to portray it in some chosen glowing light or to push a particular hypothesis. Praise for Hildreth's history has held up with the *Oxford Companion to American History* describing it as "notable for its accuracy and candor, and its acute insights into the relationship between politics and economics."

McMaster, professor of American history at the University of Pennsylvania, is best known for his eight-volume *History of the People of the United States from the Revolution to the Civil War* published from 1883 to 1913 and considered to be innovative in the writing of American social history. His 1897 *A School History of the United States* became widely used. McMaster pioneered the movement beyond pure narration in writing history, and the employment in historical writing of economic developments, the West and newspapers as important sources. McMaster, too, recognized the temporal fact that it was John Hanson who had first served as president.

As of the mid-twentieth century, well before the myth of the

Huntington and McKean presidencies was fabricated, *Encyclopedia Britannica*, *The Encyclopedia Americana*, *The Columbia Encyclopedia*, *Webster's Biographical Dictionary* and *Funk & Wagnall's New Standard Encyclopedia of Universal Knowledge* all had entries on John Hanson portraying him as the first president.

First president he was, with his colleague George Washington later serving as the first president of the nation's second form of government under the Constitution. When the time came eight years after John Hanson's term to elect a President with the full panoply of modern presidential power, Hanson was six years in his grave. George Washington is rightly honored for his irreplaceable service to his country, as the first to hold such power and the first to lead a new government that had, for the first time, the powers of a modern nation-state. He was, in that sense, the first President of the kind we know today. But he was not the first President of his country which honor belongs to John Hanson.

So, yes, John Hanson was the first president of the United States, and then, to be entirely accurate about it, George Washington was the second government's first president when the nation changed its form of government, and the nation's tenth overall. Washington followed Hanson in their first presidencies, and this was just how Hanson, Washington and Americans of their era saw it. The chronological certainty of this is uncomplicated.

Into the Maelstrom

As President John Hanson and the Congress set about establishing a government, their challenge was heightened by one of the greatest mass migrations of human beings in history up to that time. In the 150 years before the founding of the first government, the non-native population of the thirteen colonies had swelled from 4,600 to 2,800,000. The average annual population growth rate over this century and a half was 4.3 percent of which about one percent came from natural increase and the rest from net in-migration. In other words, in the typical year over this 150-year span, more than three of four who had not lived in the colonies the previous year were immigrants with the remaining one in four born in the colonies. To put this in perspective, during the 2000-2010 decade when immigration was a hot topic in the United States, annual net in-migration amounted to 0.4 percent of the population (accounting for virtually all of the population growth). In the 1780-1790 decade, this rate of net in-migration was 3.3 percent, more than eight times as rapid.

Just in the decade from 1770 to 1780 in the midst of the upheaval of a war and independence, and despite a reduction in the average annual population growth rate to 2.9 percent because of the war, United States population grew by a third from 2,100,000 to 2,800,000. Of this growth, two-thirds, or nearly a half million people, came from net in-migration. As fighting drew to a close in 1781 and the new nation began constructing its government, the tide of European immigrants swelled once more and annual growth rates rose to 3.4 percent through the rest of the decade of the 1780s with the rate of natural increase remaining at about one percent. A population growing at 3.4 percent per year will double in size every twenty years. The end of hostilities in 1781 accelerated migration to the United States: in 1790, the United States census would enumerate a population of 3,929,214, forty percent greater than only a decade before.

As John Hanson was elected president, there was much to attract European immigrants, the largest segment of the new arrivals. America's inexpensive farmland, welcoming rural settlement policies, the romantic if deceptive allure of a virgin frontier, a growing culture of immigrants, freedoms of religion, speech and association, and the very idea of joining a people who had just fashioned their own future were all powerful draws. By the millions they would come. Smaller groups of immigrants arrived from Mexico, the Caribbean and Canada.

There was nothing to attract the next most populous group of immigrants. By far the second largest group to emigrate to the United States in this period did so entirely involuntarily as they were swept up from Africa's shores, jammed into ships' holds, and, of the two-thirds who survived the journey, brought across the brutal Middle Passage enslaved. By the 1790 census, nineteen percent of Americans either had been born in Africa or were of African descent whole or in part. This one-in-five proportion would have been close to the same in 1781 as John Hanson took office. After people of English heritage, African-Americans comprised the second largest ethnic group in the United States. Scots-Irish were third, Germans fourth, Dutch fifth. African-Americans nearly outnumbered these last three groups combined. During the Hanson administration, about one in twelve African-Americans was a free Black, the rest enslaved. In 1782, during the Hanson administration, the largest enslaver in Fairfax County, Virginia, enslaving 188 souls, was George Washington.

During the 1780s and well into the next century, nineteen of every twenty immigrants to the new United States elected to settle in rural areas as opposed to cities and towns, with the rural settlement proportion nearly one hundred percent for the enslaved. Most white immigrants eschewed the areas of older European settlement where available land was scarce and expensive, and headed for the frontier. As a typical example, Frederick County, even after being carved up into three smaller counties in 1776, remained Maryland's largest county almost entirely because of rapid growth from immigrants.

The success of the United States in 1783 in negotiating the Treaty of Paris expanded American sovereignty to the Mississippi River and opened the vast trans-Appalachian reaches to settlers who began flocking there. While the nation's leaders wanted these lands to be settled to fasten the country's claim on them, one wonders if they understood that this was the beginning of the filling up of the continent. If John Hanson or other American mathematic adepts had projected the nation's population growth rate at that time into the future, they would have produced forecasts not far from what actually happened. Would they have believed that the population of fewer than three million Americans as the first government took office would, on the average, double every quarter century until there were one hundred million by 1915, then triple from that as the twenty-first century dawned? From their time when it took ninety-five farmers to feed one hundred Americans, would they have believed that the time would come when two American farmers would feed one hundred Americans plus twenty-five foreigners?

Because of the trans-Atlantic upwelling of immigrants, the new government in 1781 was confronted with the compounded challenge of getting a new government with all of its practices launched *de novo* amidst an exceptionally swift current of population growth. While this growth afforded clear opportunities to the new government — a growing labor force, readier capitalization of public and private finance, an ongoing influx of new ideas and entrepreneurial spirit, a more easily drafted military, a faster hold on western lands — the growth came with its difficulties. A population doubling every twenty years needs as often to double its food supply, arable land, post offices, roads, schools such as they were, ships, commercial establishments large and small, and much more. To be able to serve a rapidly growing population, the government would have a concomitant need to grow its revenues, its own labor force and national reach apace.

Even if the challenges of exceptionally rapid population growth had not been present, underdeveloped and fragmented national infrastructure posed a major impediment to the new government and to national development. Prior to nationhood, the responsibility for public roads, bridges, river fords, ports, postal services, other infrastructure and governance itself had devolved virtually entirely upon the thirteen state administrations. While there was some coordination among the colonies and then, after independence, the states, most national infrastructure was fragmented and had never come under any kind of central purview or coordination. The condition of American national infrastructure in 1781 was well lower than that of the poorest Third World countries today.

As mentioned, in the years following the Declaration of Independence, the thirteen new states were so independent of one another that some designated their representatives to the Second Continental Congress as ambassadors. As the first national government was about to come into being in 1781, the states still regarded themselves largely as autonomous nation-states only marginally subject to central governance by the United States in Congress Assembled and then with the full assumption of state veto rights. How then to meld thirteen postal systems, multiple currencies public and private, differing importation and exportation policies, indistinct state boundaries, discontinuous and primitive state roads, and much more? For example, much of the national transportation network in 1781 had evolved from trails, fords and water courses from aboriginal times. As European settlers began making their way inland, for the most part they adopted these routes, widening the trails enough for horses as they went, and naming the old trails as roads. Even into the nineteenth century, many of these roads were still not wide or smooth enough to take wagons or carriages making commercial and military transportation difficult or impossible in many places. In 1800 as Abigail Adams made her way from Massachusetts to the new village of Washington to move into the about to be completed White House, she would write of her coachman having difficulty finding their way on the sketchy road from Baltimore.

But the new government would prove successful in establishing a constructive dialogue among the states on coordinating national infrastructure and even more so in creating new national institutions. The one-year Hanson administration alone would create a nationalized army and navy[174], establish the nation's first central bank, issue United States coinage, inaugurate the United States Post Office, establish a successful unified international diplomatic presence, settle state boundary disputes, progress far toward formal peace with Britain, and cajole the states into beginning to coordinate their roads at state boundaries.

The government would also be called on to put into place a long list of laws, policies, codified practices, informal measures and new customs to deal not only with rapid growth itself and the coordination of national infrastructure but also with their inevitable political ramifications. Perhaps the best example was the necessity six years after launching the first government when the Constitutional Convention found it imperative to solve through a bicameral Congress the growing dispute over how shifting population patterns were to be accounted for in representation and federal spending. All of these challenges are easier for a government to meet under a regime of lesser rather than greater population growth, but it was the maelstrom of very rapid growth into which the new government and John Hanson leapt in 1781.

Forging a Government

What John Hanson and the newly minted United States in Congress Assembled inherited was not a government but a *tabula rasa* upon which could not be written a copy of any European government but only a system novel to the world. The original government's charge was to implement the revolutionary democratic ideals enshrined in the new country's audacious founding document, its Declaration of Independence, to the extent of the powers granted to the new central government by the Articles of Confederation.

A daring and novel Declaration it was. *All men are created equal. Governments derive their just powers from the consent of the governed. The right of the people to institute new government. Pledging our lives, fortunes and sacred honor.* These were concepts, ideals and words such as the world had barely ever heard and never seen boldly implemented, unprecedented aspirations for a new government to transform from ideals to reality. Such was the challenge before John Hanson and those he would choose to form the nation's first cabinet and his administration. On the day Hanson was elected president, the utterly sweeping concept of the United States of America ended its pregnancy, finally took its first breath with a functioning government, vaulted from grand theory to life, and took its emblazoned place in history.

Complicating the launching of the government was a nettlesome condition held over from the Second Continental Congress: poor attendance of the United States in Congress Assembled by too many of its delegates. After waiting for ten days beyond his inauguration to no avail for too many of the delegates to make their way to Philadelphia, President Hanson wrote to the governors of Connecticut, New York, New Jersey, New Hampshire and North Carolina urging them to compel or implore their delegates to take their seats in Philadelphia. This letter early in Hanson's term appears to have corrected the truancy as he did not write further on this matter during his presidency.[175] It appears that the states and their delegates took to heart Hanson's remonstrance and righted their roles in the new government.

The government's first order of business after the election of its president was, of necessity, organizational, and the establishment of the ranks of authority of government offices was the first step. Adopting the recommendations of a special committee establishing an official hierarchy, the Congress legislated that, " . . . the President takes precedent of all and every person in the United States; next to him, members of Congress have precedence; then the Commander-in-Chief of the Army; then the great officers of Congress in the following order: The Secretary of Congress as the nearest and most confidential; The Secretary for Foreign Affairs; The Superintendent of Finance; The Secretary of War and Secretary of Marine." The Secretary of Congress corresponds to today's Speaker of the House. There were no branches of government or separation of powers in the first government.

President Hanson then set about getting the Congress to create federal government secretary positions which were established in the order of Foreign Affairs, Finance, War, Navy and Post Office. These departments evolved into today's departments of State, Treasury and Defense, and the United States Postal Service respectively and, with the exception of the Postmaster General, now a quasi-private sector position, the order of these departments' establishment is followed in modern protocol and presidential succession. Later during President Hanson's term as we have seen, the office of

Chairman of Congress was created which seven years later evolved under the Constitution into today's vice presidency.[176]

On New Year's Eve of 1781, the Bank of North America, the nation's first central bank, was chartered by Congress and began operation one week later in Philadelphia near Independence Hall where the Congress held its meetings. After the Hanson administration and Congress enjoyed a brief recess over the new year's period, further appointments, creation of government offices and fleshing out of the administration happened in quick succession. Appointments of the cabinet positions mentioned above had occurred before the departments which the appointees would administer had been created. February 22, 1782, saw the establishment of the Office of the Secretary of the United States (predecessor of the Department of State), followed by the War Department on April 10, the Agent of Marine (predecessor of the Navy Department) on April 24 and the United States Post Office on October 18.

More than establishing the structure of the new government, the Hanson administration also set about creating the practices, customs and trappings of government, many of which are still in practice today. Among the lasting day-to-day firsts of the Hanson administration, President Hanson ordered the nation's first census; that Army uniforms be standardized nationwide doing away with the rag-tag assortment of clothing that had had to suffice up to then; charged the War Department with directing the building and management of barracks, arsenals, magazines, laboratories and foundries; ordered that the Army Quartermaster Corps be reorganized; and on September 16, 1782, entered the Great Seal of the United States into service when John Hanson authorized George Washington to exchange prisoners. Designed by Congress Secretary Charles Thomson, the Great Seal and its original impressing mechanism are still in use today. Such were some of the necessary initiatives of the nation's original government during the Hanson administration. But the greatest achievements of the nation's first presidential administration were in the arenas of national finance, foreign affairs and new national customs.

The Perils of Early National Economics

In its short year, the Hanson administration overcame many hurdles in organizing the first government, wrapping up the Revolutionary War, getting off to a superb start in foreign relations and establishing important national customs. Its record in putting government finance on an even keel, though nearly brilliant, came out mixed. An excellent appointment, astute personal financial stewardship by the president himself, and the quick founding of the nation's first central bank were offset by the barest failure of the Hanson administration to gain any rational means of financing the government. In what was arguably the top strength of the Hanson administration, John Hanson made superb appointments to his cabinet, the nation's first, none more so than in foreign affairs. His choice of appointment to the nation's top financial post was, in its own realm, nearly as astute.

The Hanson-Morris Tandem's Fast Financial Start

As his Superintendent of Finance, the new president kept in place the redoubtable Philadelphia international trade merchant Robert Morris who had led much of the debate in the full range of national financing considerations as a delegate during the waning days of the Second Continental Congress, and had occupied a vestigial position in that body as the nation's *de facto* finance chief. (Shortly after its founding, the Second Continental Congress had authorized a treasury department which was only vaguely realized during the Congress's life.) Robert Morris was regarded as the nation's foremost financier of the Revolutionary War, exceeding even Hanson's accomplishments. To finance the war, Morris had used much of the personal fortune he had accumulated from his wide-ranging business and land speculation interests, and from what today would be called war profiteering. Like Hanson, Morris would be repaid only a fraction of what had ostensibly been loans but which came to be gifts to the nation and its financially struggling first government. With his own long-honed skills in accounting and finance, visceral understanding of national financial needs, and diplomatic style, President Hanson was a well-suited counterweight to Morris's own blunter style and personality. The two made what would appear to be the best possible tandem of men of their time in the financial arena.

Regarded as the nation's most prominent merchant, Morris was also seen as its shrewdest and, in the eyes of many, as blatantly favoring the wealthy at the expense of national democratic hopes. Said John Adams of Morris, "He has vast designs in the mercantile way and no doubt pursues mercantile ends which are always gain; but he is an excellent member of our Body."[177] Adams' split assessment of Morris was typical. Though Morris's foes looked upon him with awe and gratitude for what he had been able to accomplish for their nation during the war, they simultaneously regarded him with deep suspicion, some even with hatred, for what they viewed as the rapacity of his methods.

During the rest of the 1780s and early 1790s, Robert Morris would rise to become one of the nation's most powerful political figures. Robert Morris, Alexander Hamilton and Albert Gallatin are regarded as the original architects of the United States' financial system. Only Morris and Roger Sherman signed all three of the national charters: the Declaration of Independence, the Articles of Confederation and the United States Constitution. Due to the stunning failures of his speculative investments in the founding of the nation's new capital at the District of Columbia in the 1790s, Morris fell far from grace, lost all of his fortune and the wealth of a number of others, served time in debtor's prison, and died impoverished at the home of one of his children in 1806.[178]

But in 1781, Morris was at the height of his influence and there could have been no better pick by the president to sure-handedly guide the establishment of the nation's first formal financial institutions as the government's first Superintendent of Finance. The office would in a few years evolve into that of the Secretary of the Treasury. Bringing his forceful personality and experienced methods to the office soon earned Morris the appellation of pecuniary dictator. From his own similar expertise in accounting and finance, his experience as a barely compensated war financier, and his sober financial management instincts, President Hanson was closely attuned to Morris. His letters to Philip Thomas make it clear that the president was nearly always in support of Morris and Morris's zeal in putting the nation onto a clear-headed conservative financial footing.

Robert Morris's aggressive finance agenda for the nation aimed to unshackle the government from financial dependence on the states and foreign borrowing, create the nation's first central bank, and guide the creation of government financial policy and institutions so as to strengthen — or give preference to, as some feared — the nation's business and financial community. The combination of Morris's financial brilliance, wide personal influence and powerful personality was so forceful that the Congress often found itself merely rubber-stamping policies which Morris had formulated. Morris's managerial talent, objective expense cutting, elimination of feather-bed positions, regularizing government record-keeping and re-establishment of public credit combined as the president had expected to inspire the Congress's confidence in Morris and his programs.

Too much so, some felt. During his tenure as Superintendent of Finance, Morris's financial acumen was to exceed his political skills as New Englanders and southerners saw their interests subordinated in favor of what they viewed as a middle-states financial oligarchy. "Though it benefitted from his genius, the nationalist movement under Morris paid the penalty of his leadership. It was too much the creation of Morris and his clique, savoring of personal aggrandizement and private advantage."[179]

The Nation's First Central Bank

John Hanson and his Superintendent of Finance wasted no time in proposing the establishment of a central bank for the nation, asking the Congress's approval in November 1781 within days of Hanson's election. On the last day of 1781, the Bank of North America, the nation's first central bank, was chartered by Congress and began operations in Philadelphia the following week on January 7, 1782, with an initial capitalization of four hundred thousand dollars. A week later, the president noted to Philip Thomas that "Our National Bank" had opened and was an immediate success with merchants and tradesmen large and small making deposits and beginning to take out loans. To inspire confidence and assure itself of strong liquidity and footing, the Bank of North America had a highly conservative one-hundred-percent reserve requirement, i. e., that loan volume could not exceed assets. Much to the relief of those holding them, the Bank permitted free exchange of old Continentals for new currency. To further underpin the Bank, the president noted to Philip Thomas that " . . . ten or twelve vessels are lately arrived here from the Havanna, with a large quantity of specie, which it is said will all go into the Bank."

Morris's plan was to capitalize the bank entirely through private subscription but, when this goal could be only partially fulfilled, he invested government funds in the bank's stock to sufficiently capitalize it, making the government the absolute majority shareholder. At first, most of the bank's privately owned stock was held in the hands of Morris, his business associates and other of the nation's major merchants. Legally, the joint public-private venture, though fulfilling the roles of a government central bank, operated *de facto* as a private bank under a separate charter issued by the Commonwealth of Pennsylvania which would prove to be problematical.

From the outset, Morris set the Bank of North America into motion as the depository for the United States government, as moneylender to the Congress and as issuer of a new national currency to replace the near worthless Continentals. Proceeds from foreign loans and what few remittances were made by the states to the central government were deposited in the bank. Morris also had much of his own fortune invested in and on deposit at the bank. Soon, just as with the government itself, the Bank of North America fell under the financial menace of many states ignoring the requisitions put on them and failing to remit deposits. Midway through his term, President Hanson frets to his son-in-law that, "Our Treasury is lowe. What will be the consequence of the impecuniousness of the States [if] our bank should fail?   And what is to support it if the taxes necessary for its support should be withheld? Of the last requisition little or nothing has been paid in."

Once the Bank of North America became more or less adequately capitalized, the government was able to borrow enough on terms beneficial both to it and to the bank's investors (the largest of which was the government anyway) to enable the government for the first time to begin fully servicing the nation's estimated thirty million dollars of foreign debt (a modern equivalent only in the low billions). The cautious businessmen who directed the bank used its solid capitalization to back a new national currency released in measured pace and amount so as to make its value stable and not wildly inflate as had its predecessor, the now loathed Continentals which Morris had ordered terminated as currency when he took office.

The design which John Hanson and Robert Morris had for the Bank of North America was dual: a public-sector role of maintaining government credit and a nationwide medium of exchange, and a private-sector role of growing the bank to a level of power and stability so as to bring under its influence a substantial tranche of the nation's private wealth. In this private-sector aim, it was not lost on Hanson and Morris that the coalescing of private financial interests across state boundaries would create an interdependent banking network the natural interests of which would be to promote national unity and the stronger central government that both men sought. No one accused them of thinking small.

Though able to fulfill its governmental central bank functions despite its being a hybrid public-private creature, the Bank of North America was not able to attain the full measure of the aspirations of Hanson and Morris.   Although nominally operating nationwide, the bank's activities were heavily concentrated in only three states, and in 1785, the Bank of North America fell prey to the political peculiarities from which today's central banks are insulated. Pennsylvania's legislature repealed the bank's state charter in September of that year, accusing the bank of favoritism to foreign interests and unfair competition against state banks which wished to issue their own currency. However, when its legislature swung politically after elections in 1786, Pennsylvania reinstated the Bank of North America's state charter permitting it to operate again the following year but under restrictions that kept it from serving effectively as a central bank. In a course often seen today, the Bank of North America then passed through the hands of a succession of banks by acquisition or merger right up to the present. The original Bank of North America and its successors at Sixth and Chestnut Streets in Philadelphia have been in continuous operation since January 7, 1782, the nation's oldest banking outlet. The location became a Wells Fargo branch in 2010 upon the completion of Wells Fargo's acquisition of Wachovia Bank. The address is 601 Chestnut Street next to Independence Hall.

The nation's central banks were to have multiple and fitful existences until the founding of the Federal Reserve Bank in 1913. Alexander Hamilton, Washington's Secretary of the Treasury, revived central banking in 1791 with the First Bank of the United States which had only a twenty-year life. After a five-year hiatus without a central bank, the federal government in 1816 chartered the Second Bank of the United States which, like its predecessor, lasted only twenty years before falling prey to Andrew Jackson and his fear that the bank was a tool of his enemies. The nation then saw a rocky twenty-five-year period of loosely supervised state banks followed by the National Banking Acts of 1863 and 1864 in the Lincoln administration which, though an improvement, ushered in a half century of inadequate authority of the nation's partially revived central bank apparatus. Finally in 1913, with a masterful compromise wrought by Woodrow Wilson, the United States, the last major economy in the world without a true central bank, put in place one that worked, the Federal Reserve Bank of the United States which has served the nation since. It is notable that the prime presidential friends of central banking — Hanson, Washington, Lincoln and Wilson — served at crucial times when much was at stake for their nation.

Financing the Central Government

In the earliest days of the Hanson administration, the crippling constraints on the new government imposed by limitations in the Articles of Confederation became starkly apparent. One of the most severe was the lack of authority which the central government had to raise money on its own. The first government throughout its existence was forced to go hat in hand to the state governments appealing for funds to operate, and, with the frequent failure of the states to meet their requisitions, to borrow abroad. This critical weakness came to the brink of solution early in the Hanson administration as the president, Robert Morris and the Congress labored to persuade the states to permit the national government to adequately fund itself.

Soon after his inauguration, John Hanson introduced a proposed remedy for fixing the flaw of no specified central government funding ability as the Articles had reserved all taxing authority to the states. During the first month of the Hanson administration, Hanson put forth a nearly successful attempt to amend the Articles of Confederation to permit the central government to levy a five-percent import tariff to fund the government. Proponents of federal taxation, mainly the Congress's aristocrats, understood that to pass the amendment it would have to be palatable to the tradesmen, farmers and small manufacturers who were now beginning to populate many of the thirteen statehouses which would be called on to pass such an amendment. To make the amendment more attractive to the states, the proposed import levy amendment was written with the sole purpose of retiring the new nation's heavy foreign debt remaining from the Revolutionary War.

The proposed amendment brought to a head the debates on how strong the central government ought to be and the balance of power between it and the states which uniformly still continued to view themselves, and not the fledgling central government, as possessing the highest sovereignty in the federation. The nation's rising agrarian radicals and others fearful of allowing the central government the taxing authority which it sought viewed the proposed amendment as a wedge for a usurpation of power from the states by the United States in Congress Assembled and as an opening volley for accrual of power by the aristocrats whose traditional manner and perceived superciliousness they had long resented. In his letter to John Adams, at the time away serving as United States Ambassador to Holland, Massachusetts'

Samuel Osgood, a strident opponent of strong central government, aptly summarized the fears of many when writing that, " . . . I am appreciative that if you were here, you would find it very difficult to establish funds that would not have a tendency to destroy the liberties of this country. Our embarrassments are very great. Our danger lies in this — that if permanent funds are given to Congress, the aristocratical influence, which predominates in more than a major part of the United States, will finally establish an arbitrary government in the United States."

On the other side, the propertied gentry of the nation, especially from the middle states including John Hanson's Maryland, now feared that a weak central government existing merely at the pleasure of the states could leave their class's personal and property rights open to abuses by a resentful, overbearing and increasingly vocal middle-class majority. In this early contest of life-views, we see the hardening of the political and philosophical dichotomy of privilege versus commonwealth which persists in the country today, and since the 1980s has become especially pernicious, particularly in terms of income disparity.

John Hanson urged amendment of the Articles, the federally collected import tariff and the ability of the central government to fund itself. As his whip in fashioning and gaining passage of the amendment, the new president relied on Robert Morris who had led the central taxing authority arguments since the days of the Second Continental Congress. Neither friend nor foe had reason to doubt that Morris's ulterior aim with the Articles' proposed taxation amendment was to shift power from the states and its back-country radicals to the central government stocked in the main by traditional gentry like the president and merchant kings such as himself.

Despite their all-out efforts, John Hanson, Robert Morris and their allies ran up against the central flaw in the Articles of Confederation even more limiting than the absence of any provision for raising revenues: the requirement for unanimous agreement of the thirteen states to approve any amendment to the Articles. Hanson and Morris came to the very edge of solving the government financing conundrum when they gained the consent of twelve of the states only to be thwarted by Rhode Island whose legislature unanimously rejected the proposed tax amendment. Rhode Island would long persist in its odd-man-out spoiler role by refusing to attend the Constitutional Convention in 1787 and by being the last state to ratify the Constitution and then only barely, thirty-four votes to thirty-two, more than a year after the Constitution had already been adopted and Washington had taken office. As we will see, a similar lack of a single vote later in the 1780s would prevent the government from abolishing slavery eighty years before abolition finally came about in the most difficult test which the nation would ever face.

While the Hanson administration did not succeed in passing the tax amendment despite the all-but-unanimous agreement among the states, it did in the first year of the nation's government vividly illuminate the serious shortcomings of government finance. Hanson's and Morris's thrusting of this crippling fault to center stage was vindicated six years later in the Constitutional Convention, Morris's and Alexander Hamilton's successful adoption of the Hanson-Morris position on national finance, and the United States in Congress Assembled replacing itself with a stronger government with self-financing authority becoming the law of the land.

Onto the World Stage

During the five years between the Declaration of Independence and the launching of the government, some European powers traded with the United States and lent tacit encouragement to the American quest for independence, but few were ready to grant diplomatic recognition to the breakaway nation whose future was far from certain. In 1777, the Kingdom of Morocco became the first nation to extend full formal diplomatic recognition to the United States, and Sweden and Holland extended informal recognition later in the decade. Sweden was so fond an ally that her king, Gustav III, wrote to a friend, "If I were not King I would proceed to America and offer my sword on behalf of the brave colonists." At least fourteen officers of the Army of Sweden did come to America and fight in the American or French armies.[180] France, of course, fought beside the United States and made critically important loans to it during the Revolutionary War but did not extend full diplomatic recognition until a few weeks after John Hanson had assumed the presidency.

As long as the war was still being fought, the European powers continued to hold back in formally recognizing the United States but with the victory at Yorktown and the launching of the United States' first government they became much more inclined to recognize the new nation and did. France formally recognized the new government on November 23, 1781, four more nations before the end of 1781, Holland on April 19, 1782, Sweden more formally on February 5, 1783, Denmark in February, Spain in March and Russia in July of 1783.

With the possible exceptions of Sweden's Gustav III and Louis XVI of France, no foreigner had aided the United States more in the Revolutionary War than had Marie Joseph Paul Yves Roch Gilbert du Motier, Marquis de Lafayette. So enamored was Lafayette with the ideals of the Declaration of Independence that at the age of twenty-three in 1777 he defied the King of France, purchased a ship with his own money and set sail for America. The Americans promptly made the young French nobleman a Major General in the Continental Army and Washington appointed him to his staff. In 1781, after being awarded command of the Army in Virginia, Lafayette — along with his countrymen the Comte de Grasse and General Rochambeau — played a key role in trapping and defeating Cornwallis at Yorktown, the beginning of the end of the Revolutionary War.

On the day in November 1781 that the news arrived in Philadelphia of France's formal recognition of the United States, the Marquis de Lafayette announced that he would take leave of his American friends and return home to France. A grateful President Hanson, in the florid style of his time, presented Lafayette with the written thanks of the United States: "I shall at this time only beg leave to assure you, that it is my most sincere and ardent prayer, that you may have a safe and prosperous voyage to your native country; that you may receive a gracious and welcome reception from the greatest and best of Kings; and that you may arrive at an happy and pleasing interview with your family: and permit me to indulge the Hope of your speedy return to America." Upon Lafayette's departure that November, Hanson gave Lafayette his letter to deliver to Louis XVI, the first communication from a United States head of state to another head of state.

As a guest of the John Quincy Adams administration on a fifteen-month tour in 1824 and 1825, Lafayette, then in his late sixties, would be welcomed back to America by grateful throngs in town after town including Frederick where a ball was held in his honor at the Ross Mansion. Lafayette addressed the United States Congress which rewarded him with money and land for his indispensable efforts during the American Revolution.

On July 16, 1782, three months after the fact, President

Hanson learning from Ambassador John Adams of Holland's recognition, writes delightedly to Philip Thomas that, "The States General [Holland] have acknowledged our Independence," and a week later that Adams had been received as the United States Ambassador to the "States General of the United Provinces." Holland became one of the early close friends of the United States. Along with official notification of diplomatic recognition from Holland on September 24, 1782, came cargoes of Dutch-made uniforms for American soldiers on ships putting in at Philadelphia and Boston.

During the Hanson administration, the United States Consular Service was established, ambassadors exchanged with a growing list of nations, and European diplomatic protocols of the era adopted. Among a long list of foreign affairs developments, the president in November 1781 informed the thirteen state governors of an act of Congress "respecting infraction of the Laws of Nations and the erection of proper tribunals for furnishing them," and urged the states' immediate attention in implementing the act. On January 11, 1782, President Hanson informed the thirteen governors of the nation's new diplomatic protocols and procedures of diplomatic immunity for foreign diplomats in the United States. On February 5, he authorized Benjamin Franklin, United States Ambassador to France, to accept a loan that France had offered to the United States. On April 19, John Adams, United States Ambassador to Holland, began negotiating a loan from that country to the United States, and on October 8 concluded the Treaty of Amity and Commerce with Holland.

With the United States' entry into the community of nations and the Hanson administration's thorough engagement in diplomatic relationships and the regimen that went along with it, the nation also was drawn into the peculiarly stilted bustle of diplomatic social life to which, in one of his first letters home after inauguration, President Hanson made no secret of his aversion. But it was not to be avoided. On May 13, 1782, the president presided over the nation's first state dinner in honor of the French Minister, the Chevalier de la Luzerne.[181] Perhaps the president warmed to the task: on July 16, he wrote, "I set up very late last night at the Ministers entertainment for the Dauphin [the newly born Crown Prince of France]. I shall not attempt a description of it, it far surpassed my expectations."

Concluding the War

Three weeks after his inauguration, in what must have been

a joyous reunion for the two men, the President and Congress received General Washington in a ceremony in which Washington presented Hanson with Cornwallis's sword, the formal custom of surrender in the eighteenth century. On behalf of the government and the nation, the president thanked Washington for his exemplary service in commanding the Army during the Revolutionary War and formally awarded him the new title of Commander of the Armies of United States in Congress Assembled. Days later before the Congress, Washington congratulated John Hanson "on your appointment to fill the most important seat in the United States." This well recorded and amply referenced acknowledgement by Washington is all the proof needed that he recognized Hanson and Hanson's successors in the first government as his political superiors, and that, until he resigned his commission in 1783, reported to them as his Commanders In Chief.

The National Archives' surviving official correspondence between the nation's first Commander in Chief and his Commanding General, and Hanson's letters to Philip Thomas show that correspondence between Hanson and Washington was frequent and detailed as would be expected of men in their respective positions. During his administration, Hanson, in his official capacity, wrote to no one more often than to George Washington. Their letters vividly show that the two men felt that the victory at Yorktown portended but did not guarantee the end of the Revolutionary War. Both regarded the United States as still at war with Britain though with much attenuated and more localized fighting. Hanson wrote in February 1782, four months after Yorktown, "Nor shall we have peace in my opinion until we can drive the enemy from New York and Charles Town [Charleston, South Carolina]." It was with this view that Hanson and Washington continued to prosecute the war even as the president appointed his team of Benjamin Franklin, John Adams, John Jay and Henry Laurens to negotiate the peace with Britain.

While they were creating a government, Hanson and the Congress in their foreign affairs realm also had a war to conclude, the peace to negotiate, vital aspects about the future relationship between the United States and Britain to work out, and a new nation to debut to the world.

Though Cornwallis had surrendered at Yorktown three weeks before President Hanson took office, it took months for London's order to cease fire and withdraw to reach British military units in North America, particularly those in the South, and, even when the cease-fire order did arrive, some British units and Loyalists kept fighting. Long transit times in trans-Atlantic communication meant that both the United States government and still-active British military units in the United States were not privy to London's cease-fire order or even of a change of British government until weeks after the fact at best.

On December 13, 1781, the president appointed Benjamin Lincoln as his Secretary of War. The forty-eight-year-old Lincoln had been a Major General of the Massachusetts militia when the Revolutionary War broke out and gained high notice when in June 1776 he and his militia ran British vessels out of Boston Harbor leading to his appointment as Major General in the Continental Army the following February. It was General Lincoln who at Yorktown had received the surrender sword of Cornwallis. Lincoln served as Secretary of War until 1784, and in 1787 commanded the troops which suppressed Shays' Rebellion. That year he was elected Lieutenant Governor of Massachusetts, and from 1789 to 1808 served as Collector of the Port of Boston. Though Lincoln occupied the relevant cabinet position and was technically George Washington's superior in the first government, Washington reported directly to the President and the Congress. Lincoln's primary role as Secretary of War was essentially logistical as the war wound down in 1782 and 1783.

In Britain, once news of Cornwallis's surrender reached the Parliament, change moved swiftly. On February 27, 1782, Parliament voted to cease any further war in America and six days later authorized the king to negotiate peace with the United States. On March 20, the government of British Prime Minister Lord North fell to be replaced by the government of Lord Rockingham who immediately sought faster peace negotiations with the Americans. The change in government was due mainly to the loss of Britain's American colonies.

On April 4, Major General Sir Guy Carleton replaced Lieutenant General Henry Clinton as commander of British forces in America and began implementing the new British policy of ending hostilities and the withdrawal of British troops from the United States. That Clinton was replaced by a lower-ranking officer is further indication of Parliament's waning illusions of a continued presence in what it was rapidly coming to regard as Britain's former colonies. Carleton arrived in New York on May 5. However, because of the sentiments of dissident units in the British Army in several parts of the United States and the difficulty in getting word out to cease hostilities, both Carleton and his American counterparts had to contend with continued fighting for months.

For the remainder of his presidency in 1782, President Hanson was dealing with British consolidations of their remnant forces in New York City, Charleston and Savannah, off-and-on though less frequent skirmishes between the two armies, and conflicting reports of ongoing battles in the Caribbean between the British navy and the combined allied navies of France, Spain, Holland and the United States. It was not until June 11 that Savannah was evacuated by the British. On August 27, 1782, a skirmish along South Carolina's Combahee River would prove to be the concluding armed hostility of the Revolutionary War. President Hanson notes on September 10, 1782, that the British had removed their fifteen hundred soldiers from New York City, their last major stronghold in the United States, for Halifax, Canada. On December 14, in the early days of the administration of President Elias Boudinot, the British completed their last evacuation from the United States as they departed Charleston but, in a final act of vengeance, only after torching a large part of the city.

Throughout his administration, John Hanson remained wary of British intentions, opining officially and in his correspondence to Philip Thomas that the British could be feigning retreat only to temporize and regather themselves for another try at victory on the battlefield. His doubts were shared by his commanding general as Washington remained on alert and continued to prosecute the war. On May 8, 1782, Hanson writes to Philip Thomas his doubts of being able to reach peace quickly despite recent British naval losses in the Caribbean. On June 24, he writes of the British fleet capturing American cruisers and French ships. On July 16, the president tells his son-in-law of the ongoing impasses with which General Washington is having to contend in his efforts to negotiate a prisoner exchange, but on August 14 reports that the exchange has taken place. By July 30, the president was able to report that the French fleet is "scouring the coast" for straggling British ships to make the near Atlantic safe for United States trade.

Though the nation could not know it until months after the fact, the evacuation of Charleston in 1782 would mark the last hostile act and the final chapter in the hostilities of the Revolutionary War fourteen months after the Battle of York-town. John Hanson lived long enough to witness this and had been the president who successfully wound down the war. Only the peace negotiations remained to be concluded the following year and this, too, he would live long enough to see, but barely.

First Diplomatic Victory the Greatest

The major diplomatic accomplishments of the Hanson ad-ministration stemmed from the president's dazzling foreign affairs appointments of his Secretary of Foreign Affairs and his diplomatic team to negotiate peace with Britain. Upon his election as president, John Hanson appointed Robert Livingston as his Secretary of Foreign Affairs, which office evolved into today's Secretary of State, an astute choice of temperament and political shrewdness which put an espe-cially steady hand at the helm of the fledgling nation's inter-course with other nations.[182]   Livingston's nomination by Hanson was in effect a reaffirmation from Livingston's more limited role earlier that year with the interim body.

Upon graduating from King's College (now Columbia Univer-sity) at age eighteen, Livingston studied law under New York Chief Justice William Smith, quickly became a sought-after attorney, was active in the Stamp Act revolt, and served as a New York delegate to the Second Continental Congress. There he was a member of the committee of five which drafted the Declaration of Independence.

Livingston served as United States Secretary of Foreign Af-fairs from the time of his appointment by President John Hanson in 1781 until 1783 when Livingston was appointed Chancellor of New York. In this capacity, it was he who on April 30, 1789, administered the presidential oath of office to George Washington in New York City. In 1801 President Jefferson appointed Livingston as United States Ambassador to France where in 1803 he negotiated the Louisiana Pur-chase from the French.

At least as effective as was Robert Livingston's appointment, John Hanson's appointments of Benjamin Franklin, John Adams, John Jay and Henry Laurens as the American team sent to Paris to negotiate the peace with Britain were singu-larly instrumental in what became "the greatest victory in the annals of American diplomacy."[183] Earlier, Adams had twice been sent to Europe by the Second Continental Con-gress in 1777 and again in 1779 to attempt to negotiate terms of peace with Britain.

When peace talks ostensibly began with the British in Paris on April 12, the team had its work cut out for it, but with Jay not on his way to Paris from Madrid until August and the British government at first stalling in getting its negotiators into place, the talks got off to a slow start. Nominally, the role of the French was as mediator but the American diplomats realized early on that the French had their own agenda which was not always apparent. France was bound by two conflicting treaties, one with the United States which stipulated that the United States and France would jointly agree on the terms of peace with Britain, the other with Spain not to conclude any peace with Britain until Britain surrendered Gibraltar to Spain, a dim prospect. In the background was the well-founded American suspicion that France and Spain were maneuvering to limit American westward expansion to the watershed of the Appalachians. Muddying the American diplomats' job more was that Britain sent two negotiating teams to the peace talks and that the two teams did not always agree with one another.

But it was clear that, despite their own angles on the outcome, France, Spain, Holland and other countries were actively promoting peace between the United States and Britain and this put pressure on the negotiating teams to produce. This was only intensified by, as Hanson wrote Thomas, the Irish Parliament's "spirited proceedings [which] must add greatly to the embarrassments of our enemy and dispose them to think Seriously of peace"[184] and that "The debate in the House of Commons is very interesting."[185] On May 11 the president wrote of the "total change of the Ministry" referring to the British cabinet, reflecting that the British government itself had fallen, that a change to a more sympathetic government had been brought about by the British defeat at Yorktown, and that these developments portended smoother diplomatic talks for the United States. While these favorable developments were arising, the president continued to worry that the future could still be unfavorable to the United States and deeply suspected that Britain could be licking her wounds in preparation for new offensives. But, by the autumn of his presidency, the president reported that British-allied Indian tribes, sizing up the changing balance of power, had abandoned the British for the United States.

The diplomacy, patience and shrewdness of the American delegation brought the United States major victories that had not been possible to win on the battlefield. In a nod to the aspirations of the United States, Britain recognized the independence of the thirteen former colonies (at first recognizing them separately), an outcome not entirely expected. The negotiators also persuaded Britain to include the extensive western lands which she had granted to seven of the colonies, a diplomatic triumph by the Americans which at once established a hugely expanded United States from the Atlantic Ocean to the Mississippi River and from Canada to within a few miles of the Gulf of Mexico. The American delegation was able to fashion this coup by deftly playing off French and British interests against each other, taking advantage of the British strategy of wanting to weaken the American-French alliance and adroitly ignoring certain provisions of the existing treaty with France when it counted. Some historians have reckoned that the United States has never had a brighter diplomatic team which achieved higher success against the odds than the quartet working for John Hanson to negotiate the Treaty of Paris.

A few weeks after President Hanson completed his term, President Elias Boudinot and the Congress received news that on November 30, 1782, preliminary articles of peace had been signed at Paris by Richard Oswald for Great Britain, and by John Adams, Benjamin Franklin, John Jay and Henry Laurens for the United States. Laurens, a previous president of the Second Continental Congress, had joined the American negotiating team after his release the previous New Year's Eve as a British prisoner of war held in the Tower of London, having been captured in transit in the Atlantic fifteen months earlier on his way to Holland to take up his post as the American Minister there. Upon signing the preliminary articles of peace, Laurens returned to his home in South Carolina where, when he died in 1792, he became the first recorded case of cremation in the United States.

Throughout his administration, John Hanson expressed abundant frustration over nearly an entire absence of communication from his Paris team regarding the peace negotiations. What news was received by the President and Congress came roundabout mainly through French and Dutch channels. By the time of his last letter to Philip Thomas days before completing his term, the President and Congress had not received any communication directly from the United States negotiating team throughout the seven months since the team's appointment. The reporting vacuum appears to have been deliberate on the part of the delegation which at one point even ignored its instructions from home so that it could seize unanticipated advantages which they had not been authorized to consider. Franklin, Adams, Jay and Laurens held back informing their government of their negotiations most likely from the fear that a new Congress, still trying to feel its way as it created a government, might issue weak or conflicting orders to the negotiating team. Insubordinate or not, the four brilliant negotiators were able in their eighteen months of work in Paris to produce superb results.

President Hanson was no doubt greatly relieved to learn that on February 4, 1783, two months after he had completed his presidential term, Britain's King George III had formally proclaimed an end of hostilities in the Revolutionary War. The President lived long enough to hear of the Revolutionary War officially coming to a close with the signing of the Treaty of Paris in that city on September 3, 1783, eleven weeks before he died, surely a most fitting and rewarding high point to the aged revolutionary after his long career of nation-building. The eleven weeks would have been long enough for notice of the negotiating triumph to reach America's shores. John Hanson lived barely long enough to experience the elation of this monumental capstone success of his long sacrificing career: the Revolutionary War had been officially won and put into the history books. President Thomas Mifflin and the Congress ratified the Treaty of Paris on January 14, 1784.

During his presidency, John Hanson and his government, despite weeks of delays in receiving news from abroad, remained generally well informed about events not just in North America and Europe but in the Western Hemisphere as well. For example, in his letter to Philip Thomas of February 14, 1782, the president records in detail in a full two pages — twice as long as his typical letter — recent French, Spanish and British military moves in the Caribbean and South America, an insurrection for independence in Peru, and political disquiet in St. Kitts and Martinique.

With its brilliant appointments, nation-expanding diplomatic successes, rapid wholesale foreign diplomatic recognition and sure-handed guidance by Hanson, Livingston and the American negotiating team in Paris, a fair assessment of the Hanson administration's foreign affairs performance is that it was exceptional. Brilliant would not be too strong a term. Few presidential administrations in either government since can claim a level of foreign affairs and diplomatic advances to match those attained by the nation's first administration.

And these all occurred not in a four-year span of modern presidential administrations but in a single year.

Δ

The only other cabinet position existing during John Hanson's presidential term was the office of Postmaster General. Ebenezer Hazard was appointed to the position by President Hanson on January 28, 1782, and served in the office throughout the life of the United States in Congress Assembled. The Office of Postmaster General ceased to be a cabinet position in 1971 when the United States Post Office was quasi-privatized by the creation of the United States Postal Service.

A postal undertaking of sorts had fitfully operated during the days of the Second Continental Congress, first taking shape on July 2, 1774, even before the First Continental Congress, when Baltimore newspaper publisher William Goddard launched his private all-colonies postal service which the public soon came to call Goddard's Post Offices. The impetus for this was more than pecuniary as there had been multiple instances of the colonies' British-administered Royal Colonial Post reading people's mail. In summer of 1775, the Second Continental Congress appropriated Goddard's operation, appointing Benjamin Franklin at a salary of £1,000 per year to head it with Goddard given the subordinate title of Surveyor of the Post Office. The rapid popular switch to Goddard's postal venture and then to the Second Continental Congress's brought about the dissolution of the Royal Colonial Post in the thirteen colonies in December 1775.

The true original antecedent of today's United States Postal Service is Goddard's Post Offices, often overlooked in favor of the first official postal service chartered under Franklin. It is interesting that the nation's postal operation went from private to public and back to private again. The important steps taken in national postal operations by the Hanson administration were elevating the enterprise and its head to cabinet status and regularizing postal operations. Beginning with the Hanson administration, the title of Postmaster General which Franklin had used was elevated to Postmaster General of the United States.[186]

The order of establishment of cabinet offices in the Hanson administration is carried forward today in the executive branch's Order of Precedence, protocol and, following the Presidential Succession Act of 1947, the order of succession to the presidency. Hanson's and the Congress's establishment of the offices of Secretary of Foreign Affairs, Superintendent of Finance, Secretary of War and Postmaster General, created in that chronological order, were carried forward into the second government as the Secretaries of State, Treasury and War (later Defense) and the Postmaster General, respectively. The first three of these are today's top-ranking cabinet positions in the order created.

The Department of Justice and its office of United States Attorney General did not exist during the seven years of the United States in Congress Assembled and were established as the fifth cabinet office by the Judiciary Act of 1789 in the first Washington administration. During the first government, judiciary matters were transacted by the Congress itself which sat in unitary executive, legislative and judicial capacities. When legal matters came before the United States in Congress Assembled, its presidents sat in effect as chief justices as when President John Hanson issued a decision regarding a boundary dispute between two states during his term.

New National Customs

The launching of the new government naturally led to the emergence of a number of new national customs. The first of these, occurring upon John Hanson's inauguration, was that the nation had in Jane Contee Hanson its first First Lady. "His wife, Jane Contee Hanson, because of his high office, now became the First Lady of the land, and assumed her position with a feeling of shyness, yet anxious to do her best, that her aged husband might do well in his exalted position."[187]

The title First Lady originated in the United States and is now used in a number of other countries. During the United States in Congress Assembled and well into the nineteenth century, the title had not yet come into usage, Martha Washington, for example, being referred to as Lady Washington. Nevertheless, even with the bachelor presidents, James Buchanan and Grover Cleveland until he married, and the three widower presidents, Andrew Jackson, John Tyler and Woodrow Wilson, the nation has always had at the side of its president a woman who served as the president's and the nation's hostess and has been acknowledged as such during her own time. Titled or not, capitalized or not, all of these women from Jane Hanson through Michelle Obama as of this writing served as the nation's First Ladies.

There are conflicting accounts as to when the title did first come into use. Oral tradition has it that President Zachary Taylor in his 1849 eulogy of Dolley Madison referred to her as First Lady, and that Harriet Lane, niece of President James Buchanan, was the first to be called First Lady when she served as Buchanan's White House hostess during his administration from 1857 until 1861. The first known written use of the term First Lady was diarist William Howard Russell's when in 1863 he commented on gossip about Mary Todd Lincoln, "First Lady in the Land". The title began gaining use outside of the capital in 1877 through journalist Mary Ames's frequent references to Lucy Webb Hayes, wife of President Rutherford B. Hayes, as "First Lady of the Land." Charles Nirdlinger's popular 1911 comedy *The First Lady in the Land* further entrenched the title. Florence Harding in the 1920s was the first First Lady to have a staff authorized and funded by the federal government. By the 1930s and Eleanor Roosevelt, the wives of United States presidents were routinely referred to nationwide as the First Lady. Whenever we might say the title of First Lady became accepted, it was only after a number of very dedicated American women had already served devotedly in the role without the benefit of title. Jane Hanson, simply by virtue of her position as wife of the first president, thus lays fair claim to the honor of having been the nation's and its people's first First Lady, though almost undoubtedly the term was not heard in her time. She lacked the formal title but did fully occupy the position which would later gain the title.

Another enduring national custom established during the Hanson administration is the provision of an executive mansion to the occupant of the nation's highest office. On November 21, 1781, the Congressional Committee on Arranging the President's House provided for a nearby mansion which the new government rented, a household staff of eight, a coach and horses, and presidential authority to draw on the public treasury for household expenses. The home provided to John Hanson established a lasting unbroken precedent.

The Philadelphia mansion had been built in 1767 by Mary Lawrence Masters and was among the largest in Philadelphia. In 1772, her daughter Polly married Governor Richard Penn, grandson of Pennsylvania founder William Penn, and the new home became the mother's wedding present to the couple. Richard Penn entertained First Continental Congress delegates at the home. It was Penn who was asked by the Second Continental Congress in 1775 to present the colonists' grievances to King George III and deliver the colonies' Olive Branch Petition. Failing his mission, the Penns and Mrs. Masters ended up spending the Revolutionary War in England.

On January 2, 1780, the home suffered a major fire while occupied by French Consul John Holker. Robert Morris then bought the home and restored it in 1781 to much the same floor plan as before. Morris added a third floor in 1784, expanding the home to six bedrooms.

Located at Sixth and Market Streets, the home served as the nation's President's House for John Hanson and Elias Boudinot before the seat of government was moved to Annapolis in November 1783, then to Princeton and finally to New York in the late 1780s. After being inaugurated and briefly living in New York City, George Washington occupied the President's House in Philadelphia from November 1790 to March 1797 when his second term as president expired. John Adams occupied it from then until June, 1800, when he and Abigail became the first residents of the White House (which wasn't called such until it was painted white after being burned in the War of 1812). Over an interrupted two-decade span, the Philadelphia mansion served as the public and private offices of the President and the nation's official entertaining venue. A picture of the mansion is shown here.

As with a government-provided executive mansion, the Hanson administration also established the custom of presidential portraits. During 1782, John Hanson sat for his painted by Charles Willson Peale the one-time saddle maker who in the 1760s had learned portraiture from Hanson's earlier portraitist John Hesselius. John Hanson's presidential portrait hangs in the Independence Hall portrait collection in Philadelphia.

Two other enduring customs established during the nation's first presidential administration are the annual observances of the Fourth of July and Thanksgiving established by Hanson's presidential decrees. The Fourth of July had begun being observed in 1777 with unofficial annual celebrations in towns throughout the states. By decree, John Hanson made the observances official with the imprimatur of the national government.

The Second Continental Congress had issued an earlier one-time declaration observing Thanksgiving but not as an ongoing annual observance. On March 19, 1782, John Hanson issued a proclamation that the last Thursday in November be observed annually thereafter as a national Thanksgiving Day. In 2011, John Hanson's 1782 Thanksgiving decree resurfaced when it was auctioned from the estate of his fifth-great-grandson, Mathias Oppersdorff, Jr. It's purchaser is unknown and the decree may or may not ever be seen again.

During the early part of the nineteenth century, observance of Thanksgiving Day waned. President Lincoln reaffirmed the last Thursday of November as an annual day of Thanksgiving to be observed nationwide, and succeeding presidents began issuing annual Thanksgiving proclamations. During the Franklin Roosevelt administration, Thanksgiving Day was legislated as a paid national holiday to be observed on the fourth rather than last Thursday of November so as to make a longer commercial period of the holiday season. Lincoln and Roosevelt grew the beloved American tradition which their first predecessor, John Hanson, had officially established with his decree.

Shackled

As noted, in addition to the limited ability of the government to raise funds for its own operations, an equally severe shortcoming was that the only provision which the Articles of Confederation provided for amendment of the Articles to rectify such defects was unanimous consent of the legislatures of the thirteen states. In the United States in Congress Assembled's seven-year tenure, this never happened and amendments sorely needed to facilitate better government could never muster the unanimity required to be passed.

The Articles of Confederation did not provide for the separation of powers as the Constitution later did which forced the first government to act as a unitary executive, legislature and judiciary with the inherent conflicts that this non-tripartite role posed. Congress occupied the legislative role and also approved the presidents' administrative appointees, who in effect served at the pleasure of Congress. There was only limited provision for any judicial power of the national government, leaving most disputes to be resolved in state courts. The Hanson administration in fact did carry out all three capacities as, for example, when Congress and President Hanson, acting in effect as Chief (and only) Justice, adjudicated a western lands boundary dispute between Connecticut and Pennsylvania, with the president handing down the decision on August 28, 1782.

As John Hanson and his United States in Congress Assembled successors were all too aware, the presidents of the first government were severely restricted by the Articles of Confederation in exercising executive authority. This, of course, was by design as the newly independent states, having just rid themselves of overbearing and capricious British rule, were not anxious to put much power in the hands of any individual or group as they fashioned a government. Except on routine matters, Hanson and his eight successors did not even have full authority over the departments of government reporting to them, with the Secretaries of the departments often waiting for votes of the Congress to receive direction. Though the presidents of the first government were not disputed as possessing official rank higher than that of any other American, as stated specifically by early legislation in the Hanson administration, and were clearly recognized throughout the United States and overseas as heads of state, their roles were as much ceremonial as executive.

The nine presidents[188] of the original government were not at all reluctant to apprise the Congress and the state governments of the difficulties that a weak executive was causing the nation. As the shortcomings of the Articles of Confederation and the sincere but too cautious first try at defining a government became more vexing, the original government would itself later in the 1780s call for a new stronger form of government unshackled by a too-constraining charter. By the administration of the seventh president, Nathaniel Gorham in 1786, it had become so evident that the restrictions on the office of President were holding the nation back that the Congress convened the Annapolis Convention to re-examine the Articles of Confederation with an eye toward granting presidents more power and addressing other short-comings. Instead, the Annapolis Convention recommended the wholesale replacement of the Articles through a Constitutional Convention to be convened the following year. How this led to the first government dissolving itself to launch the stronger Constitutional government operating today is dealt with later here.

The First Family in Philadelphia

On the day of his inauguration, John Hanson came under the full burden of the nation's first presidency as responsibilities both to be codified and improvised piled up rapidly. This in combination with age seems to have temporarily overwhelmed the sixty-six-year old. By November 13, eight days in office, he has written to Jane, "The load of business which I have very unwillingly and very imprudently taken on me I am afraid will be more than my Constitution will be able to bear, and the form and ceremony necessary to be observed by a president of Congress is to me Extremely irksome, moreover I find my health declining and the situation of my family requires my being at home; I shall therefore take the first opportunity of applying for a leave of absence, this to yourself." The "load of business unwillingly taken on" makes it clear not only that John Hanson had been drafted into the presidency rather than seeking it, but also that the job was more than just ceremonial.

The following day, the president put forth his leave request but was immediately dissuaded by his Congressional colleagues. Two days later, Hanson writes again to Jane, "My last was of the 13th by the post, acquainting you of my intentions of resigning my seat as president of Congress, and accordingly on Wednesday last I desired leave of absence, but some of the members Expressing their dissatisfaction of my so soon laying Congress under the difficulty of Electing Another, (for a Difficulty there would be as the votes of Seven states are necessary and only Seven states are at present represented) I shall Continue, unless the assembly of our state should leave me out of the Delegation. I therefore hope you will immediately prepare to come up if your state of health will permit it." His state did not leave him out. On November 28, 1781, the Maryland General Assembly re-elected John Hanson as one of Maryland's four delegates to the United States in Congress Assembled. As was clear in John's most recent letter to Jane, he was the only Maryland delegate present at the Congress at the time.

In this last letter dated November 16, the president asks Jane to have Philip Thomas bring her and the couple's nine-year-old daughter Elizabeth Arianna Hanson, their last child at home, to join him in Philadelphia. He extols the comforts of the executive residence provided to them and apprises Jane that the government affords the First Family's mansion with "a steward, housekeeper, necessary servants, a coach and horses." The journey was made and the nation's first First Family set up housekeeping in Philadelphia late that fall celebrating Christmas and the new year of 1782 there. (This is the Elizabeth who was the second of the couple's daughters so named, their first having died at Mulberry Grove in 1751 at the age of twenty-two months.)

Accompanying Jane and Elizabeth to Philadelphia was Dr. Thomas's daughter Catherine "Kitty" Thomas, his second youngest child, who would stay in Philadelphia with her presidential grandparents and Elizabeth. Though niece and aunt respectively, Kitty and Elizabeth are young children aged six and nine, and know each other more as sisters and playmates than in their actual relationship. It appears that Kitty was taken to live in Philadelphia with her grandparents to keep Elizabeth company as she had in Frederick. Both children will attend school in Philadelphia and, as the president noted in his correspondence to Kitty's father, both girls made friends easily. As a grandfather is prone to do, the president doted on his granddaughter and in a letter to her father the following summer praises the youngster: "Little Kitty is I think in better health than she has been for a long time but we are obliged from her tender Constitution to be very careful of her and have thought it would be injurious to send her to school this hot weather and I don't think she is losing any time. We ride every day and we let her go about as much as she can. She is really a fine girl. There is no Dancing School at present[. I]f one opens in the Fall we will send her."[189] In many of his letters, the president is extending Kitty's regards to her three siblings, James, Becky (Rebecca Bellicum Thomas) and Johny (John Hanson Thomas, Sr.). We recall that the children's mother, Jane Hanson Thomas, had died at age thirty-four, five months before John Hanson's inauguration, so Kitty lost her mother and was separated from her father during that short period.

Throughout his time in Philadelphia, the president wrote frequently to Philip Thomas noting the most important developments of the nation and government, and nearly always inquiring about the wellbeing of the president's Thomas grandchildren. The president would inquire about his Frederick business affairs and household which Dr. Thomas was overseeing for him, or give specific instructions to Thomas on these matters. For example, on April 19, 1782, Hanson instructs Philip Thomas in detail to act on his behalf in two land transactions and in doing so entrusts his son-in-law with access to the president's personal papers at home. In his letter, Hanson encloses his keys to "a trunk which stands in our room above the stairs behind the door in which are all my papers relative to the office" and to the president's "desk in the hall." One wonders what ever became of these pieces of presidential furniture. On October 26, 1943, Galton, Orsburn Co. auctioned the estate of Annie M. Hanson including a "Duncan Phyfe drop-leaf table [which] originally belonged to John Hanson." Anne Maria "Nannie" Hanson, the granddaughter of Alexander Contee Hanson, Jr., had died in May of that year at age eighty-four.

It is not known where the table is today.[190]

The First Family used its time in Philadelphia, a growing and sophisticated city by 1782, to shop for themselves and others for items which might not be found in Maryland. John Hanson had his carriage, a phaeton (a small light four-wheeled carriage typically with two seats and drawn by two horses), built in Philadelphia. In his letter of October 2, 1781, he writes, "Complements to [former] Governor Johnson and Mr. Potts. Please to tell the Latter that His carriage will be Completely finished this Week and I think it a very Genteel one." He writes of a cloak which the president had bought for "Sammy," his son Dr. Samuel Hanson before his death in June 1781 and of the delays of Saylor's, a Philadelphia hat maker, in producing a hat for Philip Thomas. In a February 1782 letter, the president details his purchases of fabrics bought on Philip Thomas's account: superfine broadcloth at $1,220 per yard and kersamere (cashmere) at $600 a yard coming to a total purchase of $5,013.50. The equivalent current value of this expense is hard to reckon because of the low worth of 1782 dollars. The month before the president's term is up and he and his family will return to Frederick, Saylor's finishes Philip Thomas's long-awaited hat, at last ready at a cost of £16-0s-9d. In these purchases, we see that for a time both the new United States dollars and British pounds were used side by side.

Reflecting John Hanson's claimed but still unproven partial Swedish heritage, the First Family attended the Old Swede's Gloria Dei Church in Philadelphia though the Hansons were Episcopalian and Old Swedes was Swedish Lutheran. The Reverend John Roak, the church's pastor in 1959, noted that, "While the Church of Sweden was Lutheran in theology, it was liturgical and Episcopalian like the Anglican Church. Many communicants of the Church of Sweden in this country have a tendency to become Episcopalians because the Lutheran Church here is too evangelical and informal in worship."[191] In fact, Old Swedes Church became Episcopalian in 1848.

John Hanson's Episcopalianism is confirmed by records of Frederick's All Saints Episcopal Church that he and his family were members, and the absence of any membership records for him or his family at Frederick's Evangelical Lutheran Church. Thomas Johnson and Francis Scott Key were also members of Frederick's All Saints Episcopal Church. The Episcopalian Church in the United States, being the Church of England, suffered before and during the

Revolutionary War. Reverend Daniel McKennon of Frederick's All Saints Episcopal Church vanished during the war. In 1814 when the All Saints parish replaced its old church on All Saints Street where the Hansons had worshipped with its new one on Church Street, Dr. Philip Thomas bought three pews from the old church.

The First Family also appears to have found a favorite Philadelphia restaurant or tavern, the Old Walnut Tree, enjoying frequent rides there in the phaeton.

John Hanson and his biographers mention that an illness overcame the president in the early spring of his presidential term. On the day after the president celebrated his sixty-seventh birthday on April 14, 1782, he fell ill. His biographers have only been able to speculate on what might have been the affliction. In his letter to Philip Thomas of April 19, 1782, the president complains that, "I am a little unwell with a cold," perhaps underplaying his illness. Writing eight days later, he reports that, "I have lately had a most severe fit of sickness but thank God am so far recovered as to be able to ride out." However, he adds, "I am hardly able to write and must conclude by tendering our love to you and the Dear little ones." It is evident in the second letter that during his illness the president was well enough to receive reports on the Congress's business at his bedside and to sign official letters and documents. By May 8, he writes, "We are now I thank God all pretty well." Even better, by June 2 the president conveys that, "Little Cate and myself are now perfectly recovered and your mother [meaning Jane, Philip Thomas's mother-in-law] is much better than she has been since she came to Philadelphia, she is getting fat fast, we ride every day and intend to continue doing so whenever the weather permits."

His biographers have conjectured toward the more severe side of the type of illness which laid up the president. While it could have been a heart attack, stroke, pneumonia or other life-threatening event, the fact that the illness appears to have begun with a cold makes a severe cold, influenza or perhaps pleurisy more likely. However, the president had complained to Jane the previous November within days after his inauguration that his health was deteriorating which could have meant heart trouble. There still is not enough evidence to answer this long-standing question but, given that the president was back at work, taking carriage rides within a fortnight or so, and in his own estimation experienced a full recovery within a month make for the hypothesis that, whatever his uncomfortable malady might have been, it was less rather than more severe. But within nineteen months, time would overtake him.

Many of John Hanson's letters home concern not only his own health but that of his wife, daughter, granddaughter, son-in-law and others, all of whom suffered their own ills during the year. In the letter commenting on the beginning of his illness, the president also mentions that Jane had a tooth ache, ear ache and fever. In several of his letters, the president writes to Philip Thomas of the president going out of his way to consult Philadelphia physicians about Thomas's health complaints and melancholy after his becoming a widower. These intimate letters are a clear window on the near total vacuum of knowledge in which patients and their physicians had to grope in their often futile attempts to dispel illness and administer cures. Eleven years after John Hanson's presidency, the most often dispensed "medicine" in Philadelphia's yellow fever epidemic was mercury. As he lay on his death bed in December 1799, the prime treatment administered to George Washington by Dr. Craik and his two other physicians was bleeding. When the president's grandson, Senator Alexander Contee Hanson, Jr., took ill probably with tuberculosis in 1812, bleeding again was the prescription. One thinks of the kind and diligent Dr. Thomas doing his best to comfort his patients in Frederick with only the scantest knowledge of what is known in medicine today, perhaps wondering if he sometimes did more harm than good.

It is clear from his letters, even after the arrival of Jane and the two girls in Philadelphia, that the president longed for his Frederick home and friends, and looked forward to returning there when his term was up. Homesickness would not be too strong a term to use. He often asks Dr. Thomas to convey his greetings to one Frederick friend or another, especially to "Mr. and Mrs. Price." This is probably Colonel Thomas Price, the militia commander who John Hanson had sent to aid Massachusetts as a Captain at the outbreak of war and who had served beside the president in Frederick County government. It is notable that when the president mentions his homesickness, he nearly always speaks of Frederick and seldom of Mulberry Grove, leaving the impression that John Hanson had become fond of his adopted hometown and county in the twelve years he had lived there leading up to his election as president.

While the president's letters to Philip Thomas often included the personal topics mentioned here, the bulk of what he wrote home dealt with getting his administration and the new government up and running, the challenges of governing, winding down the war, and the other important unfolding events of their time.

The president had for months longingly written of looking forward to returning home to Frederick, considerably reducing his schedule, and retiring from his service with the State of Maryland by then stretching over four decades. This was a man now nearly sixty-eight who complained of the weight of his years and was candid about wanting a more relaxed elder's role in his remaining time. Despite his remonstrations, there appears to have been a surreptitious friendly effort — a well-meant surprise to him — to draft John Hanson back into the Maryland General Assembly upon completion of his term as president. In the last weeks of the Hanson administration, Alexander Contee Hanson, Sr. and Philip Thomas in various guises lobbied the president to return to Frederick via Annapolis, giving faint hints of something afoot. In his replies, the president was wary and begged off, citing unconvincingly his not wanting to travel by boat down the Chesapeake in November but to take his phaeton and wagons overland through Baltimore or Lancaster, Pennsylvania. Suspecting a hero's welcome in Annapolis at which he could not easily refuse election or some appointment, Hanson adroitly declined further service in his letters to Philip Thomas, effusively recommending others by name. Citing age and fatigue, he hopes that his friends will excuse him "from standing for election to the Maryland House of Delegates the following year. I think the pubic can have no further claim to my services[.] I have performed my Term of Duty and they must give me a discharge retirement."

John Hanson did not serve again in either house of the Maryland General Assembly and there is no record that he served in any other elective or appointive capacity for the brief remainder of his life after completing his presidential term in November 1782. However, in his last existing letter to Philip Thomas of June 18, 1783, seven months after completing his term as president, he writes from the state capital, "I believe we shall leave Annapolis about the last of next week if your mother [the First Lady] can by that time return the many polite visits she has received by that time. We shall first go to Patuxent and then visit some friends in Charles, if I find my health and strength will permit. I thank God I am not worse than when you left us, and I shall be able in 8 or ten days to manage my horses in the Phaeton without too much fatigue." So after all, John and Jane did end up spending long enough in Annapolis to be lauded to the extent of needing to reciprocate courtesies and write back to Frederick. However long the stay and whatever its purpose, it undoubtedly included the warmest of thanks and congratulations from Maryland officialdom and common folk alike to the only Marylander ever to occupy the nation's highest office and to their nation's first First Lady.

During this time in Annapolis, John Hanson was asked to use his influence as the nation's first past president to help persuade the United States in Congress Assembled to make Annapolis the federal government's permanent home and the national capital. The effort nearly succeeded. That year several Annapolis opinion leaders formed a group to work with the Maryland General Assembly in a concerted effort to get the government to relocate. Touting Annapolis's virtues including its "many springs of excellent water," the Assembly offered its own statehouse as a new national capitol building, the Governor's Mansion as the presidential residence, and thirteen dwelling houses to be built at state expense, one for each state's delegates. That November upon the in-auguration of Thomas Mifflin, the third president of the United States in Congress Assembled, Maryland Delegates Daniel Carroll and James McHenry delivered the offer to the Congress which accepted it, if only temporarily as it turned out. Later that month, the Congress adjourned to make the trip from Philadelphia to Annapolis and first convened in the Maryland Statehouse on November 26. By December 13 enough delegates had arrived to make a quorum and the Congress began transacting its business in Annapolis. It was here in a long-remembered ceremony on December 23, 1783, three months after the signing of the Treaty of Paris, that George Washington tendered his resignation as Com-mander of the Army of the United States in Congress As-sembled and made it home in time to celebrate Christmas with his family.

Wealth in Satisfaction

Even with the paucity of John Hanson's personal records, it is proven without doubt that he sacrificed much in time, treasure, health and family for the Revolutionary War and then in heading the first government.

During the war Hanson often had to pay State expenses from his own pocket before being reimbursed by the Mary-land Assembly if he got reimbursed at all. "Hanson fre-quently advanced funds from his own pocket to pay jailers, soldiers, and others who threatened to quit if they were not paid on time."[192] In his letter to Philip Thomas of July 26, 1780, the month after his arrival at the Second Continental Congress, Hanson wrote, "The States pay in nothing in Comparison to what has been demanded of them. Of the one million two hundred and odd thousand Dollars required of the State of Maryland 200,000 only has been sent in. And the other States are equally deficient." In his next letter on August 4, Hanson amplifies saying that the states are "extremely backward in their payments. Little or no money to carry on its [the army's] operations." In his letter of September 19 he writes of starving Continental Army soldiers having to plunder New Jersey farms to get fed: "I am willing to believe that all our embarrassments proceed rather from the disjointed and deranged State of our finances, than the want of inclination or ability of the United States to carry on the War. Congress can do no more than recommend . . ." .

On April 10, 1781, Hanson in commenting to Dr. Thomas on Hanson's own financial situation notes that, "I have not received one farthing from the state since I have been here." He had arrived in Philadelphia in June 1780, ten months before. Delegates to the Second Continental Congress and then the United States in Congress Assembled were paid by their states, or were supposed to be. By March of 1782 and running short of funds in Philadelphia, John Hanson, now president, is pleading with his son-in-law to press the State of Maryland for long overdue reimbursements. It was a few days after writing of this financial distress when President Hanson suffered the illness which kept him from office for several weeks. John Hanson was one of a number of Revolutionary War era patriots who risked all they had for nationhood and ended up much the poorer for it financially. "Only about one-tenth of the amounts levied on the states by the Confederation was ever paid, and consequently the financial situation was desperate."[193]

The dearth of recompense was experienced by every rank of American who had been promised pay, loan repayments or other compensation from the states, the Second Continental Congress or the original government. During the war which they had won, foot soldiers went without pay and often even food and shoes. The president of their nation had to rely on his own dwindling resources in the absence of his salary. While John Hanson was president, a Frederick lieutenant who was months or years overdue to be paid for his war service beseeched Philip Thomas to plead his case to the president. The best hope that Hanson could offer the young man was forlorn: "You will inform [Lieutenant] Evans that nothing at present can be done respecting his pay[. T]here is no doubt but he will get his money but the state of our Finances will not admit of Speedy payment."

At one point in his presidency, John Hanson considers an investment in spirits as a way to produce more personal income. Hanson and Dr. Thomas assessed the financial feasibility of investing in purchases of "wine, Madeira, claret, rum" and other spirits in Philadelphia to be sold in Frederick. In the midst of the drought of 1782 and his debilitated crops, the president cannot afford to pay cash for his investment but can pay in hemp he has grown which brings a good price in Philadelphia. On the surface, this exchange would have worked but transportation costs made the prospective investment unfeasible.

During the war, his presidency and afterward, John Hanson continued to rely on the agricultural yields of his lands in Frederick County to provide the family's income. In addition to his own properties, John Hanson also rented at least one which he farmed. Toward the end of his presidency, Hanson writes Philip Thomas, "I do not propose to clear more than three or four acres a year in future not only in justice to the Landlord but to save the wood as much as possible." In the same letter, he mentions "my little farm" and proposes that Dr. Thomas order the planting of corn, wheat, rye and oats for the coming season. Even gentry plantation owners were subject to the vicissitudes of weather and rainfall: the dry summer of 1782 caused the president to worry to Philip Thomas in August that "Crops of corn will be very short. Would it not be best to stop selling any more of my corn?", and two letters later, "You alarm me much about my short Crop of corn[. P]ray sell no more grain or anything eatable."

The near complete absence of reimbursement also deeply affected John and Jane Hanson's son Alexander. In 1782 while president, John Hanson laments to Philip Thomas the situation of Alexander regarding Alexander's financial distress caused by the Maryland and national governments failing to pay Alexander for services rendered or to fully reimburse him for advances he made on the state's and Second Continental Congress's behalves. John Hanson writes that Alexander was in want of "common necessarys of life" and that the president, in the same unpaid situation, is unable to help Alexander financially. Hanson asks Dr. Thomas to send Alexander "a load of flour as soon as you can." In the summer of that year, the president and Philip Thomas assess the feasibility of bankrolling a possible commercial venture for Alexander who wants "to get into some safe species of merchandising." This idea was discussed but not implemented.

Alexander Hanson could have been owed for multiple services he had rendered as he had served in the field as private secretary and *aide-de-camp* to General Washington in 1776, then as the first Clerk of the Maryland Senate in 1777 and 1778, and from 1778 to 1789, as judge of the General Court in Frederick before becoming Chancellor of Maryland.

John Hanson also sacrificed his health, working long days late into his sixties in an era when the life expectancy was about thirty, bearing an arduous presidential load until he retired at age sixty-seven, and suffering his temporarily incapacitating illness in March 1782 while serving as president. The president completed his term with broken health which is evident from his letters. In his final letter to Philip Thomas in Summer of 1783 a few months before his death, the then former president complained of reaching the point of having difficulty managing his carriage horses during travel.

Hanson's personal life was also severely disrupted by his devotion to the Revolutionary War and his presidency. During the two and a half years which he spent mostly away from his Frederick home while in Philadelphia, his daughter, Jane Contee Hanson Thomas, wife of Dr. Philip Thomas, died in Frederick in June 1781. The president may or may not have been able to visit Frederick to be with her in her last days. A gap in the letters of John Hanson to Philip Thomas from April 10 to October 2, 1781, might mean that John Hanson was able to spend that period or some of it at home in Frederick in which case he would have been frequently at the bedside of Janey while her health declined. Nearly every letter of Hanson to Thomas through that of April 10, 1781, the last before her death, inquires pleadingly about Janey's health. This last letter mentions a trip which Janey Thomas had been able to make with her husband the previous month to Annapolis so her decline over the next two months would have been precipitous. Jane Hanson Thomas, mother of four young children, died on June 17 at the age of thirty-four.

Her death came after six more of the thirteen children of John and Jane Hanson had died before reaching adulthood, another in young adulthood, and their adult son Lieutenant Peter Hanson had given his life in the Revolutionary War.

Janey Thomas's passing was followed twelve days later by the death of her brother Dr. Samuel Hanson at the age of twenty-four, a casualty of disease in the war. It is hard to fathom the grief that befell John and Jane Hanson that summer as he was about to be drafted to assume the nation's highest office. Of their thirteen children, they were left that summer with one son, Alexander Contee Hanson, then thirty-three and already embarked on a distinguished career, and their youngest child, their second Elizabeth, then nine.

The loss of the president's daughter Janey in 1781 was also the loss of Dr. Thomas's wife. In his will filed in Frederick County that September, John Hanson left to his wife all of his estate except to his "much esteemed Son-in-law Doctr. Philip Thomas one Mourning Ring." Philip Thomas would remain a widower for the last thirty-four years of his life.

Mourning rings are memorial rings to commemorate a deceased relative, friend or historical figure. Their use dates from the Roman Empire to the early twentieth century before they went out of fashion. Mourning rings reached their height of popularity in the eighteenth century. Shakespeare's will in 1616 bequeathed money to several friends to buy them golden mourning rings.

The mourning ring willed by John Hanson to Philip Thomas came into public view again two hundred thirty years later when in 2011 it appeared in the auctioned estate of Mathias Oppersdorff, Jr., a direct descendant of John Hanson. The ring has two inscriptions, one commemorating Philip Thomas which reads "Dr. Philip Thomas / Nat. June 11, 1747 / Ob. April 25, 1815", obviously inscribed after his death; the other reading "O. H. Williams Ob 15 July 1794 Ae 45" honoring the Hansons' and Thomases' close Frederick County friend, General Otho Holland Williams, upon his death at age forty-five in 1794. Williams commanded troops in the Carolina battles of Camden, Guilford Court House, and Eutaw Springs, and, after the war, became the first Commissioner of the Port of Baltimore. Apparently, Philip Thomas had the ring which his father-in-law had willed to him inscribed with the Williams commemoration in 1794 and then the Thomas family had the ring additionally inscribed after the death of Philip Thomas in 1815. As the auction buyer of the Hanson-Thomas mourning ring is unknown, its brief public appearance in 2011 is most likely its last.

Despite the dreadful burdens of the deaths of eleven of his children, faltering health, well advanced age and the most difficult job in the nation, by all accounts President Hanson rose to the occasion, accomplished more than what was expected during his presidency, did so in the uplifting manner which had gotten him elected, and earned the grateful thanks of his colleagues and countrymen as he stepped down. The bet which the other Founding Fathers of his nation had placed on him a year earlier had paid off handsomely. The first act of Congress and of John Hanson's successor Elias Boudinot after Hanson's term had ended was the profound thanks which they gave to the nation's first past president who had successfully delivered a safe birth of the first government and, in so doing, the consummation of nationhood. John Hanson had achieved all of this at a time when presidential terms were only one year.

Perhaps the president saw that what he had lost in his deep sacrifices he had in some measure regained in the wealth of satisfaction which he must have felt at the end of his long nation-building career from his first election to the Maryland House of Delegates in 1759 to his retirement from the nation's highest office late in 1782. His nation owes a great debt to this man who as much as any sacrificed his comforts, fortune, loved ones and time to throw off the yoke of foreign tyranny and, as much as any, give birth to the United States. John Hanson deserves to have his memory and accomplishments shine as brightly today as when his one-year presidential term expired on November 3, 1782, he retired from public life after his extraordinarily long and brilliant service, and, much wearied, was at last able again to enjoy his home and friends in Frederick, if only briefly.

Vanished

By the time John and Jane Hanson and the two young girls were able to return to Frederick in November 1782, President Hanson's heath was failing and he had a difficult winter going into 1783. He rallied enough that summer to travel again to receive his accolades in the state capital but by fall entered into a last decline. The record of his final year, like much of that of the rest of his life, is thin but we are to assume that he longingly re-engaged in his domestic roles of husband, father, grandfather, merchant, planter and now past president. As the nation's first past president, he would have spent considerable time answering correspondence, receiving visitors, advising on matters of state when asked and, as his condition permitted, visiting family and friends in Maryland and perhaps elsewhere. Beginning with John Hanson, the expectations put on former presidents required their considerable time and energy.

In an oddity probably unique in United States presidential history, on March 19, 1783, a Philadelphia newspaper erroneously reported that John Hanson had died in Frederick. The error may have resulted from an illness or the declining health of the president at that time. The falsehood was soon found to be mistaken and by April 18 and May 10 papers in Baltimore and Providence, respectively, had printed corrections of articles which they had run after picking up the Philadelphia paper's blunder.

While on a trip to southern Maryland in November of 1783, John and Jane Hanson visited their twenty-three-year-old nephew, Thomas Hawkins Hanson, at his Oxon Hill Manor. The Manor home built in 1711 was located on a hill above the banks of the Potomac River in Prince George's County only twenty-one miles from Mulberry Grove where perhaps John and Jane had just visited. The past president would have savored the manor house's grand prospects up and down the Potomac, with Mount Vernon across the river seven miles downstream, and a mile upstream the small port of Georgetown and the farms which in less than a decade would become part of the District of Columbia. Quite possibly he sat one more time under his favorite spreading cherry tree where he had whiled away brief moments of leisure on previous visits to Oxon Hill Manor.[194]

While visiting at his nephew's home, President Hanson took ill a final time, lingered with much discomfort, and on November 22, a Saturday, the American whose talents and diplomacy had twice been indispensable in sweeping aside impediments to nationhood, to whom the young nation above all others had turned to first lead it, who had sacrificed so much in giving birth to his country, died at the age of sixty-eight, once more away from home. Had he lived five days longer, he would have celebrated the annual national Thanksgiving observance which by his quill had been created one year earlier. Perhaps he and Jane had planned to enjoy Thanksgiving with their nephew.

Then John Hanson vanished.

In one of the most astounding turns of events in United States history, President John Hanson's gravesite became forgotten over time, not rediscovered for two centuries and forgotten again. The crypt where he was interred was rediscovered once more in researching this book by which time it and John Hanson's body had vanished altogether in the most tragic manner detailed later here. Well into the twenti-eth century, several conjectures existed as to where he might rest. One of these has now become proven by elimi-nation of the other possibilities which are explored later here when we examine how the first president has slipped so far from the nation's memory.

Americans who now firmly reside in the pages of the nation's history revered John Hanson. Abraham Lincoln would say that Hanson should be honored equally with Washington as first presidents. Long after Hanson's passing, James Madi-son extolled Hanson's "exalted virtues," ideals, poise and diplomatic sagacity. Thomas Jefferson would state that, "President Washington accepts every condition, law, rule and authority, under the Great Seal and the first President of the United States, John Hanson."

The Maryland Gazette's eulogy of John Hanson was typical of the collective loss which the nation felt. "Thus was ended the career of one of America's greatest statesmen. While hitherto practically unknown to our people, and this is true as to nearly all the generations that have lived since his day, his great handiwork, the nation which he helped to estab-lish, remains as a fitting tribute to his memory. It is doubt-ful if there has ever lived on this side of the Atlantic, a no-bler character or shrewder statesman. One would search in vain to find a more powerful personage, or a more aggressive leader, in the annals of American history."

Jane Hanson would remain a widow for the next twenty-nine years until her death on February 21, 1812. "Died this evening in the 85th year Mrs. Jane Hanson relict of John Hanson, esq., a delegate to the old Revolutionary Con-gress."[195] This obituary appears to be the source of the myth that Jane Hanson outlived all of her children: "[S]he had lived to mourn for the last of a numerous family of chil-dren whom death had snatched from her."[196] The obituary states that until the end of life Jane Hanson " . . . still re-tained the natural clearness and vigour of her mind unim-paired . . . [t]hough distressed and enfeebled by illness."

After John Hanson had died, Jane remained at her family home in Frederick in the close care of Philip Thomas next door for the rest of her life.

In the twilight of her life, Jane Hanson lost one of her last two children. Her last surviving son, Alexander Contee Hanson, Sr., died of a stroke in 1806 at age fifty-six in An-napolis where he was living. Jane lived to see Alexander cast two presidential elector votes for George Washington, compile *The Laws of Maryland*, become president of St. John's College, and serve as Chancellor of Maryland, the second highest legal position in their state, in which position he was serving when he died.

John and Jane Hanson's thirteenth and last child, the second Elizabeth who as a youngster had lived with her parents in the presidential mansion in Philadelphia, married Daniel Floweree on March 25, 1802, at his home in Fauquier County, Virginia, when she was thirty. Until her marriage, Elizabeth had lived at home in Frederick looking after her mother. The only known images of any of the thirteen children of Jane and John Hanson are the portraits of Alexander Contee Hanson, Sr. and Elizabeth Arianna Adolphus Hanson Floweree shown here.

By 1809, the shared Hanson-Thomas household was empty of younger voices. By then, James, the eldest of Philip Thomas's four children, had died, and the other three had married and left home, leaving Philip Thomas and Jane Hanson alone in Frederick. Jane Hanson had the great satisfaction of seeing her Thomas grandchildren marry well. Catherine Hanson Thomas, the Kitty who had lived with the presidential family in Philadelphia for a year, married Dr. Ashton Alexander in 1799 and had two children. In 1805 Rebecca Bellicum "Becky" Thomas married her first cousin once removed, Judge Alexander Contee Magruder, a jurist on Maryland's highest court. The couple had four children. In 1809, the youngest Thomas child, John Hanson Thomas, married Mary Isham Colston, niece of United States Supreme Court Chief Justice John Marshall. They had one child, Dr. John Hanson Thomas, Jr. who in 1875 would write the earliest John Hanson biography.

By her eighties, Jane Hanson had nearby only the long-standing comfort of her remarkable son-in-law, himself a widower since 1781. From afar, she could take pride in her grandchildren including Alexander Contee Hanson, Jr., already a prominent statesman and journalist, and her burgeoning brood of great-grandchildren.

Compounding the mystery and astonishing accidents of history which have obscured the legacy of John Hanson, Jane Hanson would also vanish after death to an extent even greater than her husband. The rediscovery of her grave in 2011 while researching *Remembering John Hanson* is taken up later here.

Part VI

From President Hanson to President Washington

The Uncounted Nine

Remembering John Hanson would be incomplete without giving the recognition long overdue not only to Hanson but to the eight men who succeeded him as president of the original government, but first it is necessary to recollect who is not among them. It is conspicuous that entirely absent among the presidents of the original government in what Washington himself termed the highest position in the land when John Hanson was inaugurated are the major iconic figures of the late 1700s who later became enshrined as Founding Fathers.

In some measure, it is the weakness of government in the seven-year era of the United States in Congress Assembled which may have been a deterrent on recruitment of some of the nation's top talent of the time to stand for election as president. The nine presidents of the United States in Congress Assembled were well qualified and thoroughly dedicated, but, with the exceptions of John Hanson and John Hancock, at first glance today are mistaken as second-tier figures. For example, if John Hanson is not often remembered today, what of his successor as president, Elias Boudinot of New Jersey, another worthy but forgotten figure?

Among the better known personages of the 1780s, all of whom but Franklin would enter the pantheon of American greats through their roles in the second government, Adams, Jefferson, Franklin and Jay sidelined themselves abroad for much of the 1780s with the plush sinecures of ambassadorships. After his long eight-year absence during the Revolutionary War, Washington at last in late 1783 was able to retire and return home to his beloved Mount Vernon for most of the rest of the decade. Though they surely continued to enjoy attentive audiences within the government, especially Washington, these pillars of the nation had taken themselves out of central involvement with national governance. Arguably, they deprived their nation of some of its uppermost talents at a critical juncture when it could have made best use of them. What would draw them and their genius back in was the appeal of the stronger government to be wrought by the Constitution, especially the second government's far more powerful executive prerogatives.

History has amply assessed these Founding Fathers but not their nine predecessors who led the first government. One must wonder how history would have recorded the nine presidents of the first government and the first nine of the second if they had switched places.

Was it sheer charisma or weight of accomplishments or administrative brilliance which has emblazoned Washington, Adams, Jefferson and Madison onto their nation's memory, or was it that they were more able to make their mark by serving four or eight years with far greater authority under a strengthened government charter, the Constitution? Presidents Washington, Jefferson and Madison *each* served a year longer — eight years — than did all nine presidents of the first government together. (John Adams served one four-year term.) If these four had served as the first four presidents of the original far weaker government, each with a single one-year term, would they have still been able to attain their lasting recognition or would they, too, have been relegated to the far recesses of history as those who actually served have been? Certainly, they would have been able to accomplish less in single one-year terms and, as a result, would have been recorded more faintly in history.

Conversely, what kind of records would the presidents of the United States in Congress Assembled have compiled if they instead had served under the Constitution with its far more extensive presidential authority and had four or eight times longer in office during which to make their marks? Certainly, they would have been able to accomplish more, had the advantage in showing up in any list of presidents since, and been recorded far more fondly by history. If Washington had been the first president under the original government and Hanson the first under the Constitution, which of them would be better known today?

While, on the whole, the later group of first four presidents might possibly have been more talented collectively than the first group — though because of the first group's brevity of service this is entirely open to debate — the nine who led the original government were, as we are about to see, among the very most gifted the nation had to offer in the 1780s and without doubt demonstrated deep nation-sustaining measures of talent themselves which they put to work for the new United States. In fact, upon deeper inspection there doesn't seem to be much to indicate that the two groups of presidents were not equally talented and dedicated to their new nation. The record shows abundantly that the sacrifices made during the Revolutionary War and early nationhood by the two groups were on a par with one another.

Year for year in their presidencies, these two groups appear to be equally accomplished. In divining the hypothetical transposition of the two groups of presidents from one government to the other, one concludes without much difficulty that it was not so much the men but the far different opportunities afforded them under their two very disparate governing regimens that have determined their relative places in history.

Then we must ask why we see neither Washington nor Adams nor Jefferson nor Madison nor Franklin as a president in the original government. One can speculate that presiding over a weak government was unappealing or even, in their minds, beneath the dignity of Franklin and the four later presidents. This, indeed, may have been part of their calculus in taking on other roles in the 1780s but, there is much more to it than that.

At the age of seventy-five when the original government was born and he was nearing his wheelchair days, Benjamin Franklin likely regarded himself as too old to bear the burdens of the presidency. Further, with the sensation that he had caused in Paris with his persona and beaver hats, and the surfeit of young women lavished on him by the royal court, Franklin had been serving quite comfortably since 1778 as the United States Minister and the first United States Ambassador to France. In 1782, President Hanson appointed him as Minister to Sweden simultaneously with Franklin's French appointment. Franklin remained in his foreign posts until 1785 when he returned home at the age of seventy-nine. Franklin died much debilitated on April 17, 1790 at age eighty-four a year after Washington's inauguration. Twenty thousand attended the funeral of the revered publisher, scientist, diplomat, politician and sage Benjamin Franklin.

The four who became the first presidents of the second government had served in either the Second Continental Congress, the United States in Congress Assembled or both, and thus had already demonstrated their willingness to serve, at least in subordinate roles, if not presidencies. The four also served the United States in useful capacities during the seven years of the original government while trying at the same time to maintain some semblance of their family and personal lives. While Washington, Adams, Jefferson and Madison did complain justifiably of the weakness of the first government, none complained about this more vociferously than did those who actually served as presidents of the United States in Congress Assembled.

Then there are the particular circumstances of the four

which mitigated against their seeking or being drafted into the presidency until the 1790s or later.

At least until the Treaty of Paris was signed in late 1783 and he then promptly resigned his commission, Washington knew that he was indispensable in his position as Commander of the Army. It is not clear that others, had they been in charge of the Army, would have had the perseverance and willingness to sacrifice that Washington demonstrated in keeping a starving, ragged underpaid army going. Also, probably only Washington was enough of a bulwark to fend off the repeated machinations of his subordinate, General Horatio Gates, whose attempted coup in the Newburgh Conspiracy, back-channel maneuvering in the congresses, and overweening ambition at the expense of his country came at the worst times. (Rather than dismiss Gates and risk his full-time undermining from the outside, Washington kept a close eye on him by retaining Gates on his headquarters staff.) When Washington was able to resign from the Army in November 1783 barely sixty days after the Treaty of Paris formally ended the Revolutionary War, he almost certainly could then have been elected president of the United States in Congress Assembled in any term he liked, but he chose instead to retire to Mount Vernon, his long avowed plan. In part, Washington may have shunned the presidency at this juncture because of antipathy about the position and its lack of the authority that the general was used to, but, in strong measure, we must also believe Washington's diaries in which he had often written that he longed for home. In fact, Washington had a great deal of ambivalence about being drafted into the presidency when he took the job in 1789.

John Adams did not sit on his hands during the 1780s. In early 1782, President Hanson appointed Adams as the first United States Ambassador to Holland in which position Adams served until 1788 when he returned home to run for president under the Constitution, losing to Washington. From 1785 until 1788, Adams served simultaneously as the first United States Ambassador to Great Britain. So, Adams, it may certainly be said, was ably serving his country for most of the period of the United States in Congress Assembled in two key positions which were, incidentally, quite comfortable. He, too, may have eschewed being president of the first government because of its weakness and, as noted earlier, went on record with serious doubts about a government operated by what he regarded as moneyed elites. But, one must think that Adams felt especially useful to the

United States in his key dual ambassadorships.

Like Adams, Thomas Jefferson spent much of the decade of the 1780s in a vital role abroad serving as United States Ambassador to France from 1785 to 1789. Jefferson became the first United States Secretary of State of the second government when appointed by President Washington in 1789. Jefferson, too, must have appreciated the importance and comforts of his key ambassadorship in the 1780s. Until 1785, Thomas Jefferson did serve as one of the more active and able delegates to the United States in Congress Assembled, and, as we shall see, in 1784 came within a whisker's breadth of achieving what would have been a monumental good turn in the nation's fortunes.

Jefferson's young protégé, James Madison, not yet thirty at the beginning of the 1780s, did not begin to hit his political stride until the last years of the decade when his fine philosophical and theoretical bent led him to become the principal framer of the Constitution and author of over a third of the Federalist Papers. Until 1786, Madison was still serving at the state level in Virginia's House of Delegates. In that capacity, it had been Madison who had taken the lead in his state in 1780 persuading Virginia to subscribe to the Hanson Plan for federal control of the western lands and cede Virginia's own western lands to the incipient United States in Congress Assembled.

During the seven years of the original government, Washington served in his indispensible position as Commanding General of the Army before gladly retiring and then chairing the Constitutional Convention in 1787; Madison made a spectacular debut on the national scene late in the decade in authoring the Constitution; and Adams, Jefferson and Franklin served long stretches abroad in key ambassadorial roles. It can't be said that the five shrank from important service during these years. Given their key roles and their individual circumstances during the years of the original government, one cannot conclude that the five either did or did not eschew the presidency of the original government. However, once the office became more authoritative, lengthy and viable under the Constitution, it is conspicuous that we do see all but Franklin lining up over the next twenty years to run for the office, Washington and Adams in 1788 and 1792, Adams and Jefferson in 1796 and 1800, Jefferson again in 1804, and Madison in 1808 and 1812.

Two things certain are that these presidents would not have been the giants that they were had they served in the first rather than the second government, and that the first government's presidents would have attained far greater stature and been emblazoned in history books since if they had served in the second government rather than the first.

Despite the shackles of scant authority, short terms, utter newness of a nation and government finding their way, and even frequent lack of pay, there was not an ineffective president among the nine of the original government. The absence of their just historical due is not because of who they were or their performance but from the dreary circumstances in which they were nevertheless willing to serve their short presidential terms. Let us now become reacquainted with the forgotten men who did not demur in serving as the nation's chief executive when the position lacked much to make their service personally fulfilling. A table of the order and the dates of their service is provided in the appendices here.

Elias Boudinot

John Hanson's immediate successor as president was New Jersey lawyer and early American philanthropist Elias Boudinot who had a long distinguished record before, during and after his presidency but is almost entirely forgotten today.[197] Boudinot served as a New Jersey delegate to the Second Continental Congress and then to the United States in Congress Assembled throughout its seven-year existence. For a time during his tenure at the Second Continental Congress, he reported directly to George Washington as Commissary General of Prisoners of the Revolutionary Army, and later served as the Congress's *de facto* point man on foreign affairs. In the latter role, Boudinot was instrumental in controlling the receipt and disbursements of the nation's lifeline foreign aid from the French, Dutch and Spanish, and gained credit for his careful handling of relations with Canada. His acquisition of diplomatic and foreign affairs experience would prove an excellent fit during his presidency as the Treaty of Paris was being concluded.

Elias Boudinot was forty-three when inaugurated as president. Upon his taking office, the nation transitioned from the third oldest president who would serve in either the first or second governments through 2012 to the fifth youngest, perhaps from a lesson the Congress had learned from President Hanson's illness which had incapacitated him for several weeks during his presidential term as he turned sixty-seven.

Just as with his predecessor, Elias Boudinot provides an-other example of financial sacrifice for the nation to take on the intermittently paid job of an early president. The day af-ter his inauguration in November 1782, Boudinot wrote in distress to his wife Hannah, "You must not blame me hastily for a Step, which from the Nature of the Thing, must be taken before & without Consulting you. I informed you that I had this morning accepted the Chair of Congress. . . . I think you had best sell whatever you think we shall not stand in need of. . . . You must get all the Cash you can; as that all will not be sufficient. Sell one or two Horses, the largest Colt & the little Mare . . . the Waggon, Plough, Har-row, Chair . . . and supernumerary Hogs[.] . . . As to the Family, I know not what to say about them. I think if you could manage it so that Mr. P could live in the House & Mr. Remson lodge in the office, it would answer a valuable Pur-pose — but I really know not what to advise to."[198]

During the summer of his presidential term, Boudinot had to deal with a serious mutiny of unpaid soldiers which re-quired the rescue of the Congress by General Arthur St. Clair and the permanent vacating of Independence Hall for Princeton, then Annapolis, then New York where the capital remained until nearly the end of the John Adams admini-stration in early 1801. Elias Boudinot served in the United States House of Representatives during the first six years of its existence until his appointments by Presidents Washing-ton, Adams and Jefferson as director of the United States Mint at Philadelphia from 1795 to 1805. He served as a member of the Board of Trustees of Princeton University for forty-nine years. Late in life in 1816, Elias Boudinot founded and served as the first president of the American Bible Society until his death in 1821 at age eighty-one.

Perhaps most to his credit was Boudinot's life-long philan-thropic work promoting rights, education and place in soci-ety of African Americans and Native Americans. The excep-tionally gifted Yale-educated Cherokee Chief Kilikeena Watie was so touched by Boudinot's tutoring and friendship that he adopted his name.[199] His tombstone epitaph well sums the life of Elias Boudinot: "His life was an exhibition of fer-vent piety, of useful talent and of extensive benevolence."[200]

As with the Hanson-Washington contrast, most Americans today can easily identify the second president of the gov-ernment under the Constitution but surely only a bare handful can now name Elias Boudinot as the second presi-dent of the original government and of the United States.

Thomas Mifflin

The same contrast can be made between Thomas Jefferson and the original government's third president. Boudinot's successor, Thomas Mifflin, served as a Pennsylvania delegate to the First and Second Continental Congresses and then to the United States in Congress Assembled. During the Revolutionary War, Mifflin had stepped through the ranks from Major and the first *aide-de-camp* to General Washington to Major General of the Continental Army in which rank he served as the first Quartermaster General.

Thomas Mifflin was the only United States in Congress Assembled president among the nine who could be said to have had a spotty record. As Quartermaster General, Mifflin was accused of war profiteering, and upon his resignation of the post narrowly avoided being court-martialed. Mifflin fell far from favor with George Washington after participating in the rump movement to replace Washington with General Horatio Gates as Commander of the Continental Army. Thomas Mifflin was expelled from the Quaker church for his military activities and lived the rest of his life as a Lutheran. One also sees suggestions that Mifflin was too fond of the bottle.

During the Revolutionary War, Thomas Mifflin preferred the front lines where he did distinguish himself. Despite the accusations of profiteering, he excelled at securing war materiel as Quartermaster General. Mifflin served as a trustee of the University of Pennsylvania, Speaker of the Pennsylvania House of Representatives, delegate to the Constitutional Convention, and from 1790 to 1799 as Governor of Pennsylvania when his administration was marred by allegations of corruption and negligence. What seems to have carried the controversial Mifflin through his thirty up-and-down years of elective and appointive office were an affable personality and silver tongue.

When he was inaugurated as president in November 1783 at the age of thirty-nine, Thomas Mifflin would be the second youngest ever to serve in the nation's highest office through today. It was during President Mifflin's presidential term that the United States in Congress Assembled came within a single vote of abolishing slavery in future states. In tall irony, it was President Mifflin to whom George Washington tendered his resignation as Commander of the Army after the Treaty of Paris had been accepted by Mifflin, formally concluding the Revolutionary War.

Richard Henry Lee

Mifflin was succeeded by Virginia's Richard Henry Lee in November 1784. Scion of one of Virginia's most influential families over many generations before and after him, Lee had served as a Virginia delegate to the First and Second Continental Congresses from 1774 to 1779, was the sponsor of the Second Continental Congress resolution for national independence and the Declaration of Independence in 1776, was the sponsor of the Articles of Confederation, and was a signer of the Declaration.

Richard Henry Lee was one of the earliest and most strident voices in any colony against British impositions and for more colonial autonomy. As early as 1764 Lee had begun denouncing the proposed Stamp Act and, when the Act became reality, organized his county to suspend purchases of British goods until repeal of the Act. In 1774 at the First Continental Congress, he was successful in persuading the twelve other colonies to block importation of British goods and form the Continental Association, an important early move toward union. In June of 1776, had he not been called home from the Second Continental Congress because of his wife's illness, it would have been Lee who drafted the Declaration of Independence. In his absence, he assigned the job to his young Virginia protégé, Thomas Jefferson.

Though southern, high gentry and a wealthy planter with large land holdings, Lee spurned his inherited aristocratic mien and slavery. With an every-man outlook, he described America as, "an asylum where the unhappy may find solace, and the persecuted repose." In the 1787 passage of the Northwest Ordinance, Lee took a lead role in assuring that the legislation explicitly prohibited slavery in the Territory.

As a Virginia delegate to the Constitutional Convention, Lee opposed the Constitution on grounds of insufficiency. However, after his election on March 4, 1789, to the United States Senate, by which he was chosen as the Senate's first President Pro Tempore, he drove passage of the Bill of Rights which Lee felt went far in improving on the Constitution's omissions.

In a great ironic vignette of Americana, the early abolitionist Richard Henry Lee, carrier of a noble family tradition, was the great uncle of Confederate General Robert E. Lee.

John Hancock

John Hancock was nominally the fifth president of the United States in Congress Assembled but due to poor health at the time of his election could not take office. Chosen by the Congress to serve in Hancock's place was David Ramsay who was President from November 23, 1785, to May 12, 1786. Nathaniel Gorham was then elected by the Congress to serve the rest of Hancock's term. It is this case of three presidents sharing a single one-year term which resulted in nine presidents over the seven-year existence of the United States in Congress Assembled.

It is a pity that most Americans today don't remember Hancock for more than his penmanship and having an insurance company named for him. Massachusetts merchant king John Hancock, the wealthiest New Englander to champion independence, served as president of the Massachusetts Provincial Congress in 1774, then as a delegate to the Second Continental Congress from 1775 to 1778, presiding over the Congress from May 1775 to October 1777. In so doing, he served longer as the president of any of the colonial consultative bodies or the United States government than anyone until George Washington in the second government. As the presiding officer of the Second Continental Congress, John Hancock was the first signer of the Declaration of Independence. Upon his election as President of the United States in Congress Assembled, he became the only person in the nation's history, other than Grover Cleveland a century later, to be elected twice as president with a gap in service between terms.

On April 10, 1775, the opening day of the Revolutionary War, Massachusetts Patriots John Hancock and Samuel Adams had escaped capture by the British at Lexington only because of Paul Revere's warning ride. Detention of the two well known rebels had been a primary objective of the British in their march on Lexington and Concord. After being passed over for Washington to head the Continental Army, Hancock went on to serve as Senior Major General of the Massachusetts Militia during the Revolutionary War before his tenure as president of the Second Continental Congress.

John Hancock served as Governor of Massachusetts from 1780 to 1785 when he was elected to the United States in Congress Assembled, and again from 1787 until his death in 1793. As chairman of the Massachusetts constitutional ratification convention, he guided Massachusetts' endorsement of the Constitution. In doing so, Hancock rose even further in popularity and began to be mentioned for the presidency of the United States under the new government about to be launched. In 1789, he did seek the presidency, again losing out to Washington. Being eclipsed twice by Washington did not seem to lessen Hancock's affection for the other man, as Hancock and his wife Dorothy had in 1778 named their youngest son John George Washington Hancock.

Due to Hancock's illness upon his election as president of the United States in Congress Assembled, the Congress chose the following two presidents to serve Hancock's term in his place.

Dr. David Ramsay

Succeeding to the presidency at the age of thirty-six, Dr. David Ramsay, a physician, is still the youngest person ever to serve in the nation's highest office. Son of an Irish immigrant, David Ramsay was a graduate of Princeton University and of the University of Pennsylvania. He moved to South Carolina in 1773 and represented it in the United States in Congress Assembled from 1782 until 1786. In the Revolutionary War, Ramsay had served as an Army physician with field grade rank and was a prisoner of war for a year at St. Augustine, Florida, until he was freed in a prisoner exchange. His 172-day time in office is the second briefest of any United States president, longer only than William Henry Harrison's thirty-two days in 1841.

After his retirement from the Congress, Ramsay served as president of the state senate of South Carolina for seven years, authored several historical works, and was named as the first State Historian of South Carolina. At the age of sixty-six in 1815, Dr. Ramsay was shot and killed by a maniac in Charleston. Among their many errors on John Hanson, the United States in Congress Assembled and the period, most websites and even credible written histories today altogether omit David Ramsay as a president. His presidential tenure, though brief, unremarkable and all but forgotten, was actual.

Nathaniel Gorham

After Dr. Ramsay's brief service as president, Nathaniel Gorham filled in for John Hancock for twenty-two days in May and June of 1786, before being formally elected by the Congress when it met on June 6 to serve the remainder of Hancock's term, which expired on the first Monday of that November. Wealthy self-made Boston merchant Nathaniel Gorham had served in the Massachusetts state senate and during the war on the Second Continental Congress's Board of War for three years until the victory at Yorktown. Except for an interruption when he took up a judgeship in his home state, Nathaniel Gorham served in the United States in Congress Assembled from 1782 until 1788 when the Congress dissolved itself.

By the time of Gorham's presidency, the first government had been in existence for more than four years, and the shortcomings of the Articles of Confederation and the constrictions they imposed on government and its presidents were in full seed. It was during Gorham's brief time in office when the Congress began to grapple in earnest on alternatives to its existence, with Gorham taking a leading position on one prime alternative and then reversing course to a second. Because of the mounting failure of the Articles, some urged a wholesale rewriting while others, not that long removed from royal mood, began to consider abandonment of the democracy experiment in favor of the creation of some form of American monarchy. In 1786, the Congress actually considered approaching either Prince Henry, brother of Frederick II of Prussia, or the aging Bonnie Prince Charlie[201], heir to the royal Stuart line who had led the failed Scottish Jacobite Rising, to contemplate establishment of a constitutional monarchy for the United States.

While a change to monarchical government was seriously discussed, those in the Congress who treasured republicanism carried the day, and the seeds of the Constitutional Convention were sown. In September of the Gorham administration, the Congress convened the ponderously named Meeting of Commissioners to Remedy Defects of the Federal Government, quickly to be called the Annapolis Convention. Though only five states[202] attended, their delegates were sure-handed enough to bring about the Constitutional Convention the following year. Within months after completing his presidency, Nathaniel Gorham became a Massachusetts delegate to the Constitutional Convention.

In his later years, Nathaniel Gorham lost nearly all of his fortune through land speculation. In greatly reduced circumstances, he died in 1796 in Charlestown, Massachusetts, where he had been born.

Dr. Arthur St. Clair

The Scottish immigrant physician Arthur St. Clair arrived in the colonies with a wealthy inheritance, served in the British Army during the French and Indian War, as Major General in the American Continental Army during the Revolutionary War, crossed the Delaware with Washington to capture Trenton and Princeton, and was instrumental in the Continental Army victory in the Battle of Saratoga. It was General St. Clair who had come to the rescue of the Congress and President Boudinot in 1783 when they were surrounded by unpaid soldiers in Philadelphia.

Born and educated in Edinburgh, Scotland, during the last days of the Jacobite Rising, Arthur St. Clair was the only American president of either Continental Congress or either government who was foreign born. Despite the Scots' defeat in trying to restore the House of Stuart to the British throne, the Scottish St. Clair joined the British navy and came to America when assigned to help prosecute the French and Indian War. By the end of this seven-year war, by which time a third of Scotland's land area had been vacated by Scots emigrating abroad, mainly to America, St. Clair decided to join them and remained in the colonies, settling in Pennsylvania amidst a number of his newly arrived immigrant relatives. He helped organize the militias there and in New Jersey, joined the new Continental Army, commanded the Army's Canadian expedition, was accorded the rank of Major General, and was elected as a Pennsylvania delegate to the United States in Congress Assembled. For a period in the Washington presidential administration, St. Clair served as Commander of Federal Troops.

During the administration of his predecessor, Nathaniel Gorham, Arthur St. Clair had initially favored the creation of a constitutional monarchy under his former countryman, the Stuarts' Bonnie Prince Charlie, but came around to retaining the United States as a republic despite his prescient fear that a centralized federal government would have incentive to expand itself, eventually claiming, in his estimation, a quarter of national product. It took nearly two centuries, but St. Clair's prediction wasn't far off.

It is not clear why Dr. St. Clair did not take office on the first Monday of November of 1786 as prescribed in the Articles of Confederation but on February 2, 1787. Other than the Hanson administration, St. Clair's was the most eventful during the seven years of the United States in Congress Assembled. President St. Clair and the 1787 Congress rejected monarchical government, convened and oversaw the Constitutional Convention, quelled Shays' Rebellion, passed the Northwest Ordinance, and tackled slavery head on by outlawing it in the Northwest Territory.

In recognition of St. Clair's efforts in shepherding the Northwest Ordinance into law, he was appointed Governor of the Northwest Territory in the Washington administration, but was removed from the position by President Jefferson in

1802 for opposing Ohio statehood. During his governorship, Dr. St. Clair founded the city of Cincinnati, Ohio, in 1790, renaming the small village of Losantiville which had been settled two years earlier.

Arthur St. Clair died impoverished in rural western Pennsylvania in 1818 at the age of eighty-four.

Cyrus Griffin

It was Virginia lawyer and legislator Cyrus Griffin as the last president of the United States in Congress Assembled who closed the book on the first government as it put itself out of business and handed the baton of governance to George Washington and the new constitutional regime. Griffin served in the Second Continental Congress from 1778 to 1780, in the United States in Congress Assembled from 1787 to 1788 and as its president during the 1787-88 term at the age of forty. President Griffin's administration attained the ratification of the Constitution during the summer of 1788. Griffin had his own reservations about the Constitution and what it might inflict, but was later assuaged by the quick passage of the Bill of Rights.

Griffin was a close protégé of fellow Virginians Peyton Randolph, who had died two years before Griffin became president, and George Washington with whom Griffin had partnered in land development in the western reaches of their state and beyond the Appalachians. Like Randolph, Griffin had graduated in law from London's Inner Temple and was thus counted among an American legal elite.

After the Constitutional Convention made it apparent that only one more United States in Congress Assembled administration would be needed to effect a transition to the second government, the trusted Griffin became president in large part to smooth the transition from one government to the next as his mentor Washington was about to take the helm under the new Constitutional regime. In fact, everything considered, the transition from the first to the second government was remarkably smooth. Upon the advent of the second government, President Washington awarded Cyrus Griffin three federal appointments more or less simultaneously in 1789: President of the Supreme Court of Admiralty, Commissioner to the Creek Nation, and Judge of the United States District Court of Virginia.

Cyrus Griffin served in the last position until his death in Yorktown in 1810 at age sixty-two.

The nine United States in Congress Assembled presidents

comprised both variety and uniformity. In their political outlook they varied from the staid traditional gentry presidents
from the middle states to the more democratic egalitarian
ones of Massachusetts and New Jersey. At least six were, if
not outright abolitionists, non-slave owners. Boudinot and
Lee were vocal abolitionists. At least one (Hanson) was an
enslaver and so possibly were two more (Griffin and Ramsay). Geographically, the nine hailed from six states along
nearly the entire eastern seaboard, two each from Massachusetts, Pennsylvania and Virginia, one each from New
Jersey, Maryland and South Carolina. Two of the presidents
were still in their thirties when inaugurated, one just forty,
three more in their forties, two in their early fifties, and one
— John Hanson — in his late sixties. Not counting Hanson
who was thirteen years older than Arthur St. Clair, the second oldest of the nine, the average age at election of the
group was forty-five, a decade younger than the average age
at election of the forty-four presidents of the second government through 2011. The personal interests of the nine
presidents of the original government spanned a broad
range including mathematics (Hanson), human rights
(Boudinot and Lee), philanthropy (Hanson and Boudinot),
university trusteeship (Boudinot and Mifflin) and history
(Ramsay). One, Arthur St. Clair, was an immigrant, an opportunity not permitted under the later Constitution. Several others including Hanson were the sons or grandsons of
immigrants.

In contrast to their disparity in geography, demography,
personal interests and observance of human rights, the nine
had a natural consistency in their patriotism to the cause of
independence and their paths to the presidency. Three had
served in the Revolutionary War as general officers, one as a
field grade officer, and two more in high administrative civilian positions in the Second Continental Congress. Hancock
and Lee were signers of the Declaration of Independence;
Hanson, Hancock and Lee of the Articles of Confederation;
and Mifflin and Gorham of the Constitution. Lee was a
delegate to the Constitutional Convention. Boudinot, Lee,
St. Clair and Griffin served in important positions in the
early administrations of the second government. All but
Boudinot, Gorham and probably Hanson were college
graduates at what today are called Ivy League universities
(in those days colleges) or from well regarded universities in
England (Griffin) or Scotland (St. Clair).

Unlike some presidents since the Constitution — Jackson,
Lincoln, Clinton and Obama, for example — there is an ab-

sence of rags-to-riches stories among the nine presidents of the United States in Congress Assembled. No log cabins here. Only perhaps Gorham and Ramsay can be said to have come from other than privileged aristocratic backgrounds, but Gorham's middle-class upbringing and public school education appear to have been comfortable, and Ramsay, who became a physician, was the graduate of two Ivy League colleges. Unlike many of the presidents of the second government who were able to rise from humble professions such as boatman (Lincoln), haberdasher (Truman), tailor (Andrew Johnson), peanut farmer (Carter) or school teacher (Garfield, Arthur, Lyndon Johnson), there were no modest vocations among the nine earliest presidents all of whom were plantation squirearchy, major international traders, physicians or attorneys.

A telling personal contrast among the nine first presidents is how they fared at the end of life. Three served in high-level positions during the Washington administration, Boudinot as Director of the first United States Mint, Lee as the first President Pro Tempore of the United States Senate, and Griffin with three federal appointments from Washington. Boudinot went on to serve in the Adams and Jefferson administrations. Mifflin and Hancock served multiple terms as their states' governors. But, Gorham and St. Clair died either poor or outright impoverished, Ramsay was murdered, and Hanson, as we shall see, would have his tomb forgotten, then obliterated, but finally rediscovered, a unique fate among the presidents of either government.

When they are finally examined, what stands out most about this group of nine is the praiseworthy collective record which they compiled as presidents under the ultimately trying circumstance of bringing forth a national government with their hands tied by weak authority. Being fettered in this way, it is remarkable that they were able to accomplish as much as they did and, in fact, give the new nation more than a semblance of the stability and identity which it craved. The nine were also handicapped by one-year terms (or less for three of them) which made it difficult for any of them to hit his stride as head of state before handing the mace of leadership to his successor, a shortcoming which became all too obvious and was rectified when the framers of the Constitution fixed presidential terms at four years in the second government.

The nine presidents of the United States in Congress Assembled may also claim an absence of scandal in any of their administrations. While they were forced to deal with rebellions, relocate the capital three times, manage an impoverished central government with scant executive authority bestowed on them, and much more, all of which were thrust upon them, their seven-year era experienced nothing like the later government-induced scandals of the Trail of Tears, Wounded Knee, Sand Creek, Jim Crow, Teapot Dome, Japanese internment camps, Watergate or Abu Ghraib. There was not a harmful president — not a Tyler, Buchanan, Hayes, Nixon nor second Bush — among them. On the contrary, the thin collective biography on these men shows them all visibly as good as the typical president among the forty-four of the second government and more praiseworthy than many of the latter group if not most. Without doubt, if these men had served four-year terms under the second government, their intellect, character, administrative talent, dedication and ability to get things done would have made some of them especially well regarded today among presidents.

But they are unknown because their brief era is little known and that is because historians, especially presidential historians, have neglected it and them. When writing of this era, historians mention ratification of the Articles of Confederation, their weaknesses, the Battle of Yorktown, the Treaty of Paris, Shays' Rebellion, the Constitutional Convention, Washington's inauguration and usually not much more. While Washington, Adams, Jefferson, Madison and Franklin had their reasons for eschewing the presidency under the first government, withholding their talents from the presidency at a critical juncture, the nine who did serve were not so vainglorious as to take flight from the heavy responsibility under difficult constraining circumstances. They served. These nine presidents are owed their due far more than they have received. How many know of these nine today? How many could name half of them? May their nation's memory of John Hanson's eight successors be reawakened.

One among them, he who set the mark which the rest of them would strive to meet, was by far their eldest. All of his biographers have stressed that John Hanson's example of full dedication of service when he could have taken comfortable and adulatory retirement, and of sacrifice of his sons, family life, treasure, health and remaining time, established a shining standard which his eight successors felt honor bound to match. If John Hanson had not set this yardstick as the nation's first president, one wonders what quality of national leader might have followed him after 1782, and what might have become of the fledgling nation. To this man, who until now has been nearly lost in the mists of time, so much remains owed by his nation.

Not For Lack of Trying

The fourth and final form of consultative or governmental body existing during the Revolutionary War or early nationhood is that which we know today, the United States as it operates under its Constitution. To launch this second stronger government, the United States in Congress Assembled put itself out of business after writing and ratifying the Constitution and seven years governing the nation.

Though it was by design a weak government which saw the necessity to replace itself with something stronger, the United States in Congress Assembled did enjoy its share of notable, nation-defining accomplishments during its brief life and a near miss which would have radically altered the course of the nation's history and probably have averted the Civil War.

The original government's first major accomplishment was simply bringing itself into existence in 1781 and avoiding any serious missteps that first year, a tribute to John Hanson, his superbly chosen cabinet and other appointees, and an attentive Congress. Over the next seven years, despite its chronic lack of funding, the United States in Congress Assembled administered and built the nation's government, shepherded the new nation-state onto the international stage, and produced two, almost three, key undertakings which profoundly shaped the nation's and the successor government's future. The most critical of these was giving birth to the Constitution of the United States.

The first government's other key accomplishment was passage of the Northwest Ordinance in 1787 which took John Hanson's 1781 nation-saving success in solving the western lands conundrum and gave it codified bolstering by outlawing slavery in the Northwest Territory and any states to be created from it. Underground Railroad historian Owen Muelder states that "[H]ad it not been for the Northwest Ordinance, Illinois and Indiana, because their southern regions were settled first by Euro-Americans, would have been slave states."

The Northwest Ordinance was a form of compromise from an earlier nearly successful attempt to enact a much broader ban on slavery. In 1784 during the administration of President Thomas Mifflin, the ultimately conflicted Thomas Jefferson, not yet willing financially or for his own comforts to part with his slaves but believing that the continuation of slavery tainted the new nation's professed ideals and posed a long-term national threat, chaired a special committee of the United States in Congress Assembled charged with organizing all of the lands of the Northwest Territory and the Southwest Territory. This vast reach, larger in area than the original nation, was already beginning to attract settlers and within another decade would produce the first states after the original thirteen.

Jefferson's committee produced its plan which included a provision for the prohibition of slavery in not only the Northwest Territory but also the Southwest Territory which a few years hence would become the states of Tennessee, Kentucky, Alabama and Mississippi. Had this plan passed, almost certainly it would have meant that slavery would at most have been confined to the six eastern seaboard states below the Mason-Dixon Line and could not have seeped across the Appalachians or later beyond the Mississippi River when territories were organized west of there after the purchase of the Louisiana Territory in 1803. The plain choice laid before the Congress was one of either containing slavery within its 1784 southern coastal-state boundaries or opening the door for its national expansion with no western bulwark to stop it. The Jefferson Plan *was defeated by a single vote* in the Congress putting the United States on an unstoppable transit to the Civil War. Jefferson immediately saw the full import of this failed vote in his anguished lament when he wrote, "Thus we see the fate of millions unborn hanging on the tongue of one man, and heaven was silent in that awful moment."[203] Here in a raw example of the nation's torn soul on slavery, Thomas Jefferson, he of the enslaved common law African-American wife Sally Hemings and their enslaved children[204], grieved the lost chance to abolish slavery and to give uncompromised life to the soaring ideals he had penned in the Declaration of Independence eight years before.

Three years later in 1787, the Northwest Ordinance was a fashioned compromise which did manage to prohibit slavery in the six states to be formed from the Northwest Territory, but was followed the next year with a Constitution which fatally sidestepped the issue of slavery except to exacerbate it by legislating that enslaved Americans were to be counted as three-fifths of a human being and then only for purposes of apportionment for white representation in the new House of Representatives.

One might ask why the new nation simply did not keep the government it had already launched with remediating amendments to the Articles of Confederation, rather than undertaking a wholesale replacement of its governing charter. As one group of historians has explained, "During the quarrel with Britain, Americans had talked ardently of the rights of man, of government by consent of the governed, and of no taxation without representation. But the problem of giving reality to these ideas by incorporating them into institutions of government created serious disagreements. The formative period of the republic was torn by conflict."[205] In the earlier stages of rebellion, for example with the American reaction to the Stamp Act, it was almost solely the colonies' aristocrats who led among the voices of objection to Britain's actions. But as the heady ideas of nationhood and democracy took root, the far larger numbers of farmers, small merchants, colonial tradesmen and immigrants found their own voice which quickly became a good bit more strident than that of the aristocrats, creating tension between the two groups. In significant measure, it was this crystallization of divisions between the two classes which prompted the aristocratic drafters of the Articles of Confederation to incorporate into the Articles the elevated caution which prescribed weak central government.

The drafters' conservatism was matched by that of the colonial governments and Committees of Correspondence and later by many of the state legislatures which were at first stocked almost exclusively by the upper classes. After the colonies declared their independence, their new state constitutions, drawn up mainly by the elites, reflected the resentment against heavy-handed central governing authority that the colonies had just thrown off and therefore sought to limit the powers of state governments and certainly of any new national government. In addition, because they had been written mostly by the patricians of the new nation, the new state constitutions did not go far in expressing popular will, none less so than Maryland's.

American democracy, as adopted in the newly independent states, was an entirely new system of government, not one that flowed downward from a ruler as before, but one formed by the people who, aristocrat and commoner alike, were having to chart new territory in their grand experiment, a further cautioning influence. Large expressions of caution in the new state constitutions took the form of weak executives and relatively much stronger legislatures. As an example, all but one of the thirteen new state constitutions denied veto power to governors. Further, despite broadened suffrage compared to what had existed before independence, the new state constitutions were far from what is thought of today as democratic. Typical was Maryland's in which to be qualified as a voter one still had to be, as in the days of the proprietors, white, male and have at least a fifty-acre freehold or a £30 estate.

While the Articles of Confederation did create much of the lasting structure and trappings of a national government, they omitted what early on came to be seen as critical ways and means of a government. When it was born on November 5, 1781, the new nation was granted sole authority, reserved to it and not to any state, to make treaties, send and receive ambassadors, declare war, regulate the value of coinage, fix national standards of weights and measures, and regulate post offices and postal weights. But, as we have seen, the new national government had no sources of income, no taxing authority, no ability to draft men in time of war or national emergency, no disciplinary authority over lawbreakers and no control over national commerce. Furthermore, the government lacked any enforcement or even coercive authority.

Outside its limited role vis a vis the states, the original national government's legislation was too often only persuasive rather than authoritative, its judicial power improvised and only vaguely defined, and, most problematical, its executive power weak. President Hanson and his successors could order, proclaim, direct or manage little and their role was often merely ceremonial compared to that of presidents of the second government. For the most part, the responsibility of the presidents of the United States in Congress Assembled was to carry out the acts of Congress without acting on their own. President Hanson's official letters show him frequently transmitting circular letters to the state governors[206] announcing acts of Congress to which the states were requested, rarely ordered, to comply. A good bit of presidential correspondence during this time was communication of Congressional commendations of individuals. The seven Congresses of the United States in Congress Assembled did have the bulk of authority over the nationalized army and navy, and assumed responsibility for granting military promotions down to the level of Army Major. Notification of these promotions was also by official presidential letter.

As it became obvious that tying the hands of the presidents weakened the prospects of effective government and therefore of healthy nationhood, sentiment built to correct the shortcomings. As we have seen, the most crippling feature in trying to accomplish this was that the Articles of Confederation could not be amended to correct the Articles' deficiencies except by the consent of all of the states, a virtual impossibility which, in fact, never happened during the seven-year life of the first government. As we have also seen, John Hanson encountered this straight away in the first month of his administration when he and the Congress submitted to the states for ratification the Impost Amendment to the Articles calling for a modest duty on imports to finance the new national government. This measure came as close as any attempt to amending the articles, gaining twelve states' approval within a month, but not the all-important thirteenth vote required. Not a single proposed amendment to the Articles ever succeeded, locking the nation into hobbled governance which a strong frustrated majority wanted to improve but couldn't.

This deliberately constricted form of national government is what John Hanson inherited in November 1781 and within which he, his presidential successors and their administrations had to operate as best they could. During the 1780s, the critical period as John Quincy Adams aptly called it, it became increasingly evident that in their caution to preserve the states' rights and perquisites the Articles of Confederation had been written so restrictively as to hamstring national governance and therefore national development.

By 1786 the deleterious effects of limited central government, long apparent to the states' delegates to the United States in Congress Assembled, had reached a point where frustration finally prompted action. Once more it was Maryland and Virginia which took the lead when they urged that the Congress take stronger action to remedy the hobbling shortcomings of the Articles. The delegates of the two states moved that the Congress call together an all-states convention to explore ways to improve upon the Articles. Once again as he had been called on to do in 1776 in drafting the Articles of Confederation, Delegate John Dickinson a decade later was charged to lead the effort to improve upon the Articles.

Upon assembling the convention, Dickinson encountered the incandescent minds of James Madison and Alexander Hamilton who would take the meeting in an entirely different direction. Influenced primarily by Hamilton, the gifted, indefatigable and self-serving British Caribbean orphan immigrant who had been one of Washington's closest *aides de camp* in the war, delegates from five states met in Annapolis for a fast-paced and highly consequential three days in September 1786, ostensibly to discuss problems of interstate commerce in what was laboriously called the Meeting of Commissioners to Remedy Defects of the Federal Government which came to be known more simply as the Annapolis Convention.   However, their discussion was shunted by Hamilton, Madison and others away from just commerce — the precise and only charge from the Congress — and the delegates found themselves instead absorbed by the failure over the preceding five years of gaining the required unanimous approval of the states to amend the Articles of Confederation permitting the central government to raise its own operating revenues.   Primarily on the urging of the brilliant Hamilton, not yet thirty, the gathering recommended to the Congress that it convene a new commission from all of the states to amend the Articles of Confederation to better suit the needs of the nation.

The Congress agreed and called on the states to choose delegates to attend a convention the following year "for the sole and express purpose of revising the Articles of Confederation."   Maryland chose Declaration of Independence Signer Charles Carroll, Robert Hanson Harrison, former Governor Thomas Sim Lee, James McHenry and Thomas Stone as her delegates.   Robert Hanson Harrison was the first cousin once removed and Thomas Stone a close relative by marriage of President John Hanson.   The convention would go far beyond a revision of the Articles of Confederation.

The meeting encountered only tepid interest from most of the states.   Maryland, for example, saw all of its nominated delegates but McHenry decline to serve.   McHenry was finally joined by Daniel of St. Thomas Jenifer, Daniel Carroll, John Francis Mercer and Luther Martin. Jenifer was the husband of the president's niece, Elizabeth Hoskins Hanson Jenifer.

Rhode Island, mired in obstreperousness, sent no delegates at all to the Convention, in effect boycotting it. Of the twelve states which did appoint delegates, only fifty-five of the seventy-three designated attended the convention.   Some who did were so disinterested that all that remains of their participation are their perfunctory signatures.   Others were interested but their modest abilities did not make them good material for revising the government's charter.   But a providential core among the rest of the delegates comprised a rare assemblage of genius who would author one of the best conceived national documents which the world was ever to see.

Scheduled to convene on May 14, 1787, too few delegates appeared to conduct business. As more dribbled in over the next few days, the organizers decided to proceed despite small numbers and on May 25, 1787, the Constitutional Convention, as it came to be known, first met and right off disposed of the mandate merely to revise the Articles of Confederation. Instead, over the next one hundred sixteen days, the Convention produced the new nation's third revolutionary document, a plan for governance under the principles so eloquently articulated in the Declaration of Independence and a wholesale bolstering of the too-tentative governing code which had been put forth in the Articles of Confederation. The United States Constitution which the Convention was to author, with its guarded but practical ability to be amended, would stand the test of time, becoming in many eyes the best conceived and most durable governing document of any nation. In many respects, it was so well thought out that in the more than two hundred years following its adoption it would need to be amended only twenty-seven times, only fifteen after the Bill of Rights if one wants to discount Prohibition and its repeal.

Realizing the import of the Convention and the imperative that it not misfire in forging a stronger government, the delegates called on the nation's most revered figure, George Washington, to preside, stamp his unmatched imprimatur on the gathering, and give it that much more of a chance of success. Well remembering his frustration with the Second Continental Congress's and then the United States in Congress Assembled's constrained abilities to help him fund and prosecute the Revolutionary War, Washington had seen again since 1781 how the weakness of the central government now called into question the very existence of the country which he had fought to create.

To Washington, the government, essentially a coordinating body for thirteen independent-minded states, was scarcely more able to manage post-war conditions than had the Second Continental Congress been able to manage the war itself. "During the initial years of his retirement, Washington made no secret of his contempt for the [United States in Congress Assembled] which he described as 'wretchedly managed', or his conviction that the Articles of Confederation were 'fatally flawed'."[207] For the second time, his nation called on Washington to assume leadership at a critical juncture, and, coming out of his cherished retirement, he did so once again, now with the motivation to strengthen his faltering fledgling nation. Washington signed on, chaired the Constitutional Convention, taking the role of moderator leaving most of the discussion to others, and had the best seat in the house as one of the most pivotal debates the nation ever had unfolded.

The Constitutional Convention concluded that September 17 with all of the states having attended except the ever-distant Rhode Island. Going much further than just amending the Articles of Confederation, the Convention instead produced an entirely new governance blueprint, the Constitution which we know today. The new Constitution remedied many of the shortcomings of the Articles of Confederation by, among other measures, providing for three independent branches of government, a bicameral legislature which more surely guarded the interests of less populous states, a far stronger executive, the ability of the central government to levy taxes and raise its own operating revenues by other means, and the joint ability between the central government and the states of amending the new Constitution by super-majorities[208] rather than unanimity. In correcting these shortcomings of the Articles, the Constitution ended up being a third longer, 4,501 versus 3,414 words.

In drafting the Constitution, the framers had theory and their own experiences to go on, and, at this critical juncture, were loath to rely much on theory. Said John Dickinson expressing the Convention's collective mind, "Experience must be our only guide. Reason may mislead us." The experiences which the Convention delegates were able to bring directly to bear were their concrete successes and frustrations with the Articles of Confederation during the previous six years and operating with their own state constitutions over a slightly longer period. The delegates had to rely on what they themselves had witnessed. It seems to be too often overlooked today that the Constitution in virtually its entirety sprang from the sharply learned understandings of the brief eleven-year American experience of the Revolutionary War and the United States in Congress Assembled.

On September 17, the Convention concluded its drafting, submitted the draft to the United States in Congress Assembled and adjourned. The draft was read in Congress on September 20, debated through the 26th, and referred out to the states for ratification on the 28th. Shunning the unanimity requirement that had crippled the ability to amend the Articles of Confederation, and taking Rhode Island's recalcitrance into account, the Constitutional Convention prescribed that ratification by as few as nine states, a two-thirds majority, would be sufficient for enactment of the Constitution. With a good deal of trepidation, this prescription sidestepped the issue of what might ensue if some states did not subscribe.

That December 17, Delaware became the first state to ratify the Constitution. Within months, eleven of the thirteen states had ratified with only North Carolina and the chronically laggard Rhode Island, three times voting not even to elect delegates to attend the Convention, holding out. The United States in Congress Assembled, setting the stage to put itself out of business, adopted the Constitution on July 26, 1788, after New Hampshire, the ninth state, had ratified it by a vote of fifty-seven to forty-seven.

Just as it was upon the transition from the Second Continental Congress to the United States in Congress Assembled and the vaguely defined interim between the two, there was a clumsy gap between the first and second governments. After the Constitution became ratified in July 1788, it would not take effect until the following spring as called for in its provisions. The United States in Congress Assembled continued in official session until November 3, 1788, the first Monday of the month, when Cyrus Griffin's presidential term expired. No election was held to provide for a president during the six months until George Washington could be inaugurated, and the nation, for the only time since John Hanson's presidency up to the present, had no president during the interim. The first government, or at least enough of its delegates, did remain in place to administer the elections of Representatives and Senators of the new government and to maintain an official national and international presence during the six-month gap. The generous view would be that the first government, now unselfishly having given the nation the gift of a stronger successor government, passed quietly into history upon Washington's inauguration on April 30, 1789.

From the time of the First Continental Congress, through the Second, and until the end of the United States in Congress Assembled, thirty-three Marylanders had served in one of these bodies or another including John Hanson and four of his relatives: Benjamin Contee, William Hanson Harrison

Jr., Daniel of St. Thomas Jennifer, and Thomas Stone. Several other Hanson relations by marriage served. No other Maryland family, and very few in any other state, came close to this level of representation in the three bodies.

The upper class's fear of loss of its traditional influence in the selection of the occupant of the nation's highest office prompted the Convention to adopt a system of electing the president that only one other country uses. The Constitution does not provide that the president shall be elected by popular vote but by small groups of Electors from each state, collectively the Electoral College, who, with the exceptions of two states as of this writing, customarily cast their votes in state blocks for whichever presidential candidate gained the most popular votes in a state. However, Electors may cast their Elector vote for whomever they choose and on a number of occasions renegade Electors have done so, ignoring the candidate who won their state. This Electoral College design attempted to ensure that the old gentry, having much sway in their states over who served as Electors, would have the final say, or very close to it, in electing presidents. The Electoral College system of presidential elections has been criticized ever since it was devised and has led to three presidential elections in which the candidate who did not win the people's vote was awarded the electoral vote and the White House anyway (Hayes in 1876, Cleveland in 1888 and Bush the younger in 2000). Among democracies today, only the United States and Argentina use electors instead of voters to choose presidents.

The first election under the Constitution was an unusual one. Electoral votes were allocated more or less proportionally according to estimated state populations. Rhode Island, North Carolina and New York did not cast votes at all in the election. Each of the sixty-nine electors casting votes from the ten other states had two votes, and all sixty–nine each cast one of their votes for George Washington electing him unanimously as president. Eleven other candidates split the other sixty-nine votes, each receiving at least one vote. Among the second sixty-nine votes, coming in first with thirty-four votes was John Adams who thereby became the nation's first Vice President since the office had not existed under the United States in Congress Assembled. After voting for Washington for president, Maryland Electors Alexander Contee Hanson, Sr. and his brother-in-law Dr. Philip Thomas voted for their relative by marriage, Robert Hanson Harrison[209] of Maryland. Hanson and Thomas were chosen as presidential electors by popular vote in Maryland, one of only two states to choose electors in this manner in the first election. Connecticut's Samuel Huntington, president of the Second Continental Congress at the time of ratification of the Articles of Confederation in 1781, received two electoral votes for vice president in the 1789 election.

The new Congress of the United States was scheduled to first meet on March 4, 1789, but its upper house, the new United States Senate, did not organize itself until April, and, as specified in the Constitution, it was the Senate which was to count the electoral votes and announce the winners of the offices of president and vice president. With the elections certified by the Senate when it finally met, Charles Thomson, by then having served continuously for fifteen years as Secretary of the First Continental Congress, the Second Continental Congress, the United States in Congress Assembled and now the new government, rode to Mount Vernon to inform Washington of his election. In fact, when the United States in Congress Assembled wound down after the first Monday of November 1788 when Cyrus Griffin's presidential term expired, Thomson simply continued in place on his own, acting, in effect, as the nation's sole officer.

Washington's journey to New York, the nation's capital at the time, amounted to a triumphal procession for this most respected of all Americans. In town after town, city after city, he was greeted by throngs, speeches, well-wishers and outright adoration. On April 30, 1789, John Hanson's fellow nation-builder George Washington — his very old neighbor, friend, confidant and general — was inaugurated at New York City's Federal Hall on Wall Street as the nation's first president under the Constitution, and, to be historically precise, as the nation's *second* first president and tenth overall. By their sublime partnership during the Revolutionary War, the two first presidents had done as much as any duo to deliver the safe birth of their nation, one as political rescuer, the other as military master.

When the Hansons still resided at Mulberry Grove, John Hanson and George Washington had visited each other's homes beginning probably in the 1750s when Washington was in his twenties, Hanson in his forties, and in their talks planted the seeds of independence and nationhood. In the 1770s and 1780s, they as much as any brought forth a nation. What an anointed relationship fate thrust upon the two men, certainly to their nation a supremely providential friendship. It had been Hanson who had come to the aid of

Washington in Massachusetts at the outbreak of war sending him his first companies of reinforcements. It had been
Washington who had inspired these impoverished soldiers to
keep fighting while Hanson broke through the western lands
impasse to permit formation of a government and actual union among the states. Upon his inauguration, it would be
hard to imagine that the new President Washington did not
reflect intently upon his old friend Hanson, then in his grave
nearly six years, and all that the nation's first president had
done to usher the United States into being. Washington
would have been grateful for the brighter presidential prospects which he had been dealt than those under which Hanson had had to labor: a four-year term, a much stronger
government, executive authority and the adoration of his
countrymen. These advantages would shift posterity from
Hanson to Washington who before long would in error be
called the first president.

The Deepest Shadow:
Washington's Long Tenure at Center Stage

An account of John Hanson and his era would not be complete or in sure context without an examination of the pre-
dominant figure of Hanson's time and later. By 1789,
George Washington had been called on to guide the nation
at three of the five most critical junctures in the birth of the
United States: by the Second Continental Congress in 1775
to command the army, by the United States in Congress Assembled in 1787 to chair the Constitutional Convention, and
by the Electoral College in 1789 to lead the nation as its first
president under the Constitution. At the two other critical
moments, it was John Hanson in 1781 who had been
tapped as the nation's first president and Thomas Jefferson
in 1776 as the prime author of the Declaration of Independence.

There is historical consensus today, as in his own era, that
George Washington rose above all other Americans in regard
from 1775 when he assumed command of the Continental
Army until his death in December 1799. As Washington biographer Joseph J. Ellis has put it, ." . . Benjamin Franklin
was wiser than Washington; Alexander Hamilton was more
brilliant; John Adams was better read; Thomas Jefferson
was more intellectually sophisticated; James Madison was
more politically astute. Yet each and all of these prominent
figures acknowledged that George Washington was their un-
questioned superior. Within the gallery of greats so often
mythologized and capitalized as Founding Fathers, Wash-

ington was recognized as *primus inter pares*, the Found-ingest Father of them all."[210] During a long day's worth of eulogies at Washington's memorial service in 1799, a line from his fellow Virginian Patrick Henry best epitomized Washington in the minds of many, and became lastingly emblazoned as the nation's and world's remembrance of Washington: "First in war, first in peace, and first in the hearts of his countrymen."

Lending to his stellar nation-binding accomplishments, there was sure method to Washington. One of the most dili-gent diarists of his time, Washington took career-long care to guard his image for posterity. At the same time, Wash-ington would modestly demur when the heaviest duties were pressed upon him, further prompting the three draftings into his most prominent roles, with the demurrals them-selves doing much to burnish the image which he safe-guarded. The now accepted view on this aspect of the Washington persona is that his public bearing of modesty both veiled and bolstered the adept public relations efforts of a supremely ambitious man. As Washington biographer John Ferling has put it, "But none of them, including such assiduous memorialists as Franklin, Jefferson, and John Adams, [was] as earnest in courting posterity as Washing-ton."[211] The result of the combination of his singular ac-complishments and astute image management was that no one of his era approached the esteem in which Washington was held by his countrymen. To be sure, the starting place of his fame and adoration was Washington's singularly matchless nation-building accomplishments, but his self-branding acumen is now accepted to have gone far in ce-menting his lasting appeal. While Hanson was first to vault to the highest position in the land in 1781, neither he nor anyone else then or through the rest of the century occupied a higher position in the minds of their countrymen than did George Washington.

Washington's legacy also has the pronounced advantage of the longevity of his accomplishments, with Washington oc-cupying one central position after another in the nation's founding over a forty-five-year span beginning with the French and Indian War in the 1750s. Washington's long stay on the national stage, unparalleled popularity and attentive care of his image for posterity lay in contrast to the more modest John Hanson whose contributions to the nation all occurred over a far briefer period. The time from when Han-son began raising Frederick County militias in 1775 through his meteoric rise to the presidency to his passing in 1783 spanned only a brief eight years. In addition to Washington, the other major figures of the time also lived until much later than did Hanson to establish their own posterities and thus were able put much more of themselves into the historical record than Hanson had opportunity to do. Franklin, with an exceptionally long public career begun as a printer even before Washington was born, occupied many roles and lived to see the promulgation of the Constitution and election of Washington. The voluminous correspondents and diarists Adams and Jefferson both famously lived fifty years to the day after the signing of the Declaration of Independence and, with Hamilton, Madison and Monroe, well onto the nineteenth century. Hancock and Henry lived into the 1790s and the period of the second government. All of the eight other presidents of the United States in Congress Assembled outlived Hanson, some by decades well into the nineteenth century.

While the contrasts of career longevity and fame between Hanson and Washington are plain enough, there is abundant indication of the long and lasting affection between the two men beginning probably in the 1750s as riverine neighbors to one another, through Hanson's passing in 1783, and, for Washington, beyond that in memory. Two examples of John Hanson's and his army commander's firm alliance suffice.

From his letters to Philip Thomas, it is clear that Hanson was an unfaltering supporter of Washington. From these candid letters, written in confidence to Philip Thomas, there is no indication that in their long relationship Hanson ever waivered in his friendship or in his support of the general in the conduct of the war even after Washington's error in judgment in attempting to defend Fort Washington cost Hanson his son Peter. In this steadfastness, we see not only constancy of friendship but, again at work, John Hanson's astute judgment of character. As history has concluded, so did Hanson that George Washington was the best, perhaps only one up to the job of winning the Revolutionary War on the battlefield.

During 1778, General Horatio Gates openly maneuvered through friendly delegates in the Second Continental Congress to replace Washington with himself as Commanding General of the Army. This came even after Washington had made Gates his first general's appointment in the war in 1775, given Gates plum assignments and named him as the nation's first Army Adjutant General. When Gates's perfidy was detected and then roundly put down by Washington's simple threat of resignation, Gates was shunted into a lesser position late 1778. In July of 1780, Washington transferred Gates to the undesirable command of the Army in the Carolinas. Gates then took to groveling in his supplications to Washington and the Congress to regain some position of renewed personal influence. In his letter of October 2, 1780, John Hanson, speaking of Gates's supposed repentance and clearly in Washington's corner, wrote to Philip Thomas, "How is the mighty fallen and the proud humbled."

In 1782 during Hanson's presidency, Gates was still at it when his New England supporters in the Congress came to his aid once more by quashing a congressional board of inquiry into Gates's conduct in the defeat of his Army at the Battle of Camden. On August 23, 1782, President Hanson wrote Philip Thomas that, "This will be handed you by Gen. Gates[.] Congress have rescinded the resolution ordering a Court of Inquiry on his Conduct at Camden, and directed that he join the main Army as General Washington may direct." Throughout the Hanson administration, he and Washington held Gates at bay by confining him to the sidelines on Washington's staff then headquartered at Newburgh, New York. Even then, Gates tried to unseat Washington and install a military government to replace the United States in Congress Assembled, again being detected with the Newburgh Conspiracy roundly put down. After the war, Gates, to his credit, freed his slaves at the urging of his friend John Adams and retired to Manhattan. His support of Jefferson's presidency ended his friendship with Adams. Horatio Gates served a term in the New York legislature in 1800 and died in 1806.

In the same letter of October 2, 1780, Hanson told Philip Thomas of the recent attempt by Benedict Arnold — who had already changed sides as the most infamous traitor the country would ever produce — to lay a trap for Washington by trying to lure him under false pretenses to West Point and capture. Eleven days after his inauguration in 1781, Hanson wrote to Thomas of what Hanson hoped would be Benedict Arnold's imminent apprehension and of the recent capture, trial and hanging in Philadelphia, all within five days, of an Arnold accomplice. Benedict Arnold avoided capture and died in London in 1801.

Solidly and unfailingly in support of Washington, it appears that John Hanson was not averse to burnishing Washington's image when he was too modestly unpretentious to promote his own. Throughout his official record, surviving personal correspondence and passed-down family oral tradition, there is no indication that John Hanson took any particular measures to polish his own image and no record of Hanson even keeping a diary though this could have been one of the important Hanson personal records that went missing in 1836. Beginning with the first John Hanson biography written by his great-grandson John Hanson Thomas, Jr. in 1875, Hanson's biographers uniformly portray him as a figure of modest demeanor who made his mark not so much by show, posturing or bluster as through outstanding abilities at quiet persuasion, analysis, organization, execution and judgment of character. An important aspect of Hanson's nature seems to have been shared with Washington in that both were men of action in contrast to some of the more intellectually elegant philosophers and political theoreticians who surrounded them.   In Hanson's case, there is every indication that it was because of his superior abilities to recruit, analyze, organize, persuade, overcome difficult obstacles and find ways to get things done that his contemporaries in the United States in Congress Assembled chose him as their nation's first president.

While Hanson had to have been deeply admired to be chosen, it is clear that, if Washington had not needed to remain in the field fighting the war, the first presidency in 1781, or for that matter any presidency later, would have been Washington's for the taking.   But from two months after the Treaty of Paris in 1783 until he was called back to chair the Constitutional Convention in 1787, Washington vacated center stage by retiring to Mount Vernon where for the eight years of the war he had longed to be. Throughout the administrations of the original government, its presidents and all of the other Founders worked in the long shadow of the living icon, George Washington, still eminently visible in the wings.   Not to take anything away from Washington, his iconic presence in combination with the limiting constraints placed on the United States in Congress Assembled did much to relegate most of the 1780s and the first government's nine presidents to near obliteration in the nation's memory. When historians write of this period, it is of Yorktown, the Treaty of Paris, Shays' Rebellion, the Constitutional Convention, the election of Washington and perhaps — but only perhaps — the Articles of Confederation, but rarely of the nation's original government and those who ably led it. At the same time, too many of Washington's biographers have so attentively deified Washington as to become the handmaidens of American historical amnesia.

Like President Hanson, President Washington wore the laurels from his peers for his performance as president, became worn down by the burdens of office, and died weary not long after retiring from the presidency. Unlike Hanson's, Washington's tomb, easily visited, has become a shrine.

The Historical Hollow of the 1780s

The dearth of more explicit historical study of the 1780s puzzles a number of well qualified historians who the author queried on the matter. They agree that it is unmistakable that much that was indispensible to the birth of the newly declared United States and to getting nationhood and the governmental machinery successfully up and running bore fruit in the early 1780s. In his later labeling the decade the critical period, John Quincy Adams wrote of how the future of the new nation hung in the balance in the 1780s. The decade opened with John Hanson's arrival at the Second Continental Congress in 1780 with the Hanson Plan which would finally open the door to nationhood and ended as the first government relegated itself to posterity by ushering in its more successful successor which took the stage in 1789. We have seen here some of what transpired in between, particularly in the context of the United States in Congress Assembled. With the possible exceptions of the 1860s and 1930s, there would appear to be no other decade in the nation's history in which more decisive and pivotal national configuration took place than in the 1780s.

Then why don't we hear more about the decade? Why is much of the 1780s so often glossed over in historical writing? Why are there innumerable writings on the personages and various aspects of the 1780s but little on the decade *per se*? What explains the historical inattention by a trained profession which one would think would have wanted to dig much further into Quincy Adams' fascinating and crucial critical period?

In exploring these questions, let us first examine what is usually missing in writings on the 1780s.

Despite the limitations put on it by the cautions of the Articles of Confederation, the United States in Congress Assembled may be reckoned to have succeeded as well as it could have under its constraints or, indeed, beyond what could have been expected given the limits of its powers. In its first year alone during the Hanson administration, the United States in Congress Assembled consummated the union of the thirteen states, thus completed nationhood, effected a smooth if impoverished transition to national government, began winding down the Revolutionary War, inaugurated and got far in peace talks, organized the structure of government and the first cabinet, launched the first central bank, regularized monetary exchange, formalized a national postal service, gathered disparate state militias into a national army and navy, quickly established formal diplomatic relations on several continents, gave birth to cherished national customs still observed today, saw the citizenry joyously celebrate the consummation of nationhood and the birth of government, garnered the approbation of a grateful people, and accomplished all of this amidst the strains of rapid population growth.

Succeeding administrations of the original government concluded the Revolutionary War entirely in the United States' favor, produced a lasting peace, attained nation-making diplomatic triumphs in the Treaty of Paris, more than doubled the territory of the nation, opened the rapid settling of the western lands, put down the Newburgh Conspiracy by a few of Washington's generals thus thwarting military government, shook off the brief but deep recession of 1784-85, quelled Shays' Rebellion against Massachusetts debt collectors, defeated proposals of installing an American monarchy, quashed North African piracy of American ships, three times relocated the seat of central government, far more directly grappled with the issue of slavery than did the second government for its first seventy-five years, outlawed slavery in the Northwest Territory, ushered the United States prominently onto the world stage, enthused peoples the world over with a successful democratic republic, called the Constitutional Convention, and had the courage to replace itself by creating a new stronger government which it fashioned.

From beginning to end of the first government's brief existence, these are mighty achievements, collectively amounting to a sterling record by a shackled government, and set the stage for a gathering which would produce a better blueprint for national governance. Remaining utterly unexplained is why historians, histories and history textbooks in writing on the 1780s more often than not neglect the very existence of the United States in Congress Assembled and its indispensable nation-making accomplishments, or, if the first government is mentioned at all, gloss it over as only a failure.

In concluding the writing of *Remembering John Hanson*, a

number of historians were queried in an attempt to divine the answer to the lack of attention paid to the indispensible formative national evolution of the 1780s, but collectively these astute correspondents, too, were not able to ascertain any particular reason for the neglect, or as one put it, "the glaring gap in historians' treatment of the 1780s." None asked could report any major book explicitly and comprehensively devoted to the period. Some of the hypotheses which they offered for the historical lacuna bookended by Yorktown and the Constitutional Convention are that, "when the period is addressed, it tends to be in bits and pieces," that "the era of the Articles of Confederation served as a kind of on-the-job training period prior to the establishment of the United States," that "the Articles period has been slighted by comparison to the high peaks of drama that went before and came afterward," and that "political history generally has been rather out of fashion for the last generation or so, as historians who want to make names for themselves in academia focus on race, gender, class, and other more 'populist' forms of history."

Each of these incisive observations rings true but even collectively they still do not explain the historical inattentiveness to the 1780s.

This negligence to the period may have begun early. Even in Frederick where one would think that special attention would be accorded the period in which its native son was the first president, the time of his presidency was skipped over by a Frederick County newspaper. In 1799, the masthead of, *Bartgis's Federal Gazette,* a local weekly newspaper displayed "Independence 24th Year – Federal Government 11th Year" referring to 1776 and 1789.[212] (At that time, anniversaries of events were often counted from the beginning of a year since the event rather than from the end as now.) Here, independence and the launch of the second government are bannered but not the consummation of nationhood, inauguration of national government nor election of Frederick's own John Hanson with, one would think, "Nationhood 19th year." The editors of *Bartgis's Federal Gazette*[213] seem to have regarded the United States in Congress Assembled as a kind of transitory misstep to be omitted.

The lack of conclusiveness to the questions on omission brings us back to the contrast between the relative presidential arenas in which the presidents of the first and second governments operated: the one-year versus four-year presidential terms, the crucial weak-versus-strong contrast in the relationship of the two central governments to the states, the vast gap in presidential powers and perquisites between the first government and the second, and the far different leeway accorded the two governments and their presidents by their respective charters. In comparison, the promise of the first government paled to that of the second, but this was certainly not for lack of trying by the first government or its unblemished presidents, cabinets and delegates.

One year and out versus four-year terms. One term versus, at the time, an unlimited number of terms. Central government subordinate to the states versus a strong measure of central authority. No means of bringing in central government financial support versus viable ways and means. Weak versus strong charter. Inability to improve on a flawed first charter versus a cautious but workable method of doing so with the second.

Looking at these contrasts, it becomes clear why the early presidents of the second government have been accorded the mantle of Founding Fathers but their presidential predecessors remain uncounted. As historian Owen Muelder has aptly distilled it, "Beatification of the men described as 'our Founders' obscured the accomplishments of their predecessors. The desire of most Americans, including many historians and political scientists, to glorify the founders and cast them in a romantic glow has resulted in a tendency to dismiss the Articles and that period as mere prelude to the Constitutional period."

Professor Muelder's observation of "mere prelude" would seem to sum up the evolved view of the period of the United States in Congress Assembled. But, as did the early presidents of the second government, the nine of the original United States government put their all into their presidencies, given the weak hands which they had been dealt. One might even conclude that the great strides which they did manage to accomplish under the constraints within which they had to function amounted to a collective record — year for year, administration for administration — which in many respects actually exceeded what occurred in the early administrations of the second government. In an opposite contrast, it is revealing to note that when President Hanson completed his term, he had benefitted greatly from political comity, was not fed up with politics, and had hope and not despair for his nation's political prospects. By all accounts, Washington keenly suffered the opposites as he completed his second term in early 1797.

Where one comes out in analyzing the historical mistreatment of the 1780s is that the hypotheses, contrasts and facts elaborated above are not so much explanations as symptoms of the root of the neglect of the period which is sheer neglect itself. It is high time for a good political history of what John Quincy Adams correctly ascertained as the critical decade of the United States.

Part VII

Defenseless In Repose:

John and Jane Hanson's Rediscovered Graves

The Obliteration of John Hanson's Tomb

After spending considerable time over three years researching possible burial sites of Jane and John Hanson, the
pieces necessary to solving both mysteries fell together
quickly, though independently of each other, in spring of
2011.

Certainly a primary cause of the nation's faded memory of
John Hanson is the astonishing historical misfortune that
the location of his grave was forgotten for a long period in
the twentieth century, and that the Hanson tomb, rediscovered in the late twentieth century, was robbed of its coffins
and mysteriously destroyed after the property was acquired
by a developer. This, too, had been forgotten until fortuitous discoveries in researching *Remembering John Hanson*
once more identified the Hanson gravesite and what happened to it.

By about 1930, by which time all but a few people had lost
track of John Hanson's tomb, a number of places began to
be hypothesized as his burial place. Before evaluating the
three most likely possibilities, it is useful to provide a fuller
record which disproves other sites which had been proposed.

A faint possibility of John Hanson's gravesite is beside that
of his father, Judge Samuel Hanson, in the ancient Stone
burial ground at Equality where Samuel died in 1740 while
visiting his daughter Sarah. At the time, the Equality estate
was owned by Samuel Hanson's son-in-law, David Stone,
who had married Sarah. The graveyard, which contains
only five other identifiable grave markers at this writing, is
located near the hamlet of Faulkner, Maryland, in Charles
County. There is no indication that John Hanson is buried
in this graveyard other than the remote possibility that his
body could have been transported here upon his death as
has once or twice been proposed. This graveyard lies
twenty-six miles from Oxon Hill Manor where he died and
four miles from Samuel's Mulberry Grove home. Samuel
Hanson's grave was identified in 2004 by Anne Braun who
has done outstanding work rediscovering and cataloguing
old Charles County graveyards many of which had been entirely lost to time. The small Stone family graveyard where
Judge Samuel Hanson rests is surrounded by a nondescript
farm field. The graveyard is preserved and tended by a duti-
ful farmer. This graveyard is visible on Google Earth at coordinates 38ª 26' 34.67" N, 76ª 59' 17.07" W.

Most other hypotheses as to where John Hanson might rest were diligently gathered over two years of research by Hanson writer Aldan Weinberg. In his investigations for a 2003 article on John Hanson, Weinberg came across faint suppositions of John Hanson's burial or reinterment in Annapolis, in the Contee burial ground at Oaklands near Laurel, Maryland, or in the sub-basement of All Saints Episcopal Church in Frederick.[214] In an October 3, 1956, postcard from Hanson researcher Herbert Stoekel to Mary Edelen, Stoekel wrote, "Mr. A. T. Robinson of Brandywine, Prince George's County, gave me the following: John Hanson was buried in a home graveyard beside his mother near old Durham Church, near Welcome, in Charles County. Graveyard long neglected and overgrown and difficult to get to. Some or none of the graves are not marked (*sic*)."

However, these possibilities are remote to the vanishing point when put up against the following three contenders.

When the nation's first past president died at the home of his nephew Thomas Hanson[215] at Oxon Hill, Maryland, probability is virtually complete that he would have been buried in one of three places: there at his nephew's Oxon Hill Manor, twenty-one miles away in his old family cemetery at Mulberry Grove which, however, John Hanson had not owned for fourteen years, or fifty-two miles away in Frederick where he and his family lived and his daughter Jane had been buried in the Episcopal graveyard two years before. Consistent oral tradition and a newspaper article existing since the time of his death state that Hanson was buried right away at his nephew's Oxon Hill Manor estate, a practice not uncommon at the time. One of two known remaining newspaper accounts at the time reported, "On Saturday last departed this life at Oxon Hill, the seat of Mr. Thomas Hanson, in the sixty-third year of his age, the Hon. John Hanson, Esq.: He had long been a servant to his country in a variety of employments, the last of which was that of President of the Congress."[216] (The article had the president's age wrong by five years. He was sixty-eight.) Harry Newman wrote in 1940 that, "He was interred in the ancient burying ground of the Addison family at Oxon Hill," but did not cite a source for this.[217]

The Addisons were relatives by marriage of the Hansons through Thomas Hawkins Hanson, owner of Oxon Hill Manor at the time of the president's death. Thomas Hanson had purchased Oxon Hill Manor from his in-laws, the Addisons, five years before John Hanson died there in 1783.

When a mausoleum with burial crypt on a hillside and several old burial tablets in the estate's graveyard were rediscovered in the twentieth century, it was theorized correctly that the crypt was John Hanson's tomb. When the other possibilities for his gravesite are examined, the crypt emerges as the certain burial place.

Ordinarily, the strongest clue to the president's gravesite would be the location of the grave of Jane Contee Hanson. Before Jane died in Frederick in 1812, at the age of eighty-four, she could have instructed that she be buried beside her daughter Jane in Frederick, beside her husband at Oxon Hill Manor, or at Mulberry Grove, the couple's first home where at least two of her children were buried. As we will see shortly, Jane was buried in Frederick.

The Mulberry Grove cemetery, a half day's wagon ride from Oxon Hill Manor in 1783, includes the graves of thirty-five identified souls and at least one unmarked grave but no grave of John or Jane Hanson. If either was buried there, almost certainly there would be a grave marker and record. The oldest of the identified graves are those of two of Jane and John Hanson's children, the couple's second set of twins born December 9, 1751. Elizabeth died October 12, 1753, at the age of one year, ten months; her twin John "died in infancy." Jane and John Hanson still owned and resided at Mulberry Grove when these two children died. (The couple's last child, the Elizabeth who lived with them in Frederick and Philadelphia, was their second daughter named Elizabeth. Another son who died young would also be named John.)

The only other close Hanson family relative listed as being buried in the Mulberry Grove cemetery is Jane Contee Hanson's brother Peter Contee who purchased Mulberry Grove from William Hanson on December 21, 1771. Peter Contee is listed as the occupant of a grave marked by a large horizontal tablet beside the graves of the two Hanson children. The tablet's inscription is barely legible today.

Local lore sometimes had it that this is the grave of Jane Hanson but cemetery records and a twenty-first century archeological survey indicate that it is her brother Peter who rests beneath the tablet. Beside Peter Contee's grave is a sunken depression indicating most likely a collapsed coffin and an unmarked grave. For several years until early 2010 before a list of those buried at Mulberry Grove was discovered in the process of writing this book, it was believed that the tablet grave could be that of Jane Hanson and that the sunken grave beside the tablet could be the unmarked grave of John Hanson or *vice versa*. However, the discovered grave list belies this by not listing any Hansons other than the two children. Mulberry Grove's current owners commissioned archeological work at Mulberry Grove and have considered an exhumation of the person in the mystery grave for DNA analysis, but it would appear based on current evidence that chances are very remote that this person is either John or Jane Hanson.

Another unexplained mystery of this cemetery is the absence of marked graves or names in the grave list of the six other Hanson children beside the first John and the first Elizabeth who died before Jane and John Hanson moved to Frederick.   Infant twins Anne and Mary Hanson died in 1744 early in their parents' marriage.   In their birth order, Heloise died in 1763 at the age of nineteen or twenty; Catherine died March 11, 1767, at the age of twenty-two; the couple's second son named John died March 6, 1760, twelve days short of his seventh birthday; and Grace died August 10, 1763, at the age of ten months.   It is certain that these six children died while their family still lived at Mulberry Grove but their gravesites remain unknown. One possibility is that they were buried in the now long neglected Episcopal church graveyard in Port Tobacco, a half mile from Mulberry Grove. Nearly all of the tombstones and other grave markers are now missing there. Far less likely is burial in the Port Tobacco public cemetery now underwater in the shifted Port Tobacco River. Another remote possibility is that the children were buried in the cemetery at nearby Equality beside their grandfather, Judge Samuel Hanson, but there are no grave markers there indicating this. Perhaps the most likely possibility to explain the absence of the six children's graves is that there are as yet undiscovered Hanson graves on the Mulberry Grove premises.

More than half of the identified Mulberry Grove graves are those of the Ferguson[218] family which owned Mulberry Grove for much of the nineteenth century and whose burials there range from 1812 to 1938. Eight members of the Mitchell family whose burials range from 1852 to 1902 are also buried in the cemetery.   The Ferguson and Mitchell burials overlap in time most likely because the two families are known to have been related to each other or possibly because the Fergusons continued to be buried there after the Mitchell ownership of Mulberry Grove began. In Pundt's genealogy of President John Hanson's extended family, only one Ferguson is present, Jennie Ferguson who died in 1896, wife of Frederick Stone, a great-great-grandnephew of the president. Assuming this extensive genealogy to be correct in this regard, the Fergusons then were Mulberry Grove owners related by marriage to the Hansons.

The same genealogy shows forty persons with the Mitchell surname including Walter Hanson Jenifer Mitchell, Jeanette Hanson Mitchell, John Hanson Mitchell, Robert Ferguson Mitchell and Bettie Ferguson Mitchell. The first two of these are related to President John Hanson as, respectively, his great-grandnephew and grandniece. The last three are unrelated to John Hanson. The last two establish consanguinity between the Ferguson and Mitchell families which would explain the joint graveyard.

A search of gravesites in Frederick has turned up in Mount Olivet Cemetery those of John and Jane Hanson's daughter Jane, son-in-law Philip Thomas, Philip and Jane's daughter Rebecca Bellicum Thomas Magruder, the couple's son John Hanson Thomas, Sr., and an unidentified Hanson or Thomas grave. This cemetery was not opened until May 28, 1854, and these Hanson descendants were reinterred in Mount Olivet in 1901 from the old Episcopal graveyard on Frederick's All Saints Street before the parish relocated to its present site on West Church Street in 1913.

Though not beyond possibility, it is improbable that John Hanson's body would have been taken the fifty-two miles from Oxon Hill to Frederick. The decision as to where to bury him would have been made by Jane who had accompanied the president to Oxon Hill on his fateful visit. There is no church or civil record, oral tradition or other suggestion of John Hanson having been buried in Frederick at the Episcopal cemetery or at Mount Olivet. Based on this lack of evidence, the possibility that the president rests in Frederick is virtually eliminated.

It is also possible that President John Hanson was first buried at his nephew's Oxon Hill home as reported shortly after his death and was later reinterred at Mulberry Grove or Frederick, but these remote possibilities also do not explain the lack of a gravestone or any record of burial in either place. Based on the evidence, it is highly implausible that the president rests at Mulberry Grove which he no longer owned upon his death and which has no John Hanson burial marker or record, or in Frederick where there is also no record or hint of his burial.

With Mulberry Grove and Frederick both ruled out as to the location of John Hanson's grave, this takes us back to Oxon Hill Manor and the four known remaining pieces of documentation pointing to his burial place: the two newspaper notices shortly after his death stating that he was buried at Oxon Hill Manor, Jacob Nelson's mention of this as the burial site in his 1939 John Hanson biography, and Harry Wright Newman's statement to the same effect in 1940. However, the latter two sources could have relied on one or both of the old newspaper notices, and the second newspaper notice appears certain to have been picked up from the first so, in effect, the sole extant original documentation for John Hanson's gravesite is the earlier-cited first newspaper account which appeared in the *Maryland Gazette* the Saturday after the president's passing. Bolstering this account exactly is the long and consistent Hanson family oral tradition that the president was buried at Oxon Hill Manor.

Oxon Hill Manor, another of the grand old Tidewater Maryland plantations, was established by the Addison family in 1687. By 1767, Thomas Addison had surveyed and patented a total of 3,663 acres, nearly six square miles, and named the estate Oxon Hill Manor. On March 2, 1778, Thomas's widow, Rebecca Dulaney Addison, married Thomas Hawkins Hanson, the president's nephew. Thomas's father was the president's brother, Samuel Hanson, Jr.

Oxon Hill Manor was owned by the Addison family or its Hanson in-laws until 1810, the property then passing through a succession of owners until the manor house burned on November 5, 1895. After being abandoned for a generation, 245 acres of the original estate were bought in 1927 by Sumner Welles, at the time the United States Ambassador to Cuba and later Franklin Roosevelt's Undersecretary of State. Welles built a forty-nine room Georgian-style manor house designed by Count Jules Henri de Sibour fifteen hundred feet east of the original home site. President Roosevelt was a frequent visitor, and it is said that Welles once hosted, or perhaps offered to host, a meeting between Roosevelt and Winston Churchill at Oxon Hill Manor. The mansion at one time was considered for the official residence of the Vice President.

From the time of the newspaper obituary immediately after John Hanson's death reporting that he had been buried among the Addisons until sometime in the early twentieth century, there appears to have been unchallenged acceptance that the president was buried at Oxon Hill Manor based not just on the one or two early obituaries but on un-questioned passed-down oral tradition which had diffused widely beyond the Hanson and Addison families. For exam-ple, two of the president's earliest biographers, George Han-son in 1876[219] and Douglas Hamilton Thomas in 1898[220], state that the president died at Oxon Hill Manor without feeling it necessary to be explicit that he was also buried there. In the mentions of the president's passing by several members of Congress in the ceremony placing the John Hanson statue in National Statuary Hall in 1903, there is no mention of or wondering about his burial place.[221] If at that time the location of his gravesite had been mysterious, it surely would have been mentioned as a major historical point in this ceremony.

In 1933, the John Hanson Society of Maryland, accepting apparently unquestioningly the then long tradition of Han-son's grave at Oxon Hill Manor, commissioned a statue of John Hanson to be placed at his gravesite there, but the sculptor, Karl Skoog of Boston, died in the midst of the pro-ject which then never went forward to completion.[222]

Nothing which the author has seen suggests doubt over the Oxon Hill Manor burial site or the need for speculation over other possible burial sites until the 1930s when at least some John Hanson biographers began to wonder. In his 1932 Hanson biography, Seymour Smith tells of Hanson's passing while visiting Oxon Hill Manor but makes no men-tion of a burial place.[223] Jacob Nelson was definitive, stating that "for years" John Hanson's burial site had been a mys-tery but that it had been rediscovered at Oxon Hill Manor not long before Nelson's 1938 Hanson biography.[224] In 1939, Bruce Kremer, either unaware of the Nelson biogra-phy or in disagreement with it, wrote, "It seems possible that he was buried on his nephew's estate, as would have been the custom. If so even the exact location of his grave is lost to time."[225] During the 1930s, the Federal Writers Project reported to Frederick archeologist E. Ralston Goldsborough that John Hanson's grave had been located at Oxon Hill Manor which Goldsborough then confirmed. In his 1940 history of the Hanson, Edelen and Dent families, Harry Newman states flatly that, "He was interred in the ancient burying ground of the Addison family at Oxon Hill."[226]

Thus we see that sometime after the turn of the century John Hanson's gravesite began to be thought of by some as a mystery. By the time of the Great Depression, Newman continued to accept the oral tradition that Oxon Hill Manor was the site, Smith seems to assume the same by not mentioning a site, to Kremer it had been lost to time, and to Nelson and Goldsborough it had been lost and rediscovered. (It would have been most helpful if Nelson could have provided the basis on which he understood that there had been a rediscovery.) Certainly, the prime reasons why doubt arose are the lack of burial documentation and of a marker of John Hanson's gravesite. When biographies a century and a half after a subject's death get put into the works, their writers look for something as basic as proof of the whereabouts of a gravesite, and if they can't find any, are then prone to speculate. Thus a mystery is born where none was considered to have existed before.

In his 1939 John Hanson biography, Jacob Nelson wrote, "After the search for years for this precious sepulchre it has only recently been found in Prince George's County on the estate of the Honorable Sumner Welles, Undersecretary of State, at Oxon Hill, not far from the scene of his [John Hanson's] death."[227]   Nelson referred to the research by Bethesda, Maryland, attorney William Nelson Morrell who had tracked down and authenticated a mausoleum forgotten by all but a few.[228]   The sepulcher refers not to the Addison graveyard but to the family crypt found in the hillside sloping down from Oxon Hill Manor and the graveyard toward the Potomac. This crypt is known to have existed since the eighteenth century during the Addison period of ownership and to have been where the more prominent members of the Addison family were buried. Within a generation after the 1930s rediscovery, the crypt again appears to have been forgotten by all but a few and become further obscured by overgrowth.

The Welles home and fifty-five acres of the original Oxon Hill Manor, but not the Addison burial ground or crypt site, are owned today by the Maryland-National Capital Park and Planning Commission. The beautiful Welles home, formal gardens and grounds are now operated and well maintained by the Prince George's County Department of Parks as Oxon Hill Manor, a rental venue for weddings and other events.

In the 1980s as Maryland and the federal government planned an immensely large road interchange for Interstate Route 495, Interstate Route 95, Maryland Route 210, Oxon Hill Road and the Woodrow Wilson Bridge where it crosses the Potomac River, archeological surveying was performed on the Oxon Hill Manor site. As a result, the layout of the enormous interchange was replanned to preserve the newer

Oxon Hill mansion and, barely, the Addison family crypt and cemetery. The remnant of Oxon Hill Manor containing the Welles mansion is cheek by jowl beside National Harbor, an exceptionally large commercial development of several square miles along the banks of the Potomac. The Addison Cemetery, or what remains of it, lies within the development. A Google Earth photograph of the cemetery is shown here.

The Maryland-National Capital Park and Planning Commission states that the cemetery was to be cleaned up and preserved as required in the development plans which Prince George's County approved for National Harbor. The Commission points out that "There are six inscribed stones for members of the Addison family, in poor condition, and certainly more burials the markers of which have not survived." During commercial development of the site, several illegible grave tablets, the olden kind placed horizontally over a grave, were discovered and then disappeared. There are no grave markers in this cemetery for John or Jane Hanson.

The cemetery has been designated as a Prince George's County Historic Site protected under the County's Historic Preservation Ordinance. Peterson Companies, the developer of National Harbor, also signed a memorandum of agreement with the Maryland Historical Trust conferring permanent protection to the cemetery. Shortly before completion of *Remembering John Hanson* in 2011, the author visited the Addison cemetery. If Peterson Companies is required to be maintaining the cemetery, the opposite is happening. Except for a narrow path and the area immediately around the tombstones, the site is entirely overgrown with dense blackberry vines and weeds. Small trees are beginning to grow among the graves.

In April 1971 Paul Lanham, about to become president of the Prince George's County Historical Society, attended a meeting of the Society at the Welles mansion hosted by its then owner, wealthy oilman and art collector Fred N. Maloof. At the meeting, Mr. Maloof mentioned the "discovery of a burial crypt on the river cliff which he assumed to be the burial location of John Hanson known to have passed away ay Oxon Hill."[229] After the meeting, Lanham asked Maloof to show him the crypt, the interior vault of which Lanham reported was bricked up protecting the coffins inside.

Crypts are special burying places. At the time of John Hanson's death in 1783, it was the most distinguished of the Addisons who were being buried in the crypt, lesser souls in the graveyard. This, and the fact that no John Hanson inscription appears in the graveyard, point to the crypt as the burial site of a figure as prominent as John Hanson. Based on the evidence and deductive logic presented above, the author is now virtually certain that John Hanson was buried in the Addison family crypt when he died in 1783, just as oral tradition has had it all along.

In the fall of 1971, the Reverend Alan Freed, a Lutheran clergyman from Dundalk, Maryland, and the then president of the now defunct John Hanson Society of Maryland, completed an examination which he had begun that April of the refound crypt by then well overgrown by a large swath of honeysuckle. Freed determined that the underground chamber had once been capped with "an elaborate stone mausoleum," not long gone by the time of his exploration. This finding squared with oral tradition. Excavation that year of the outer crypt leading to a sealed vault produced only the bones of small animals. A newspaper account at the time states that the inner vault measuring twelve feet wide by eight high, and constructed of thick granite slabs was unsealed at that time and that a dig was taking place in the vault. Freed's later report that he was certain that he had found John Hanson indicates that occupied coffins were found in the vault corresponding with all oral tradition that they would be there.[230, 231] During his research on the crypt, Freed was told that the above-ground mausoleum had only recently been destroyed either as an ill-conceived prank by workers said to have blown it up on their lunch hour, or intentionally to eliminate a historical obstacle to development. Despite the destruction of the mausoleum, the vault and crypt built into the hillside and their coffins remained intact as of 1971. At the time, there was a flurry of press attention that the first president's tomb had been rediscovered.

Before moving on, mention should be made that the John Hanson Society of Maryland was incorporated as a membership organization on March 2, 1932, to honor President John Hanson on the one-hundred-fiftieth anniversary of his inauguration as president. The Society existed until at least 1982, had a distinguished board of trustees, and for a half century did what it could to keep alive the nation's memory of John Hanson.

Vanished Once More

Naji Maloof, son of Fred Maloof, grew up at Oxon Hill Manor, played in and around the crypt as a child during the mid-twentieth century, and clearly remembers that its interior vault was sealed at that time. In 1998, Mr. Lanham, who

seventeen years previously had been shown the crypt by
Fred Maloof, requested Susan Pearl, Historian of the Prince
George's County Historical Society, to research the files of
the Maryland-National Capital Park and Planning Commission for any reference to the crypt or the John Hanson burial. Pearl's responding research determined that the crypt
had been well documented as part of the proposed development and that, according to the developer's archeological
consultant, it had "been totally destroyed by recent grading"
as of 1987. The documentation found by Pearl indicated
that, shortly before the time of destruction, the archeologists
reported that the interior vault was *unsealed and empty.*
Pearl concluded that, "It is assumed that this structure was
the 1783 burial place of John Hanson."[232]

The questions are, who broke into the vault, when, why did
those who did so remove its coffins, what happened to the
coffins and corpses, and who then finished the desecration
by destroying the crypt and its vault? Since vandals probably would not have bothered to remove coffins and bodies,
their confiscation would appear to have been for a purpose.

From 1980 until early 1986, several extensive archeological
investigations were conducted on behalf of the Maryland
State Highway Administration by the Maryland Geological
Survey, the University of Maryland Laboratory of Archeology,
and Garrow and Associates, Inc. on the portion of the Oxon
Hill Manor property near the proposed highway inter-
changes. These investigations concentrated on the original
Oxon Hill Manor home site, crypt, cemetery and their environs. A total of 345 features and more than 300,000 artifacts were found and catalogued during these investigations.
Throughout the six-year period of the digs, the crypt, vault
and coffins were intact. In 2011, the author conducted several interviews of the Maryland-National Capital Park and
Planning Commission's Jennifer Stabler who had personally
inspected the crypt and vault in 1984 and again in 1985.
Ms. Stabler is emphatic that they were sealed and intact
with their coffins at that time.

In 1984, the majority of the Oxon Hill Manor estate, including the area researched by the State, was purchased by
James T. Lewis Enterprises, Inc. for the purpose of developing the property into Lewis's proposed PortAmerica, a very
large mixed use community and riverside commercial venture which never reached fruition. In 1986, after the State
Highway Administration had completed the archeological
work which it had commissioned to be able to site the inter-

changes, Lewis Enterprises hired John Milner Associates, Inc. to conduct surveys of eighty-two acres which included the crypt, cemetery and original manor house site located within the PortAmerica development near the highway right-of-way. These investigations, conducted for the purpose of securing development permits, were concluded in 1988. A Milner report completed in 1987 states that, "About 70 to 80 feet below the site of the plantation house, on the slope, there was observed a deteriorating brick vaulted structure built into the hillside." This report states that the structure was empty, "*had been robbed*," and "It is assumed that this structure was the 1783 burial place of John Hanson." The Maryland-National Capital Park and Planning Commission reports that the Milner firm was never paid by Lewis Enterprises for the archeological work Milner had performed.

To recapitulate, the 1985 archeological survey done on behalf of the State found the crypt and vault intact and the vault sealed, and the 1987 survey by Milner Associates found them robbed and empty. So, sometime between 1985 and 1987, John Hanson and whoever else had been interred in the crypt disappeared.

Not long after that, so did the entire crypt and its vault. A 1993 aerial photograph in the possession of the Maryland-National Capital Park and Planning Commission shows the crypt site having mysteriously vanished and its location graded flat into a parking lot. So, between 1987 when the crypt and vault are known to have still been intact, though emptied, and 1993, they, too, disappeared. For the entire 1984-1993 period, Lewis Enterprises was the owner of the crypt where John Hanson was buried. James T. Lewis, a Virginia lawyer, headed Lewis Enterprises. Later in the 1990s, Lewis's PortAmerica project ran out of funding and the property was sold to the Peterson Companies, the current owner and developer of National Harbor. Efforts to track down James Lewis have so far proved futile.

Through protection conferred by the Maryland Historical Trust and the County of Prince George's, the Addison grave-yard managed to escape destruction, though today the graveyard is a pathetic sight. When the Peterson Companies bought most of the Oxon Hill Manor property to build the enormous fifteen-hundred-acre National Harbor, the purchase severed the graveyard from the Welles mansion which was retained by Prince George's County. As part of the purchase agreement, the Peterson Companies are required to tend the cemetery which became designated as a Prince

George's County Historic Site at the time of purchase. The cemetery is situated on a high knoll with one of the best views in the surrounding area of the Potomac River. The graveyard is now enclosed by two concentric locked fences in roughly circular configurations about four hundred feet in diameter. With the exception of the immediate area of the gravestones, vegetation within the fenced area has been left to grow unchecked. The cemetery is untended despite the preservation requirement by which the Peterson Companies are bound. As of this writing, the graveyard is surrounded by commercially zoned property graded into parking lots and used as contractor staging areas in various stages of development and construction disruption. The noisy sixteen-lane Interstate Route 495, one of the nation's busiest, lies less than four hundred feet from the graveyard. One may view this forlorn sight on Google Earth at coordinates 38° 47" 51.92" N, 77° 00' 21.01" W.

The National Harbor development has caused other considerable controversy due to environmental impacts. The Sierra Club voiced strong objections in 1999 saying that construction of National Harbor would prevent forever the completion of the Potomac Heritage Trail which so far it has.[233] National Harbor was linked to a discharge of hundreds of thousands of gallons of untreated sewage into the Potomac River in 2008.[234] In its rush for commercial tax dollars, Prince George's County government has been accused of turning the formerly bucolic Oxon Hill Manor and its adjoining Eagle Cove into a county "sacrifice zone" by allowing it to be overdeveloped. Where the iconic national bird once roosted, there are now four thousand hotel rooms built or on the drawing boards, vastly boosting the County's tax base.

It is ironic to note the contrast between Oxon Hill Manor which has suffered the assaults of development, rapacity, interstate highways, noise, neglect and the destruction of the first president's tomb, and Mount Vernon seven miles downstream on the opposite bank of the Potomac, wonderfully protected and managed by the Mount Vernon Ladies Association, the property owner since 1853 and the oldest historic preservation organization in the country. George Washington's abundantly documented tomb at Mount Vernon has rightfully evolved into a revered national shrine visited by thousands every year. Even the view across the Potomac from Mount Vernon has been expensively protected. By preventing development, Piscataway Park, occupying six miles of prime Maryland riverfront directly across the Potomac from Mount Vernon, preserves the view as

Washington saw it. The large tract was purchased by the
federal government in 1961 and is managed by the National
Park Service. The contrast in how Oxon Hill Manor and
Mount Vernon, resting places of the two first presidents,
have evolved is emblematic of the gaping disparity in how
Hanson and Washington have been remembered and honored in their posterity.

John Hanson's rediscovered burial place was obliterated,
and Jane Hanson's was rediscovered by the author and
others in a mass grave. If the grave of John Hanson had not
been destroyed and if Jane had one of her own, these would
be among the most remarkable historical finds in the nation's history and stunning news events. Modern DNA
analysis would have been able to determine if the graves'
occupants were a Hanson and a Contee, and in which generation of their families the two individuals had lived. But,
the remains of John Hanson were stolen in the late twentieth century, a ghoulish fate, and the greatest of the historical insults which has befallen this neglected Founding Father, his family and his nation. And Jane's fate was not
much better.

The author's Internet search for the gravesites of the presidents of both governments turned up two lists in under a
minute showing all but John Hanson's. What happened to
John Hanson's robbed remains may yet be solved, and is
being investigated, but for now he is the only missing president, an astoundingly tragic fate.

The Rediscovery of Jane Hanson's Grave

It was well documented that Jane Hanson died at home in
Frederick on February 21, 1812. Jane, an Episcopalian,
was buried in the graveyard of the church where she wor-
shiped, the All Saints Episcopal Church which at that time
was located on All Saints Street in Frederick. She could
have given instructions to her son-in-law, Philip Thomas, or
grandson, Alexander Contee Hanson, Jr., to transport her
body to Oxon Hill Manor to be buried beside her husband
but either had instructed a Frederick burial instead or had
left no instructions which is doubtful. It has been possible
to conclusively document through church, cemetery and
newspaper records that Jane lay in the ancient Episcopal
graveyard in Frederick from 1812 until 1913 when all of the
bodies there were exhumed and reburied at nearby Mount
Olivet Cemetery so that the church could sell the graveyard
for development. For much of the twentieth century, the
former graveyard site was occupied by a Greyhound bus sta-

tion until that was demolished to make way for condominia a few years ago.

The church where Jane and John Hanson and their family worshipped was founded in 1742 at the All Saints Street site and existed until 1814, two years after Jane Hanson's death. Founded even before Fredericktowne had been laid out or Frederick County had been created, All Saints is the oldest Episcopal parish in western Maryland. In 1814 the parish relocated to a new larger building a few blocks away on Court Street in Frederick. At that time, Philip Thomas, a church vestryman, bought three pews from the old church. Records do not indicate when the original church building on All Saints Street was torn down. In 1855 the newer building was converted into a parish hall when the parish's present church was opened around the corner on West Church Street. In 1793 when Jane Hanson was a parishioner at the original church, All Saints was the site of the first Episcopalian confirmation of an American citizen, by Bishop Thomas John Claggett, the first Episcopal bishop consecrated on American soil. In addition to Jane and President Hanson, a number of other prominent Americans including Philip Thomas, Maryland's first governor Thomas Johnson and National Anthem author Francis Scott Key were members of the All Saints congregation.

About seventy of those exhumed from the old Episcopal graveyard and reinterred at Mount Olivet in 1913 were able to be identified from their tombstones which were intact enough to be read. Those with legible tombstones were reburied beside each other in the same area at Mount Olivet in their own graves with their original tombstones mounted above them. In many cases, the church could not find sufficient records in its archives to be able to associate specific names with those from the old cemetery who had illegible or no tombstones, or who had been buried in crypts unless with a marked coffin. Apparently no grave map had been kept for the old cemetery. These unidentifiable souls whose remains were transferred numbered two hundred eighty-six.

Four Hansons or Hanson relatives whose legible gravestones permitted them to be individually reinterred along with their gravestones in Mount Olivet were Jane Hanson Thomas, her husband Dr. Philip Thomas, the couple's daughter, Rebecca Bellicum Thomas Magruder, and the couple's son, John Hanson Thomas. They are buried side by side in Mount Olivet Cemetery. However, these four Hansons were brought over to Mount Olivet Cemetery not in 1913 in the mass reinterment, but on November 20, 1901, shortly after Douglas Hamilton Thomas, great-grandson of Philip Thomas, had purchased five burial plots in Mount Olivet Cemetery and paid thirty-two dollars to its president, Lewis S. Clingan, to effect the transfer.[235] The fifth plot is occupied with an unidentified person reinterred by Douglas Thomas from the old cemetery at the same time as the other four and is marked with a sizeable horizontal tablet inscribed "Unknown." Possibly this grave is occupied by Jane and Philip Thomas's first child, James, who died young and would have been buried at the old Episcopal cemetery. In 2011, Mount Olivet Cemetery cleaned the five gravestones in preparation for the installation of a plaque by the Frederick chapter of the Sons of the American Revolution commemorating Philip Thomas and his important contributions to the nation. All five of these gravestones, including the oldest, Jane Hanson Thomas's which dates from 1781, are easily legible today.

Jane Hanson Thomas died young that year and her widower Philip Thomas in 1815. Rebecca Bellicum Thomas Magruder died at age thirty-seven on October 27, 1814, of an unrecorded cause, the year before her father's passing. She left behind four young children and her husband Alexander Contee Magruder who would serve as Associate Justice on Maryland's highest court from 1844 until 1851. John Hanson Thomas, Sr. died on May 2, 1815, six days after his father's death, having contracted the yellow fever which killed him at his ailing father's bedside. In addition to his only child, John Hanson Thomas, Jr., John Hanson Thomas, Sr. left behind his wife Mary Isham Colston Thomas, niece of United States Supreme Court Chief Justice John Marshall. The graves and handsome grave markers of Jane and Philip Thomas, their children Rebecca and John, and the unknown are easily located and plainly identifiable in area MM at Mount Olivet today.

There were six burial crypts in the old Episcopal cemetery including one belonging to the Hanson family. Those interred in crypts do not have a gravestone and their coffins within their crypts are usually unmarked. That the Thomas couple, their children Rebecca and John, and the unknown did have gravestones indicates that they had not been interred in the Hanson crypt but in graves of the old graveyard.

A sketch of the old Episcopal cemetery displaying its appearance before it was dismantled shows a hillside crypt with the inscription "Hanson" carved into the large capstone over the crypt's entrance. The most prominent Hanson to have died in Frederick before the crypt was emptied in 1913 and later destroyed was Jane Hanson.[236] There is no theory put forth that when Jane Hanson died in 1812 she was buried anywhere other than in the Episcopal graveyard, and church records clearly show her as having been buried there. It is not known when the Hanson crypt was constructed but it was after the death of Jane the younger or otherwise she would have been interred in it. The crypt was constructed sometime after 1781 when Jane the younger died and before 1812 when Jane the elder died, but there are no known church or other records which reveal the construction date.

In the 1913 reinterment, either there was no gravestone for Jane Hanson the elder if she had been laid to rest in the crypt, or there was an illegible gravestone if she had been buried in the graveyard. The latter possibility does not seem plausible given that Jane the younger's gravestone from 1781 was still legible in 1913 (and remains so today). Church records do clearly show that Jane Hanson was laid to rest in the old cemetery, but do not show whether she was buried in the crypt or the graveyard. Almost certainly, Jane Hanson had been laid to rest in the Hanson crypt. At any rate, in whichever place she had been laid to rest, lack of any means of being able to specifically identify her coffin led to the situation in 1913 in which the coffin became one of the many taken to Mount Olivet for anonymous reinterment.

Mount Olivet Cemetery's well-kept records indicate that how a body from the Episcopal graveyard was interred once it arrived at Mount Olivet in 1913 depended solely on whether the body had had a legible gravestone at the old cemetery. Those with legible gravestones were reburied in ordinary graves at Mount Olivet and identified by their gravestones beneath which they rest. Those with illegible gravestones, those who had been buried in crypts with unmarked coffins, those for whom there were church records but no way to identify their coffins in the old graveyard, and those with no gravestone or record at all were buried together in a mass grave in Mount Olivet Cemetery. Those with illegible gravestones had their gravestones buried with them. Reburied, these two hundred eighty-six unidentified bodies created a burial mound about thirty feet in diameter in section MM of Mount Olivet Cemetery. The cemetery's records show a deep excavation through clay, an underground brick enclosure built to accommodate the two hundred eighty-six coffins, and an underground slate cap overlaying the edifice. What one sees today is a gentle circular unadorned grassy rise at the site. There is no marker.

A contemporary 1913 newspaper account[237] notably states that the body of Jane Hanson the elder was removed from the church graveyard for reinterment at Mount Olivet. Church and Mount Olivet records show the same. However, Mount Olivet records do not show a grave there for her. Jane Hanson either had been in the Hanson crypt with an unmarked coffin or, less likely, had had a regular grave with an illegible gravestone, over a century old by 1913. The unknown person reinterred along with Jane and Philip Thomas and their two children in 1901 came to Mount Olivet Cemetery that year, so this unknown is not the First Lady. Given that Jane Hanson is reliably listed as having been reburied at Mount Olivet in 1913 but that she has no grave marker there, the only place she could be is in the mass grave resting in close with more than two hundred of her countrymen, the mystery of her burial place at last solved. One would think that she longs to be beside her husband but is in contented peace from the closeness in rest with so many early American citizens whom she long did her part to make such. May Jane Hanson rest in peace, and may the nation which she did her part to give birth to honor her now that her resting place is known.

The Johnson crypt in the Episcopal cemetery belonged to the family of Thomas Johnson, the close friend of Jane and John Hanson, political ally, and first governor of Maryland after independence. The church's cemetery records were too incomplete in 1913 to be able to identify which body in the Johnson crypt was that of Governor Johnson. To properly place Johnson under the memorial which was erected to honor him in Mount Olivet, all of the bodies from the Johnson crypt were buried together to ensure that Governor Johnson ended up under his memorial. The Johnson grave lies a few feet from the Thomas graves and the burial mound of the unknowns. It is most fitting that a monument was erected to honor Thomas Johnson at his second gravesite. One is being considered to honor Jane Hanson a few feet away.

Ronald Pearcey, Superintendent, and C. Larry Bishop, volunteer, of Mount Olivet Cemetery deserve special credit for the many hours they have spent in complicated research on the Hansons, Thomases and their burials, and for helping the author to unravel the mystery of where Jane Hanson was finally laid to rest.

Robbed tomb and mass grave: there is no story of an American First Couple that begins to approach this except perhaps the Lincolns' assassination and asylum.

The John Hanson National Memorial

In 1943 Hanson biographer Jacob Nelson proposed that a commemorative monument to John Hanson be constructed in Frederick. It took sixty-eight years to make it a reality.

In 2009, an active movement arose to revive national awareness of John Hanson, his indispensable roles in independence and the Revolutionary War, and the accomplishments of his presidency. Current efforts involve the John Hanson Memorial Association, the John Hanson National Memorial, the planned John Hanson Institute, this biography, John Cummings' forthcoming history of the John Hanson era, correction of modern Internet inaccuracies in the Hanson record, and a permanent public education campaign to reacquaint Americans with John Hanson.

If any place should rekindle John Hanson's name and honor him today, it would be Frederick to which Hanson moved late in life and refashioned his career for the sake of nationhood. As we have seen, Hanson adopted Frederick and brought credit to the young town and county, and Hanson and Frederick forged a political bond with one another that propelled both into the historical forefront of the founding of the United States. To those now rekindling the national memory of him, it seemed fitting that it be Frederick to host an enduring and noble John Hanson landmark. If Frederick could honor with a bust before its City Hall its native son Roger Taney who brought infamy to himself by authoring the Dred Scott decision, it could certainly honor John Hanson, the deliverer of nationhood. For at least these reasons, Frederick was the logical choice where to locate a John Hanson National Memorial.

The John Hanson Memorial Association was incorporated in 2009 with the initial purpose of founding the John Hanson National Memorial. In addition to the author, the other founding directors of the Association are Hanson writer Aldan Weinberg, Professor of Journalism and Director of the Communication Arts Program at Frederick's Hood College; Judge John Hanson Briscoe, former Speaker of the Maryland House of Delegates and a descendant of John Hanson's sister Chloe; Edward Edelen, owner of Mulberry Grove, John Hanson's first home, and founder of the John

Hanson Institute; long-time Montgomery County, Maryland, civic leader Robert Hanson; and his son John Hanson, also a civic leader and, appropriately, the first donor to the John Hanson National Memorial.

The site chosen for the Memorial was the courtyard of the Frederick County Courthouse directly adjacent to the site of John and Jane Hanson's Frederick home. The County of Frederick which owns the courtyard was very enthusiastic to have the Memorial located there, and the County's Board of County Commissioners and government staff were unfailingly helpful throughout the planning and construction of the Memorial. The Memorial became a donation from the John Hanson Memorial Association to the County of Frederick which became the owner of the Memorial.

The government of the State of Maryland was likewise excited to honor the only Marylander ever to occupy the nation's highest office and legislated a matching grant which provided half of the Memorial's funding. Maryland General Assembly Delegate Galen Clagett and State Senator David Brinkley carried the 2009 legislation which brought the State matching grant to the John Hanson Memorial Association. They and the six other members of the 2009 Frederick County Delegation to the State Assembly were unanimous in support of the project. The county's delegation elected in 2010 has been equally supportive and enthusiastic.

The other half of the funding for the Memorial came from private donations raised by the John Hanson Memorial Association. Many Frederick County residents, foundations, corporations, civic organizations and even churches, retired groups and arts organizations made donations, as did others beyond the county and a number of Hanson family descendants. Special mention is deserved by the Randall Family Charitable Trust of Frederick which has been especially generous in its support of the John Hanson National Memorial.

After a nationwide competition, the acclaimed sculptor Antonio Tobias Mendez was selected by the John Hanson Memorial Association as the sculptor for the John Hanson National Memorial. Mendez sculpted the John Hanson statue of bronze and designed the full Memorial shown here. Installation of the Memorial was completed on May 20, 2011. This and other examples of Mendez's work may be seen at TobyMendezStudios.com.

Funds raised to construct the Memorial comprised the first phase of fundraising which is continuing on a lasting basis to support a permanent national public education campaign already begun to reacquaint Americans with their first president and first government, and to support the operation of a future John Hanson National Memorial visitor center. Support from readers of *Remembering John Hanson* and others is most welcome. More information on the Association and on donating is available at JohnHansonMemorial.org.

In the absence of President John Hanson's grave or any known epitaph, the new John Hanson National Memorial in Frederick, Maryland, now serves as the place where Americans may go to honor the nation's first president. Perhaps the observation of his son Alexander Contee Hanson, Sr. is John Hanson's most fitting epitaph. Here are Alexander's words which he wrote in *The Laws of Maryland* in 1787 and later delivered as a toast honoring his father.

> "During the whole memorable interval between the fall of the old and the institution of the new form of government, there appeared to exist amongst us such a fund of public virtue as has scarcely a parallel in the annals of the world."[238]

Public virtue indeed. We may praise John Hanson with the same words. The record is clear that Hanson did as much as any to give birth to a nation which ever since has been emulated the world over for its ideals of independence and democracy. Among those deserving credit for this including the much more revered American icons, it was John Hanson who was chosen to first lead the new nation as it gave birth to its government, the consummation of nationhood. John Hanson was in the very top rank among the deliverers of the United States.

May his nation's memory of him be forever reawakened.

Epilogue: Remembering John Hanson

How Hanson Faded in the Nation's Memory

How John Hanson has slipped so far from the nation's memory is owing to several causes: most of his personal papers and possessions having been lost, his Frederick home being torn down, a heretofore aging biographical record, his line of the Hanson family dying out, very confused Internet information on John Hanson, and, most tellingly, his burial place long being lost until its obliterated site was rediscovered in research for *Remembering John Hanson.* This unfortunate combination makes it not so surprising that there has been an ebbing of the first president in the nation's memory. His most recent biographies, none annotated and only one with a short bibliography, date to the 1930s. Especially clouding the Hanson record are several unfounded myths that have grown up about John Hanson in recent decades, now propagated widely by the Internet.

Personal Papers of President Hanson Lost

A prime cause of the dimmed national memory of John Hanson is that much of his personal papers and a relevant period of George Washington's diaries have gone missing. Many of Hanson's and Washington's personal papers vanished in 1836 when a historian borrowed them from the Hanson and Washington families to write a history of the official collaboration between the two men during Hanson's presidency.[239] This loss wiped out much of the Hanson personal record, though most if not all of his official record remains intact in the National Archives and the Archives of Maryland. Very conspicuous is the loss of the pages of Washington's borrowed diaries beginning precisely on November 5, 1781, the day Hanson was elected and inaugurated as president, until well into 1784, a year after Hanson's death. The diary reappeared but its pages for those dates were torn out at an unknown time. It is no wonder that these two gaps in the national historical record make it difficult to research John Hanson.

John Hanson Possessions Surface Then Vanish

In researching *Remembering John Hanson* for what happened to the president's estate after his death, only snippets of information turned up, almost entirely from very obscure, hard-to-find sources. In his will, John Hanson left nearly all of his estate to his wife Jane, with his mourning ring passing to his son-in-law, Philip Thomas, and a few token objects to his grandchildren. John and Jane's two surviving children, Alexander and Elizabeth, were not mentioned in the will. It appears that Jane retained most of what she had received until her death in 1812 twenty-nine years after her husband's, and that then the couple's belongings remained in place in their home in the possession of Philip Thomas next door. By this time, only Elizabeth survived among the First Couple's children.   The records of Philip's grandson, Dr. John Hanson Thomas, Jr., show that when Philip Thomas died in 1815, the Hanson possessions came down through John Hanson Thomas, Sr. to John Hanson Thomas, Jr., probably when his widowed mother died in 1844. (His father had died in 1815 after contracting yellow fever at his father Philip's bedside.)

When he died in 1881, Dr. John Hanson Thomas, Jr. passed the John Hanson possessions, mostly if not entirely, to his son, Douglas Hamilton Thomas, Sr. who during his lifetime sourced and purchased a number of other John Hanson items including his original Thanksgiving declaration.   The volume of what Douglas Thomas possessed indicates that he amassed the most significant collection of Hansoniana since the time of the president himself.

This regathered John Hanson estate then apparently remained whole until 1919 when Douglas Thomas died in a late-night automobile accident in Baltimore.   Douglas and Alice Thomas had three children: Douglas Hamilton Thomas, Jr., John Hanson Thomas III and Alice Lee Thomas Stevenson. Extant records show that, upon the passing of Douglas Hamilton Thomas, Sr., the presidential possessions passed to Douglas Hamilton Thomas, Jr. and his sister Alice Lee Thomas Stevenson. A portion probably also went to John Hanson Thomas III but no record of this has been found.

Upon her death in 1972, Alice Lee Thomas Stevenson bequeathed some portion of the Hanson collection which she had inherited to the Maryland Historical Society. The bequest included the midlife portraits of Jane and John Hanson, a portrait of Dr. Philip Thomas, John Hanson's letters to Philip Thomas, the president's two journals, his memorandum book, many letters of members of the Thomas family particularly during the Civil War, and a trove of other Hanson and Thomas ephemera. The Contee silver brought from Europe by the original Contee immigrant which Jane Hanson had inherited as her parents' oldest surviving daughter was not included in the Maryland Historical Society bequest and is thought to have remained in the Stevenson family.

The two daughters of Baltimore architect Douglas Hamilton Thomas, Jr. both married Silesian Counts who were brothers, Katherine Thomas to Count Matias Oppersdorff, and Rosamond Thomas to Count Edward Oppersdorff. Silesia is a non-national region of Europe mostly in Poland but extending into Austria, Germany and the Czech Republic. In 1975 Rosamond Thomas Oppersdorff donated the portrait of Dr. John Hanson Thomas, Jr., her great-grandfather, to the Maryland Historical Society.

It would appear that the bulk of the passed-down Hanson and Thomas possessions inherited by the two sisters ended up with Matias Oppersdorff, Jr. On September 17, 2011, part of the estate of Matias Oppersdorff, Jr. was auctioned by Crocker Farm auctioneers of Sparks, Maryland. The aggregate of this auctioned part of the estate was enormous, containing exactly one hundred lots comprising thousands of individual items which had either belonged to or were intimately related to John Hanson, his descendants, the Thomas family or the in-laws of them. Some of the items auctioned were John Hanson's presidential Thanksgiving proclamation, his family bible printed in London in 1760, the mourning ring which he willed to Philip Thomas, the president's personal seal stamp, the Hanson family genealogy, the family's English and, purportedly, Swedish coats of arms, an unopened bottle of port which had belonged to the president, a National Statuary Hall John Hanson medallion, and a collection of out-of-print books and other publications on John Hanson and the Hanson family.

Other items auctioned included four other Hanson and Thomas family bibles and prayer books, an oil portrait of United States Senator-elect John Hanson Thomas, Sr., the Revolutionary War diary of the president's brother-in-law, Thomas Contee, which includes historically important contemporaneous mentions of John Hanson, rare Revolutionary War era currency, a large Thomas family archive, and letters and invitations from and to Lafayette, President Zachary Taylor, Vice President John C. Breckinridge, Lincoln's Secretary of War Edwin Stanton, several Maryland governors, governors of other states, several Civil War generals and Henry Wadsworth Longfellow, among many others.

A few weeks before the auction, the John Hanson Memorial Association, the Maryland Historical Society, the author and one other Hanson descendant conferred at the Society on who should bid on which auction items for the Society's already unparalleled Hanson collection. Decisions were reached on which Hanson and Thomas items the Society would bid on. The board of directors of the John Hanson Memorial Association decided that, as any items which the Association could seek should go to the Historical Society's Hanson collection anyway, the Association would support the Maryland Historical Society's auction budget with a back-up donation if the Society's budget should become used up during the auction.

In a complete surprise to the John Hanson Memorial Association, the Maryland Historical Society bid on no John Hanson items at the auction nor even used the John Hanson Memorial Association's offered donation to do so. The Society acquired the portrait of John Hanson Thomas, Sr., one large lot of Civil War letters written to and from three Thomas brothers, boxes of photographs of the Thomas family taken in the latter half of the nineteenth century, and slave material of distant nineteenth century Thomas in-laws. Thus the entire trove of John Hanson's belongings which would have shed so much light on him and been invaluable additions to the Maryland Historical Society's John Hanson Collection was scattered to anonymous bidders and probably lost forever. The Society's change of plans in its bidding and its not fulfilling the agreement made with the John Hanson Memorial Association and the Hanson family went unexplained.

One will always now wonder what would have been revealed by what was lost. John Hanson's 1760 bible and the Hanson genealogy which it is known to contain would very likely have solved the ambiguity over his birth year and quite possibly his family's European origins. The Thomas Contee diary, which luckily was transcribed in full by the auctioneers, provided detail and context on his and John Hanson's 1776 mission to General Washington and the Second Continental Congress as earlier presented here. The family genealogy and the two coats of arms would probably have put to rest the John Hanson European ancestry dispute dissected in an appendix here. John Hanson's Thanksgiving declaration, personal seal stamp and mourning ring would have been unparalleled additions to the Maryland Historical Society's Hanson collection, rounding it out in a personal dimension now lacking.

But all of this was lost. This most recent affront to the memory and indispensible accomplishments of John Hanson, at the hands of the very institution which is the prime beneficiary of his legacy, is inexplicable. This was a failure of stewardship by an otherwise commendable institution.

Before moving on, the Oppersdorff family is worth further mention. The Oppersdorff brothers grew up in the Austrian part of Silesia in the 1930s before their family emigrated to the United States after opposing Nazism. The brothers' aristocratic father was Count von Oppersdorff of Oberglogau, Austria. An ancestor, another Count von Oppersdorff, had commissioned Beethoven's Fourth Symphony which the composer dedicated to the Count. Matias "Mo" Thomas Oppersdorff, Jr., whose estate was auctioned, was a nationally known photographer and world traveler who spent most of his career with *Gourmet* magazine. He died at his home in Matunuck, Rhode Island, on January 26, 2010, at the age of seventy-five after a long battle against Parkinson's disease.

John and Jane Hanson's Frederick Home Lost

After John Hanson and his family moved to Frederick in 1769, they purchased lots in 1773 near the corner of Patrick and Court Streets in downtown Frederick and constructed two large adjoining homes there, one the couple's residence for the rest of their lives, the other the residence of their daughter Jane and her husband Dr. Philip Thomas. After the president's passing in 1783, First Lady Jane Hanson continued to live in the Frederick home until her death in 1812. The long widowered Dr. Thomas continued living in his home next door to the First Lady until his death in 1815.

The two homes remained in the Thomas and related families until 1836. The adjoining John Hanson House and Thomas home then passed through several owners during the remainder of the nineteenth century and into the twentieth. Its last owner was the Frederick County government which bought John Hanson House in 1969 when the County began planning for the building of the Frederick County Courthouse complex on the site. The last occupant of John Hanson House was Frederick Underwriters, a local insurance agency. Former Maryland Senator Jack Derr who was employed by Frederick Underwriters in the 1970s states that the building had been reconfigured inside to accommodate offices but that many of the fine original interior features from the president's day remained intact. Senator Derr says that the building was structurally sound but in need of significant refurbishment.

As the County formulated its plans for the new courthouse, it leaned more and more toward razing John Hanson House and the Thomas home. This caused alarm resulting in the

Historical Society of Frederick County, the Frederick County Landmarks Foundation, the Frederick County Chamber of Commerce, the county's two daily newspapers, other groups and many individuals springing to the aid of the two historic homes, urging their preservation. As a result of these efforts, John Hanson House and the Thomas home were placed on the National Register of Historic Places on January 25, 1972. Later that year, a joint resolution passed by the Maryland House of Delegates and Senate requested "the Mayor and Board of Aldermen of the City of Frederick to abey the demolition of John Hanson House pending consideration by the Maryland General Assembly to restore this historically significant building."[240]   This brought a nine-year reprieve. During most of this time, John Hanson Briscoe, a descendant of the president's sister Chloe, was Speaker of the Maryland House of Delegates and kept a close eye on the matter. Though John Hanson House's having been listed on the National Register of Historic Places presumably conferred a strong measure of protection, the Maryland Historic Trust's consent to the City of Frederick to demolish the home wiped out this shield. Overriding widespread community and official State disapproval, the County in 1981 tore down all but the front façades of the homes and a very few of their external appurtenances. It is stunningly tragic that demolition of the home of the nation's first president occurred in the year of the two-hundredth anniversary of his inauguration as president.

The two historic homes just missed being saved. In his sixteen years in office, Frederick Mayor Ronald Young, an ardent historic preservationist and as of 2012 a State Senator, implemented his far-reaching vision of a restored downtown Frederick and was the moving force behind the transformation of a fifty-block area from a drab, decaying, depopulating eyesore into a superb national example of careful period restoration of an entire small-town downtown. Bert Anderson, Curtis Bowen, Donald Linton, Peggy Pilgram, Landon Proffit and others were also instrumental in this revival. Young, first elected mayor in 1973, vigorously opposed the Hanson and Thomas homes being torn down and points out that they would still be standing national landmarks and restored as well if the homes had been on City rather than County property. Young recommended an architect who favored saving the homes and was sensitive to period motif in designing the new county courthouse, but this recommendation fell prey to politics and to an eventual design which emphasized expedience and dull utilitarian architecture.

Thus a national treasure was lost. It is difficult to fathom that, while successive owners of Mulberry Grove have cherished and promoted its and John Hanson's history, that same flame of pride was absent in Frederick County government when it counted.

After destroying the two homes, the County then put up its Public Defender's Office on the site using the original front façade and one other exterior wall of John Hanson House and the Thomas home in constructing the new building. The original marble front entry stairs to John Hanson House and their wrought iron handrails remain as do the extensive adjoining basements of the two homes. The previously mentioned spring in one basement was sealed off. In a departure from the rest of the courthouse complex architecture, the exterior of the Public Defender's office was rendered in typical eighteenth century residential design which, though a significant divergence from the configuration of John Hanson House, does at least reflect the period.

Thin Biographical Record on John Hanson

Contributing to the neglect of John Hanson is the scarcity of recent or any known deeply researched biography on him. Other than the official record, there are only three sketchy biographical mentions of Hanson from the nineteenth century: a brief 1875 account of his life by his great-grandson, John Hanson Thomas, Jr., George Hanson's even more succinct 1876 distillation, and the 1898 compilation of John Hanson's accomplishments by the president's great-great-grandson Douglas Hamilton Thomas. In his early twentieth century work on Swedish Americans, Amandus Johnson wrote on John Hanson but not a biography.

Three John Hanson biographies came in the 1930s. Of these, the most authoritative, complete and erudite remains J. Bruce Kremer's *John Hanson of Mulberry Grove* published in 1938. Seymour Wemyss Smith's 1932 *John Hanson: Our First President* provides a detailed and obviously well sourced chronology of Hanson's late adult life and his political accomplishments with, however, no bibliography or annotations as to sources. Jacob Nelson's 1939 Hanson biography, also well sourced but lacking any annotation or bibliography, comes across as somewhat hagiographic. These useful books have occasionally been unduly maligned in some quarters including Wikipedia, apparently because, as the most complete of the Hanson biographies until now, they are frequently mentioned when the question of who was the first president arises, and some, neglecting to dig for the facts, have been quick to wrongly dismiss Hanson's first presidency as myth and Kremer's or Smith's book along with it.[241]

The best annotated John Hanson work is Ralph Levering's *John Hanson: Public Servant* published in 1976 as part of the nation's bicentennial celebrations. However, at thirty-six pages this commendable monograph is brief, hard to find and not cited by contemporary writers on John Hanson as often as it should be. It deserves a much wider readership than it has received.

John Cummings is preparing a history on the John Hanson presidential administration which in its early drafts appears well researched and documented, especially as to the president's American and European ancestry.

The President's Family Line Grows Faint

The four of President and Jane Hanson's thirteen children who managed to reach maturity produced a total of eighteen grandchildren for the couple. Of these, thirteen were male with five of these carrying the Hanson surname from their two Hanson fathers, Alexander and Peter Hanson, as in the following table. The five were Peter, the son of Peter Hanson; and another Peter, Charles Wallace, Alexander Contee, and Edward P. Hanson, the sons of Alexander Contee Hanson, Sr. According to Pundt's Hanson genealogy, which could be incomplete as to the president's heirs, President and Jane Hanson's five male Hanson grandchildren produced four male Hansons, three of whom were the sons of Senator Alexander Contee Hanson, Jr.: Alexander Contee Hanson III (1807-18??), James Lingan Hanson (1813-18??) and Charles Grosvenor Hanson (1816-1880). The fourth great-grandson of the president carrying the Hanson surname was James Hanson (1796-1867) whose father and grandfather were both Peter Hansons, the first of whom was the president's son who died in battle in the Revolutionary War.

Among the eight known Hanson-surnamed great-great-grandsons of the president, James Hanson's only son William lived until 1912; Alexander Contee Hanson III had at least one son, Alexander Contee Hanson IV who died in his teens; and six of Charles Grosvenor Hanson's ten children were male, all born in the 1840s and 1850s. The last to die of these identified Hanson-surnamed great-great-grandsons, Charles Grosvenor Hanson's son Murray Hanson, passed away March 5, 1918, at the age of sixty-six. (The last of Charles Grosvenor Hanson's children to die, Anne Maria "Nannie" Hanson who died unmarried May 25, 1943, at the age of eighty-four, was the donor of the portraits shown here of Alexander Contee Hanson, Sr. and his family. She gave the paintings to the Hanson Collection of the Maryland Historical Society.)

As George Hanson noted in his 1876 *Old Kent*[242], with only eight identifiable direct male descendants of the president known to exist less than a hundred years after John Hanson's passing, we see a rapid thinning of the president's line of the family. Pundt's extensive Hanson genealogy shows no direct descendants of the president carrying the Hanson surname alive today. However, the eight she has identified as above, at least four of whom lived until the early twentieth century, would seem to be enough to have perpetuated President Hanson's direct line through the time of this writing, but if they have Hanson-surnamed descendants alive today, they have not been identified.

A 1933 article cites one Walter Carpenter Young, identified as a direct descendant of President John Hanson, as having officiated at the unveiling of a John Hanson memorial tablet at Oxon Hill Manor that year.[243]

As of 1959, the John Hanson Society of Maryland possessed a short list of living Hanson descendants. Of those with the Hanson surname, most appeared to descend not from the president but from a collateral line headed by his uncle Robert Hanson through the author's great-grandfather, Frances Alban Hanson.[244] One Hanson on this list who apparently descended from some other line in the family was Brigadier General Thomas Grafton Hanson who was born in 1865, retired from the United States Army in 1919, and was serving on a national advisory council of the John Hanson Society in the 1930s. Though General Hanson does not appear in it, the extensive Hanson family genealogy mentioned shows several Hansons with first or middle name of Grafton including Grafton Dulaney Hanson, the first Congressional Page. General Hanson appears to descend from the president's nephew, Thomas Hawkins Hanson, owner of Oxon Hill Manor.

The present analysis of the descendants of President John Hanson has turned up no known direct living male descendants of his but the probability is that, with at least four known to have lived within the last one hundred years, the president has more than a sparse likelihood of having living direct male descendants as of 2011, Hanson-surnamed or otherwise. If so, they remain unidentified.

Some of the demographics of John and Jane Hanson's children and grandchildren are as follows. Only Catherine, Jane, Alexander, Peter and the second Elizabeth ever married.

Child	Born	Died	Age	Children
Heloise	1743	1763	19 or 20	0
Anne (twin) [245]	1744	1744	"Died young"	0
Mary (twin)	1744	1744	"Died young"	0
Catherine	November 16, 1744	March 11, 1767	22	0
Jane	February 23, 1747	June 17, 1781	34	2M, 2F
Alexander	October 22, 1749	January 16, 1806	56	4M, 1F
Peter	December 9, 1750	December, 1776	25 or 26	1M, 0F
Elizabeth (twin)	December 9, 1751	October 12, 1753	22 months	0
John (twin) [246]	December 9, 1751	1751 or 1752	"Died young"	0
John[247]	March 18, 1753	March 6, 1760	6	0
Samuel	August 25, 1756	June 29, 1781	24	0
Grace	September 19, 1762	August 10, 1763	10 months	0
Elizabeth[248]	1772	1825	52 or 53	2M, 6F

In several known twentieth century events honoring John Hanson to which his descendants were invited, all both male and female bore a surname other than Hanson. These particular descendants appear to derive from one of two lines: through the president's daughter Jane and her husband Dr. Philip Thomas, and through the Thomas couple's great-grandchild, Douglas Hamilton Thomas; or the aforementioned line from the president's uncle Robert Hanson through Francis Alban Hanson to the author and others.

Modern Misinformation and Myths About John Hanson

Partly because most of John Hanson's personal papers were lost and his biographical record is sparse, but also to an extent because of confusion over the two early national governments, quite a bit of modern disinformation concerning John Hanson and his official record has come about, most of it only in the past decade. Following are some of the elements of this disinformation and their sources when known, the fourth cause of the nation's faded memory of President John Hanson.

Wikipedia

Today, the worst of the distorted record on John Hanson are Wikipedia's Internet entries entitled John Hanson and another, John Hanson Myths, both heavily suffused in historical inaccuracies.[249] For the uninitiated, Wikipedia is an Internet web site purporting to be an encyclopedia. Wikipedia entries may be made or edited by anyone and often are not well vetted for accuracy. Because of the ubiquity of Wikipedia, Internet searches on a very wide variety of subjects often turn up Wikipedia's entry, accurate or not, as the top search hit.

Exemplifying its notoriety for posting inaccurate history, the Wikipedia website incorrectly lists the three men elected as presidents of the 249-day interim body in 1781 not just as United States in Congress Assembled presidents but as the first three of the first government, clearly disproven earlier here. For this reason and for other errors sown by Wikipedia concerning John Hanson, it is most unfortunate that the site's confused entry on John Hanson finishes high, even at the top, in Internet searches on John Hanson.

Since Wikipedia's first posting of its John Hanson article on November 23, 2001, the entry had been edited over 500 times by at least 285 different "editors" as of 2011, an average of more than once a week. Some of those who edited the John Hanson entry go by the names Smackbot, Soltak, Viper Daimao, Cluebot, Hermit, Icewedge, Isomorphic, Closed Mouth, Jack of Oz, Snowolf, Discospinster, Obi Wan Kenobi and worse. Looking at the entire history of Wikipedia's John Hanson article entries and edits, one finds no indication whatsoever of any input by Hanson scholars or actual historians.

How Wikipedia's John Hanson article came about and has evolved is typical of the site and the reason why teachers and college faculty now routinely prohibit their students from quoting Wikipedia sources in term papers, theses, dissertations and other work. Snopes.com's entry on John Hanson, apparently picking up on Wikipedia and other erroneous sources, is, if anything, even more misguided. As of this writing, there is effort underway by the John Hanson Memorial Association to correct entries on John Hanson at Wikipedia, Snopes and other websites.

"Third (or Fourth) President"

Typical of the kind of error found at Wikipedia, and especially misleading, is the Wikipedia contention that John Hanson "was the third presiding officer of the Congress of the United States, and he considered himself a successor to the first two men to hold the office, Samuel Huntington and Thomas McKean."[250] This short phrase is shot through with falsehood. First, the Congress of the United States did not exist until 1789 when government under the Constitution came into being six years after Hanson's death. Second, Samuel Huntington and Thomas McKean were the first and third presidents of the virtually powerless interim body which existed for 249 days in 1781 before the election of the first government which was not yet in existence when Huntington and McKean served as presidents for a few weeks each before resigning. Hanson was president of a different body than were Huntington and McKean. Third, the record shows that this is certainly how Hanson, Huntington, McKean and others in 1781 and later saw it.

"Caribbean Immigrant"

Two genealogists and a few amateurish twenty-first century bloggers have confused President John Hanson's namesake grandfather with a John Henson (*sic*) who immigrated to Maryland from Barbados as an indentured servant in the 1660s several years after President Hanson's well-connected grandfather John Hanson appears in colonial records. President Hanson's European family lineage before his grandfather is uncertain and contested, but it is proven later here that the immigrant John Hanson could not have been the Caribbean John Henson. See the appendices here on John Hanson's ancestry which clearly demonstrates that President Hanson did not descend from the Barbados immigrant John Henson.

"First Black President"

Picking up on the Barbados immigrant yarn, the comedian Dick Gregory hypothesized that the Caribbean immigrant Henson was black or part black, that President John Hanson was this immigrant's grandson and, ironically using the one-drop rule, that Hanson was therefore the nation's first black president. Hanson family descendants would be proud if this were true, but it is the most fallacious and easily disproven myth about John Hanson.

"The Two-Dollar Bill"

Gregory and others spin further by purporting that one of the individuals shown on the back of the two-dollar bill is African-American and therefore John Hanson. The back of the bill shows an engraving of the signing of the Declaration of Independence. John Hanson was the key Signer of the Articles of Confederation but was not a Signer of the Declaration of Independence.

"Signer of the Declaration of Independence"

Simple inspection of the signed Declaration of Independence shows that John Hanson was not a signer. On August 2, 1776, when the Second Continental Congress delegates signed the Declaration of Independence ratifying it, Hanson was not yet a Maryland delegate to the Second Continental Congress which authored the Declaration. Five years later, he was a signer — and the key signer at that — of the Articles of Confederation when he was a Second Continental Congress delegate. However, some Internet posters, weak on their United States history, have incorrectly listed John Hanson as a Signer of the Declaration of Independence, not even mentioning the Articles of Confederation.

"Jane Hanson Outlived All of Her Children"

On this, one virtually always sees that Jane and John Hanson had twelve children and that when Jane died in 1812 she had outlived them all. The couple actually had thirteen children including two sets of twins, and Jane was survived only by her youngest child, Elizabeth Adrianna Adolphus Hanson Floweree, who lived until 1825. The likely reasons for the miscounting of the children are that all of the twins died in infancy or early childhood, and that two of them, John and Elizabeth, had later-born siblings, including Elizabeth Floweree, named for them. Elizabeth and Daniel Floweree had eight children at least two of whom were born before their grandmother Jane died.

Most Prevalent Muddle: Two National Governments and Two Consultative Bodies

Easy-to-debunk myths aside, what has led to much modern misinformation about John Hanson and his role in national government, as we have seen, is the confusion surrounding the four successive national bodies that were consultative arrangements among the colonies before and during the Revolutionary War or actual governments afterward, all existing in the short fifteen-year span from 1774 to 1789. As demonstrated earlier here, only two of these were governments, and John Hanson was the first president of the original government, the United States in Congress Assembled.

We have seen how some, even in its day, confused the United States in Congress Assembled with its predecessor body, the Second Continental Congress, which did not function as a government. Further, the First Continental Congress and the interim body, though powerless and existing for only twenty-one and two hundred forty-nine days respectively, nevertheless became widely confused with the other bodies of the era then and since.

For example, the nation saw the Second Continental Congress and the interim body, both consultative, and then the first government, the United States in Congress Assembled, in existence and two of these entities go out of existence all in an eight-month period in 1781. This must have confused many people of the time and certainly does today. A clear delineation of the bodies, the reasons for the creation of each and the means of transition from one to another have been detailed here.

Δ

So John Hanson's family line has died out, much of his personal papers are missing, his biographical record until now is thin and misinterpreted, John Hanson House no longer stands, the Internet sows wild misinformation on the president, he escaped an attempt in 2011 to remove his statue from National Statuary Hall, and until the completion of the John Hanson National Memorial in 2011, the nation had no place to honor John Hanson. These are tragic turns for the man to whom, at the birth of his country, our nation's founders and early heroes looked to lead them and to symbolize their new nation, the man the young nation's stellar array of leaders thought best for the job, the one to whom as Commander In Chief they had Washington report. Reading the Hanson record, it is conspicuous that one does not find criticism but only gratitude and high praise for Hanson from his contemporaries. In his long political career, John Hanson seems to have altogether avoided any major personal controversy other than from the British perspective. It is difficult to fathom the coincidences of history that have nearly obliterated the legacy of one who as much as any other deserves our lasting gratitude for his pivotal role in founding the United States and being the first to lead it.

Four Centuries of Public Service

Before concluding with how the first president has been memorialized past and present we pause to recount the long legacy of high public service and social prominence which the president inherited, lived himself, and passed on to generations of his descendants. We keep in mind that with the early deaths of so many of his children, the president hadn't many descendants who lived to produce their own. However, the few there were lived up to the family legacy established by their immigrant forebear, his son Judge Samuel Hanson and Samuel's son, President John Hanson. The heritage of Hanson public service begun with the immigrant John Hanson in the seventeenth century reached its apogee with his namesake presidential grandson in the eighteenth, was continued by the president's son and grandson, the two Alexander Hansons, in the nineteenth, and by the president's great-great-grandson Douglas Thomas into the twentieth century.

This legacy of public service continued after President Hanson with a United States Senator, a member of the House of Representatives, two presidential electors, a Chancellor of Maryland, a United States Centennial Commissioner, a Maryland Centennial Commissioner, the United States Congress's first Page, a bank president, two publishers and several of the nation's most distinguished families marrying into the Hanson family. Altogether, we see a family which contributed heavily and continuously to the public welfare first of the Maryland colony and then of the state and of the nation during the seventeenth, eighteenth, nineteenth and twentieth centuries over a series of eight generations.

It is not an exaggeration to say that only a few other families in the history of the United States have a record of public service to match that of the Hansons over so long a period. While history keeps illuminated the Adamses, Cabots and Kennedys of New England, the Washingtons, Randolphs, Lees and Marshalls of Virginia, the Roosevelts of New York, and other families, it borders on the out of the ordinary that the Hansons have become so overlooked.

Jane Hanson

As with all of her American compatriots, Jane Hanson was swept along in the amazing tide of history that was the plantation age, the Revolutionary War, independence and finally nationhood and beyond. She was born in the age of the Maryland proprietors and died as the War of 1812 began.

During her lifetime, her nation came into being, her husband served as its first president, her son occupied some of the highest legislative and judicial positions in Maryland, the Constitution bolstered her country, further importation of slaves into the United States was outlawed, her son and son-in-law were George Washington electors, a vaccine against smallpox was discovered, a permanent national capital was established, the Treaty of Paris doubled the size of the United States, the Louisiana Purchase doubled it again, and Lewis and Clark mapped the continent all the way to its western ocean. Four years after her passing, her grandson would become a United States Senator.

A separate work on Jane's distinguished family, the Contees, would be justified, lengthy and fascinating. Aside from her royal French ancestry and high-ranking English forebears examined in an appendix here, Jane Contee Hanson's American family occupied a number of important political positions from the earliest days of the Maryland colony through the end of eighteenth century. As one example, her nephew Benjamin Contee served as a Maryland delegate to the United States in Congress Assembled in the 1787-1788 term and then as Member of the United States House of Representatives in its first term from 1789 to 1791 after which he ordained as an Episcopal priest. Benjamin's mother, Sarah Fendall Contee, Jane's sister-in-law, was the great-granddaughter of Josias Fendall, the earlier mentioned first Governor of the colony of Maryland from 1658 to 1660.

In an age when women had practically no way to make their own mark on society aside from through their husbands, Jane Hanson lived far more than a life of devoted wife, mother and daughter and being at the side of John Hanson for the thirty-nine years of their marriage. Jane Hanson was called on to sacrifice more than most, giving up her comfortable life at Mulberry Grove to move to the frontier, starting anew in Frederick County which only shortly before her arrival had been ravaged by Indian raids, losing two sons to war and then outliving all but one of her other children, watching the family fortune ebb, having her husband away for long periods, and living out the last twenty-nine years of her life as a widow.

Certainly, aside from her family, the highlight of Jane Hanson's life was the thoroughly unexpected role of serving as the nation's original First Lady. Despite her long service and sacrifices for her nation, Jane Hanson, like her husband, has slipped into virtual anonymity, her gravesite unknown until rediscovered in 2011. To her, her nation also owes a debt of gratitude and renewed recognition.

Alexander Contee Hanson, Sr. and His Descendants

Alexander Contee Hanson, Sr. was the only son of President and Mrs. Hanson to survive beyond the Revolutionary War. Alexander Hanson attended the College of Philadelphia, later studied law in Annapolis, and was admitted to practice in the Provincial Court, the Frederick County Court and the Charles County Court in 1773, and to the Prince George's County Court in 1774.

In 1775 Alexander was appointed with the rank of Colonel as Assistant Private Secretary to General Washington, reporting to his cousin, Colonel Robert Hanson Harrison, Washington's Chief Secretary. In 1776 Alexander had to resign his commission, having lost his health from exposure in a violent rain at the battle of Brandywine. He was taken by Washington to a farmer's house where Washington insisted that Alexander take the only bed available. Washington slept on the floor as did Alexander Hamilton in a corner. Of Hamilton, Colonel Hanson would later say that he "never saw a man look so like a cat."[251]

After his war service as George Washington's private secretary and *aide-de-camp*, Alexander Hanson returned to Frederick and compiled a career nearly as distinguished as his father's.

Alexander Contee Hanson, Sr. was a member of the Annapolis Convention from Frederick County for the first session in 1774, and in 1774 and 1775 was elected to the Committee of Observation of Frederick County. Alexander then served as the first Clerk of the Maryland Senate in 1777 and 1778. From 1778 to 1789 he served as the first judge of Maryland's General Court, the state's highest.

Alexander Contee Hanson authored *The Laws of Maryland* in 1787, compiled a volume of Maryland testamentary laws published in 1798, and authored numerous well-read political pamphlets urging adoption of the new form of government under the Constitution, writing under the pseudonym Aristides. He was an articulate supporter of the ratification of the United States Constitution and served as a delegate to the Constitution Ratification Convention held in Annapolis in 1788. In 1789 and in 1793 he was a presidential elector from Maryland, both times casting his vote for George Washington.

In 1789 the president of the new government, Alexander Hanson's old family friend, George Washington, offered Hanson a seat on the United States Supreme Court. However, at the same time the State of Maryland asked Hanson to assume the chief justiceship of the Supreme Chancery Court of Maryland. Alexander Contee Hanson served as Chancellor of the State of Maryland from 1789 until his death by stroke on January 16, 1806, at age fifty-six. The office of Chancellor was a holdover from the English office of colonial times and functioned as the chief justice of equity courts. A Maryland chancery or equity court was one authorized to apply principles of equity, as opposed to law, to cases brought before it. Decisions of the state's equity courts were not precedent-setting. Equity courts existed in Maryland side by side with courts of law and handled lawsuits and petitions requesting remedies other than damages, such as writs, injunctions, and specific performance. United States bankruptcy courts are an example of federal courts which operate as courts of equity. Except in five states, equity courts were eventually merged with courts of law. The High Court of Chancery of Maryland ceased to exist on June 4, 1854.[252] As Chancellor of Maryland, Alexander Contee Hanson was also charged with being the keeper of the Great Seal of Maryland.

Alexander Contee Hanson served on the Board of Visitors of St. John's College in Annapolis and at one time as the college's president.

As a judge, Alexander Contee Hanson gained a degree of notoriety by handing down what must be one of the most draconian sentences ever levied by an American court. As Frederick author and historian John Ashbury describes it, "Those loyal to the crown of England during our war of independence faced almost certain death. In February of 1781, the 'Associated Loyalists of America' was formed with the expressed purpose 'of annoying the seacoasts of the revolted provinces and distressing their trade.' Many men loyal to King George III were enlisted in the organization with a royal commission to rob and murder inhabitants. A disguised British officer was to meet a messenger at a designated place in Frederick 'to put him in possession of all the plans relating to the conspiracy.' A watchful patriotic soldier in civilian garb was standing in the designated place at the appointed time and was given the plans, thus revealing them and the men involved locally. Among those arrested were seven Fredericktonians: Peter Suemans, Nicholas Andrews, John George Graves, Yost Plecker, Adam Graves, Henry Shett and

Casper Fritchie. At their July 25, 1781, trial they were all found guilty and sentenced by Judge Alexander Contee Hanson to 'be hanged . . . . cut down alive and your entrails . . . taken out and burnt while you are yet alive, your heads shall be cut off and your body divided into four parts'. Records suggest that three of the men were merely hanged in the courtyard of the jail . . . and the other four were pardoned. Among those put to death was Casper Fritchie, father of John Fritchie who married Barbara Hauer in 1806."[253]

(It was Barbara Hauer Fritchie who was immortalized in the John Greenleaf Whittier poem for her supposed defiance of Confederate soldiers who had ordered her to take down the Union flag at her Frederick home during the Civil War. Historians dispute whether it was Barbara Fritchie, then ninety-five, who made this stand, another woman who lived a few doors down from her, yet another woman in Middletown, Frederick County, or a conflation of two or three of them.)

Perhaps Alexander Contee Hanson's severe sentencing of the seven was influenced by his having lost his brother, Dr. Samuel Hanson, and sister, Jane Hanson Thomas, only the month before.

Land records show that Alexander Contee Hanson owned at least 364 acres in Frederick County and property in Annapolis at the time of his first election to public office. Before his death, he patented 64 more acres and sold at least 109 acres in Frederick County. He rented two lots in Annapolis and lived on Church Street there from 1775 to 1806 during which period he spent much time in the colonial and then state capital.[254]

Alexander Contee Hanson, Sr., his wife Rebecca and two of their children are shown here.

Alexander Contee Hanson, Sr. and his wife Rebecca had five children including Charles Wallace Hanson who became an Associate Judge of the Sixth Judicial Circuit Court. Charles Wallace Hanson married Rebecca Dorsey Carnan Ridgely, daughter of Charles Carnan Ridgely, Governor of Maryland from 1815 to1819.

Alexander Contee Hanson, Jr.

Another of Alexander and Rebecca's sons, Alexander Contee Hanson, Jr., also carried on the Hanson family tradition of high public service in his brief life.

Fifty-seven surviving letters of Alexander Contee Hanson, Jr. possessed by the Maryland Historical Society show a man who travelled in the nation's highest political and social circles two generations after his presidential grandfather did. Alexander Contee Hanson, Jr. founded and published *The Federal Republican*, a Federalist newspaper. On June 26, 1812, four days after the War of 1812 was declared, a mob destroyed his newspaper office in Baltimore because of Hanson's published opposition to the United States entering the war. Hanson continued publishing the paper from a nearby building until the mob attacked again on July 28, injuring Hanson with a serious head wound, crippling General Lighthorse Harry Lee for life, and killing James McCubbin Lingan, the Revolutionary War General who had been captured at the Battle of Fort Washington in 1776 in which Alexander Contee Hanson, Jr.'s uncle, Lieutenant Peter Hanson, was killed. After the mob had first attacked the newspaper's offices, General Lingan had rallied to the defense of the paper and its publisher. During the second, more violent attack, Alexander Contee Hanson, Jr., General Lingan, General Lee and others sought refuge in the Baltimore jail but it was there that the mob found and murdered Lingan. He was sixty. The murderers thought that they had also gotten Hanson who was severely beaten and left for dead on the jail floor.

After the destruction of his Baltimore offices, life moved quickly for Alexander. He fled Baltimore for Georgetown which by that time had been incorporated into the relatively new federal territory of the District of Columbia. A few days after the sacking of his Baltimore office, he wrote to his wife Priscilla, then in Rockville, Maryland, "There is no further news of any violence in Baltimore. More of the murderers have been apprehended & committed to prison." In the same letter, Hanson comments on the planning of General Lingan's funeral in Georgetown where Lingan had been serving as the Collector of the Port of Georgetown: "On no account must Mrs. Lingan & family fail to be here. The General's horse and sword must be brought by Crabb." In this letter, he mentions that he is on the way to Mr. Custis's house.

While setting up household in Georgetown, Hanson conferred with friends about the war and the future of his newspaper. In another letter to Priscilla a few days after arriving in Georgetown, Alexander writes, "I spent last night with Mr. Custis at Arlington. He gave me a distinguished reception and requested that I would sleep in the very bed on which Genl. Washington drew his last breath. . . . He has offered and pressed me to use Genl. Washington's celebrated tent which he used throughout the war, for the heroes of Charles Street to hold their consultations under." The latter reference refers to his allies and other who had tried to protect his Baltimore newspaper offices. In this letter, Alexander writes to Priscilla that, "I have just received information that the Grand Jury has presented us all for manslaughter which is a bailable and not a capital offense. You have therefore no reason to be uneasy." The Custis here is a relative of Martha Custis Washington who inherited Mount Vernon upon her husband George Washington's death. Judging by this letter, Mr. Custis would appear to have been the owner of Mount Vernon at the time.

Hanson moved his newspaper to Georgetown where he was able to continue publishing it safely. He then moved his family to Georgetown where he and Priscilla quickly entered the high tier of the capital's social life. On January 8, 1813, he writes to an associate of a concert and ball held in Georgetown as a fundraiser for the new village of Washington saying that "Mrs. Washington was so good as to join Mrs. H. and me by my fire." (This would not be Martha Washington who died in 1802.) The fundraiser brought in $1,000. In an 1813 letter to his Baltimore attorney, Edward Johnson Coale, Alexander writes, "[Supreme Court Chief Justice] Judge [John] Marshall has been sitting with us all the evening, and a charming companion he is."

After a few years in Georgetown, Alexander Contee Hanson, Jr. moved his family, himself and his newspaper to Rockville, Maryland, in Montgomery County not far from Frederick. There, he was elected as a Federalist to the United States House of Representatives serving from March 4, 1813, until his resignation in 1816 to run for election to the Maryland House of Delegates. During the campaign for this election, he fell seriously ill on the campaign trail and had to be transported to his home where his recovery took several weeks. One of his letters describes his coughing up blood in this episode and before. His absence from the campaign cost him the election. However, within weeks after this defeat, he was elected as a Federalist by the Maryland General Assembly to the United States Senate to fill the vacancy caused by the resignation of Senator Robert G. Harper, and took his seat January 2, 1817 when was just thirty years old, the minimum permissible age for a United States Senator as prescribed by the Constitution. [255]

In his letters, Alexander Contee Hanson, Jr. writes of trips to Berkeley Springs, Virginia (now West Virginia) and to York Springs, Pennsylvania, in search of relief from ailments which he described as acid after each meal, pains in the liver and lungs, and difficult emitics for worms. The young man's health troubled him continually until his early death. Alexander Contee Hanson, Jr. served as United States Senator from his appointment on December 20, 1816, until April 23, 1819, when he died in office at the age of just thirty-three. From what one can gather from his letters, he felt vigorous enough to bear the duties of his office through his last extant letter written on New Year's Day, 1819, in which he mentions selling tickets for First Lady Elizabeth Monroe's coming fundraising event in Georgetown.[256] This leads to the conclusion that Senator Hanson's death is perhaps more likely to have resulted from an acute rather than chronic illness. Among the condolences received by Priscilla Dorsey Hanson was an effusive letter from Rufus King, the Federalist Party candidate for Vice President in 1804 and 1808 and the last Federalist candidate for President in 1816.

In 1805 Alexander Contee Hanson, Jr. and Priscilla Dorsey had had to elope to marry when Priscilla's guardian would not consent to the marriage of his nineteen-year-old orphan charge. Alexander spirited Priscilla away from her Baltimore home in a chaise which promptly broke down. However, with the foresighted planning for which he would become known, Alexander had prepared a packet of repair materials just in case, and the couple were soon on their way again. Their destination was the Annapolis home of the highest chancellery juror of Maryland, his father Alexander Contee Hanson, Sr. who married the couple and lodged them in his home until his death a year later.

Alexander Contee Hanson, Jr. is buried in the family graveyard at Belmont where he died, the Howard County, Maryland, estate of his wife's family, the Dorseys.[257] Belmont was occupied by the Hansons until 1917 when it was sold to the family of David K. E. Bruce, a distinguished United States ambassador to Great Britain, France and Germany. Today, Belmont, a Registered National Historic Landmark, is owned by the Smithsonian Institution and operates as a conference center.

The year after Alexander Contee Hanson, Jr. died, the western Massachusetts town of Pembroke, first settled in 1632, incorporated and renamed itself Hanson in honor of Alexander Contee Hanson, Jr.'s opposing the War of 1812 and continuing to publish his newspaper in defiance of the Baltimore mob.

There were two more Alexander Contee Hansons who continued the family line until Alexander Contee Hanson IV died at the age of sixteen in 1857.

A portrait of Senator Alexander Contee Hanson, Jr. is shown here.

Jane Contee Hanson Thomas, Her Husband Dr. Philip Thomas and Their Descendants

In an undated letter written in 1813 or 1814, Alexander Contee Hanson, Jr. worries about the health of his brother-in-law, Dr. Philip Thomas, as Alexander's cousin Kitty Thomas, Philip's daughter, was to have joined Alexander and his family at York Springs, Pennsylvania, but did not arrive. Dr. Philip Thomas, who had been of inestimable value to John Hanson when he was serving in Annapolis and then as president in Philadelphia, died on April 25, 1815, at his home in Frederick at the age of sixty-seven. His *bona fides* have been earlier described. Healer of the sick, public servant, founder of his state's medical society, two of Frederick's first schools, and a newspaper, widowered father of four for more than half of his life, devoted son-in-law to a president and then for twenty-nine years to a widowed first lady, Philip Thomas, like his parents in law, is an undersung American hero. May he, too, be better remembered. Philip Thomas died of the yellow fever epidemic which swept Frederick in 1815.

Jane and Philip Thomas are buried in Frederick's Mount Olivet Cemetery with their daughter Rebecca "Becky" Thomas Magruder and their son, John Hanson Thomas, Sr. Their graves lie next to the unmarked grave of Jane Hanson; the grave and monument of President Hanson's friend and ally, Thomas Johnson, Maryland's first governor; and the grave of Barbara Fritchie. Becky's husband, Judge Alexander Contee Magruder, a justice on Maryland's highest court, was the first cousin of the First Lady and thus Becky had married her first cousin once removed, not uncommon at the time.

John Hanson Thomas in 1809 married Mary Isham Colston, niece of John Marshall, the fourth and still longest serving United States Supreme Court Chief Justice who served from 1801 to 1835. One of Mary's ancestors was William Brewster, a Mayflower pilgrim who became the first elder of the Plymouth colony. Mary Isham Colston's father, Rawleigh

Colston, had married Elizabeth Marshall, sister of the Chief Justice. At the time of his marriage, John Hanson Thomas was a twenty-nine-year-old Federalist member of the Maryland House of Delegates. In 1815, he was elected a United States Senator but died on May 2 that year at age thirty-five before he could take office. He died six days after Philip Thomas, having contracted yellow fever at his father's bedside.[258]

He left but one child, Dr. John Hanson Thomas, Jr., born in 1813, who became a physician, Baltimore City Councilman, and member of the Maryland General Assembly from 1861 to 1865. He died at the age of sixty-six in 1881 while trying to recuperate from illness at the While Sulfur Springs resort in Virginia.

The middle of the three children of John Hanson Thomas, Jr. and Annie Campbell Gordon Thomas was Douglas Hamilton Thomas, Sr. who became president in 1886 of Merchant Mechanics National Bank of Baltimore and served in that capacity for thirty-five years until his death in 1919. Douglas Thomas served as an appointed Commissioner of the Maryland Centennial Commission of 1876, and in 1898 wrote a biography of President John Hanson, his great-great-grandfather. Mr. Thomas wrote a companion publication[259] at the request of the Maryland General Assembly as it prepared its case to have President Hanson's statue accepted by the United States Congress for inclusion in National Statuary Hall of the United States Capitol. The companion piece presents a compilation of President Hanson's accomplishments, press commentary on him from his time forward, and the successful case for the president's enshrinement in Statuary Hall.[260]

Douglas Hamilton Thomas, Sr. inherited, or gathered through acquisition, many Hanson Family objects including some which had belonged to the president, and the Contee family's earlier mentioned silver punch bowl, silver plate and the tea service with muffineer and waiter bearing the 1620 Tower of London stamp. He fathered Alice Lee Thomas Stevenson who inherited much of the Hanson family memorabilia including John Hanson's presidential portrait which she donated to the Independence Hall Portrait Collection, and the midlife portraits of Jane and John Hanson and portraits of Alexander Contee Hanson, Sr., Alexander Contee Hanson, Jr. and Dr. Philip Thomas, all of which she donated to the Maryland Historical Society. She also inherited and donated to the Maryland Historical Society the priceless letters of John Hanson to Philip Thomas and John Hanson's two ledgers, all of which have been critically important in compiling *Remembering John Hanson*. Without Alice Lee Thomas Stevenson's donations and foresight to posterity, this biography would not have been possible in anything close to its present degree of completeness. She is the eighth generation of the Hanson family since her immigrant forebear to heighten the national good.

Mathias Oppersdorff, Jr., grandson of Douglas Hamilton Thomas, Sr. and fifth-great-grandson of the president, inherited a treasure trove of Hanson memorabilia including several pieces which had belonged to the president himself. Many items which had belonged to John and Jane Hanson, other Hansons, the descendants of Philip and Jane Thomas, in-laws of these families and the Contees were auctioned from the estate of Mr. Oppersdorff on September 17, 2011, by Crocker Farm Auctioneers of Sparks, Maryland.

Another of the children of Dr. and Mrs. Philip Thomas, their daughter Catherine Hanson Thomas — the Kitty who as a child had lived with her presidential grandparents in Philadelphia for a year — married Dr. Ashton Alexander. In 1820 the Alexanders' daughter Elizabeth Maria married John Marshall III, son of Chief Justice John Marshall. As John Marshall III was the first cousin of Mary Isham Colston mentioned above and they found their marriage partners only a few years apart, it is quite possible that one couple introduced the other.[261]

The only other child of Jane and Philip Thomas was their first-born, James, who is believed to have died young and unmarried.

Other Notable Relations of President John Hanson

Several of John Hanson's nephews and their children attained important positions from the Revolutionary War on into the nineteenth century. His cousin, Colonel Robert Hanson Harrison, grandson of the president's uncle Robert Hanson, served as Military Secretary to George Washington during the Revolutionary War and was appointed by Washington as one of the first United States Supreme Court justices. The president's nephew, Daniel of St. Thomas Jennifer, son of the president's sister Elizabeth, was a Signer of the Constitution.

Another of John Hanson's nephews, Thomas Stone, son of the president's sister Jane, was a Signer of the Declaration of Independence, delegate to the Second Continental Congress, and delegate to the United States in Congress Assembled. His great-great-grandfather William Stone, who had served as Maryland's third colonial governor, had come to the Port Tobacco area with the immigrant John Hanson where the two friends settled, laid out their plantations and built their manor homes. After studying law in Annapolis under future Governor Thomas Johnson, Thomas Stone settled in Frederick County in 1765 before returning to Port Tobacco and his family's Habre de Venture estate where he built a new home in 1771. While he was serving as a Maryland delegate to the United States in Congress Assembled in 1787, Thomas's wife Margaret died on June 1 after a ten-year illness contracted either from a smallpox inoculation or mercury treatment. In despair, Stone resigned, deciding that an ocean voyage might allay his grief. Thomas Stone died October 5, 1787, at age forty-five in Alexandria, Virginia, awaiting passage to Europe. He is buried at Habre de Venture, now restored as the Thomas Stone National Historic Site open to the public.[262]

John Hoskins Stone, the eighth governor of Maryland from 1794 to 1797, was a relative by marriage of the Hansons. Another nephew and child of the president's sister Jane, Michael Jennifer Stone, was a Member of Congress in the First Congress under the Constitution. Frederick Stone, great-grandson of Michael Jennifer Stone, served in the United States House of Representatives from 1861 to 1871. John Mitchell, a grandnephew of the president through his brother Judge Walter Hanson and Walter's daughter Anne, rose to the rank of Brigadier General during the Revolutionary War. John Hanson Thomas Magruder[263] served as the Maryland State Librarian in the mid-nineteenth century.

On the recommendations of Senators Henry Clay and Daniel Webster, Grafton Dulaney Hanson at the age of nine was appointed as the first United States Congressional Page in 1829, serving in the Senate. Grafton Dulaney Hanson was the president's grandnephew and the son of Thomas Hanson, owner of Oxon Hill Manor. The young Grafton was apparently an autograph collector: on a single sheet which came up at auction in 2011 appear twelve early political autographs including those of immediate past president John Quincy Adams, Henry Clay and Daniel Webster. In August 2011 House of Representatives Speaker John Boehner terminated the House's 182-year-old Page program as a cost-cutting move turning out seventy teenage Pages. The $5 million saved represented about one one-hundred-thousandth of planned deficit reduction at the time. The

United States Senate controlled by Democrats said that its Page program, in which Grafton Dulaney Hanson was the first to serve, will continue.[264]

The southern Maryland and Virginia Harrisons, who produced a Virginia governor, a Signer of the Declaration of Independence, President William Henry Harrison, President Benjamin Harrison and Benjamin Harrison III, a member of the House of Representatives from Wyoming in the mid-twentieth century, were related by marriage to the Hansons through both the Hansons and the Contees. The Hanson-Harrison relationship is by marriage through President John Hanson's niece Chloe Hanson Lingan's marriage to William McKinney. The Contee-Harrison relationship is through Jane Contee Hanson's sister Catherine's marriage to John Harrison.

The Washingtons and Hansons are said to have been related.

Jane and John Hanson's portraitist, John Hesselius, married into the Addison branch of the family.

In a very unusual confluence of several bloodlines already mentioned in *Remembering John Hanson*, Zelda Fitzgerald, wife of F. Scott Fitzgerald (Francis Scott Key Fitzgerald), wrote in a fascinating article of her descent from the immigrant John Hanson, the Charles County Briscoes who several times married into the Hanson family, and Thomas Cresap, the Frederick County frontier Indian fighter, all. Zelda descended on her mother's side from the president's sister Chloe Hanson who married Philip Briscoe, and on her father's side from the Cresaps. Thomas Cresap was also the fifth great-grandfather of F. Scott Fitzgerald so F. Scott and Zelda were distantly related.[265]

In these various connections among the great families of the era, we see that as late as five generations after President John Hanson, his descendants remained within the most influential social and political circles in the land and were contributing in significant ways to the betterment of society. But by the late nineteenth century, few Hansons of the president's line of the family remained and fewer still were prominent.   Other than perhaps his daughter Alice, no prominent Hanson descendant is apparent after Douglas Hamilton Thomas who died in 1919 at the age of seventy-two, and none identified with the Hanson surname in the twentieth-first century. With Alice Lee Thomas Stevenson who died in 1972, a dynasty begun by the first John Hanson, the immigrant progenitor upon his arrival in the seventeenth century, apparently ended eight generations of national leadership and prominence.

Commemorating President John Hanson Today

The John Hanson Institute

Edward and Lexy Edelen's John Hanson Institute, a companion project to the John Hanson National Memorial, envisions several buildings designed in colonial architectural style including a conference center situated along the Port Tobacco River adjacent to Mulberry Grove. Site plans have been drawn up and archeologists have examined the site and nearby Port Tobacco. Talks with Johns Hopkins University are ongoing to forge a collaboration between the institute and the university. The John Hanson Institute will be a very handsome and useful facility when up and running. While there isn't a formal relationship between the Institute and the John Hanson Memorial Association, there is close communication between the two, and the two projects will of course very nicely complement one another. The work on the John Hanson Institute proceeds in parallel with the commendable reassembling of the old Mulberry Grove estate through land purchases by Ed and Lexy Edelen and their sponsorship of the Port Tobacco Historic Trail through the Institute and Mulberry Grove.

Mulberry Grove

At least prior to the unveiling of the John Hanson National Memorial and the John Hanson Institute, many would regard the most moving extant remembrance of John Hanson to be his first home, Mulberry Grove. Ownership of the ancient estate went out of the Hanson and Contee families early in the nineteenth century, being owned by the Hanson-related Ferguson and Mitchell families until after 1900. In the early 1930s, Mulberry Grove was purchased by John Hanson biographer J. Bruce Kremer, and later by the Edelen family which owns Mulberry Grove today.

After more than two centuries of sturdy service, the Mulberry Grove home where John and Jane Hanson lived from 1744 until 1769 burned on July 25, 1934. Some of the original paneling was saved and is now displayed as an example of an early colonial room at the Philadelphia Museum. The farm was afterward largely untended for more than fifteen years falling into a decrepit state until Dr. Edward J. and Mary Keech Edelen, parents of Edward Edelen III, today's owner, bought Mulberry Grove and three hundred surrounding acres, restored the grounds, gardens and fields, reintroduced farming, and rebuilt the home, faithfully replicating its original plan, facades and period interior and exterior materials. Along with the Hansons and the Dents, the Edelens are one of the oldest families of Charles County, Maryland, and for generations have been closely familiar with Mulberry Grove and the Hansons. All that was left of the original home were its basement, chimneys and, ironically, a two-ton fire bell. During the two-year restoration, Dr. and Mrs. Edelen meticulously sourced from around the state very old used eighteenth and nineteenth century building materials including pegged walnut flooring, windows, solid walnut doors, paneling, moldings, hardware and other fittings. Upon completion of the restoration, the couple and their family moved into the home, reviving Mulberry Grove into a living working estate once again and bringing it back from the brink as an important national landmark.

Dr. and Mrs. Edelen's son Edward III and his wife Lexy purchased Mulberry Grove from his parents and have continued the older generation's preservation work in a number of important ways, most notably the reassembling through land purchases of the original Mulberry Grove estate and several surrounding farms as buffers to Mulberry Grove. Ed and Lexy Edelen are in the process of establishing a foundation to operate Mulberry Grove in perpetuity along the lines of the Mount Vernon Ladies' Association, a private, non-profit organization founded in 1853 by Ann Pamela Cunningham, and the oldest national historic preservation organization in the country.

From the attentions of two generations of the Edelen family, Mulberry Grove is in better condition today than it has been for decades if not centuries. In touring Mulberry Grove's woods and fields, its streams and ponds, riding by its several old tenant farmhouses, barns and outbuildings, and especially visiting the Hanson family cemetery, one is transported back to a quieter hallowed time of the nation. Once the senior Edelens reconstructed John Hanson's home, the estate reverted to something much akin to its original state — beautiful, rustic, tranquil and deeply reminiscent of a bygone time.

The Mulberry Grove home today is at least as evocative as the farms of which it is the centerpiece. With its broad center hall staircase and lengthy parlour wings, the home retains its classic original layout from the 1700s. Its brick walls, slate roof, colonial interior colors, old paneling and fittings in most cases exactly match the originals. Spending the night at the beautifully reconstructed Mulberry Grove home is a special treat summoning a reverence for the place and its most famous son, and for what the Edelen family has done in bringing back to life this national treasure. The nation owes a debt of gratitude to the Edelen family for rescuing Mulberry Grove.

Independence Hall and National Statuary Hall

The John Hanson Memorial Association and John Hanson Institute enjoy the benefit of being able to build on a fair amount of existing iconography on John Hanson.   Other than the John Hanson National Memorial, the most notable images of John Hanson are his presidential portrait in the Independence Hall Portrait Collection and his statue in National Statuary Hall of the United States Capitol.

John Hanson's presidential portrait was one of the first painted by Charles Willson Peale, the foremost portraitist of the late eighteenth century and probably the most esteemed in the nation's history. With Peale's oblique pose of Hanson, bust scale and classical background, his early painting of President John Hanson set the style for Peale's later portraits of United States presidents and others.   John Hanson's presidential portrait and the portraits of a number of other major Revolutionary War figures are owned by the National Park Service and are displayed in the Independence Hall Portrait Collection which is now housed in the Second National Bank Building next to Independence Hall.

Each state gets to have monument-scale[266] statues of two of its sons or daughters in National Statuary Hall of the United States Capitol. National Statuary Hall was authorized by Congress and signed into law by President Lincoln on July 2, 1864. The first statue, that of Rhode Island Revolutionary War General Nathaniel Greene, was placed in 1870. By 1971 all fifty states had contributed at least one statue and by 1990 all but five states had contributed two. As of 2012, there had been one hundred three Americans memorialized in Statuary Hall, with three states permitted since 2000 to replace the statues of one their previous honorees with statues of new honorees. The three replacements are Kansas' Dwight D. Eisenhower in 2003, Alabama's Helen Keller in 2009, and most recently California's Ronald Reagan in 2009.

The two Marylanders honored in National Statuary Hall are John Hanson and Charles Carroll of Carrollton, Maryland's first United States Senator and the last signer of the Declaration of Independence to die. Hanson's National Statuary Hall statue is shown here. John Hanson is one of only six presidents honored in National Statuary Hall, the others being George Washington, Andrew Jackson, James Garfield, Dwight Eisenhower and Ronald Reagan. After a certain point, the room in the Capitol designated as National Statuary Hall became full and the National Statuary Hall collection began spilling out into the Capitol rotunda until the weight of the statues there reached the limit of the floor's carrying capacity. Because of these constraints, most of the statues of the National Statuary Hall collection are now displayed at a number of other places scattered about in the Capitol. John Hanson's statue resides beside the entrance to the Senate Gallery and Charles Carroll's is on display in the Crypt. Since 9/11, heightened security practices have meant that most of the statues are in parts of the Capitol which are no longer open to the public.

In the 2011 session of the Maryland General Assembly, identical bills were introduced in the State Senate and House of Delegates at the urging of the Maryland chapter of the National Organization of Women and Equal Visibility Everywhere to replace the John Hanson statue in National Statuary Hall with a statue of American Underground Railroad heroine Harriet Tubman. While there was widespread support in both houses for Tubman's inclusion in the Hall, intense opposition arose against replacement of the Hanson statue. The original bill's sponsors fought back causing a flurry of press attention. The author testified on behalf of the John Hanson Memorial Association urging a Maryland request to permit expansion of National Statuary Hall or to put a Tubman statue in the Capitol on its own and not as a part of the National Statuary Hall collection as has been done with statues of others.

Speaker of the House of Delegates Michael E. Busch, State Senate President Thomas V. "Mike" Miller, State Senator Thomas Middleton (a John Hanson relative) and the author led the opposition, getting the Senate bill amended to request the United States Congress either to permit Maryland a special exception with a third statue or a Tubman statue separate from the Hall collection. The amended bill passed the Maryland Senate unanimously but, in the waning days of the session, never made it to the floor of the House of Delegates for a vote. The ill-conceived approach of the bill's sponsors had at least temporarily cost a very deserving American her place of honor in the United States Capitol.

Underground Railroad Free Press, the nation's top-circulation Underground Railroad news publication, editorialized for inclusion of Harriet Tubman into National Statuary Hall but not at the expense of anyone already honored there. A *Free Press* survey in 2011 showed nearly nine-tenths of the international Underground Railroad community in favor of an approach that would not involve removal of a statue of a person already honored in National Statuary Hall.[267]

In 1973 when John Hanson Briscoe was Speaker of the House of Maryland, the Maryland Assembly passed a bill that declared April 14, John Hanson's birthday, as John Hanson Day in Maryland every year. When Charles Brooks sculpted the John Hanson statue for National Statuary Hall in 1903, he began with a smaller maquette from which to fashion the final product. The maquette, now covered in gold leaf, resides beside the dais in the Senate chamber of the Maryland General Assembly, the maquette of Brooks' Charles Carroll statue on the other side of the dais.

Other John Hanson Official Remembrances

Other than his presidential portrait, the best known painting of John Hanson is his portrait painted by John Hesselius in the 1750s or 1760s when John Hanson was in his forties. The Hesselius portrait is shown earlier here. There is also a retrospective drawing of President Hanson done by H. B. Hall in 1871.

The Hesselius portrait of John Hanson, and the portraits of Jane Hanson, John and Jane Hanson's son Alexander Contee Hanson, grandson Senator Alexander Contee Hanson, Jr. and son-in-law Dr. Philip Thomas, are all shown here. These and portraits of eight other Hanson family members are in the possession of the Maryland Historical Society and were donated mostly by Alice Lee Thomas Stevenson. Ms. Stevenson was a third-great-grandchild of Jane and President John Hanson and the granddaughter of Douglas Hamilton Thomas, Sr. earlier mentioned.[268] A full listing of the Maryland Historical Society collection of twelve Hanson family portraits is provided in the bibliography here on the Maryland Historical Society's Hanson holdings.

In addition to the John Hanson statue in National Statuary Hall, there is a monument-scale bronze bust of the president mounted on a five-foot, seven-sided pedestal of pink Swedish granite at Mulberry Grove. This bust was commissioned by the Vasa Society, a Swedish-American civic organization, sculpted in the 1950s, and until 2008 resided at Gloria Dei Old Swedes Church in Philadelphia before being purchased by Edward and Lexy Edelen and moved to Mulberry Grove.

Also at Mulberry Grove is an obelisk of pink marble about seven feet in height which was donated and dedicated there on October 17, 1959, by the Vasa Society honoring President Hanson and his presumed Swedish-American background.

There is a similar obelisk in white marble honoring John Hanson at Oxon Hill Manor. This monument was donated by the former John Hanson Society and dedicated November 26, 1933.

In the mid-twentieth century, the Maryland State Roads Commission erected two roadside historical plaques noting John Hanson. One is on Chapel Point Road near Port Tobacco at the entrance to the lane leading up to the Mulberry Grove estate. The other is on Oxon Hill Road in Oxon Hill, Maryland, about a mile east of Oxon Hill Manor.

In 1981 the United States Postal Service honored President Hanson with a twenty-cent John Hanson stamp commemorating his election as president. The first issue of this stamp from the United States post office in Frederick, Maryland, was on November 5, 1981, the two-hundredth anniversary to the day of John Hanson's election as president. The stamp was designed by artist Ronald Adair. In the ceremony held in Frederick that day, the Postmaster General of the United States, the Ambassador of Sweden and United States Senator Charles Mathias, a Frederick County native, spoke. The United States Post Office had earlier issued a six-cent John Hanson post card in the 1960s.

On March 24, 1983, the United States and Sweden issued stamps commemorating the two hundredth anniversary of the Treaty of Amity between the two countries. John Hanson had gotten the treaty into the works during his administration and lived long enough to see it become reality.

In October 1981 in preparation for the stamp issue, a bronze commemorative medal struck in limited quantity was issued by the United States Capitol Historical Society commemorating John Hanson's inauguration as president and the two-hundredth anniversary of Cornwallis' surrender. The face of the medal shows President John Hanson with the inscription "John Hanson First President Under Articles of Confederation" inscribed inside the rim. The reverse of the medal shows Cornwallis' surrender at Yorktown with the inscription "1781 * 200th Anniversary – Surrender of Cornwallis * 1981" inscribed at the rim.   The medal is shown here. The sculptor was Miko Kauffman.

In 1981 the Maryland Sons of the American Revolution commissioned a limited issue of 100 Maryland bicentennial medals honoring the two-hundredth anniversary of President John Hanson's inauguration.

There is a privately struck medal commemorating President Hanson, the Articles of Confederation and the period when the Second Continental Congress was forced from Philadelphia and met in York, Pennsylvania. The face of the medal shows a bust of John Hanson with the incorrect inscription "3rd President of the United States." The reverse with the inscription "Articles of Confederation-1777" shows the old courthouse in York where the Second Continental Congress met.

In 1976 upon the completion of his book, *John Hanson, Public Servant*, Ralph B. Levering, then an assistant professor of history at McDaniel College (then called Western Maryland College) in Westminster, Maryland, arranged for the college to award John Hanson a posthumous honorary Doctor of Humane Letters degree.

During World War II, John Hanson had a liberty ship named for him.[269]

Finally, John Hanson Memorial Association director Robert Hanson reports seeing in the 1940s an oil portrait of President John Hanson at Mount Republic, a colonial-era Charles County estate a few miles from Mulberry Grove.

John Hanson Place Names

US Route 50 from Washington, DC, to Annapolis, dedicated on November 21, 1961, is named the John Hanson Highway. There is a middle school in Charles County, Maryland, named for Hanson; a Montessori school in Oxon Hill, Prince George's County, Maryland, named for him; and a Maryland savings and loan association, since merged out of existence, that had been named for him. The City of Frederick named a group of low-income apartments after John Hanson but these were torn down in 2007 much to the approval of the Hanson family. Hansonville and Hansonville Road in Frederick County, Maryland, are named for John Hanson.

As recently as 1977, there was an ill-fated attempt, not the first, to split Prince George's County, Maryland, into two and name the new county John Hanson County.   This effort went as far as a bill being submitted in the Maryland General Assembly.

As mentioned, Hanson, Massachusetts, was renamed such in 1820 in honor of United States Senator Alexander Contee Hanson, Jr., grandson of President John and Jane Contee Hanson, a year after the Senator's death.

Dr. Philip Thomas purchased a farm property a few miles from Frederick which he named Mount Philip which is located on today's Mount Philip Road just west of Frederick.

John Hanson Artifacts

The only known personal possessions of John Hanson the whereabouts of which are known today are his and Jane Hanson's portraits, his 54 letters, his two journals and a memorandum book in the Maryland Historical Society's John Hanson collections. In his letters to Philip Thomas, Hanson referred to his desk and storage chest at his Frederick home but, with the few exceptions following, there is no record of how these or other of the couple's furnishings might have been passed down in the family or how long they existed.

In 1973 a gold quill which belonged to John Hanson was used by Maryland Governor Marvin Mandel to sign legislation creating John Hanson Day in Maryland. In 1943 a Duncan Phyfe drop-leaf table owed by Jane and John Hanson was auctioned as part of the estate of Nannie Hanson, John and Jane's great-great-granddaughter. The oldest reference to John Hanson's true birth year of 1715 is the family bible owned by the couple's great-grandson, Dr. John Hanson Thomas, Jr., as late as 1875.[270] This is the bible auctioned in 2011. The Contee silver which had come to Maryland with the immigrant family in 1703 and was inherited by Jane Hanson was owned by her great-great-grandson, Douglas Hamilton Thomas, when he died in 1919. The whereabouts of the quill, table, bible and silver are unknown today. These Hanson artifacts had come down in two lines of the Hanson family as Nannie Hanson and Douglas Hamilton Thomas were third cousins.

Publicity and Books on John Hanson

John Hanson's biographies and all other Hanson publications which the author could locate are listed in the bibliographies of *Remembering John Hanson*.

Beginning with its fourteenth edition in 1929 (but not until then), *The Encyclopedia Britannica* has featured an entry on

John Hanson.   In that edition, John Hanson's entry was fourteen lines long, George Washington's, seven pages.

Under the direction of John Hanson Memorial Association director Aldan Weinberg, a national publicity campaign was launched in 2008 which has resulted in a number of articles on John Hanson and the John Hanson Memorial Association by the Associated Press, *The Washington Post, The Baltimore Sun,* a cover story in *The Frederick News-Post* and mention in other publications and on National Public Radio's *All Things Considered.*   Through press releases and a newsletter published periodically by the Association, this publicity campaign issues regular updates on progress made by the Association and the Institute, on John Hanson discoveries revealed by ongoing research and on other matters of interest.

Background information, a slide show and other materials on John Hanson and the John Hanson Memorial Association are available at the Association's website, JohnHansonMemorial.org.

In addition to *Remembering John Hanson,* the first biography of the president in over seventy years, John Cummings is preparing a history of John Hanson's presidency.

The John Hanson Memorial Association presses ahead on its several fronts, and Edward and Lexy Edelen are bringing forth the John Hanson Institute and a reassembled Mulberry Grove.   With any luck, Wikipedia and Snopes will be convinced to begin disseminating accurate information on John Hanson. The coming years should see visitors discovering the John Hanson National Memorial, the John Hanson Institute reach fruition, more national press coverage and at least the beginning of a national reawakening of the memory of President John Hanson.   As has been the case for far too long with John Hanson, time will tell.

Appendix One

Timeline of John Hanson's Life and Remembrances

Early and Midlife of John Hanson, 1715-1772[271]

April 14, 1715[272]	Born at Mulberry Grove, his parents' plantation in Charles County, Maryland, "about 2 or 3 in ye afternoon,"[273] son of Judge Samuel Hanson and Elizabeth Story Hanson, and grandson of his namesake
September 28, 1728	Future First Lady Jane Contee Hanson born at her family's estate in Prince George's County, Maryland
1731	Hanson visited England
1743	John Hanson marries Jane Contee. He is 28, she is 15. Date unknown.
1750	Appointed as Sheriff of Charles County, Maryland
1757-58, 65-66, 68	Represents Charles County in the Maryland House of Delegates
February 14, 1758	Appointed by House of Delegates to two finance committees beginning Hanson's specialized and prominent role in field of public finance
During Hanson's time in the Maryland House of Delegates	Becomes a leader of the Country Party which seeks more colonial rights and opposes the Proprietary Party which owes allegiance to the Maryland Proprietor, the owner of Maryland
March 22, 1765	British Parliament passes the Stamp Act to take effect November 1, 1765, taxing the North American colonies
September 23, 1765	The Maryland Assembly meets to discuss the Stamp Act after having been forbidden by the British to meet in 1764
September 24, 1765	John Hanson one of seven appointed by the Maryland Assembly to draft instructions for Assembly delegates to the colonies' Stamp Act Congress

October 19, 1765	Stamp Act Congress, a meeting of the colonies to oppose the Stamp Act, meets
November 1, 1765	Stamp Act takes effect. British agents attempt to collect new taxes.
November 15, 1765	The twelve judges of the Frederick County Court decide unanimously that the county need not comply with the Stamp Act, thus becoming the first official body in the colonies to oppose the Stamp Act[274]
November 23, 1765	Frederick County Sons of Liberty holds a mock funeral of the Stamp Act
During this period	Stamp act riots occur in the colonies. The British governor of Georgia defends himself at gunpoint from a mob storming the governor's mansion.
During this period	John Hanson among the most vocal in the Maryland Assembly opposing the Stamp Act and advocating more independence for the colonies
March 18, 1766	Stamp Act repealed by the British Parliament
June 29, 1767	Britain passes Townshend Acts taxing imports into North American colonies, creates admiralty courts trying colonists for defiance of Acts.
Soon afterward	Riots and widespread defiance of the Townshend Acts ensue
June 22, 1769	John Hanson is one of 43 signers from the American colonies of the Non-Importation Resolution which prohibits "ships laden with goods from England to land at Annapolis, [Port] Tobacco Creek in Charles County, and elsewhere."[275] Hanson oversees inspection of British ships putting into Port Tobacco where he resides at his Mulberry Grove home.
1769	Becomes a charter member of the Association of Maryland Freemen
Fall 1769	Gives up his seat in the House of Delegates from Charles County

Fall 1769	Appointed Deputy Surveyor of Frederick County, Maryland, which comprised all of Maryland from Georgetown and Westminster west to present-day Garrett County and from the Potomac River to Pennsylvania.
1769	For better political opportunity and a stronger power base, John Hanson moves to Frederick County.
November 25, 1769	John Hanson sells most of Mulberry Grove including the home to his brother William Hanson.
March 5, 1770	Boston Massacre takes place when British troops fire on protesting civilian colonists. The first casualty of resistance against the British is the African-American Crispus Attucks.
April, 1770	Britain repeals the Townshend Acts
December 21, 1771	William Hanson sells Mulberry Grove to Jane Hanson's brother, Peter Contee
Spring, 1772	John Hanson confers with George Washington at Mount Vernon about the future of the colonies
February 18, 1773	John and Jane Hanson's daughter, Jane Contee Hanson, marries Dr. Philip Thomas, Frederick's first physician and prime aide to John Hanson
Sometime in 1773	John Hanson builds two homes near the corner of West Patrick and Court Streets in Frederick
Fall, 1773	Jane and Philip Thomas settle next door to Jane and John Hanson in Frederick.

Hanson In the Drive for Independence, 1773-1776

1773	Pennsylvania's Benjamin Franklin proposes that representatives of the thirteen colonies meet to discuss relations with Britain and more colonial autonomy
September 27, 1773	Samuel Adams of Massachusetts calls for a continental congress to be formed to discuss Britain's imposition of taxes on the colonies

December 16, 1773 — Boston Tea Party occurs

March 24, 1774 — In response, Britain imposes the Intolerable Acts, also known as the Coercive Acts, on the North American colonies

April 19, 1774 — Last Maryland colonial Assembly adjourns

May 28, 1774 — In response to Massachusetts' plea, Maryland House of Delegates leaders establish the colony's Committee of Correspondence which requests Maryland county leaders to cease trade with Britain and proposes an association to enforce the trade ban

May 1774 — New York City's Committee of Fifty-One calls for a continental congress to respond to the Intolerable Acts

June 20, 1774 — Frederick County Committee of Observation, a new extra-legal body, meets in response to the May 28 request, elects John Hanson to head the body[276]

June 20, 1774 — Frederick County Committee of Observation appoints John Hanson, son Alexander Contee Hanson and son-in-law Dr. Philip Thomas as Frederick County delegates to the General Congress at Annapolis

June 22-25, 1774 — General Congress, later to be named the First Convention of the Province of Maryland, another extralegal body, held in Annapolis

Summer 1774 — First Continental Congress planned by Committees of Correspondence of the thirteen colonies

September 5, 1774 — First Continental Congress convenes in Philadelphia. Maryland represented by Samuel Chase, William Paca, Matthew Tilghman and Frederick's Thomas Johnson. Georgia is the only colony not attending.

September 5, 1774 — Peyton Randolph of Virginia elected president of the meeting

October 20, 1774 — Articles of Association, precursor to the Declaration of Independence, drafted

October 22, 1774	Henry Middleton of South Carolina elected First Continental Congress president, serves for four days
During the Congress	Resolution passed to hold a Second Continental Congress in 1775.
October 26, 1774	First Continental Congress dissolves after fifty-two days
November 18, 1774	John Hanson re-elected to head Frederick County Committee of Observation
November 18, 1774	John Hanson and other officials charged "to carry into execution the association agreed on by the American Continental Congress."[277]
November 21-25, 1774	Second Convention of Maryland held in Annapolis
December 8-12, 1774	Third Convention of Maryland held in Annapolis
January 24, 1775	Public meeting held at the Frederick County Courthouse with Hanson presiding puts into effect resolutions of the recent provincial convention for financing and formation of militias. Hanson re-elected as a Frederick County delegate to the next provincial convention.
February 17, 1775	Hanson as presiding officer of the Frederick County Committee of Observation sends £1,200 to Boston on behalf of the Committee to support Boston's ability to resist the British blockade of the port of Boston
March 22, 1775	Patriots of Bush River in Harford County, Maryland, call for independence with the Bush Declaration
April 19, 1775	Revolutionary War begins with the battles of Lexington and Concord
April 20, 1775	British begin laying siege to the city of Boston
April 25 - May 3, 1775	Fourth Convention of Maryland held in Annapolis

During Revolutionary War	Hanson's eldest son, Alexander Contee Hanson, appointed by General Washington as his private secretary during Revolutionary War, spends most of his service in the field. Middle son Peter Hanson serves as an Army Lieutenant. Youngest son Dr. Samuel Harrison Hanson serves as surgeon on Washington's staff.
May 10, 1775	Second Continental Congress convenes. Peyton Randolph elected president, serves thirteen days.
May 24, 1775	John Hancock begins nearly two and a half years of service as president of the Second Continental Congress, succeeded in order by Henry Laurens, John Jay and Samuel Huntington
May 25, 1775	British reinforcements led by Generals William Howe and John Burgoyne arrive in Boston
June 14, 1775	Second Continental Congress appoints George Washington as commanding general of what will soon be named the Continental Army
June 17, 1775	Battle of Bunker Hill occurs
June 21 - 25, 1775	Delegates from throughout Maryland meet in Annapolis to plan Maryland's Revolutionary War efforts
June 21, 1775	Hanson receives request from the Second Continental Congress that he organize militias to be sent to aid Massachusetts after the Battle of Bunker Hill. The same day, the Frederick County Committee of Correspondence authorizes Hanson to raise the militias.
June 21, 1775	Hanson elected Treasurer of Frederick County
June 22 - July 18, 1775	Hanson organizes two companies of trained riflemen

June 26, 1775	The American people begin learning of the Revolutionary War through accounts in the press. Among the first of these is a broadside on the Battle of Bunker Hill published in Lancaster, Pennsylvania.
During this period	Hanson persuades the Frederick County Committee of Observation to pledge all county males as prospective soldiers
During this period	Hanson organizes manufacture of arms, gun locks, gunpowder, ammunition and army equipment for the Continental Army
July 3, 1775	George Washington takes command of colonial forces in Massachusetts, begins organizing colonial militias into the Continental Army.
July 26, 1775	Second Continental Congress appoints Benjamin Franklin to organize a postal service, precursor to the United States Postal Service to be formed during the Hanson administration in 1782
July 26 – August 14, 1775	John Hanson serves as a Frederick County delegate to the Fifth Convention of Maryland, most important of the nine Maryland Conventions
July, 1775	In the Convention of Maryland, Hanson is first to pledge that he and his followers will repel British by force and support opposition to the British
July 26, 1775	The seventy-nine delegates from all Maryland counties to the Fifth Convention of Maryland sign the *Association of Freemen of Maryland* which vows to "repel force by force"
August 9, 1775	After a twenty-two-day march, Hanson's rifle companies are the first assistance to arrive in Massachusetts
August 29, 1775	Maryland Council of Safety, an extralegal body, organized by patriot leaders as the breakaway colony's presence between meetings of the Conventions of Maryland
September 12, 1775	Hanson re-elected president of Frederick County Committee of Observation. "The

Committee . . . was the government of the area from the fall of 1775 until the state constitution went into effect in the spring of 1777."[278]

December 7, 1775 – January 18, 1776	Sixth Convention of Maryland held in Annapolis
January 20, 1776	Hanson appointed by the Maryland Council of Safety to collect donations in Frederick County to aid the colonies' fight against the British
March 17, 1776	British forces withdraw from Boston
May 8 – 25, 1776	Seventh Convention of Maryland held in Annapolis
June 7, 1776	Virginia's Richard Henry Lee exhorts independence to the Second Continental Congress, makes a formal motion for same seconded by Massachusetts' John Adams.
June 17, 1776	Hanson proposes that Freemen of Frederick County issue a resolution urging to the Convention of Maryland that Maryland not decline to join in the Declaration of Independence and that Maryland recommend to the other colonies that they authorize independence
June 21 – July 6, 1776	The Eighth Convention of Maryland is held
June 26, 1776	Robert Eden, Maryland's last colonial governor, abandons his office and departs Maryland for Britain
June 28, 1776	The Hanson-authored Freemen of Frederick County Resolution for independence and nationhood put forth by Hanson is adopted by the Convention of Maryland as the position of Maryland which subscribed the state to the Declaration of Independence and " . . . took the first decided action on the part of the colony looking to an armed contest with Great Britain."[279]
July 2, 1776	Maryland's agreement to the Declaration of Independence authored by John Hanson

reaches the Second Continental Congress in Philadelphia ensuring unified nationhood. The Second Continental Congress passes the Declaration of Independence declaring the collective nationhood of the thirteen colonies.

July 4, 1776	A revised version of the Declaration of Independence, including rewording in a few places as agreed upon on July 2, is accepted by the Congress
July 6, 1776	Eighth Convention of Maryland declares independence from Great Britain and adjourns
August 2, 1776	The colonies, now becoming states, ratify the Declaration of Independence
August 14 – November 11, 1776	The Ninth Convention of Maryland, the last, is held in Annapolis, authors the Constitution of Maryland and the Maryland Declaration of Rights. The Conventions are replaced by the soon-to-be-organized State government.
October 19, 1776	Hanson appointed to reorganize Maryland troops and exhort them to enlist for the duration of the Revolutionary War
November and December 1776	John and Jane Hanson's son Lieutenant Peter Hanson is wounded in the battle of Fort Washington, New York, dies the following month as a prisoner of war, first of two Hanson sons to die in the war
November 10, 1776	Ninth Convention of Maryland adopts the Declaration of Rights and Constitution of Maryland, establishes bicameral legislature of Senate and House of Delegates
December 17, 1776	Elections held for State positions. Frederick County's Thomas Johnson, a Hanson friend and political ally, elected as Maryland's first governor.
February 5, 1777	The First General Assembly under the state Constitution convenes in Annapolis
February 13, 1777	Thomas Johnson sworn in as Maryland's first governor, serves two one-year terms

| June 14, 1777 | Stars and Stripes adopted as the nation's flag by the Second Continental Congress |

Formation of the First Government, 1777-1781

September, 1777	British occupy Philadelphia forcing the Second Continental Congress to remove to Lancaster, then York, Pennsylvania
November 15, 1777	At York, the Second Continental Congress passes the Articles of Confederation calling for the first national government to be formed. The Articles are sent to the states for ratification.
December 16, 1777	Virginia becomes the first state to approve the Articles of Confederation
December 17, 1777	France recognizes United States independence but withholds full diplomatic recognition
July 2, 1778	After British occupation of Philadelphia ends, Second Continental Congress returns from York, again meets in Independence Hall
November 1778	Frederick County elects John Hanson to serve as its Delegate in the new state legislature
1779-1782	Frederick County's Thomas Sim Lee serves three one-year terms as Maryland Governor, serves two more terms 1792-1794
May 21, 1779	Following Hanson's proposal, Maryland instructs her Second Continental Congress delegates not to sign the Articles of Confederation unless the new nation controls the western lands. Proposal comes to be known as the Hanson Plan.
December 22, 1779	Hanson elected as one of five to represent Maryland at Second Continental Congress. Hanson and Daniel Carroll only two to attend and serve.
June 1780	Hanson arrives at the reconvened Second Continental Congress
Over the next eight months	Hanson leads effort to get colonies with western lands to cede these territories to the nation, holds out Maryland's ratification until agreement, solves western lands impasse, es-

tablishes himself as national statesman and bridge-builder.[280] All states eventually agree to the Hanson Plan.

December, 1779	Virginia agrees to discussions on ceding her western lands
March 7, 1780	New York begins discussion on ceding her western lands
September 6, 1780	A Second Continental Congress committee recommends adoption of the Hanson Plan
October 10, 1780	Second Continental Congress passes resolution supporting the Hanson Plan, recommends it to the states for adoption
January 5, 1781	American traitor and British Brigadier General Benedict Arnold has his most dubious success as a British commander when his naval expedition burns the undefended Richmond, Virginia
February 2, 1781	Upon receiving New York's agreement to cede her western lands, Maryland withdraws opposition to approve Articles of Confederation
February 2, 1781	Maryland property of British subjects and loyalists confiscated
March 1, 1781	John Hanson and Daniel Carroll of Maryland are last to sign Articles of Confederation and Perpetual Union thus chartering the United States' original government. Hanson for the second time ensures unified nationhood. Articles of Confederation establish a new government, the United States in Congress Assembled, to come into being on the first Monday of November 1781. Articles provide for election of presidents to one-year terms on the first Monday of each November.
March 2, 1781-November 4, 1781	An attenuated interim body with scant powers and some delegates and officers from the Second Continental Congress continues to function as an official presence pending the launching of the first government
March 2-July 9, 1781	Samuel Huntington serves 130 days as president of the interim body

June 17, 1781	John and Jane Hanson's daughter Jane Contee Hanson Thomas, thirty-four, wife of John Hanson confidant Dr. Philip Thomas, dies in Frederick
June 29, 1781	John and Jane Hanson's son Dr. Samuel Harrison Hanson, twenty-four, is killed in the Revolutionary War less than four months before its last major battle
July 9, 1781	Samuel Johnston elected President of interim body *in absentia*, next day refuses to serve saying he does not want to preside over a temporary government not meeting often and only waiting for the United States in Congress Assembled to commence in November
July 10, 1781	Thomas McKean elected "Provisional President" with understanding that he will retire from the position upon regular presidential election on first Monday of November as provided in the Articles of Confederation
July 10-November 4, 1781	McKean serves 118 days as President of interim body. Persuaded to withdraw his resignation In October after resigning for the same reason that Johnston had.
September 20, 1781	John Hanson's will filed in Frederick County
October 19, 1781	Cornwallis surrenders at Yorktown. United States wins independence on the battlefield.
Soon after this	Revolutionary War winds down. British begin withdrawing troops. British House of Commons votes against further war in America.
November 4, 1781	Interim body eases to exist, to be replaced by the United States in Congress Assembled

The Hanson Administration, 1781-1782

| November 5, 1781 | United States in Congress Assembled, nation's first government, springs into being, meets in Independence Hall |
| November 5, 1781 | As its first act, the new United States in Congress Assembled unanimously elects John Hanson to a one-year term as the nation's first president. Hanson becomes first president elected to a stated fixed term under any |

form of United States government and first in the nation's history to be recognized at home or abroad as head of state.

November 5, 1781	Charles Thomson, Secretary of the United States in Congress Assembled, certifies President Hanson's election, informs the states, foreign nations and dignitaries
November 1781	Ranks of government officials established by the new government as: • President of the United States • Members of Congress • Commander in Chief of the Army • Secretary of the Congress (today's Speaker of the House) • Cabinet Secretaries as below
During Hanson's term	Departments of the government established. Chronological order of first three observed to-day in department seniority protocol and line of succession to the office of President: • Foreign Affairs (became Department of State under the Constitution) • Finance (became Department of Treasury under the Constitution) • War (Became Department of Defense in 1949) • Marine (Became Department of the Navy under the Constitution. Absorbed into the Department of War in 1947) • United States Post Office (became United States Postal Servicein 1971)
During Hanson's term	United States Consular Service established
During Hanson's term	Hanson appoints four who negotiate a peace treaty with Great Britain
During Hanson's term	Position of Chairman of Congress created, becomes today's United States Vice President
During Hanson's term	Jane Contee Hanson becomes first First Lady

During Hanson's term	President Hanson first to be provided an official residence
November 23, 1781	France formally recognizes the United States, calls for exchange of ambassadors
November 28, 1781	President Hanson and Congress receive General Washington and officially thank him for his service as Commander of the Army. Washington delivers Cornwallis's surrendered sword to Hanson and the Congress.
November 29, 1781	Upon departure for France, Marquis de Lafayette is given President Hanson's letter to Louis XVI, King of France, the first communication from a United States head of state to another head of state
November 30, 1781	Washington congratulates Hanson "on your appointment to fill the most important seat in the United States"
Before end of 1781	Four more nations recognize the United States. United States ambassadors posted to these nations' capitals in 1782.
December 11, 1781	First United States census ordered
December 31, 1781	Bank of North America, nation's first central bank, chartered by Congress
January 7, 1782	Bank of North America begins operation in Philadelphia
January 11, 1782	President Hanson informs thirteen state governors regarding the nation's new protocols and procedures of diplomatic immunity
January 28, 1782	President Hanson appoints first United States Postmaster General
January 29, 1782	President Hanson orders General Greene to mop up British Army resistance in the South.
February 5, 1782	President Hanson authorizes Benjamin Franklin, United States Ambassador to France, to accept loan which France has offered to the United States
February 11, 1782	Hanson orders United States Army uniforms standardized nationwide

February 22, 1782	Office of the Secretary of the United States, today's Secretary of State, created. Diplomatic protocols and procedures established.
April 10, 1782	Congress authorizes new War Department to direct building and management of barracks, arsenals, magazines, laboratories, foundries
April 12, 1782	Peace talks with Great Britain begin in Paris
April 15, 1782	President Hanson falls ill. Suggestions to name a temporary president or to elect a Vice President fail. Maryland Delegate Daniel Carroll chosen to preside temporarily with title of Chairman until Hanson's return.
By May	President Hanson resumes his duties.
April 19, 1782	Holland recognizes the United States, receives John Adams as United States Ambassador, begins negotiating a loan to the United States
April 24, 1782	The Agent of Marine (the future office of Secretary of the Navy) reports to Congress on construction of ships for the new United States Navy
May 13, 1782	Hanson presides over the nation's first state dinner in honor of the French Minister, the Chevalier de la Luzerne
June 20, 1782	Congress adopts the Great Seal of the United States, authorizes its fabrication. The original Seal and impressing mechanism are still in use today.
June 24, 1782	President Hanson orders state governors to suppress "illicit traffic and intercourse with enemies of the United States"
July 16, 1782	President Hanson presides over a state dinner honoring the Dauphine, the Crown Prince of France
August 28, 1782	President Hanson hands down a decision adjudicating a western lands boundary dispute between Connecticut and New York
September 14, 1782	President Hanson endorses ratification of a treaty with Holland

September 16, 1782	President Hanson authorizes Washington to exchange prisoners with Great Britain
September 16, 1782	President Hanson enters the Great Seal of the United States into service
September 1782	The United States and Sweden, which had recognized each other and entered into diplomatic relations during the Second Continental Congress, sign a Treaty of Amity and Commerce
October 11, 1782	President Hanson decrees the last Thursday of November to be observed annually nationwide as Thanksgiving Day (observed today as a national holiday on the fourth Thursday)
October 18, 1782	United States Post Office established
October 23, 1782	Army Quartermaster Corps reorganized
November 3, 1782	President Hanson's one-year term as president expires. He becomes first president in United States history to serve as a central government president and first of any entity to have and serve a full fixed term as president. At age sixty-seven and in declining health, he returns to his family in Frederick after spending nearly all of the previous thirty-four months in Philadelphia.
September 3, 1783	Treaty of Paris signed officially ending the Revolutionary War. Great Britain formally recognizes the United States.
November 22, 1783[281]	John Hanson, aged sixty-eight, dies at the home of his nephew Thomas Hanson in Oxon Hill, Maryland. Burial place becomes forgotten in twentieth century until rediscovered,
November 26, 1783	United States in Congress Assembled moves the government from Philadelphia to Annapolis, moves back to Philadelphia June 3, 1784
December 23, 1783	General George Washington resigns as Commander of the army, retires to private life at his Mount Vernon, Virginia, home
January 14, 1784	Treaty of Paris signed, formally ending the Revolutionary War

April 13,   John Hanson's will proved in Frederick
1784   County Court. Estate passes to his wife Jane
                Contee Hanson and then to their sole surviv-
                ing son Alexander Contee Hanson after
                Jane's passing but she will outlive Alexander.
                Will mentions widower Dr. Philip Thomas and
                his children.[282]

Transition to Constitutional Government, 1783-1789

April 23,   Jefferson Plan organizing the Northwest Ter-
1784   ritory and Southwest Territory passed by
                Congress. Earlier version in which Jefferson
                included prohibition of slavery in these terri-
                tories defeated by one vote in the Congress.

September   Annapolis Convention discusses improving
11-14, 1786   the Articles of Confederation

July 13,   In what is often regarded as its most impor-
1787   tant act, the United States in Congress As-
                sembled unanimously passes the Northwest
                Ordinance providing for westward expansion,
                statehood and outlawing of slavery for new
                states created from the ceded lands of the old
                Northwest Territory

September   Constitutional Convention, also known as the
17, 1787   Philadelphia Convention, George Washington
                presiding, concludes meeting to improve on
                Articles of Confederation, authors Constitu-
                tion of the United States

September   Proposed Constitution read in United States
20-28, 1787   in Congress Assembled, debated, referred to
                the states

December   Delaware by a 30-0 vote is first state to ratify
17, 1787   the Constitution

June 21,   New Hampshire by a 57-47 vote is ninth state
1788   to ratify. United States in Congress Assem-
                bled deems nine states, a two-thirds majority,
                enough to adopt the Constitution.

November 2,   Term of Cyrus Griffin, last president of the
1788   United States in Congress Assembled, ex-
                pires. United States in Congress Assembled
                goes out of business

November 2, 1788-April 30, 1789	For the only time, United States has no president. United States in Congress Assembled Secretary Charles Thomson remains on duty as sole official presence of the nation.
December 23, 1788	Maryland and Virginia give one hundred square miles (ten miles square) to the incipient second government to establish a national capital district named the District of Columbia. Virginia later takes back its part.
January 7, 1789	Presidential electors appointed by ten states to choose the first president of the new government under the Constitution. Maryland electors include Alexander Contee Hanson, Sr. and Dr. Philip Thomas.
February 4, 1789	Electors unanimously elect George Washington President of the United States
March 4, 1789	Constitution takes effect
April 30, 1789	George Washington inaugurated for his first term as president
October 3, 1789	Alexander Contee Hanson, Sr. replaces John Rogers as Chancellor of Maryland
November 21, 1789	North Carolina is the twelfth state to ratify the Constitution
May 29, 1790	Rhode Island the last (thirteenth) state to ratify by a bare 34-32 vote

Remembering John Hanson, 1790-Present

February 21, 1812	Jane Contee Hanson, the nation's first First Lady, widowed for twenty-nine years, dies at age eighty-four at her Frederick home. She outlived all but one of her thirteen children. "Died this evening in the 85th year Mrs. Jane Hanson relict of John Hanson, esq., a delegate to the old Revolutionary Congress."[283]
November 3, 1812	Alexander Contee Hanson, Jr., grandson of President John and Jane Hanson, elected from the third district of Maryland to the United States House of Representatives

December 20, 1816	Alexander Contee Hanson, Jr. begins service as a United States Senator
July 2, 1864	President Lincoln signs into law Congress's provision for a National Statuary Hall to be created in the United States Capitol.
1875	First John Hanson biography written by his great-grandson, John Hanson Thomas, Jr.
1876	George Hanson publishes his compilation of John Hanson and others in *Old Kent*
1898	Compilation of the John Hanson official record, written by his great-great-grandson Douglas H. Thomas, for Maryland's case to enter John Hanson into National Statuary Hall
January 31, 1903	Statue of President John Hanson, sculpted by Richard E. Brooks, presented by the State of Maryland and placed in National Statuary Hall in the United States Capitol.[284]
1930s	Three biographies of John Hanson published
1950s	The Vasa Society, a Swedish-American group, donates the John Hanson bust to Gloria Dei Old Swedes Church in Philadelphia, and a marble obelisk commemorating John Hanson to Mulberry Grove
Mid-century	Various Maryland landmarks named for John Hanson
1971-1981	Frederick, Maryland, historians, preservationists and others exert in vain strenuous efforts to preserve John Hanson's Frederick home
1973	Maryland Assembly under leadership of Speaker John Hanson Briscoe passes bill declaring April 14 each year as John Hanson Day
1981	Frederick County government tears down nearly all of John Hanson House. Front façade, basements, entry stairs and handrails preserved.
November 5, 1981	From the post office at Frederick, Maryland, the United States Postal Service issues a twenty-cent stamp with President John Han-

	son's presidential portrait commemorating the two-hundredth anniversary of his inauguration as president. The United States Capitol Historical Society issues a bronze medal commemorating the same.
1982	The John Hanson Society, a Maryland organization no longer active, operates until at least this year
2000 and later	Various myths and misinformation about John Hanson and the Hanson presidential record arise, make their way onto the Internet
February 25, 2002	Wikipedia entry on John Hanson begins, incorporates much of myth and misinformation about Hanson from unreliable sources and contributors' personal guesses, nevertheless becomes a top hit on Internet searches for John Hanson
May 21-23, 2007	Edward Edelen, owner of Mulberry Grove, John Hanson's first home, convenes group of officials, architects, historians and interested parties, launches planning of forthcoming John Hanson Institute at Port Tobacco, Maryland, adjacent to Mulberry Grove
April 14, 2008	On the 293rd anniversary of his birth, the John Hanson Memorial Association and the John Hanson National Memorial project are launched in Frederick, Maryland. First private donations and pledges of financial support begin arriving.
September 18, 2008	After purchase, bust of John Hanson and pedestal moved by Edward Edelen from Old Swedes Church in Philadelphia to Edelen's Mulberry Grove
January 6, 2009	John Hanson Memorial Association, Inc. incorporated in Maryland
May 19, 2009	Maryland Governor Martin O'Malley signs into law bond bill funding the John Hanson National Memorial
July 28, 2009	Board of County Commissioners of Frederick County, Maryland, authorizes John Hanson National Memorial

September, 2009	Nationally prominent sculptor Antonio Tobias Mendez chosen to design and produce the John Hanson National Memorial
April 14, 2011	Peter Michael rediscovers the plundered gravesite of John Hanson
May 22, 2011	Construction of the John Hanson National Memorial is complete
June 6, 2011	Peter Michael, Ronald Pearcey and C. Larry Bishop rediscover the unmarked mass grave of Jane Hanson
May 21, 2012	Formal dedication of the John Hanson National Memorial planned for this date with President Barack Obama presiding

Appendix Two

Continental Congress and Government Presidents

Presidents of the First Continental Congress (two)

Peyton Randolph (September 5, 1774 – October 21, 1774)

Henry Middleton (October 22, 1774 – October 26, 1774)

Presidents of the Second Continental Congress (five)

Peyton Randolph (May 10, 1775 – May 23, 1775)

John Hancock (May 24, 1775 – October 31, 1777)

Henry Laurens (November 1, 1777 – December 9, 1778)

John Jay (December 10, 1778 – September 27, 1779)

Samuel Huntington (September 28, 1779 – March 1, 1781)

Presidents of the 249-Day Interim Body of 1781 (two or three)

When the Articles of Confederation were ratified on March 1, 1781, elections were not held to choose a new president of the interim body, with Samuel Huntington continuing to serve as the presiding officer until stepping down on July 9, 1781. That day, Samuel Johnston of North Carolina was chosen *in absentia* as Huntington's successor but declined the office the next day without ever actually serving. On July 10, Thomas McKean of Delaware was then chosen as presiding officer for the remainder of the body's life with the understanding that he would stand down on November 4.

Samuel Huntington (March 2, 1781 – July 9, 1781)

Samuel Johnston (July 9-10, 1781) Elected but refused to serve

Thomas McKean (July 10, 1781 – November 4, 1781)

Presidents of the United States in Congress Assembled (eight or nine)

John Hanson (November 5, 1781 – November 3, 1782)

Elias Boudinot (November 4, 1782 – November 2, 1783)

Thomas Mifflin (November 3, 1783 – October 31, 1784)

Richard Henry Lee (November 30, 1784 – November 6, 1785)

John Hancock (elected to the November 1, 1785 – November 5, 1786 term) Due to poor health, Hancock did not serve. The following two men served in Hancock's place during his term.

David Ramsay (November 23, 1785 – May 12, 1786)

Nathaniel Gorham (May 15 – November 5, 1786)

Arthur St. Clair (February 2, 1787 – November 4, 1787)

Cyrus Griffin (January 22, 1788 – November 2, 1788)

Presidents of the United States (forty-four as of 2012)

George Washington followed by forty-three others as of 2011[285]

Appendix Three

The Declaration of Maryland

Following are the complete instructions issued by the Maryland General Assembly on December 15, 1778, to the state's Second Continental Congress delegates to withhold Maryland's ratification of the Articles of Confederation unless the Articles were to include wording satisfactory to Maryland resolving the western lands impasse. Aside from providing clear guidance to the Maryland delegates, the Assembly's additional motivations in issuing the instructions were to articulate to the Congress and the legislatures of the other states a carefully drawn exposition of Maryland's reasoning on the western lands issue, and to soften the Assembly's more strident position previously put forth. Henceforth, the instructions came to be known as the Declaration of Maryland.

Δ

Having conferred upon you a trust of the highest nature, it is evident we place great confidence in your integrity, abilities and zeal, to promote the general welfare of the United States, and the particular interest of this State, where the latter is not incompatible with the former; but to add greater weight to your proceedings in Congress, and take away all suspicions that the opinions you there entertain and the votes you give may be the mere opinions of individuals, and not resulting from your knowledge of the sense and deliberate judgment of the State you represent; we think it our duty to instruct as followeth on the subject of the Confederation; a subject in which, unfortunately, a supposed difference of interest has produced an almost equal division of sentiment among the several States comprising the Union. We say a supposed difference of interests, for if local attachments and prejudices, and the avarice and ambition of individuals, would give way to the dictates of a sound policy founded on the principles of justice (and no other policy but what is founded on those immutable principles deserves to be called sound), we flatter ourselves this apparent diversity of interests would soon vanish, and all the States would confederate on terms mutually advantageous to all; for they would then perceive that no other confederation than one so formed can be lasting. Although the pressure of immediate calamities, the dread of their continuance from the appearance of disunion, and some other peculiar circumstances, may have induced some States to accede to the present confederation contrary to their own interests and judgments, it requires no great share of foresight to predict that, when those causes cease to operate, the States which have thus acceded to the Confederation will consider it as no longer binding, and will eagerly embrace the first occasion of asserting their just rights and securing their independence. Is it possible that those States who are ambitiously grasping at territories to which, in our judgment, they have not the least shadow of exclusive right, will use with greater moderation the increase of wealth and power derived from those territories, when acquired, that what they have displayed in their endeavors to acquire them? We think not. We are convinced the same spirit which hath prompted them to insist on a claim so extravagant, so repugnant to every principle of justice, so incompatible with the general welfare of all the States, will urge them on to add oppression to injustice. If they should not be incited by a superiority of wealth and strength to oppress, by open force, their less wealthy and less powerful neighbors, yet depopulation, and consequently, the impoverishment of those States, will necessarily follow, which, by an unfair construction of the Confederation, may be stripped of a common interest and the common benefits desirable from the Western country. Suppose, for instance, Virginia, indisputably possessed of the extensive and fertile country to which she has set up claim, what would be the probable consequence to Maryland of such an undisturbed and undisputed possession? They cannot escape the least discerning.

Virginia, by selling, on the most moderate terms, a small proportion of the lands in question, would draw into her treasury vast sums of money; and, in proportion to the sums arising from such sales, would be enabled to lessen her taxes. Lands comparatively cheap, and taxes comparatively low, with the lands and taxes of the adjacent State, would quickly drain the State thus disadvantageously circumstanced of its most useful inhabitants; its wealth and its consequence in the scale of the Confederated States would sink of course. A claim so injurious to more than one-half, if not to the whole of the United States, ought to be supported by the clearest evidence of the right; yet what evidence of that right has been produced? What arguments alleged in support, either of the evidence or the right ? None that we have heard of deserving a serious refutation.

It has been said that some of the delegates of a neighboring State have declared their opinion of the impracticability of governing the extensive domain claimed by that State; hence, also, the necessity was admitted of dividing its territory and erecting a new State, under the auspices and direction of the elder, from whom, no doubt, it would receive its form of government, to whom it would be bound by some alliance or confederacy, and by whose councils it would be influenced; such a measure, if ever attempted, would certainly be opposed by the other States, as inconsistent with the letter and spirit of the proposed confederation. Should it take place, by establishing a sub-confederacy, *imperium in imperio,* the State possessed of this extensive dominion must then either submit to all the inconveniences of an overgrown and unwieldy government, or suffer the authority of Congress to interpose at a future time, and to lop off a part of its territory, to be erected into a new and free State, and admitted into the confederation on such conditions as shall be settled by nine States. If it is necessary for the happiness and tranquility of a State thus overgrown, that Congress should hereafter interfere and divide its territory; why is the claim to that territory now made and so pertinaciously insisted on? We can suggest to ourselves but two motives; either the declaration of relinquishing, at some future period, a portion of the country now contended for, was made to lull suspicion asleep, and to cover the designs of a secret ambition, or, if the thought was seriously entertained, the lands are now claimed to reap an immediate profit from the sale. We are convinced, policy and justice require that a country unsettled at the commencement of this war, *claimed by the British crown,* and *ceded to it by the treaty of Paris,* if wrested from the common enemy by the blood and treasure of the thirteen States, should be considered *as a common property,* subject to be parceled out by Congress into free, convenient and independent governments, *in such manner* and at such times as the wisdom of that assembly shall hereafter direct.

Thus convinced, we should betray the trust reposed in us by our constituents were we to authorize you to ratify on their behalf the Confederation, unless it be further explained. We have coolly and dispassionately considered the subject; we have weighed probable inconveniences and hardships against the sacrifice of just and essential rights; and do instruct you not to agree to the Confederation unless an article or articles be added thereto in conformity with our declaration. Should we succeed in obtaining such article or articles, then you are hereby fully empowered to accede to the Confederacy.

Appendix Four
The Articles of Confederation

Following is the exact text of the Articles of Confederation ratified on March 1, 1781, including its spellings and other English usages of the era.

The Articles of Confederation and Perpetual Union

Between The States of New Hampshire, Massachusetts-bay, Rhode Island and Providence Plantations, Connecticut, New York, New Jersey, Pennsylvania, Delaware, Maryland, Virginia, North Carolina, South Carolina and Georgia.

ARTICLE I. The Stile of this Confederacy shall be "The United States of America."

ARTICLE II. Each state retains its sovereignty, freedom, and independence, and every power, jurisdiction, and right, which is not by this Confederation expressly delegated to the United States, in Congress assembled.

ARTICLE III. The said States hereby severally enter into a firm league of friendship with each other, for their common defense, the security of their liberties, and their mutual and general welfare, binding themselves to assist each other, against all force offered to, or attacks made upon them, or any of them, on account of religion, sovereignty, trade, or any other pretense whatever.

ARTICLE IV. The better to secure and perpetuate mutual friendship and intercourse among the people of the different States in this Union, the free inhabitants of each of these States, paupers, vagabonds, and fugitives from justice excepted, shall be entitled to all privileges and immunities of free citizens in the several States; and the people of each State shall free ingress and regress to and from any other State, and shall enjoy therein all the privileges of trade and commerce, subject to the same duties, impositions, and restrictions as the inhabitants thereof respectively, provided that such restrictions shall not extend so far as to prevent the removal of property imported into any State, to any other State, of which the owner is an inhabitant; provided also that no imposition, duties or restriction shall be laid by any State, on the property of the United States, or either of them.

If any person guilty of, or charged with, treason, felony, or other high misdemeanor in any State, shall flee from justice, and be found in any of the United States, he shall, upon demand of the Governor or executive power of the State from which he fled, be delivered up and removed to the State having jurisdiction of his offense.

Full faith and credit shall be given in each of these States to the records, acts, and judicial proceedings of the courts and magistrates of every other State.

ARTICLE V. For the most convenient management of the general interests of the United States, delegates shall be annually appointed in such manner as the legislatures of each State shall direct, to meet in Congress on the first Monday in November, in every year, with a power reserved to each State to recall its delegates, or any of them, at any time within the year, and to send others in their stead for the remainder of the year.

No State shall be represented in Congress by less than two, nor more than seven members; and no person shall be capable of being a delegate for more than three years in any term of six years; nor shall any person, being a delegate, be capable of holding any office under the United States, for which he, or another for his benefit, receives any salary, fees or emolument of any kind.

Each State shall maintain its own delegates in a meeting of the States, and while they act as members of the committee of the States.

In determining questions in the United States in Congress Assembled, each State shall have one vote.

Freedom of speech and debate in Congress shall not be impeached or questioned in any court or place out of Congress, and the members of Congress shall be protected in their persons from arrests or imprisonments, during the time of their going to and from, and attendance on Congress, except for treason, felony, or breach of the peace.

ARTICLE VI. No State, without the consent of the United States in Congress Assembled, shall send any embassy to, or receive any embassy from, or enter into any conference, agreement, alliance or treaty with any King, Prince or State; nor shall any person holding any office of profit or trust under the United States, or any of them, accept any present, emolument, office or title of any kind whatever from any King, Prince or foreign State; nor shall the United States in Congress Assembled, or any of them, grant any title of nobility.

No two or more States shall enter into any treaty, confederation or alliance whatever between them, without the consent of the United States in Congress Assembled, specifying accurately the purposes for which the same is to be entered into, and how long it shall continue.

No State shall lay any imposts or duties, which may interfere with any stipulations in treaties, entered into by the United States in Congress Assembled, with any King, Prince or State, in pursuance of any treaties already proposed by Congress, to the courts of France and Spain.

No vessel of war shall be kept up in time of peace by any State, except such number only, as shall be deemed necessary by the United States in Congress Assembled, for the defense of such State, or its trade; nor shall any body of forces be kept up by any State in time of peace, except such number only, as in the judgment of the United States in Congress Assembled, shall be deemed requisite to garrison the forts necessary for the defense of such State; but every State shall always keep up a well-regulated and disciplined militia, sufficiently armed and accoutered, and shall provide and constantly have ready for use, in public stores, a due number of filed pieces and tents, and a proper quantity of arms, ammunition and camp equipage.

No State shall engage in any war without the consent of the United States in Congress Assembled, unless such State be actually invaded by enemies, or shall have received certain advice of a resolution being formed by some nation of Indians to invade such State, and the danger is so imminent as not to admit of a delay till the United States in Congress Assembled can be consulted; nor shall any State grant commissions to any ships or vessels of war, nor letters of marque or reprisal, except it be after a declaration of war by the United States in Congress Assembled, and then only against the Kingdom or State and the subjects thereof, against which war has been so declared, and under such regulations as shall be established by the United States in Congress Assembled, unless such State be infested by pirates, in which case vessels of war may be fitted out for that occasion, and kept so long as the danger shall continue, or until the United States in Congress Assembled shall determine otherwise.

ARTICLE VII. When land forces are raised by any State for the common defense, all officers of or under the rank of colonel, shall be appointed by the legislature of each State respectively, by whom such forces shall be raised, or in such manner as such State shall direct, and all vacancies shall be filled up by the State which first made the appointment.

ARTICLE VIII. All charges of war, and all other expenses that shall be incurred for the common defense or general welfare, and allowed by the United States in Congress Assembled, shall be defrayed out of a common treasury, which shall be supplied by the several States in proportion to the value of all land within each State, granted or surveyed for any person, as such land and the buildings and improvements thereon shall be estimated according to such mode as the United States in Congress Assembled, shall from time to time direct and appoint.

The taxes for paying that proportion shall be laid and levied by the authority and direction of the legislatures of the several States within the time agreed upon by the United States in Congress Assembled.

ARTICLE IX. The United States in Congress Assembled, shall have the sole and exclusive right and power of determining on peace and war, except in the cases mentioned in the sixth article -- of sending and receiving ambassadors -- entering into treaties and alliances, provided that no treaty of commerce shall be made whereby the legislative power of the respective States shall be restrained from imposing such imposts and duties on foreigners, as their own people are subjected to, or from prohibiting the exportation or importation of any species of goods or commodities whatsoever -- of establishing rules for deciding in all cases, what captures on land or water shall be legal, and in what manner prizes taken by land or naval forces in the service of the United States shall be divided or appropriated -- of granting letters of marque and reprisal in times of peace -- appointing courts for the trial of piracies and felonies committed on the high seas and establishing courts for receiving and determining finally appeals in all cases of captures, provided that no member of Congress shall be appointed a judge of any of the said courts.

The United States in Congress Assembled shall also be the last resort on appeal in all disputes and differences now subsisting or that hereafter may arise between two or more

States concerning boundary, jurisdiction or any other causes whatever; which authority shall always be exercised in the manner following. Whenever the legislative or executive authority or lawful agent of any State in controversy with another shall present a petition to Congress stating the matter in question and praying for a hearing, notice thereof shall be given by order of Congress to the legislative or executive authority of the other State in controversy, and a day assigned for the appearance of the parties by their lawful agents, who shall then be directed to appoint by joint consent, commissioners or judges to constitute a court for hearing and determining the matter in question: but if they cannot agree, Congress shall name three persons out of each of the United States, and from the list of such persons each party shall alternately strike out one, the petitioners beginning, until the number shall be reduced to thirteen; and from that number not less than seven, nor more than nine names as Congress shall direct, shall in the presence of Congress be drawn out by lot, and the persons whose names shall be so drawn or any five of them, shall be commissioners or judges, to hear and finally determine the controversy, so always as a major part of the judges who shall hear the cause shall agree in the determination: and if either party shall neglect to attend at the day appointed, without showing reasons, which Congress shall judge sufficient, or being present shall refuse to strike, the Congress shall proceed to nominate three persons out of each State, and the secretary of Congress shall strike in behalf of such party absent or refusing; and the judgment and sentence of the court to be appointed, in the manner before prescribed, shall be final and conclusive; and if any of the parties shall refuse to submit to the authority of such court, or to appear or defend their claim or cause, the court shall nevertheless proceed to pronounce sentence, or judgment, which shall in like manner be final and decisive, the judgment or sentence and other proceedings being in either case transmitted to Congress, and lodged among the acts of Congress for the security of the parties concerned: provided that every commissioner, before he sits in judgment, shall take an oath to be administered by one of the judges of the supreme or superior court of the State, where the cause shall be tried, 'well and truly to hear and determine the matter in question, according to the best of his judgment, without favor, affection or hope of reward': provided also, that no State shall be deprived of territory for the benefit of the United States.

All controversies concerning the private right of soil claimed under different grants of two or more States, whose jurisdictions as they may respect such lands, and the States which passed such grants are adjusted, the said grants or either of them being at the same time claimed to have originated antecedent to such settlement of jurisdiction, shall on the petition of either party to the Congress of the United States, be finally determined as near as may be in the same manner as is before prescribed for deciding disputes respecting territorial jurisdiction between different States.

The United States in Congress Assembled shall also have the sole and exclusive right and power of regulating the alloy and value of coin struck by their own authority, or by that of the respective States -- fixing the standards of weights and measures throughout the United States -- regulating the trade and managing all affairs with the Indians, not members of any of the States, provided that the legislative right of any State within its own limits be not infringed or violated -- establishing or regulating post offices from one State to another, throughout all the United States, and exacting such postage on the papers passing through the same as may be requisite to defray the expenses of the said office -- appointing all officers of the land forces, in the service of the United States, excepting regimental officers -- appointing all the officers of the naval forces, and commissioning all officers whatever in the service of the United States -- making rules for the government and regulation of the said land and naval forces, and directing their operations.

The United States in Congress Assembled shall have authority to appoint a committee, to sit in the recess of Congress, to be denominated 'A Committee of the States', and to consist of one delegate from each State; and to appoint such other committees and civil officers as may be necessary for managing the general affairs of the United States under their direction -- to appoint one of their members to preside, provided that no person be allowed to serve in the office of president more than one year in any term of three years; to ascertain the necessary sums of money to be raised for the service of the United States, and to appropriate and apply the same for defraying the public expenses -- to borrow money, or emit bills on the credit of the United States, transmitting every half-year to the respective States an account of the sums of money so borrowed or emitted -- to build and equip a navy -- to agree upon the number of land forces, and to make requisitions from each State for its quota, in proportion to the number of white inhabitants in such State; which requisition shall be binding, and thereupon the legislature of each State shall appoint the regimental officers, raise the men and cloath, arm and equip them in a solid-like manner, at the expense of the United States; and the officers and men so cloathed, armed and equipped shall march to the place appointed, and within the time agreed on by the United States in Congress Assembled. But if the United States in Congress Assembled shall, on consideration of circumstances judge proper that any State should not raise men, or should raise a smaller number of men than the quota thereof, such extra number shall be raised, officered, cloathed, armed and equipped in the same manner as the quota of each State, unless the legislature of such State shall judge that such extra number cannot be safely spread out in the same, in which case they shall raise, officer, cloath, arm and equip as many of such extra number as they judge can be safely spared. And the officers and men so cloathed, armed, and equipped, shall march to the place appointed, and within the time agreed on by the United States in Congress Assembled.

The United States in Congress Assembled shall never engage in a war, nor grant letters of marque or reprisal in time of peace, nor enter into any treaties or alliances, nor coin money, nor regulate the value thereof, nor ascertain the sums and expenses necessary for the defense and welfare of the United States, or any of them, nor emit bills, nor borrow money on the credit of the United States, nor appropriate money, nor agree upon the number of vessels of war, to be built or purchased, or the number of land or sea forces to be raised, nor appoint a commander in chief of the army or navy, unless nine States assent to the same: nor shall a question on any other point, except for adjourning from day to day be determined, unless by the votes of the majority of the United States in Congress Assembled.

The Congress of the United States shall have power to adjourn to any time within the year, and to any place within the United States, so that no period of adjournment be for a longer duration than the space of six months, and shall publish the journal of their proceedings monthly, except such parts thereof relating to treaties, alliances or military operations, as in their judgment require secrecy; and the yeas and nays of the delegates of each State on any question shall be entered on the journal, when it is desired by any delegates of a State, or any of them, at his or their request shall be furnished with a transcript of the said journal, except such parts as are above excepted, to lay before the legislatures of the several States.

ARTICLE X. The Committee of the States, or any nine of them, shall be authorized to execute, in the recess of Congress, such of the powers of Congress as the United States in Congress Assembled, by the consent of the nine States, shall from time to time think expedient to vest them with; provided that no power be delegated to the said Committee, for the exercise of which, by the Articles of Confederation, the voice of nine States in the Congress of the United States assembled be requisite.

ARTICLE XI. Canada acceding to this confederation, and adjoining in the measures of the United States, shall be admitted into, and entitled to all the advantages of this Union; but no other colony shall be admitted into the same, unless such admission be agreed to by nine States.

ARTICLE XII. All bills of credit emitted, monies borrowed, and debts contracted by, or under the authority of Congress, before the assembling of the United States, in pursuance of the present confederation, shall be deemed and considered as a charge against the United States, for payment and satisfaction whereof the said United States, and the public faith are hereby solemnly pleged.

ARTICLE XIII. Every State shall abide by the determination of the United States in Congress Assembled, on all questions which by this confederation are submitted to them. And the Articles of this Confederation shall be inviolably observed by every State, and the Union shall be perpetual; nor shall any alteration at any time hereafter be made in any of them; unless such alteration be agreed to in a Congress of the United States, and be afterwards confirmed by the legislatures of every State.

And Whereas it hath pleased the Great Governor of the World to incline the hearts of the legislatures we respectively represent in Congress, to approve of, and to authorize us to ratify the said Articles of Confederation and Perpetual Union. Know Ye that we the undersigned delegates, by virtue of the power and authority to us given for that purpose, do by these presents, in the name and in behalf of our respective constituents, fully and entirely ratify and confirm each and every of the said Articles of Confederation and perpetual Union, and all and singular the matters and things therein contained: And we do further solemnly plight and engage the faith of our respective constituents, that they shall abide by the determinations of the United States in Congress Assembled, on all questions, which by the said Confederation are submitted to them. And that the Articles thereof shall be inviolably observed by the States we respectively represent, and that the Union shall be perpetual. In Witness whereof, we have hereunto set our hands in Congress.

DONE at Philadelphia, in the State of Pennsylvania, the 9th day of July, in the Year of our Lord 1778, and in the third year of the independence of America.

The aforesaid articles of confederation were finally ratified on the first day of March 1781; the state of Maryland having, by their Members in Congress, on that day acceded thereto, and completed the same.

New Hampshire: Josiah Bartlett, John Wentworth, jun.

Massachusetts Bay: John Hancock, Samuel Adams, Elbridge Gerry, Francis Dana,
James Lovell, Samuel Holten

Rhode Island and Providence Plantations: William Ellery, Henry Marchant, John Collins

Connecticut: Roger Sherman, Samuel Huntington, Oliver Wolcott, Titus Hosmer,
Andrew Adams

New York: James Duane, Francis Lewis, William Duer, Governeur Morris

New Jersey: John Witherspoon, Nathaniel Scudder

Pennsylvania: Robert Morris, Daniel Roberdeau, John Bayard Smith, William Clingan,
Joseph Reed

Delaware: Thomas M'kean, John Dickinson, Nicholas Van Dyke

Maryland: John Hanson, Daniel Carroll

Virginia: Richard Henry Lee, John Banister, Thomas Adams, John Harvie,
Francis Lightfoot Lee

N. Carolina: John Penn, Cornelius Harnett, John Williams

S. Carolina: Henry Laurens, Will Henry Drayton, John Mathews, Richard Hutson,
Thomas Heyward, jun.

Georgia: John Walton, Edward Telfair, Edward Longworthy

Appendix Five
European Origins of the Hanson Family

While the question of the European origins of President John Hanson is of interest, it has no particular bearing on the president himself, his contributions toward the founding of the United States or his presidency. Of necessity in discussing John Hanson's family origins is to settle two fiercely contending theories on the family's origins, demonstrate that neither is proven, and present two other conjectures, one of them compelling but also unproven. This appendix provides the full historical detail of the four competing theories on the European lineage of the Hanson family as completely as the author has been able to research the topic as of the time of publication of *Remembering John Hanson*. If what follows seems overly detailed, it is to put to rest the now proven fallacy of one claim, preserve and present in one place this historical detail much of which is newly gathered, and show that no theory yet offered on the European ancestry of President John Hanson is conclusive.

Here, we revisit the controversy over President John Hanson's ancestry mentioned briefly at the beginning of *Remembering John Hanson*. We recall that four scenarios have been put forward regarding the immigrant ancestor of President John Hanson. Two of these, here called the Six Hansons Scenario and the Lord Mayor of London Conjecture, have been previously suggested with only cursory investigation by others, and have never been advanced as actual claims as to the origin of the immigrant Hanson from whom President John Hanson descends, but it is conceivable that either could be a correct claim, particularly the latter. The two more prominent scenarios explored here as full claims of Hanson family ancestry are George Hanson's Four Brothers Claim of 1876 and a modern genealogist's Barbados Immigrant Claim in 1988. These two claims have elicited strong contention against one other.

George Hanson's "Four Brothers" Claim

The origins of President John Hanson's family line are seemingly well traced by the president's claimed distant relative[286], the historian and author George Hanson in his 1876 book *Old Kent*[287] which shows the immigrant ancestor of President John Hanson as one of four English-Swedish brothers who emigrated together to America from Sweden in 1642. George Hanson claimed that the genealogy of President John Hanson's family is primarily English and traced it to one Roger de Rastrick[288] of Rastrick, Halifax Parish, York County, England, in the year 1251. According to this account, Roger de Rastrick's great-great-great-grandson, John de Rastrick, son of Henry de Rastrick, in 1330 assumed the name John Hanson, the new surname meaning "son of Henry" following the era's custom of one's surname coming from the father's first name.[289] After this first John Hanson, President John Hanson is the tenth in his line so named according to George Hanson. See the chart at the end of this appendix for George Hanson's claimed line from Roger de Rastrick to President John Hanson and to himself.

More than two centuries after the sixth John Hanson are three others of the same name. Writes George Hanson, "John Hanson, of London, son of John Hanson and Frances Pritchard, while taking a summer tour in Sweden, fell in love with and m. a Swedish lady, who was closely connected, in friendship, at least, with the Royal Family. He and his wife d. young, leaving a son, who was reared in familiar intimacy with [future Swedish king] Gustavus Adolphus, then a youth about the same age. At a suitable time he entered the army, served with credit, rose to the rank of Colonel, became a trusted officer, and was always retained near the royal person in action. While defending and attempting to shield his King, he fell, slain in battle, with Gustavus Adolphus, at Lutzen, 16th Nov. 1632. He left four sons, viz. Andrew Hanson, — Randal or Randolph Hanson, — William Hanson and John Hanson, all of whom were taken under the immediate protection of the Royal Family of Sweden. In August 1642 Queen Christina placed them in the special care of Lieutenant Colonel John Printz, Governor in New Sweden, with whom they came to the Delaware, and remained there on Tinicum Island, until the year 1653, when they came to Kent Island."[290]

The New Sweden colony had been first settled in 1637 when the *Key of Kalmar* and the *Bird Grip* landed 150 Swedes at Tinicum Island in the Delaware River near present day Philadelphia. There the group established Fort Christina, the seat of New Sweden.

Kent Island, to which George Hanson claims the brothers relocated in 1653, lies in the Chesapeake Bay on the Eastern Shore of Maryland and in August 1631 became the first place in Maryland settled by Europeans when William Claiborne, coming from the Jamestown colony in Virginia, began trading with Native Americans. Claiborne named the island for Kent, England, his birthplace. By 1634 the settlement included a mill and courthouse in addition to Claiborne's trading station. After Maryland was officially formed as a British colony that year, Claiborne continued claiming Kent Island as part of Virginia but lost the argument to Caecilius Calvert, second Baron Baltimore of Maryland, who three times expelled Claiborne from the island until he left permanently in 1658. Virginia continued to claim Kent Island until 1776.

George Hanson is correct that Gustavus Adolphus died in the Battle of Lutzen on November 6, 1632. "Moving a conquering hero from the borders of Hungary and Silesia to the banks of the Rhine and from the Lake of Constance to the Black Sea, beholding cities and warriors yield to the force of his arm, uplifted in the cause of religious liberty, Gustavus Adolphus finally met a soldier's death on the battlefield of Lutzen."[291] He was succeeded on the throne by his daughter Christina (1626-1689) who never married and ruled from 1632 to 1654 when she was succeeded by her first cousin Charles X Gustav. Christina thus took the throne at the age of six. She was sixteen when the four Hanson brothers allegedly emigrated to New Sweden so the brothers would have been raised by someone else in the royal household if George Hanson is correct that these boys actually existed and had resided in Sweden. Though their queen, the brothers probably would have known Christina more as their cousin, which she was.

One hears the debate as to whether the immigrant Hanson brothers were English or Swedish. If George Hanson's account here and Anna Dorsey's below are correct, then by having an English grandfather and a Swedish grandmother, they were of both national strains obviating debate. Though the name Hanson is common in both England and Sweden, in this case it is English.

Modern genealogical research confirms the line from Roger de Rastrick to John and Mary Frances Pritchard Hanson at the end of the sixteenth century in London as claimed by George Hanson[292] who either identified or hypothesized this couple as the parents of the claimed John Hanson traveler to Sweden. A modern genealogy of the Rastrick/Hanson line does show a John Hanson of London, born in 1586, as son of John and Frances Pritchard Hanson.[293] However, another genealogy of this line of the Hanson family shows a Thomas and an Edward but not a John as son of John and Mary Frances Hanson.[294]   As the first-cited genealogy shows a more complete array of descendants of John and Mary Frances Pritchard Hanson and others in the genealogy, it is accepted as the more authoritative.

According to the history which George Hanson provided, Governor Printz, the four young Hanson brothers and the Governor's party arrived at the New Sweden colony aboard the *Swan* and *Fama* in 1642.   It is known that these two ships did, in fact, arrive at the New Sweden colony that year.[295]   The question then is who was aboard. George Hanson claims that the youngest of the brothers was the John Hanson who was the immigrant grandfather of President John Hanson and that the boy was twelve upon arrival in America.   He thus would have been born in 1630.   If his great-grandparents were John and Mary Frances Pritchard Hanson, then the ostensible immigrant John was born when his great-grandfather was forty-four which is biologically possible but barely.   This assumes that the genealogies inspected for this analysis are correct.

Much of the area of present-day Delaware and Pennsylvania claimed by Sweden was claimed by the Dutch as well. Within a few decades of the settlement of New Sweden, the Dutch had prevailed, claiming the residents of New Sweden as Dutch subjects.   Some of the Swedes of New Sweden acceded to this tide taking Dutch citizenship in the New Amsterdam colony, while others left.   According to George Hanson, all of the other John Hanson biographers, and the rendition of Anna Hanson McKinney Dorsey below, the four Hanson brothers left New Sweden travelling south about eighty miles to Kent Island, Maryland, in the 1650s.

George Hanson claims descent from Andrew, eldest of the four immigrant brothers, and says of the youngest immigrant brother John Hanson, "Col. John Hanson, youngest son of Col. Hanson of the Swedish Army, was b. in Sweden, about the year 1630, came to New Sweden, on the Delaware, in 1642, removed to Maryland in 1653, and after a short sojourn on Kent Island, went to St. Mary's: finally, about, or after, the year 1656, he settled in Charles County, and lived there until his death."[296]   George Hanson believed this ostensible immigrant Colonel John Hanson to be the same Charles County Colonel John Hanson reliably identified as the grandfather of President John Hanson.

Partly on the basis of George Hanson's *Old Kent* but also on the scholarship of University of Pennsylvania Professor

Amandus Johnson[297], the Vasa Society, the Swedish-American organization previously mentioned, donated two monuments in memory of President John Hanson. One of these is the marble obelisk dedicated at Mulberry Grove, on October 17, 1959,[298] the other, the John Hanson bust given to Gloria Dei Old Swedes Church in Philadelphia at about the same time. As mentioned, the bust is now at Mulberry Grove.

Expanding on George Hanson's Four Brothers claim is the letter of Anna Hanson McKinney Dorsey (1815-1896) to Josephine Ridue in 1882, two years after George Hanson died.[299] Ms. Dorsey is the great-grandniece of President John Hanson. In her letter, she better defines the Hanson English-Swedish relationship which George Hanson left incomplete in his *Old Kent*: Dorsey writes that the four brothers' father was the child of a John Hanson of England — George Hanson's traveler — and specifically of Margaret Vasa, sister of the Swedish King Gustavus Adolphus. If true, this explains how the four orphaned boys would have been raised in the Swedish royal household as they would have been the grandnephews of the King. Revealingly, Anna Dorsey also comments in detail on the continuation of the de Rastrick coat of arms into the 1600s and provides the only known reference found by the author to a Swedish modification of the coat of arms to indicate the Swedish royalty of the four brothers. Ms. Dorsey wrote that she possessed both versions of the coat of arms at the time of her letter in 1882. These are probably the two coats of arms auctioned in 2011.

If Anna Hanson McKinney Dorsey was in fact George Hanson's distant cousin as she states *and* since she descends from the president's father Samuel Hanson which, in fact, she does, then the common ancestor of her, George Hanson, Samuel Hanson, the president and many others precedes the known immigrant John Hanson of southern Maryland and therefore could be the Colonel Hanson of the Swedish Army as George Hanson claimed.[300] Anna Dorsey's specificity regarding the grandparentage of the four brothers and the modified coat of arms lends significant credence to the Four Brothers claim. However, it is possible that, for whatever reason, Anna Dorsey might have assumed incorrectly that she was related to George Hanson when she wasn't. Her verified line from the immigrant John Hanson is shown in the genealogical chart at the end of this appendix.

Anna Hanson McKinney Dorsey was the mother of the

author Ella Loraine Dorsey mentioned earlier who had written the precise account of John Hanson's solving the western lands impasse permitting the Articles of Confederation to be brought to life.

John Hanson biographer J. Bruce Kremer provides a detailed genealogy of the Hanson family from the John Hanson he believes to have died in the battle of Lutzen in 1632, through his presumed four sons who emigrated to New Sweden, through President John Hanson and his siblings, to two generations later including Alexander Contee Hanson, Jr. in 1819. In a genealogical chart, Kremer provides as much detail on the four brothers as seems to be available anywhere except in George Hanson's *Old Kent*.[301]

Kremer shows the eldest of the four brothers, Anders (Andrew) Hanson having married his wife Annika in Sweden before their arrival in America and fathering the well-researched Colonel Hans Hanson of Kimbolton, among his other children. It is well recorded that Hans Hanson represented both Kent and Cecil Counties in the colonial Maryland Assembly and served as a judge in Kent County.

Kremer has the second brother, Randal (Randolph) Hanson (without his wife's name) as fathering Barbara Hanson who married Thomas Hatton. Kremer notes that an unnamed descendant of this couple built the southern Maryland estate West Hatton thirteen miles from Mulberry Grove.

William Hanson, the third brother, is noted by Kremer as having married Alice, no last name given. According to Kremer, after a brief period across the bay in St. Mary's County, William returned to Kent County on the Maryland Eastern Shore where he lived out his life as a planter, dying in 1684. William and Alice may have had children but, if so according to Kremer, none survived William who was survived only by Alice according to probate records.

Kremer provides a mostly complete family tree for the youngest brother, John Hanson, but when he gets to this John Hanson's grandson, President John Hanson, omits five of the latter's thirteen children.

As does George Hanson, Kremer shows the four brothers moving from New Sweden to Kent Island, Maryland, and then Randal and John showing up in Charles County, Maryland, by the 1650s. As of 2012, about a dozen websites, mostly genealogical records, show the English traveler John Hanson having married Margaret Vasa and the couple having the four sons named above. However, as of 2012, the provenance of this could not be discerned at any of these websites.

The most deeply researched genealogy supporting George Hanson's four brothers claim found in the author's research was complied in 1974 by attorney William N. Morrell, Sr., president of the Federal Bar Association, who at one time served as president of the John Hanson Society of Maryland. This genealogy is the best sourced of those inspected in preparing *Remembering John Hanson*. As did George Hanson, Morrell shows the four brothers' grandfather as an English John Hanson traveler to Sweden whose parents were John Hanson and Frances Pritchard. Morrell shows the traveler marrying a Swede by the last name of Vasa with unrecorded first name. Coming down a generation, Morrell writes, "The names of the Swedish Colonel and his wife are unknown to the writer, but the four sons were wards of the Crown, Queen Christina and the great Chancellor Axel Oxenstjern being appointed guardians. The four sons were Andrew(as), Randal or Randolph, William and John born 1630. They were given a coat of arms based as to crest and motto on John Hanson's own, but giving the history and claims of the Swedish Colonel and his sons." Here, Morrell's research on the two Hanson coats of arms reprises that of Anna Hanson McKinney Dorsey. Morrell then goes on to recount the emigration of the four boys to New Sweden and their later removal to Kent Island, Maryland.

Morrell's specificity regarding the identities of the boys' guardians is the most definite and convincing evidence found that the four boys existed. Morrell's failure to conclusively identify their parents leaves some doubt as to their descent from the English traveler Hanson rather than perhaps a line of Swedish Hansons. However, Morrell's ascertainment of the coat of arms awarded the boys being the same as that of President John Hanson lends strong credibility that the president and the boys were directly related, whoever their ancestors might have been.

A Modern Genealogist's "Barbados Immigrant" Claim

More than a century after George Hanson's Four Brothers account of his family history but only a few years after William Morrell's work, contention over the Swedish influence on the Hanson bloodline arose through an article in a genealogical journal. In 1988, the American genealogist George Russell researched President Hanson's genealogy, especially George Hanson's claim of the president's partial Swedish ancestry, and concluded that the president's grandfather was not the English-Swedish immigrant brother John Hanson claimed by George Hanson but one John Henson (*sic*), an indentured servant who arrived in Maryland from Barbados in 1661.[302]   Russell proves Henson's entry into Maryland under indenture in 1661 and his being sold to a series of Maryland owners through 1666 when Henson fulfilled the obligations of his servitude and was freed.

Russell claims that the marriage between the English Hanson and a Swedish woman, who he does not identify, never happened, that three of the four brothers including John never existed, that there is no record of their father having served in the Swedish Army or having died in the Battle of Lutzen, that George Hanson descends from one Anders Hansson for whom Russell did find a record from the New Sweden colony, and that George Hanson entirely fabricated the story of the four brothers and therefore President Hanson's partial Swedish bloodline.   Russell's further assertion is that later scholars gullibly and uncritically reprised George Hanson's Four Brothers account.   To be clear, George Russell specifically accuses George Hanson of deliberate fabrication.   The late Peter Craig, a Fellow of the American Society of Genealogists, supported George Russell's contentions.   Russell and Craig used terms such as "hoax," "made up," "total fraud," "fabricated" and "nonsense" in describing George Hanson's version of President John Hanson's partial Swedish ancestry.

Russell's research did collect several strong indications which seem to say that the original American John Hanson had come to the colonies as an Englishman and not a Swede.   Most tellingly, if he had been a Swede, he would have had to become a naturalized British citizen before being permitted to pass on property through his will, but Russell could find no naturalization record for the immigrant who did pass on all of his property.   Russell also noted no indication that the immigrant Hanson associated with Swedes, and that his children had typically British given names and married persons with British surnames: Hoskins, Parry, Harrison, Maconchie, Hussey, Goodrick, Story and Swift.

However, Russell played down signs that his proposed John Henson was not the Hanson immigrant: Russell does not address the very facts which he has verified that the indentured servant who came into the Maryland colony in 1661 had had his name officially recorded as Henson, not Hanson, not only upon entry but twice when he was sold.   John

Henson was sold in 1661 by contract into Maryland by the Barbados Quaker William Plumley to Edward Keene of Calvert County, Maryland, who sold Henson to John Geere in 1663. It is apparently under Geere's ownership when in 1666 Henson worked off his indenture and became free.

It would also seem that Russell should have made more than he did when he wrote of John Hanson's bequeathing "one Large Book of Sr. Walter Raleigh works . . . and sundry other books" when he died. These and "one pair of spectacles" are the accoutrements of a literate and financially comfortable man, not of an indentured servant.

George Russell's brief three-page article conspicuously lacks a bibliography or any source citations but, for the most part, so does George Hanson's *Old Kent*. The late Peter Craig kindly provided the author with fairly detailed responses to a number of questions posed to him about the differences between George Russell's Barbados Immigrant claim versus George Hanson's Four Brothers claim.[303]

Picking up on Russell's Barbados Immigrant contention, the modern-day comedian Dick Gregory has hypothesized that the Barbados immigrant John Henson was black or part black, that Henson is the ancestor of President John Hanson as claimed by Russell, ironically by the one-drop rule that President John Hanson was therefore the nation's first black president, and that an African-American President John Hanson is pictured on the back of the two-dollar bill. The scene pictured on the two-dollar bill is the signing of the Declaration of Independence; John Hanson was not a Signer of the Declaration of Independence.

The author and his immediate family which is tri-racial would be proud if this were true but Gregory's hypothesis has precisely no reliable factual support. Nevertheless, when one conducts an Internet search on President John Hanson, among the tops hits are sites devoted to Gregory's spurious claim. It would be too generous to call the contrast between researched accounts including those of George Hanson, George Russell and Peter Craig versus comedians' and bloggers' contentions mere differences of opinion. These contentions run the gamut from the occasionally well researched to the wildly fallacious, the latter readily disproved without too much sleuthing.

Russell claimed that three of the four brothers — John, Randal (Randolph) and William — claimed by George Hanson as immigrants to New Sweden never existed but that an

Anders Hansson (*sic*) did in fact emigrate from Sweden to New Sweden on Delaware Bay and that George Hanson's line does descend from Anders Hansson. George Hanson, George Russell, Peter Craig and the author all agree that Anders Hansson moved to Kent Island in the Chesapeake in the 1650s, at some point anglicized his name to Andrew Hanson, and was George Hanson's fourth-great-grandfather.

Confirmation of Anders Hansson's arrival in America is found in civil and church records of the New Sweden colony showing that he arrived at the colony from Sweden at the age of twenty-four with his wife Annika. The records of Philadelphia's Gloria Dei Old Swedes Church begun by Johannes Campanius, who founded this church in 1646 four years after Anders' arrival, indicate that, "Their [Andrew and Annika's] daughter Catherine Hanson d. on Tinicum Island and was buried on 28th of Oct. 1646. Campanius recorded that hers was the first corpse ever interred upon that Island."[304, 305] Colonial Maryland civil records show the colony's prominent Colonel Hans Hanson as the son of Andrew and Annika Hanson. Further cementing George Hanson's claim to Swedish ancestry is that his middle name is Adolphus in honor of the Swedish king who author George Adolphus Hanson's ancestor is claimed to have died defending. His being so named indicates that his parents thought of their ancestry as Swedish and handed this down through George Hanson nearly two hundred years after their Swedish ancestors' arrival in America.

On the basis of Russell's claims, Gloria Dei Old Swedes Church concluded in 2008 that it would no longer accept the Four Brothers version of President John Hanson's ancestry and decided to rid itself of the bust of President John Hanson that had been given to the church by the Swedish-American Vasa Society in the 1950s. Hearing of this decision, Edward and Lexy Edelen purchased the bust and its large granite pedestal and moved them to Mulberry Grove in November 2008, a wonderful addition to the first home of President John Hanson.

A John Hanson (rather than Henson), listed as an immigrant from Barbados, does show up in Charles County records in 1678. This could possibly be the same John Henson indentured servant found by George Russell. Baptismal records for Christ Church near Nanjemoy in Charles County show "Anno Domini 1678, September, was bapt. ye: 8th. Francis ye sonn of John and Ann Hanson." This record is found in John Camden Hotten's revealingly entitled *The*

Original Lists of Persons of Quality; Emigrants; Religious Exiles; Political Rebels; Serving Men Sold for a Term of Years; Children Stolen; Maidens Pressed; and Others who Went from Great Britain to the American Plantations 1600-1700.[306] "Serving Men Sold for a Term of Years" is the indentured servitude condition of John Henson until 1666. This could possibly be George Russell's indentured servant John Henson who, on his own or by his church's misspelling, had had his name changed to John Hanson by the time of the 1678 baptism of his son.

Pundt's extensive Hanson genealogy shows no Hanson couple with first names John and Ann, and the first Francis Hanson in the extended family not born until 1807, so the John Hanson who had his son christened in 1678 is not the immigrant progenitor of the president. Given the chronology of his origin in Barbados and that the christening occurred twelve years after John Henson's indenture had been worked off, this John Hanson and John Henson could possibly be the same person. There are a few identifiable cases of the spellings Hanson, Henson and Hynson being used for one another in early Maryland records. Given the high literacy of the immigrant John Hanson — the reader of the works of Sir Walter Raleigh "and sundry other books" — it is more than improbable that the immigrant progenitor of President John Hanson would have allowed his name to be misspelled repeatedly.

The "Six Hansons" Scenario of Harry Newman

This third possibility put forth by Harry Newman in 1940[307] has not been made a claim of President John Hanson's ancestry but does constitute a possibility and a revealing presentation of documented civil records apparently not explored by George Hanson, George Russell or Peter Craig. Newman found evidence that six persons with the surname Hanson arrived together in Maryland in 1658 at the same time aboard the same ship and settled on Kent Island, the long-time seat of George Hanson's family. One cannot discern from the recorded names of the six — Andrew, Anibeck, Catherine, Frederick, Hance (Hans) and Margaret — their ages or the relationship among them but, with all having the same surname, they are almost certainly related to one another. They could be a couple with children or other possible familial relationships. A civil record for this Hans Hanson shows him on his naturalization application in 1671 stating that he had been born at Delaware Bay of Swedish parents so this is almost certainly the son Hans of the Anders and Annika Hansson of New Sweden mentioned above. The most likely familial relationship among the six is father (Andrew), mother (Anibeck) and four children, but this is not certain. George Hanson says that Anders Hansson (Andrew Hanson) would be the great-uncle of the president while Russell contends that Anders Hansson was not related to the president.

If Russell's research of old Swedish military and civil records, which he mentioned but did not cite in his 1988 article, should prove to be complete and correct, then the evidence leans heavily toward President John Hanson not descending from either of the other two males who arrived in Maryland with Anders or from any of the three alleged immigrant brothers attributed to Anders by George Hanson. Again, neither Russell's article nor Craig's responses to the author's questions produced any confirmation of Russell's assertions of incorrectness of George Hanson's Four Brothers claim which leaves the Four Brothers claim as a live possibility. The author did not attempt to research the Swedish records which Russell claims omit three of the four brothers at the New Sweden colony and their father in Swedish military records.

Clouding the picture is the presence of a John Hanson in an official role in Kent County in 1687 in which this John Hanson, whoever he was, requested of the Commissioners of Kent County that his resignation as a Commissioner be accepted.[308] There are several possibilities as to the identity of this John Hanson: (1) that he is one of the four immigrant brothers claimed by George Hanson and therefore the uncle of Hans (Hanse) Hanson, also a Kent County Commissioner at the time; (2) that this John Hanson is the Charles County John Hanson known to be the president's grandfather; (3) that these are the same person; (4) that this is someone else. Given the timing, 1687, it is doubtful that the John Hanson mentioned is the Charles County John Hanson known to be the president's grandfather as he had been well established in Charles County for thirty years by that time and it is unlikely that he would have been doing business as an official of Kent County all the way across the Chesapeake Bay. If the Kent County John Hanson was one of George Hanson's claimed four immigrant brothers but was not the Charles County John Hanson, then he was not the president's grandfather as claimed by George Hanson. Then who was he? We now have a deeper mystery. As argued below, it is especially doubtful that he is the John Henson (*sic*) claimed by the twentieth century genealogists.

Summing up Newman's Six Hansons scenario, there is little in it to support it being the explanation of President John Hanson's immigrant ancestor.

The "Lord Mayor of London" Scenario of Harry Newman

The fourth scenario is the intriguing conjecture also put forth by Harry Newman that the president's immigrant ancestor was a John Hanson not mentioned by either George Hanson or George Russell. Newman wonders if the immigrant John Hanson was the son of Sir Robert Hanson, Lord Mayor of London, and cites two pieces of corroboration for this theory. First, the known John Hanson of early Charles County (President John Hanson's grandfather) named his eldest son Robert[309] possibly following the English custom of the eldest grandson being named for the paternal grandfather. Second, Newman shows that the immigrant John Hanson ranked among the "first families in the Province in culture as well as society of that period" suggesting high family status, such as a Lord Mayor father, before he immigrated to Maryland.[310]

Sir Robert Hanson was appointed Lord Mayor of London in 1672 and served the 1672-1673 term. "In 1672 the Lord Mayor's procession for Lord Mayor Robert Hanson, a grocer, was led by a negro riding a camel scattering fruit to the crowd, with Plenty and Concord on either side of him. There was also a throned Indian emperor with Princes of Peru and Mexico at his feet. *Two extra great giants each of them 15ft high were drawn by horses in two separate chariots, moving, talking and taking tobacco as they ride along to the great admiration and delight of all the spectators.*' "[311] (Emphasis in the original)

Despite lengthy attempts by the author and a skilled researcher, Sir Robert Hanson's birth year has not been able to be ascertained, but several sources indicate that he was about sixty when he was mayor so it is chronologically feasible that he was the father of the American immigrant John Hanson who was born about 1630. Sir Robert Hanson had previously served as High Sheriff of London, having been appointed on September 28, 1665.[312]

Newman's Lord Mayor of London conjecture is intriguingly bolstered by recalling the ancestry of President John Hanson's in-laws, the Contees. As noted earlier, Jane Contee descended from Adolphe de Contee who had served as High Sheriff of London in 1643, within a few years of when Sir Robert Hanson served as High Sheriff and then Lord Mayor of London. (Another of Wikipedia's errors is claiming that Adolphe de Contee also served as Lord Mayor of London which he did not. The City of London provides an easily found online list of Lord Mayors of London back to the thirteenth century which does not include a Contee, de Contee or similar name.)

Jane Hanson was the great-great-granddaughter of Sheriff de Contee. Given that Mayor Hanson and Sheriff de Contee inhabited the same official and social circles in London at the same time, and if indeed the immigrant John Hanson was the son of Mayor Hanson, it would be a virtual certainty that the American Hansons and Contees would have known one another. That the two families did settle in close proximity to each other in the same colony at the same time and then joined their families by marriage gives quick rise to deeper speculation. Two final clues are that Sheriff de Contee's wife and one daughter were named Grace and Elizabeth, respectively, and that Jane and John Hanson gave their daughters these same names.

Harry Newman never advanced this scenario as a claim of John Hanson's ancestry but offered it as conjecture. There is no indication that Newman was aware of the Hanson-de Contee affinity in London which probably would have encouraged Newman's stronger suggestion of this scenario.

Robert Hanson, Lord Mayor of London, appears to have descended from the Rastrick/Hanson line. The John Hanson who married Frances Pritchard in 1611 sold his share in Rastrick Hall to a brother Robert, moved from the town of Rastrick near Halifax to London and became a grocer, the profession of Lord Mayor of London Robert Hanson. That the Robert Hanson who was Lord Mayor of London was a grocer further suggests the likelihood of this line of Hansons. John Hanson and Frances Pritchard's eldest son John, born in 1612, could have been the John Hanson immigrant to Maryland. It is known that this John's brother Thomas was an immigrant to New Hampshire where he died in 1666.

The top-level social and political relationships of the immigrant John Hanson corroborate his arrival in Maryland with high social status, a good fit with the Lord Mayor of London conjecture. For example, two of the immigrant John Hanson's grandsons married into the families of early colonial Maryland governors. William Hanson (immigrant John-Robert-William is the lineage) married Mary Stone, a great-granddaughter of William Stone, Maryland governor from 1649 to 1656; and the Hansons and Contees had nine relationships by blood or marriage to the Fendall family which produced Maryland Governor Josias Fendall who served from 1657 to 1660. In 1719, the immigrant John's son Robert Hanson and Luke Barber served as guarantors to the estate of John Parry. Barber was the son of a caretaker governor of the same name who Josias Fendall had appointed to serve in Fendall's absence from the colony from June 1657 to February 1658.[313] These relationships not only lend credence to Newman's Lord Mayor of London conjecture but also thoroughly belie the Barbados immigrant claim.

Sorting Out President John Hanson's Ancestry

Having eliminated the Six Immigrants scenario, we are left with the other three mutually exclusive alternatives as to the origins of President John Hanson's family plus the possibility that none of these is true. We now examine the strengths and weaknesses of each of the remaining three alternatives.

On at least the following key point George Hanson, Russell, Craig, Newman, Morrell and the author all agree: that an immigrant John Hanson lived in Charles County, Maryland, and fathered Judge Samuel Hanson who was the father of President John Hanson.

Bona Fides of the Claimants

George Hanson, George Russell, Peter Craig, Harry Newman and William Morrell all appear to be well qualified commentators on President John Hanson's ancestry, Hanson from his vantage point as Hanson family chronicler, Russell and Craig as expert genealogists, and Newman and Morrell for their meticulously documented research.

Lending credence to the voluminously sourced and cross-referenced detail of his 1876 book *Old Kent*, George Hanson was a college graduate in an era when fewer than one percent of American males went to college, went on to receive his master's degree, practiced law, gained a federal appointment as a member of the United States Centennial Commission, was prominent in the Maryland Historical Society, and served as an advisor to the Governor of Maryland. George Adolphus Hanson died in 1880 at the age of fifty.

George Russell was elected a Fellow of the American Society of Genealogists and served as Editor of the *National Genealogical Society Quarterly*. A resident of Maryland, he researched and wrote extensively on a number of Maryland genealogical topics.

The late Dr. Peter Craig, a historian, genealogist and Fellow of the American Society of Genealogists, was named by the King of Sweden to the Order of the Polar Star, the highest award given to foreigners, for his scholarship on early American immigrants from Sweden.

During the half-century from 1933 until 1983 when he died at the age of eighty-nine, Harry Wright Newman authored more than a dozen books and genealogies on the oldest families of southern Maryland, tidewater Virginia and elsewhere. His works employ meticulously annotated searches of civil, church, family and other records in establishing the histories of the families and individuals about whom he wrote. Harry Newman was a professional researcher employed by the Bureau of Foreign and Domestic Commerce of the United States Department of Commerce where he authored studies on international trade.

William N. Morrell, Sr. was an attorney from Bethesda, Maryland, who served as the 1939-1940 president of the Federal Bar Association and later as the president of the former John Hanson Society of Maryland.

We now examine several issues bearing on the Four Brothers and Barbados Immigrant claims, the Lord Mayor of London conjecture, and competing arguments among the three.

Independent Oral Traditions of Hanson Swedish Blood

The story of partial Swedish ancestry of the Hansons was also handed down in the author's line of the family. Upon query, one of the genealogists was able only to suggest that somehow the author's line had to have been aware of George Hanson's book and picked up the Swedish claim from it. This is remotely possible but unlikely as there is no indication that the author's line of the family ever knew of George Hanson's Eastern Shore family or of his book until the author came across the book several years ago. In addition, there is the rendition of Anna Hanson McKinney Dorsey on Hanson Swedish ancestry which is consistent with and more precise than George Hanson's. So we have three independent lines of the Hanson family regarding partial Swedish ancestry that would seem to square with one another closely.

There are two other clues in the author's line of the family that point to Swedish ancestry. One is that the nickname of the author's uncle, Robert Bennett Hanson, was "Swede." The other is the passed down story that the author heard growing up that the first John Hanson, the president's grandfather, moved to Charles County from Kent Island because of the island's mosquitoes. This placement of the grandfather John Hanson on Kent Island for a period is consistent with the Four Brothers claim and a possibility with the Lord Mayor of London conjecture but not with the Barbados Immigrant claim.

On his English side, George Hanson records that the American Hansons and their English relatives continued to correspond at least up to the time of the Revolutionary War. ". . . Col. Hans Hanson, of Kimbolton, did keep up the intercourse with his grandfather's [English] family, and it was maintained until the Revolutionary War. A magnificent silk dress, inwrought with bullion thread, was sent over as a wedding present to the bride of his grandson Gustavus Hanson, by the family in England, and a portion of it is in possession of her great-grandson." This account also involves both English and Swedish given names in the same family and is consistent with George Hanson's claim of dual English and Swedish lineage. We keep in mind George Hanson's proven Swedish ancestry. It is also very implausible that sometime not later than the Revolutionary War, among second-generation American Hansons, an English Hanson family is sending wedding gifts woven in gold to the children or grandchildren of an immigrant indentured servant.

Two other clues to the possible Swedish connection to the American Hansons involve John Hanson himself. First, it is conspicuous that his youngest child was named Elizabeth Arianna *Adolphus* Hanson. Also, when John Hanson chose an artist to paint his and Jane's portraits in the mid-eighteenth century, he hired John Hesselius, son of the Swedish immigrant, Gustavus Hesselius, the continent's most prominent painter and frequent portraitist of the Maryland tidewater elite.[314]

Finally, as we have seen, when Jane and John Hanson lived in Philadelphia during his presidency, they chose to attend Gloria Dei Old Swedes Church, a Swedish Lutheran parish at the time, rather than an Episcopalian church. John and Jane were Episcopalians.

Presence of Two of the Alleged Four Brothers and the Descendant of a Third in Charles County

Using Maryland colonial records, Harry Newman finds a John Hanson, a Randal Hanson and a Colonel Hans Hanson all in Charles County in the mid-1600s.[315] Here we have two of the alleged four brothers — John and Randal — and their apparent nephew Hans, son of Anders Hansson (Andrew

Hanson), a third of the four brothers. George Hanson records Randal Hanson (anglicized to Randolph) as going from the New Sweden colony to "St. Mary's to carve out his fortune at the point of his sword."[316] St. Mary's County borders Charles County. Kremer's research for his John Hanson biography, completed independently before Newman's, has identically the same findings, and Morrell's genealogy finds the same. However, it is possible that all three could have used George Hanson's *Old Kent* as their source.

At odds with George Hanson's Four Brothers account is that Harry Newman found that a Randal Hanson had entered the colony as an indentured servant, having worked off his indenture to Dr. Luke Barber of St. Mary's County by 1659. Randal's indentured servitude is inconsistent, though not impossible, with the claimed Swedish royal lineage claimed by George Hanson for Randal.[317]

Russell claimed that these three documented Charles County Hansons were not related, that their surnames are coincidental, and that they are not three of the Hansons from the Four Brothers claim. However, Russell's assertions that the three were unrelated and that George Hanson deliberately conflated a familial relationship among them are hypotheses with no conclusive proof offered. There is no evidence that George Hanson engaged in any kind of intentional fabrication though it is possible that he got the facts wrong in his research or stretched his assumptions.

Imprimatur of Writers, Scholars and Organizations on the Four Brothers Claim

In 1898, President John Hanson's great-great-grandson, Douglas H. Thomas, Sr., wrote in his publication supporting the State of Maryland's choice of John Hanson to be represented in National Statuary Hall that the Hanson family was of partial Swedish descent. Mr. Thomas could have gotten this from family oral tradition or possibly from George Hanson's *Old Kent* published twenty-two years before. Professor Amandus Johnson in his 1911 doctoral dissertation and in some of his later writings including a 1921 monograph on Swedish-American contributions to the nation mentions the Hanson family, its professed partial Swedish descent and John Hanson's presumed Swedish heritage.[318] The three John Hanson biographers of the 1930s and one scholar in the 1970s mention the same.[319] In the 1950s, the Vasa Society, a Swedish-American organization, donated the John Hanson monument to Mulberry Grove and the John Hanson bust to Gloria Dei Old Swedes Church based on the Society's own examination that the immigrant ancestor of President John Hanson had Swedish blood. In 1981, at the first-issue ceremony in Frederick, Maryland, of a United States postage stamp dedicated to President Hanson, the Swedish ambassador was present and spoke of the president's Swedish background. Mormon genealogical records, generally very well researched, show President Hanson's grandfather being born "about 1630" squaring exactly with the Four Brothers claim of his arrival at the New Sweden colony in America in 1642 at the age of twelve. A modern Hanson genealogy complied by Walter G. Hodge delineates George Hanson's claimed line from John Hanson and Frances Pritchard in England in the sixteenth century through two generations of John Hansons in Sweden to the four brothers in America just as claimed by George Hanson but with more detail regarding the Hanson marriage into the Swedish royal Vasa family.[320] The Hodge genealogy also shows that the full name of President and Jane Hanson's youngest child was Elizabeth Arianna Adolphus Hanson. Her parents could have given her this extra middle name from Swedish background on her father's side or from the French background on her mother's but the spelling is northern European rather than French. In either case, the name is conspicuous and goes back to the family's European roots at least four generations before Elizabeth.

Peter Craig suggested that, excepting the Hodge work which Craig was apparently unaware of, all of the above references including those of the scholars, scholarly organizations and Swedish government were somehow adopted wholesale without question from George Hanson's 1876 work. Though this is possible, so many errors of incaution and failure to perform their own research by multiple scholars over so long a period does seem to be quite a reach.

It is quite possible that George Hanson and his possible distant cousin Douglas Thomas, Sr. might have known each other before Hanson's death in 1880. In 1876 George Hanson served on the United States Centennial Commission and Douglas Thomas on the Maryland Centennial Commission so it might well have been that the two met in this connection or some other way though they lived on opposite sides of the Chesapeake.[321]

Independent Claim and Amplification on the Swedish Parentage of the Immigrant John Hanson

In his discussion of the John Hanson who was the president's grandfather, George Hanson mentions that the grandfather's father married "a Swedish lady, who was connected, in friendship, at least, with the Royal Family"[322] but does not mention her name. In his 1932 biography of John Hanson, Seymour Wemyss Smith gets specific, writing that the president's great-grandfather, ". . . met, wooed, and married Margaret Vasa, granddaughter of the famous Gustavus Vasa, founder of the Vasa line of kings."[323] That Smith was able to identify the immigrant John Hanson's alleged grandmother while George Hanson was not (he would certainly have mentioned her by name if he had identified her) indicates Smith's research as separate from George Hanson's rather than being based entirely on it. If this bloodline is correct, then the son of Margaret Vasa and the English John Hanson, also named John Hanson who was father of the alleged four brothers, was the second cousin of Gustavus Adolphus II. It was these two cousins who are claimed by Smith, George Hanson, other John Hanson biographers and others to have fallen in the Battle of Lutzen.

Smith also provides the fullest accounting of the alleged four brothers, citing Andrew's progeny including the amply recorded Colonel Hans Hanson; Randolph's move to southern Maryland, his military career, and his daughter's marriage into the prominent Hatton family (thus belying any indentured servitude); William's move to southern Maryland and back to Kent Island, and his leaving no heirs; and the rest of the book about the youngest brother John, grandfather of the president. It is conspicuous that the last three all moved to southern Maryland at nearly the same time.[324]

Hanson vs. Henson: Impossibility of the Barbados Immigrant Claim

What is most improbable with the genealogists' Barbados Immigrant claim is that a family which in its first American-born generation had extensive land holdings, moved in the highest social circles of the colony, saw its immigrant progenitor rise to the rank of colonel, married into the elite of the colony including the families of its earliest governors, included a judge, a colonial legislator and another colonel, and produced a president could somehow have been spawned by an impoverished bound servant with a different surname less than a decade after attaining his freedom. The author is as fond of American immigrant success stories as anyone, has witnessed this first hand in one of his own children, and would be pleased if the Henson servant from Barbados in his lifetime had actually founded an American political dynasty which was to last for centuries. But, the overwhelming unlikelihood of this in combination with the wrong surname casts profound doubt on the genealogists' theory that Henson was related to the Hansons.

Most telling and entirely definitive, Henson's arrival in Maryland in 1661 is too late for him to be the John Hanson, the president's grandfather, who shows up in colonial records five years previous to this. "While his older brothers were thus variously making records of success and useful life, young John Hanson had gone on into St. Mary's County and as early as 1656 appears in Charles County, the newly developing section centering around Port Tobacco where groups of Protestant settlers were clearing land and building homes."[325] The original land grant to Colonel John Hanson was in 1656 five years before Henson arrived in Maryland.

This John Hanson continues to show up in church, civil and land records through 1666 while John Henson was still an indentured servant. Though it is certain from Charles County civil records that this John Hanson resided in Charles County as early as 1672 and that he was the grandfather of President John Hanson, the genealogists do not offer any proof that this John Hanson is somehow their John Henson and have shown no evidence of a connection between Henson and the Hansons. The genealogists' acknowledge their not being able to identify from colonial records the European origin of the known John Hanson who was the president's grandfather. What they do offer is only the very thin conjecture without any conclusive corroboration that their bound servant John Henson for whatever reason changed his name to Hanson and somehow managed to vault into the colony's top social stratum within a few years *even before* attaining his freedom. This theory goes beyond improbability.

John Hanson author John Cummings has found correspondence among Church of England records[326] showing John Hanson (the president's grandfather) and Hans Hanson both serving as Church of England vestrymen in Maryland. In their era, vestrymen enjoyed "standing considered to be one of wealth in one the most respectable positions in the Province of Maryland."[327] It is Mr. Cummings' "opinion that the grandfather John Hanson's standing in the community is the furthest away from an indentured servant and [is] that of an established leader to the community and church."[328]

Unreasonable Protestations By the Barbados Immigrant Claimants

As troubling as George Russell's Hanson-versus-Henson conundrum are his untoward personal attacks levied on George Hanson. Accusing George Hanson of deliberately perpetrating a hoax, calling him a fraud and labeling the part of his 1876 *Old Kent* on the four brothers as total fabrication, it is too apparent that Russell went out of his way to unduly malign George Hanson.   Russell's intemperate descriptions of George Hanson and his work, and Peter Craig's unquestioning support of them, are for no good reason so highly pejorative as to further detract from the credibility of the genealogists' Barbados Immigrant claim of Hanson family ancestry.

There is not the slightest indication in a word-for-word reading of *Old Kent* or in any later commentary about it, other than that of the two genealogists, which would indicate that in any way George Hanson set out to deceive, deliberately fabricated any Hanson family ancestry or did anything other than record what he believed to be true based on his research and his family's oral tradition.   While the genealogists contend that George Hanson erred in his work, they have presented no valid reason not to see his account fairly in the light of mutual honest factual disagreement.   There is no evidence to conclude that George Hanson did anything less than put forth with honesty and good intent the family history he believed.   While the genealogists could be factually correct in some of their challenges to George Hanson's Four Brothers claim, this gives them no reason to engage in personal vilification of George Hanson which does nothing to help their own claim.

Conclusion On President John Hanson's Ancestry

To conclude, we begin by distilling the questions of Swedish ancestry and Barbados origin, deferring for the moment the Lord Mayor of London conjecture.

The modern genealogists' work on attempting to disprove Swedish ancestry of President John Hanson is far from airtight, and their theory of the president's descent from the immigrant servant Henson is clearly impossible.   Here, the former appears to be based on purportedly well-sourced but unidentified documentation while the latter presents itself as a very stretched attempt to conjure some immigrant ancestor of President John Hanson once George Russell satisfied himself that the ancestor was not one of the four brothers.

Without replicating the genealogists' work which has not been attempted here, one must question their apparently well-researched doubts about the Four Brothers Claim.   However, if the immigrant Hanson in fact had no Swedish blood, this leaves open the question of how the author's, George Hanson's and Anna Dorsey's lines of the family all have the same independently handed-down oral tradition that the family is part Swedish. This remains unexplained as do John Hanson's choices of giving one of his daughters a Swedish middle name, choosing a first-generation Swedish-American portraitist, and attending a Swedish church in Philadelphia.

The Barbados Immigrant claim is much too tenuous, expedient and far-fetched to be possible. The rationale of one of the genealogists for the claim is that "there was only one known John Hanson in the relevant period of time" but in the next breath he identified this person as actually the John *Henson* indentured servant from Barbados.[329]

The weight of evidence does cast some doubt on the John Hanson who George Hanson thought was at New Sweden being President John Hanson's ancestor, if this immigrant John Hanson existed at all, though a strong question remains because of the triple oral traditions in the Hanson family to the contrary. Any relationship of John Henson to President John Hanson remains entirely unsupported and indeed disproved by the timing of Henson's arrival in Maryland. With regard to these two proposals of President John Hanson's European ancestry, one may fairly conclude that the Barbados Immigrant claim is disproven, and that the Four Brothers claim is neither proven nor disproven but does involve some doubt.

This leaves us with Harry Newman's Lord Mayor of London conjecture and the recent expansion on it here by examining the Contee family history. This scenario, as far as it goes, seems consistent and as convincing as the Four Brothers claim. However, while there are no apparent flaws in the Lord Mayor of London conjecture, there is no proof either. Confirmation of John Hanson's descent from Sir Robert Hanson, Lord Mayor of London, will rest on genealogical corroboration yet to be found. Online information on Sir Robert's children is vanishingly sparse and extensive searching by a skilled genealogist has not turned up any reference to his children.

A fourth barely explored possibility is that President John Hanson's namesake grandfather was not the immigrant Hanson but the son of an as yet unidentified immigrant. Given when the grandfather John Hanson shows up in Maryland colonial records by the 1650s, it is highly doubtful that another Hanson generation preceded his in America.

The first European settlement in Maryland was on Kent Island in August 1631, the second at St. Clement's Island in March 1634. St. Clement's Island lies in the Potomac River about thirty miles upstream from its discharge into the Chesapeake Bay. The island belongs to St. Mary's County, the state's oldest, and lies about ten miles from John Hanson's Charles County.

The impossibility of the Barbados Immigrant claim, the doubts around the Four Brothers claim, and the convincing but yet-to-be-proven Lord Mayor of London conjecture lead to the conclusion that John Hanson's European family ancestry still remains uncertain, the last unsolved mystery about the nation's first president. The most fruitful line of inquiry at this point would seem to be identifying the children of Robert Hanson, Lord Mayor of London.

While the question of whether or not President John Hanson had Swedish blood is intriguing, useful for the historical record and of great interest to Hanson descendants, it has little bearing on the president himself, his contributions toward the founding of the nation or his presidency.

Following here is the six-hundred-year Hanson family genealogy from Roger de Rastrick to President John Hanson and George Adolphus Hanson as believed by George Hanson, J. Bruce Kremer and William N. Morrell. Added to this is the line from the immigrant John Hanson to Anna Hanson McKinney Dorsey.

George Hanson's Genealogy of the Hanson Family

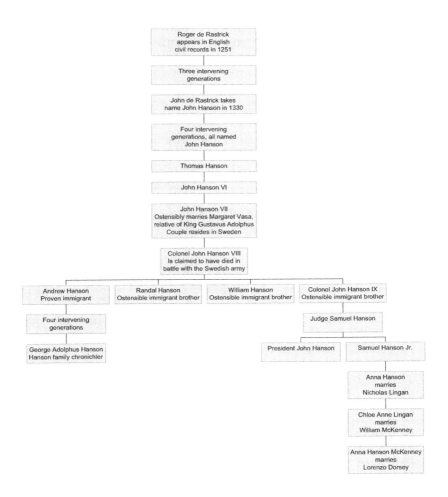

Bibliographies

The bibliographies here are arranged in six parts. They are references on John Hanson's life, family and ancestry; references on John Hanson and his family in Frederick; references on the Continental Congresses and governments of the United States; the Hanson and related collections of the Maryland Historical Society; the Mary Keech Edelen Collection of the College of Southern Maryland; and general references.

For his public and political life, the most definitive references on John Hanson are the official federal and state sources listed below much of which consists of primary source documents. Especially useful are the several collections, particularly that of the Maryland Historical Society, of Hanson's extant correspondence, mainly his many letters to his son-in-law and confidant Dr. Philip Thomas of Frederick who looked after John Hanson's personal interests for the years that Hanson spent away in Annapolis and Philadelphia. These letters often comment confidentially on important historical and political matters as they were happening. Among nonofficial sources, Levering provides an accurate, formally annotated but brief chronology of John Hanson's public life for the most part after Hanson's move to Frederick. Smith provides a detailed, reliable and more extensive but unannotated chronology of Hanson's presidency in his 1932 John Hanson biography.

The best John Hanson biography listed below is that by J. Bruce Kremer, owner of Mulberry Grove in the mid-twentieth century. Excepting Levering's thirty-six-page monograph, Kremer's *John Hanson of Mulberry Grove* published in 1938 is the only John Hanson biography prior to *Remembering John Hanson* which provides a bibliography and much discussion of sources, though the Kremer bibliography is thin and unaccompanied by any notes in the body of his book. *John Hanson of Mulberry Grove* is written with a fluid engaging skill providing many insights into less studied historical aspects of the period and into the thinking of its major players. A third biography written in the 1930s is *John Hanson and the Inseparable Union* by Jacob A. Nelson, an Iowa judge and John Hanson aficionado.

The extant record of Hanson's personal life is much thinner. Here, the best sources are Kremer, Smith, Newman, George Hanson and particularly John Hanson's letters to Philip

Thomas. Kremer and Smith provide reasonably good chronologies of the events of Hanson's early and midlife, while Newman provides an especially detailed and definitively sourced inventory of Hanson-related events such as land transactions, probating of wills, posting of bonds and such which appear in the Charles County, Maryland, and other civil and church records. The sources which Newman provides extend over seven generations from the immigrant John Hanson to four generations beyond President John Hanson. John Hanson's extant account books from the years 1730 to 1737 and 1776 to early 1779 provide vivid detail of his large war loans to the Second Continental Congress and his personal accounts and life at Mulberry Grove and then in Frederick.

George Hanson provides an exceptionally detailed though not fully substantiated background on Hanson family history dating back to the twelfth century, the Hanson family's professed two-generation sojourn through Sweden in the sixteenth and seventeenth centuries, the contested version of the Hanson family's arrival in America, and an extensive tracking of Hanson descendants and their relatives by marriage up to 1876. Amandus Johnson provides a more recent account of President John Hanson. Not listed below are some of Johnson's many publications on the New Sweden colony and the roles of Swedish-Americans in early America which may be found at the websites of online booksellers.

References on John Hanson's Life, Family and Ancestry

1. "A Letter from Baltimore," *The Pennsylvania Gazette*, December 3, 1783. This is a notice of John Hanson's death.

2. Andrews, Matthew P., *History of Maryland: Province and State*, Doubleday, Doran & Company, Garden City, New York, 1929. Reprinted by Tradition Press, Hatboro, Pennsylvania, 1965.

3. *The American*, Frederick, Maryland, February 25, 1812

4. *Archives of Maryland,* various collections and single holdings

5. Ashbury, John W., "Thomas Stone," *Frederick Magazine*, Frederick, Maryland, issue 314, August 2011, p. 110

6. *The Bangor Daily News*, "First President Was John Hanson," Bangor, Maine, September 9, 1972. Article reprinted from *The Washington Star*, author unattributed, date unknown.

7. Benson, Adolph B. and George H. Ryden, "John Hanson, American Patriot," *The American Scandinavian Review*, vol. VIII, July 1920

8. Boardman, Liz, "Mathias Oppersdorff, photographer, adven-

turer, dead at 75," *South County Independent,* Wakefield, Rhode Island, February 2, 2010

9.   Boles, Nancy G., "The John Hanson Collection," *Maryland Historical Magazine,* 65 (Fall 1970)

10.   Braun, Anne, "Stone Family Cemetery, Faulkner, Charles County, Maryland," as of November 30, 2010, at http://www.interment.net/data/us/md/charles/stonefam_fa ulk/index.htm

11.   Bykowicz, Julie, "A historical battle over Maryland statues," *The Baltimore Sun,* Baltimore, Maryland, February 23, 2011

12.   Bykowicz, Julie, "Statue debate: Tubman, Hanson backers make case," *The Baltimore Sun,* Baltimore, Maryland, February 24, 2011

13.   Cavanaugh, John W., "Our Two First Presidents, John Hanson and George Washington," *The Gold Book of United States History,* New York, 1932

14.   Clay, Rev. Jehu Curtis, *Annals of the Swedes On the Delaware From Their First Settlement in 1636 to the Present Time,* Gloria Dei Old Swedes Episcopal Church, Philadelphia, 1834. Reprinted, H. Hooker & Company, Philadelphia, 1858. Digitized, University of Michigan, 2006.

15.   Claypool, David C., *Journals of Congress and of the United States in Congress Assembled for the Year 1781,* Philadelphia, 1781

16.   Cohen, Richard M., "John Hanson Honored as the Very First U. S. President," *The Washington Post,* April 15, 1971

17.   Coldham, Peter C., *The Complete Book of Immigrants, 1607-1660,* Genealogical Publishing Company, 1987

18.   Craig, Peter, personal correspondence to the author (email), February 2, 3, 9 and 12, 2009

19.   Cummings, John, personal correspondence to the author (email), February 9, 2009, *et seq.*

20.   Delaplaine, Edward C., *The Life of Thomas Johnson,* New York, 1927. See pp. 29-31 *et seq.* for mention of John Hanson.

21.   Dent, Richard J., Karen L. Orrence, Jonathan Wright, Gloria Judges, and Anne Dilorenzo, *Final Report on the Preliminary Site Examination (Intensive Reconnaissance) of the Oxon Hill Manor Project Area Interstate Route 95/Maryland Route 210 and Interstate 295 Interchange Modification Project,* prepared for Envirodyne Engineers of Baltimore, Maryland, and the Maryland State Highway Administration, 1983

22.   Dorsey, Anna Hanson McKinney, *Letter to Josephine Ridue,* August 9, 1882, (transcription), Catholic University library.

http://genforum.genealogy.com/ingram/messages/5116.ht
ml.

23. Dunlap, John, *Journal of the United States in Congress assembled: containing the proceedings*, Library of Congress, control number 54046177. (Under the old Library of Congress
catalogue, this journal was listed under United States, Continental Congress, Journals of Congress and United States,
Continental Congress, Resolutions, acts and orders of Congress.

24. Eberlein, H.D. and C.V. Hubbard, *Diary of Independence Hall*,
Philadelphia, 1948

25. Fanelli, Doris Devine, Karie Diethorn and John C. Milley, *His-
tory of the Portrait Collection, Independence National Historical
Park*, American Philosophical Society and Diane Publishing
Company, 2002

26. Foster, Joseph, *Alumni Oxonienses,1715-1886*, University Archives, The Bodleian Library, Oxford University

27. "Fourteenth Congress: March 4, 1815, to March 3, 1817,"
website of the United States House of Representatives,
http://artandhistory.house.gov/house_history/bioguide-
front/14.pdf.

28. Frederick County Wills, 1784, Maryland Hall of Records, Annapolis

29. Freed, Reverend Alan C., letter to John Hanson Mitchell, La
Plata, Maryland, March 19, 1970. Copy in the John Hanson
Collection of the Historical Society of Frederick County.

30. Freed, Reverend Alan C., letter to Judge Edward S. Delap-
laine, Frederick, Maryland, March 22, 1971. Copy in the
John Hanson Collection of the Historical Society of Frederick
County.

31. Freed, Reverend Alan C., letter to Judge Edward S. Delap-
laine, Frederick, Maryland, April 9, 1971. Copy in the John
Hanson Collection of the Historical Society of Frederick
County.

32. Freed, Reverend Alan C., "John Hanson Was Missed for a
Change," *The Baltimore Evening Sun*, March 17, 1971

33. Frost, Karolyn Smardz, *The Life of Josiah Henson: Sources
and Documents*, Report for the Ontario Heritage Trust: Uncle
Tom's Cabin Historic Site Project, March, 2007

34. Galton Orsborn Co., Auctioneers, "Special Auction Sale of Antiques from the Estate of Annie M. Hanson, Elkridge, Maryland, Great-Great-Granddaughter of John Hanson," *The Sun*,
Baltimore, Maryland, October 26, 1943 (auction date)

35. Garrow, Patrick H. and Thomas R. Wheaton, Jr., editors, *Final Report, Oxon Hill Manor, Archaeological Site Mitigation Pro-*

ject, I-95/MD 210/I-295, vols. 1 and 2, report prepared for the Maryland Department of Transportation, Garrow and Associates, Inc., 1986

36.   Gewehr, Wesley M., Donald C. Gordon, David S. Sparks and Roland N. Stromberg, *The United States: A History of a Democracy*, McGraw-Hill, New York, 1960

37.   Gibb, James G., and April M. Beisaw, *Seeking Port Tobacco: An Intensive Archeological Investigation of a Maryland Town Site*, parts 1 and 2, Gibb Archeological Consulting, Annapolis, Maryland, July 2008

38.   Hanson, George A., *Old Kent: The Eastern Shore of Maryland*, original publisher unknown but possibly the author, Baltimore, 1876. Reprinted by Regional Publishing Company, 1967

39.   Hanson, John, *Book of Accounts and Journal, 1730-1737*, in the John Hanson Collection of the Maryland Historical Society

40.   Hanson, John, *Book of Accounts, 1775-1779*, in the John Hanson Collection of the Maryland Historical Society

41.   Hanson, John, *Letters to Dr. Philip Thomas, 1780-1783*, in the John Hanson Collection of the Maryland Historical Society

42.   Hanson, John, *Memorandum Book*, undated, in the John Hanson Collection of the Maryland Historical Society

43.   "The John Hanson Family Archive & Collection," *The Maryland Sale*, (auction catalogue), Crocker Farm Auctioneers, Sparks, Maryland, August 2011

44.   Hanson, Laura, *The Hanson Family*, unknown publisher or publication date. A single obscure internet reference was found on this book and an internet search for it has turned up nothing. This is most likely the Laura Hanson who is the great-aunt of the author of *Remembering John Hanson*. The two never met.

45.   Heitman, Francis Bernard, *Historical Register of Officers of the Continental Army During the War of the Revolution*, Rare Book Shop Publishing Company, Washington, DC, 1914

46.   Henson, Josiah, *The Autobiography of Josiah Henson, Formerly a Slave, Now an Inhabitant of Canada, as Narrated by Himself*, Arthur D. Phelps Publisher, Boston, 1849

47.   Henson, Josiah, *Uncle Tom's Story of his Life: an Autobiography of the Rev. Josiah Henson, 1789-1876; with a preface by Harriet Beecher Stowe and an Introductory Note by George Sturge and S. Morley; edited by John Lobb*, London: Christian Age Office, 1876

48.   Historical Society of Pennsylvania Collection of Richard Peters, Jr. Papers, Philadelphia

49. Historical Society of Pennsylvania Connaroe Collection of John Hanson Papers, Philadelphia

50. Historical Society of Pennsylvania Etting Collection of John Hanson Papers, Philadelphia

51. Historical Society of Pennsylvania Simon Gratz Autograph Collection, Philadelphia

52. Holm, John Campanius, *Description of the Province of New Sweden*, circa 1690

53. http://www.colonialswedes.org/Churches/GloDei.html, web site of the Swedish Colonial Society of America

54. http://www.old-swedes.org/History4522.php, the web site of Gloria Dei Old Swedes Episcopal Church of Philadelphia, Pennsylvania

55. http://www.womenhistoryblog.com/2010/10/jane-contee-hanson.html

56. Hughes, Thomas Patrick and Frank Munsell, editors, *American Ancestry: Giving the Name and Descent, in the male line, of Americans Whose Ancestors Settled in the United States Previous to the Declaration of Independence, A. D. 1666,* vol. III, Joel Munsell's Sons, Publishers, Albany, New York

57. Hurry, Silas D., *Intensive Archeological Testing of the Oxon Hill Manor Site*, (Maryland Geological Survey File Report Number 187), report prepared for the Maryland State Highway Administration, 1984

58. Hurry, Silas D. and Maureen Kavanagh, *Additional Intensive Archeological Testing at the Oxon Hill Manor Site: An 18th Through 19th Century Plantation in Maryland*, (Maryland Geological Survey File Report Number 189), report prepared for the Maryland State Highway Administration,1985

59. "John Hanson Marker Unveiled," *The Baltimore Evening Sun*, November 23, 1933. Reprinted in *The Prince George's County Star*, November 26, 1933.

60. *John Hanson Papers Collection*, The Maryland Historical Society, Baltimore.

61. *John Hanson, President of the United States in Congress Assembled, 1781-1782*, Cushing Publishing Company, Baltimore, 1892 (author unattributed)

62. JohnHansonMemorial.org

63. *The John Hanson Monolith*, The Swedish Colonial Society and the Vasa Order of America in Sweden, 1966. This is the dedication booklet for the John Hanson bust originally at Old Swedes Church in Philadelphia, now at Mulberry Grove.

64. Johnson, Amandus, *John Hanson: First President of the United States Under the Articles of Confederation*, original pub-

lication information unknown. Reprinted by the Swedish Colonial Society, Philadelphia, 1966

65.   Johnson, Amandus, *Swedish Contributions to American National Life, 1638-1921*, Committee of the Swedish Section of
America's Making, New York, 1921

66.   Johnson, Amandus, *The Swedish Settlements on the Delaware: Their History and Relation to the Indians, Dutch and English, 1638-1664 : With an Account of the South, the New Sweden and the American Companies, and the Efforts of Sweden to
Regain the Colony*, two volumes, 1911

67.   Johnson, Amandus, *Swedish Contributions to American Freedom, 1776-1783: Including a sketch of the background of the
Revolution,*

68.   Johnson, Amandus, *Swedish Contributions to American National Life, 1638-1921,* Committee of the Swedish Section of
America's Making, Inc., New York, 1921. Republished by
Nabu Public Domain Reprints, Breinigsville, Pennsylvania,
2010.

69.   *Journals of the Continental Congress*, United States Government Printing Office

70.   Kremer, J. Bruce, *John Hanson of Mulberry Grove*, Albert &
Charles Boni, Inc., New York, 1938

71.   Lanham, Paul, "The Crypt on the Cliff," *News & Notes*, Prince
George's County Historical Society, vol. XXVII, no. 5, June
1998

72.   Lantz, Emily Emerson, "Hanson Lineage and Arms," (1) *The
Sun*, Baltimore, Maryland, July 29, 1906

73.   Lantz, Emily Emerson, "Hanson Lineage and Arms," (2) *The
Sun*, Baltimore, Maryland, August 5, 1906

74.   Lantz, Emily Emerson, "The Hanson Family Again," *The Sun*,
Baltimore, Maryland, August 12, 1906

75.   Levering, Ralph, *John Hanson: Public Servant*, monograph as
part of the United States Bicentennial observance, Western
Maryland College, Westminster, Maryland, 1976, also as
"John Hanson: Public Servant," *Maryland Historical Magazine*
(Summer 1976)

76.   Library of Congress, *The Diaries of George Washington*, 51
volumes, 1748-1799

77.   Mackenzie, George Norberry, *Colonial Families of the United
States of America,* (seven volumes), Seaforth Press, Baltimore,1917. Reprinted by Genealogical Publishing Company,
1966, and others since.

78.   Manley, Reverend F. H., "Notes on the History of Great
Somerford," *The Wiltshire Archaeological and Natural History*

Magazine, volume XXXI, no. XCV, June 1901

79. Marbury, William L., "The High Court of Chancery and the Chancellors of Maryland," address given to the annual meeting of the Maryland State Bar Association, 1905

80. *The Maryland Sale* (auction catalogue), Crocker Farm, 15900 York Road, Sparks, Maryland, August, 2011

81. *Master Plan Charrette Summary: John Hanson Institute and Village*, The Wiles Group, Annapolis, 2007

82. Mathias, Senator Charles M., "A Tribute to John Hanson: Maryland Day 1981," *The Congressional Record*, United States Congress, March 25, 1981

83. McCarthy, John P., Jeanne A. Ward, George D. Cress, and Charles D. Cheek, *Intensive Archeological Survey of the Addison Plantation Site and Intensive Archeological Testing of the Addison Manor Foundations, Beltway Parcel, PortAmerica Development, Oxon Hill, Prince George's County, Maryland*, report prepared for James T. Lewis Enterprises, Ltd., John Milner Associates, Inc., 1989

84. McCarthy, John P., Jeffrey B. Snyder, and Billy R. Roulette, Jr., "Arms from Addison Plantation and the Maryland Militia on the Potomac Frontier," *Historical Archaeology*, vol. 25, no. 1, pp. 66-79, 1991

85. "Memorial to Patriot Judges, First to Repudiate the British Stamp Act," *New York Times*, November 23, 1904

86. Michael, Peter H., *Remarks made to the Board of County Commissioners of Frederick County, Maryland, on the proposed John Hanson National Memorial*, July 28, 2009, (private publication in possession of the author)

87. Michael, Peter H., "Historian Seeks to Honor First President," *The Washington Times*, October 13, 2008.

88. Michael, Peter H., "John Hanson: Frederick's Indispensible National Founder, *The Frederick News-Post*, Frederick, Maryland, October 23, 2011. This was the first of a series of six articles published by *The Frederick News-Post* on John Hanson on the fourth Sunday of the month through March, 2011, the last five appearing after the publication of *Remembering John Hanson*.

89. Michael, Peter H., "Keep John Hanson and Install Harriet Tubman in National Statuary Hall," testimony presented before the Maryland Senate Committee on Education, Health and Environmental Affairs hearing on Senate Bill 351, Request to Place a Statue of Harriet Tubman in the National Statuary Hall Collection, February 23, 2011, Maryland State Senate, Annapolis, and in possession of the author

90. Michael, Peter H., "Let John Hanson Remain Standing," *The*

Frederick News-Post, Frederick, Maryland, February 27, 2011

91. Michael, Peter H., private letter to Aldan Weinberg, March 15, 2003

92. Michael, Peter H., *The John Hanson Memorial Project*, privately published memorandum, 2008

93. Morris, Richard B., *Seven Who Shaped Our Destiny*, New York, 1973

94. Murdock, Myrtle Cheney, *National Statuary Hall in the Nation's Capitol*, Monumental Press, 1955

95. Negas, Kristina, "The Real First President," *The Frederick News-Post,* Frederick, Maryland, August 31, 2008, p. 1

96. Nelson, Jacob A., *John Hanson and the Inseparable Union,* Meador Publishing Company, Boston, 1939

97. Nelson, Jacob A., *John Hanson and the National Domain*, paper presented at the Smyrna Society, May 5, 1933. In possession of the Luther College Library, Luther College, Decorah, Iowa.

98. Newman, Harry Wright, *Charles County Gentry*, published by the author, Washington DC, 1940. Reprinted in 150 copies by Higginson Book Company, Salem, Massachusetts, undated. Republished by Clearfield Publishing, Clearfield, Pennsylvania, 1997

99. Newman, Harry Wright, *Seigniory In Early Maryland, Descendants of the Lords of the Maryland Manors*, Baltimore, 1949

100. Newman, Jeff, "Hanson or Tubman? Legislators pick sides," *The Enterprise*, Lexington Park, Maryland, February 18, 2011

101. *New York Times*, "Douglas H. Thomas Dead," March 13, 1919

102. Papenfuse, Edward C., *et al.*, *A Biographical Dictionary of the Maryland Legislature, 1635-1789*, 2 volumes, Johns Hopkins University Press, 1979 and 1985

103. Papenfuse, Edward C., *Accident, Maryland,* en.wikipedia.org/wiki/Accident,_MD. The author is reluctant to cite Wikipedia entries because of the well-known high inaccuracy of this thinly vetted website as, for example, with the many mistakes in its John Hanson entry. However, this Wikipedia article on the village of Accident, Maryland, which John Hanson surveyed, is written by Edward Papenfuse, the State Archivist of Maryland, who provides correct information in the article.

104. Papenfuse, Edward C. and Joseph M. Coale III, *The Maryland State Archives Atlas of Historical Maps of Maryland, 1608-1908*, Johns Hopkins University Press, 2003

105. Pearl, Susan G., "Archeology at Oxon Hill Manor," memorandum, Maryland-National Capital Park and Planning Commis-

sion, April 8, 1998

106. Power, Mark, "Matias T. Oppersdorff," (obituary), *The Salt Mine*, http://markpowerblog.com, February 20, 2010

107. "Program and Exercises at the Dedication of the John Hanson Memorial Monument," Vasa Oder of America, October 17, 1959. Copy in possession of the author.

108. *Proceedings of the Council of Maryland, 1687/8-1693,* Archives of Maryland Online, http://aomol.net/megafile/msa/speccol/sc2900/sc2908/00 0001/000008/html/am8--23.html

109. *Proceedings in the Senate and House of Representatives Upon the Reception and Acceptance From the State of Maryland of the Statues of Charles Carroll and of John Hanson Erected In the Statuary Hall of the Capitol,* United States Government Printing Office, Washington DC, January 31, 1903

110. Pundt, Mary Jo, *Descendants of John Hanson*, in the private collections of Ms. Pundt, A. Gulbransen and Peter H. Michael, July 10, 2002, and as updated

111. Richardson, Hester Dorsey, *Side-Lights of Maryland History with Sketches of Early Maryland Families,* Williams and Wilkins Company, 1913. Republished by Bay Country Publishing Company, 1967.

112. Rodgers, Bethany, "In search of John Hanson," *The Frederick News-Post*, Frederick, Maryland, October 16, 2011.

113. Russell, George, "John Hanson of Maryland; A Swedish Origin Disproved," *The American Genealogist*, October 1988, vol. 63, pp. 211-213.

114. Scharf, John Thomas, *Essay on John Hanson*, Typescript biographical essay, Library of Congress, Miscellaneous Manuscripts Collection, MSS2184,1892

115. Scharf, John Thomas, *History of Western Maryland*, vols. I, II and III, Clearfield Company, 1968 (reprint)

116. Schirm, United States Representative Charles R., "Address of Mr. Schirm of Maryland," in *Proceedings in the Senate and House of Representatives Upon the Reception and Acceptance From the State of Maryland of the Statues of Charles Carroll and of John Hanson Erected In the Statuary Hall of the Capitol*, United States Government Printing Office, Washington DC, January 31, 1903

117. "Searchers Hunt Mausoleum for Body of John Hanson," *The Sun*, Baltimore, Maryland, April 14, 1973

118. Smith, Seymour Wemyss, *John Hanson: Our First President*, Brewer, Warren & Putnam, New York, 1932. Reprinted by Invest In America National Council, 1976.

119. Smith, Scottie Fitzgerald, "The Maryland Ancestors of Zelda Sayre Fitzgerald," *Maryland Historical Magazine*, vol. 78, no. 3, Fall 1983

120. Steele, John Francis, "First Page of the United States Was Grafton Dulaney Hanson," *The Washington Star*, unknown publication date in 1929

121. Steiner, Bernard C., *Western Maryland In the Revolutionary War*, Publisher unknown, Baltimore, 1902

122. Stiverson, Gregory A., "Hanson, John," *American National Biography Online*, Oxford University Press, 2000, http://anb.org/articles/01/01-00369.html.

123. Stoeckel, Herbert J., *The Strange Story of John Hanson, First President of the United States: A Guide to Oxon Hill Manor and Mulberry Grove in Maryland*, 1956. Reprint by Hanson House, Hartford, Connecticut, 1958

124. Stowe, Harriet Beecher, *A Key to Uncle Tom's Cabin, Presenting the Original Facts and Documents Upon Which the Story is Founded, Together with Corroborative Statements Verifying the Truth of the Work*, Applewood Books, 1998, reprint of 1853 edition

125. Taylor, Walter Hanson Stone, letter to George A. Hanson, May 30, 1874. Excerpts from this letter may be found in Hanson, George A., *Old Kent: The Eastern Shore of Maryland*, original publisher unknown, Baltimore, 1876. Reprinted by Regional Publishing Company, 1967

126. "The John Hanson Family Archive & Collection," *The Maryland Sale*, (auction catalogue), Crocker Farm Auctioneers, Sparks, Maryland, August, 2011

127. *The Maryland Gazette*, Annapolis, March 22, 1781

128. Thomas, Annie Campbell Gordon, Letters to her husband Dr. John Hanson Thomas, Jr., September 13, 1861, through February 22, 1862, Hanson-Thomas Collection, Maryland Historical Society. The approximately eighty letters were written to her husband when he was a prisoner of war.

129. Thomas, Douglas H., *John Hanson, President of the United States in Congress Assembled*, Cushing and Company, Baltimore, undated. Republished for the Maryland General Assembly in support of the Assembly's case for inclusion of the John Hanson statue in National Statuary Hall, Baltimore, 1898

130. Thomas, Dr. John Hanson, Jr., Letters to his wife Annie Campbell Gordon Thomas, September 13, 1861, through February 21, 1862, Hanson-Thomas Collection, Maryland Historical Society. The approximately sixty-five letters were written when Dr. Thomas was a prisoner of war.

131. Thorsell, Elisabeth, "Was the First President of the United States a Swede?," *Sveriges Slaktforskarforbund*, genalogi.se, 2003. (Cited despite its errors.)

132. Tully, Meg, "Fighting for John Hanson: Senate leader makes plea," *The Frederick News-Post*, March 6, 2011

133. Tully, Meg, "New John Hanson statue planned for downtown," *The Frederick News-Post*, July 29, 2009

134. Tully, Meg, "Ousting John Hanson? Some legislators want prominent Frederick County historical figure to remain on view in a national hall," *The Frederick News-Post*, Frederick, Maryland, February 27, 2011

135. United States Congress, *Biographical Directory of the United States Congress, 1774-Present.* See http://bioguide.congress.gov/scripts/biodisplay.pl?index=H0 00177 for the John Hanson entry.

136. Venn, John, *Alumni Cantabrigienses, a biographical list of all known students, graduates and holders of office at the University of Cambridge, from the earliest times to 1751*, 4 volumes (1922–27)

137. *Washington Post*, "Eisenhower Salutes Hanson as 'First' President," October 17, 195?

138. *Washington Star,* "Rites to Mark Anniversary of Hanson, 'First President' ," November 12, 1933

139. *Washington Star,* " 'First President' Is Honored on Anniversary of Death: Site of Hanson Home Marked in Maryland," November 16, 1933

140. *Washington Star,* "Bill to Split P. G. (Price George's) County Again Filed in Annapolis," January 29, 1977

141. Weinberg, Aldan, "Hanson Mysteries Persist," *Frederick* magazine, Frederick, Maryland, November 2004

142. Weinberg, Aldan, "No Respect," *Frederick* magazine, Frederick, Maryland, February 2003

143. Wellington, United States Senator George L., "Address of Mr. Wellington of Maryland," in *Proceedings in the Senate and House of Representatives Upon the Reception and Acceptance From the State of Maryland of the Statues of Charles Carroll and of John Hanson Erected In the Statuary Hall of the Capitol*, United States Government Printing Office, Washington DC, January 31, 1903

144. Williams, T.J.C., *History of Frederick County, Maryland*, vol. I, p. 95, L.R. Titsworth & Company, 1910

145. Wills, Liber GM no. 2, folio 75, Frederick County, Maryland

146. Wilstach, Paul, *Patriots Off Their Pedestals,* Bobbs-Merrill Company, Indianapolis, 1927

147. Wilstach, Paul, *Tidewater Maryland,* Bobbs-Merrill Company, Indianapolis, 1931

148. Zahner, Robert, *The Legacy of the John Hanson Society of Maryland,* The John Hanson Society of Maryland, Baltimore, 1982

149. Zipp, Barbara, transcriptions of letters of Dr. John Hanson Thomas, Jr. to his wife Annie Campbell Gordon Thomas when he was a prisoner of war, Crocker Farm, 2011. Transcriptions in the possession of the transcriber and the author. See the entry above for Dr. Thomas.

150. Zipp, Barbara, transcriptions of letters of Annie Campbell Gordon Thomas to her husband Dr. John Hanson Thomas, Jr. when he was a prisoner of war, Crocker Farm, 2011. Transcriptions in the possession of the transcriber and the author. See the entry above for Annie Thomas.

References on John Hanson and His Family in Frederick

The record of John Hanson's personal life in Frederick is thin, with his letters to Philip Thomas the best guide from 1769 when Hanson moved his family to Frederick until 1783 when he died. The following sources mostly provide civil transactions and major life events such as marriages and deaths in the Hanson family from 1769 until the death of Jane Contee Hanson in Frederick in 1812 and later. The letter to Aldan Weinberg provides some illumination of Hanson's life not found elsewhere. Some references listed above also reveal John Hanson's Frederick period.

151. Ashbury, John W., *And All Our Yesterdays, A Chronicle of Frederick County, Maryland,* Diversions Publications, 1997

152. Bishop, C. Larry, *Frederick's Other City,* Mount Olivet Cemetery 150th Anniversary Committee, Frederick, Maryland, 2002

153. Delaplaine, Judge Edward S., "John Hanson- a study in controversy," *The News,* Frederick, Maryland, August 1, 1981

154. Delaplaine, Judge Edward S., "John Hanson- Part 1: Hanson Returns to US Capitol," *The News,* Frederick, Maryland, February 27, 1970

155. Delaplaine, Judge Edward S., "John Hanson- Part 2: Hanson Chosen With Carroll," *The News,* Frederick, Maryland, March 3, 1970

156. Delaplaine, Judge Edward S., "John Hanson- Part 3: Hanson Statue Finds a Home," *The News,* Frederick, Maryland, March 6, 1970

157. Engelbrecht, Jacob, *Death Ledger,* 1820-1890, Eader and Long. Reprinted by Paw Prints Publishing, 1995.

158. Engelbrecht, Jacob, *Marriage Ledger,* 1820-1890, Eader and Long. Reprinted by Paw Prints Publishing, 1994.

159. Engelbrecht, Jacob, *Property & Almshouse Ledgers*, Eader & Long. Reprinted by Paw Prints Publishing, 1996.

160. Evangelical Lutheran Church, *Evangelical Lutheran Church Records 1780-1811*, vol. 4, Frederick, Maryland

161. Evangelical Lutheran Church, *Evangelical Reformed Church Records 1746-1789*, vol. 5, Frederick, Maryland

162. Evangelical Lutheran Church, *Evangelical Reformed Church Records 1790-1828*, vol. 6, Frederick, Maryland

163. Evangelical Lutheran Church, *Monocacy Lutheran Congregation and Evangelical Lutheran Church, Frederick, 1742- 1779*, Frederick, Maryland

164. Holdcraft, Jacob M., *75,000 Cemetery Inscriptions From Frederick County, Maryland; Reprinted With More Names in Stone*, Monocacy Book Company, 1999

165. Holdcraft, Jacob M., *More Names In Stone: Cemetery Inscriptions From The Peripheral Areas of Frederick County, Maryland*, Monocacy Book Company, 1972

166. Holdcraft, Jacob M., *Names in Stone: 75, 000 Cemetery Inscriptions From Frederick County, Maryland*, two-volume set, Monocacy Book Company, 1963

167. Jourdan, Elise G., *Early Families of Southern Maryland*, volume 10, Heritage Books, 2007

168. msa.md.gov/megafile/msa/speccol/sc2900/sc2908/html/chancery.html, the page at the website of the Maryland State Archives dealing with the office of Chancellor of Maryland and the Chancery Courts.

169. Miller, Nancy, "108 West Patrick Street, Frederick," *Maryland Historical Trust* magazine, January 11, 1972

170. Myers, Margaret, *Marriage Licenses of Frederick County 1778-1810*, Family Line Publications, 1986. Updated version, Family Line Publications, 1994

171. Myers, Margaret, *Marriage Licenses of Frederick County 1811-1840*, Family Line Publications, 1987

172. Noyes, Theodore W., "The Heart of Maryland," *The Washington Star*, January 14, 1930. Noyes was Editor of the newspaper at that time.

173. Rogers, A., "The Open Door," *The Frederick Post,* March 3, 1975

174. Sanner, Patricia, transcript of her talk given to the annual meeting of the John Hanson Society of Maryland, delivered in Frederick, Maryland, April 29, 1973

175. Scharf, John Thomas, *History of Frederick City, the Districts & Villages of Frederick County From Early Historical Writings,*

Louis H. Everts Publishing Company, Philadelphia, 1882

176. Scharf, John Thomas, *History of Western Maryland*, vol. I, Louis H. Everts Publishing Company, Philadelphia, 1882

177. Schildknecht, C. E., *Monocacy and Catoctin*, vol. II, 1898, reprinted 1998

178. *Session Laws, 1972*, Maryland State Archives

179. Skaggs, David C., *Roots of Maryland Democracy, 1753-1776*, Greenwood Press, 1973

180. Smith, J. F. D., *A Tour of the United States of America*, London, 1784

181. *The Frederick Post*[330], "The John Hanson House" (editorial), December 12, 1974

182. *The Frederick Post,* "Was the oldest section of Hanson House razed?," June 25, 1977

183. *The Frederick Post,* "John Hanson Fiasco," June 23, 1981. Editorial reprinted from *The Valley Register*, Middletown, Maryland, date unknown.

184. *The News,* "Group Strives for Preservation of Hanson House," October 9, 1971

185. *The News,* "First day of issue ceremonies held for John Hanson stamp," November 6, 1981

186. *The Post,* "Groups Strive for Preservation of Hanson House," October 11, 1971

187. *The Post,* "Foundation to Restore Hanson House," May 9, 1974

188. *The Post,* "Saving the Hanson House: A 'Complex' Problem," August 19, 1974

189. Tracey, Grace L. and John P. Dern, Pioneers of Old Monocacy: The Early Settlement of Frederick County, Maryland, 1721-1743, Clearfield Company, (reprint edition), 2001

190. Weld, Isaac, *Travels through the States of North America and the Provinces of Upper and Lower Canada During the Years 1795, 1796, and 1797*. London, John Stockdale, 1807

References on the Continental Congresses and Governments of the United States

The author has personally inspected most but not all of the references below. The most authoritative are the official federal and state records listed. The National Archives' revealing *John Hanson Letter Book* comprises the full record of John Hanson's official correspondence while he was president of the United States in Congress Assembled.

191. Adams, Herbert B., *Maryland's Influence upon Land Cessions to the United States*, Baltimore, 1885

192. Adams, John, *John Adams autobiography, John Adams through 1776, part 1*, Adams Family Papers, Massachusetts Historical Society

193. Adams, John, letter to Abigail Adams, July 3, 1776, Letters of Delegates to Congress: Volume 4, May 16, 1776 - August 15, 1776, Library of Congress

194. Adams, John, letter to Abigail Adams, July 3, 1776. Original manuscript from the Adams Family Papers, Massachusetts Historical Society

195. Adams, John, letter to Samuel Chase, June 14, 1776, *The Works of John Adams*, vol. IX

196. Adams, Willi Paul, The First *American Constitutions: Republican Ideology and the Making of the State Constitutions in the Revolutionary Era, University of North* Carolina Press, 1980

197. Ammerman, David, "Annapolis and the First Continental Congress: A Note on the Committee System in Revolutionary America," *Maryland Historical Magazine*, LXVI, pp. 169-180, 1971

198. Bancroft, George, *History of the United States of America, From the Discovery of the American Continent,* (1854-78), vols. 4-10, online edition

199. Baxter, James, "Review of *The Diplomacy of the American Revolution*", *The New England Quarterly*, vol. 8, no. 4, December 1935

200. Bemis, Samuel Flagg, *The Diplomacy of the American Revolution*, The American Historical Association and Appleton-Century Publishing Company, 1935

201. Boudinot, Elias, *Letter to Hannah Boudinot*, November 4, 1782. Statesmen Collection, New Jersey Historical Society and at etext.virginia.edu/toc/modeng/public/DelVol19.html.

202. Boudinot, Elias, *Journal on Historical Recollections of American Events During the Revolutionary War*, F. Bourquin, Philadelphia, 1894

203. Burnett, Edmund Cody, *Letters of the Members of the Continental Congress,* eight volumes, Carnegie Institution of Washington, Washington, DC, 1921

204. Burnett, Edmund Cody, "Who Was the First President of the United States?," *News Service Bulletin*, The Carnegie Institution of Washington, Vo. 11, no. 32, May 29, 1932

205. Burnett, Edmund, The *Continental Congress,* Norton, 1941. Reprinted by Greenwood Publishing, 1975

206. Cogliano, Francis D., Revolutionar*y America, 1763-1815: A*

Political History, 2000

207. Contee, Thomas, *The Original Diary of Thomas Contee Esqr., of Prince George's County, Maryland. In Octr., 1776, to Genl. Washington's Camp near New York, in company with John Hanson, Esq., who married the sister of said Contee,* unpublished diary, 1776. This diary was sold at auction in 2011. It is fully transcribed in the bibliography entry for Crocker Farm above.

208. Dorsey, Ella Loraine, letter to the editor of *The Baltimore Sun,* in Letters of Alexander Contee Hanson, Jr., Maryland Historical Society, MS.408. The letter is undated but would have been written between 1898 when the John Hanson statue in National Statuary Hall of the United States Capitol had been authorized by the Maryland General Assembly and before January 31, 1903, when it was formally donated by Maryland to Statuary Hall.

209. Eisenberg, Gerson G., *Marylanders Who Served the Nation,* Maryland State Archives, 1992

210. Force, Peter, editor, *American Archives,* 9 vols., 1837-1853. This is a major compilation of documents from 1774 through 1776.

211. Fowler, William M., *The Baron of Beacon Hill: A Biography of John Hancock,* Houghton Mifflin, 1980

212. Masthead, *Bartgis's Federal Gazette,* vol. VII, no. 381, Frederick, Maryland, Wednesday, August 28, 1799

213. Garver, Frank Harmon, "The Transition from the Continental Congress to the Congress of the Confederation," *Pacific Historical Review,* vol. 1, no. 2, June, 1932, pp. 221-234, University of California Press

214. Grant, George, "John Hanson, American Patriot and First President of the United States," in *The American Patriot's Handbook: The Writings, History, and Spirit of a Free Nation,* Cumberland House Publishing, 2009

215. Hakim, Joy, *The New Nation,* Oxford University Press, 2003

216. Hanson, John, *Letter Book of John Hanson,* in *Letter Books of the Presidents of Congress 1781-1787,* National Archives. These letter books may be found in the original and on microfilm at the Washington, DC, headquarters of the National Archives and Records Administration. The microfilm location of the John Hanson letter book is microform 247, cabinet 67A, roll 24, item 16. This is the full record of President John Hanson's official correspondence during his presidency.

217. Hanson, John, *Letter* to George Washington, March 28, 1782 in George Washington Papers, 1741-1799: Series 4, General Correspondence, 1697-1799, United States Library of Congress

218. Henderson, H. James, *Party Politics in the Continental Congress*, Rowman & Littlefield, 1974. Reprinted 2002

219. http://memory.loc.gov/ammem/amlaw/lwjclink.html. Full text of *Journals of the Continental Congress, 1774-1789*

220. Hunt, Gaillard et al., editors, *Journals of the Continental Congress*, 1774-1789, Library of Congress and the Government Printing Office, 34 volumes published 1904 to 1937

221. Jefferson, Thomas, *Autobiography*, draft dated January 6, 1821, The Thomas Jefferson Papers, Library of Congress

222. Jensen, Merrill, *New Nation: A History of the United States During the Confederation, 1781-89,* 1950

223. Ketchum, Richard, *Divided Loyalties, How the American Revolution came to New York*, 2002,

224. Kruman, Marc W., *Between Authority and Liberty: State Constitution Making in Revolutionary America,* University of North Carolina Press, 1997

225. Lankford, Richard E., "Extension of Remarks of Hon. Richard E. Lankford of Maryland in the House of Representatives," *Congressional Record*, appendix A558, January 29, 1957

226. Launitz-Schurer, Leopold, *Loyal Whigs and Revolutionaries, The Making of the Revolution in New York, 1765-1776*, 1980

227. Library of Congress, *Journals of the Continental Congress*, (34 volumes published by the Library of Congress, 1904-1937). See volumes 21-23 for the Hanson administration.

228. Library of Congress, *The Diaries of George Washington, 51 volumes, 1748-1799*

229. Library of Congress: Major documents from the Congress, with journals, letters and debates

230. Maier, Paulin, *American Scripture:* Making *the Declaration of Independence,* 1988

231. *Maryland Gazette*, issue of March 22, 1781

232. McKinsey, Folger, *History of Frederick County, Maryland, Continued from the Beginning of the Year 1861 Down to the Present Time*, L.R. Titsworth & Co., Frederick, Maryland, 1910. Reprinted by Regional Publishing Company, Baltimore, 1967 and 1979. Reprinted by Genealogical Publishing Company, Baltimore, 1997 and 1903.

233. McLaughlin, Andrew C., *A Constitutional History of the United States,*1935, online version

234. Miller, John C., *Origins of the American Revolution*, 1943, online edition

235. Miller, John C., *Triumph of Freedom, 1775-1783*, 1948

236. Montross, Lynn, *The Reluctant Rebels; the Story of the Conti-nental Congress, 1774–1789*, Barnes & Noble, 1950. Re-printed 1970

237. Morris, Richard B., "The Confederation Period and the Ameri-can Historian," *William and Mary Quarterly*, 3rd Ser., vol. 13, no. 2, April 1956, pp. 139-156

238. Morris, Richard B., *The Forging of the Union, 1781-1789*, 1988

239. Morris, Robert, *Letter to John Hanson*, January 15, 1782 in Thomas Jefferson Papers Series 1, General Correspondence, 1651-1827, United States Library of Congress

240. Morris, Robert, *The Papers of Robert Morris, 1781-1784*, Elmer James Ferguson and Elizabeth M. Nuxoll, editors, Uni-versity of Pittsburgh Press, 1999

241. Ohio Historical Society, *Ohio History*, Volume II, 1887

242. *Papers of the Continental Congress* (Digitized Original Docu-ments)

243. Puls, Mark, *Samuel Adams, Father of the American Revolution*, 2006

244. Rakove, Jack N., *The Beginnings of National Politics: An Inter-pretive History of the Continental Congress*, Knopf, 1979

245. Roper, Daniel C., *The United States Post Office*, Funk & Wag-nall Company, New York, 1917

246. Sobel, Robert, and John Raimo, editors, *Biographical Direc-tory of the Governors of the United States, 1789-1978*, 4 vol-umes, Meckler Books, 1978

247. Stoekel, Herbert J., "Mulberry Grove- New National Shrine?," *The Hartford Courant*, Hartford, Connecticut, March 18, 1950

248. Stoekel, Herbert J., "The People's Forum: Further Credentials for John Hanson," *The Hartford Courant*, Hartford, Connecti-cut, March 18, 1950

249. *The Continental Congress - History, Declaration and Resolves, Resolutions and Recommendations*, at AmericanRevolu-tion.com

250. Time.com/time/magazine/article/0,9171,742964-1,00.html

251. Tolzman, Donald Heinrich, *The German-American Experience*, Red Rose Studio, Willow Street, Pennsylvania, 2000

252. Van der Mei, William, personal communication to the author (email), May 14, 2009

253. Warfield, Joshua Dorsey, *The Founders of Anne Arundel and Howard Counties, Maryland*, Kohn and Pollock Publishers, Baltimore, 1905

254. Washington, George, "Letter to Pennsylvania Governor Jo-

seph Reed," in *The George Washington Papers*, Manuscript Division, United States Library of Congress, May 28, 1780

255. Washington, George, *Letter to John Hanson*, November 30, 1781, in *The George Washington Papers*, 1741-1799: Series 4, General Correspondence, 1697-1799, United States Library of Congress; and in Fitzpatrick, John C., Editor, *The Writings of George Washington from the Original Manuscript Sources, 1745-1799*, United States Library of Congress.

256. White, Frank F., Jr. *The Governors of Maryland, 1777-1972*, Maryland Hall of Records Commission, 1970

257. Williams, Thomas John Chew, *History of Frederick County, Maryland, from the Earliest Settlements to the Beginning of the War Between the States*, L.R. Titsworth & Co., Frederick, Maryland, 1910. Reprinted by Regional Publishing Company, Baltimore, 1967 and 1979. Reprinted by Genealogical Publishing Company, Baltimore, 1997 and 1903.

258. Worthington C. Ford, et al. editors, *Journals of the Continental Congress, 1774-1789,* 34 vols., 1904–1937, online edition

259. Young, Christopher J., "The Goddard Broadside: Mary Katherine Goddard's Printing of the Declaration of Independence," *Maryland Historical Society News*, Fall, 2011

The Hanson and Related Collections of the Maryland Historical Society

The Maryland Historical Society in Baltimore possesses the most extensive and useful collections on John Hanson and his extended family.

260. Boles, Nancy G., "Notes on Maryland Historical Society Manuscript Collections: The John Hanson Collection," *Maryland Historical Magazine*, 65 (Fall 1970), pp. 304-5

261. Maryland Historical Society, *Hanson Family Papers*, MS.408. One volume and two portfolios of ninety letters from and to Alexander Contee Hanson, Jr. including miscellaneous Hanson family letters and correspondence from Alexander Contee Hanson, Jr. to George Corbin Washington; Alexander Contee Hanson, Jr. to John Elihu concerning the burial of General James Lingan; accounts and other business papers concerning the Elk Ridge Company (Caleb Dorsey & Company Iron Furnaces).

262. Maryland Historical Society, *John Hanson Papers*, MS. 1785. Letters written by Hanson (1715-1783) to his son-in-law Dr. Philip Thomas of Frederick, Maryland covering military campaigns, scarcity of food and money, difficulties in fulfilling Maryland's quotas of men and supplies during the Revolutionary War, the weakness of the government, the Andre-Arnold plot to capture West Point, the surrender of Cornwallis, naval engagements off the West Indies, the peace ne-

gotiations, the opening of the Bank of North America in 1782, family health, management of his plantation and slaves, and other topics. During this period, Hanson was a member of the Second Continental Congress and then President of the United States in Congress Assembled.

263. Maryland Historical Society, *John Hanson Ledgers*, 1775-82, MS. 1785.1. Records of Maryland planter and politician (1721-1783): accounts of household and plantation expenses, accounts of the Council of Safety for purchasing guns, blankets, and other materials, the Continental Congress's account with the Frederick County Committee of Observation, and the Continental Congress's account for prisoners.

264. Maryland Historical Society, *John and Walter Hanson Papers, 1776-1791* (nine items), MS.1579. Correspondence and petitions to the Maryland General Assembly concerning the sum of 1,000 pounds of tobacco lent to John and Walter Hanson by the Council on Safety, Annapolis, 1776, for the building of a powder mill.

265. Maryland Historical Society, John Hanson Society Records, 1932-1974 (eighty-four items), MS. 2086. Organized in 1932 to honor Hanson as the first president of the United States: correspondence, newspaper clippings, papers concerning Swedish-American groups.

266. Morell, William Newman, form letter to "Dear Associate," November 3, 1933. John Hanson Society of Maryland papers, Maryland Historical Society

267. Morrell, William N., letter to Hon. Nels Johnson, October 1, 1959. John Hanson Society of Maryland papers, Maryland Historical Society

268. Morrell, William N., "One Hundred and Fiftieth Anniversary of the Death of John Hanson," *The Maryland Club Woman*, vol. VII, no. 2, October, 1933

269. Morrell, William N., untitled genealogy of the Hanson family from Roger de Rastrick through the Hanson generation including John Hanson, 1974. Among the papers of the Mary Keech Edelen Collection, Southern Maryland Studies Center, Southern Maryland College, La Plata, Maryland.

The following twelve entries are paintings held by the Maryland Historical Society,

270. John Hanson (1721 (*sic*) - 1783) He was the great-great-great grandfather of the donor.
Donor: Estate of Alice Lee Thomas Stevenson (Mrs. Robert H. Stevenson, Jr.)
Year donated to the Maryland Historical Society: 1972

271. Jane Contee Hanson the elder (Mrs. John Hanson) (1728-

1812), daughter of Alexander Contee (1691-1740) of Charles County and his wife, Jane Brooke. She was the great-great-great grandmother of the donor.
Donor: Estate of Alice Lee Thomas Stevenson (Mrs. Robert H. Stevenson, Jr.)
Year donated to the Maryland Historical Society: 1972

272. Alexander Contee Hanson, Sr. (1749-1806)
Donor: Mrs. W. Winchester White
Year donated to the Maryland Historical Society: 1947

273. Alexander Contee Hanson, Sr. (1749-1806), Chancellor of Maryland
Donor: Estate of Miss Nannie Hanson. Anne Maria "Nannie" Hanson(1858-1943), the unmarried daughter of Charles Grosvenor Hanson (1816-1880) who married Anne Maria Worthington in 1840. Her ancestral home was Belmont, built by Caleb Dorsey, and the burial place of Alexander Contee Hanson, Jr.
Year donated to the Maryland Historical Society: 1961

274. Rebecca Howard Hanson (Mrs. Alexander Contee Hanson, Sr.) (1759-1806)
Donor: Estate of Miss Nannie Hanson
Year donated to the Maryland Historical Society: 1961

275. The family of Alexander Contee Hanson, Sr. (1749-1806)
Donor: Partial purchase by the Dr. Michael and Marie Abrams Memorial Purchase Fund, the John D. Teeter Fund, the G.H. Powder Fund and the Dangerfield Fund, and the partial gift of Elaine M. and Terrance O. Winner
Year donated to the Maryland Historical Society: 1985

276. Jane Contee Hanson the younger (Mrs. Philip Thomas) (1747-1781), daughter of John and Jane Hanson. She was the great-great-grandmother of the donor.
Donor: Estate of Alice Lee Thomas Stevenson (Mrs. Robert H. Stevenson, Jr.)
Year donated to the Maryland Historical Society: 1972

277. Dr. Philip Thomas (son-in-law of President John Hanson) (1747-18150
Donor: Estate of Alice Lee Thomas Stevenson (Mrs. Robert H. Stevenson, Jr.)
Year donated to the Maryland Historical Society: 1972

278. Alexander Contee Hanson, Jr. (1786-1819)
Donor: Mrs. Henry J. Bowdoin
Year donated to the Maryland Historical Society: 1943

279. John Hanson Thomas, II (1813-1881) He was great-grandfather of the donor.
Donor: Rosamond Whitridge Thomas Oppersdorff (Mrs. Edward Oppersdorff)
Year donated to the Maryland Historical Society: 1975

280. Eleanor Williams Hanson (1883-1925). The donor is the daughter of the sitter. Eleanor Hanson was the only child of Elizabeth Hazlett Williams (1859-1927) and Earnult Hawkins Williams (1857-1922). Portrait was exhibited at the 1893 World's Fair in Chicago.
Donor: Mrs. Roger W. Collins
Year donated to the Maryland Historical Society: 1991

281. Walter Hanson (1710 or 1711-1794)
Donor: Historical Society of Charles County, Maryland
Year donated to the Maryland Historical Society: 1996

The Mary Keech Edelen Collection
of the College of Southern Maryland

In a bequest, Mary Olivia Keech Edelen, gave her collection of Hansoniana and other Charles County and southern Maryland records and memorabilia to the College of Southern Maryland upon her death in 1990 at age eighty-two. The collection is housed in the Southern Maryland Studies Center at the library of the College's main campus near LaPlata, Charles County, Maryland, a few miles from Mulberry Grove.

Mary and Dr. Edward Edelen, Jr. were the owners of Mulberry Grove from 1950 when they bought and restored the Mulberry Grove home until the 1980s when their son, Edward Edelen III and his wife Lexy purchased the Mulberry Grove estate and began acquiring nearby farms which had once been part of Mulberry Grove. With the Hansons, Briscoes and Dents, the Edelen family is one of the oldest and most distinguished in Charles County.

Mary Keech Edelen was an active community leader, local researcher and genealogist. She served on the boards of the Charles County Tercentenary Commission and the John Hanson Society. Among many community and civic organizations, she was a member of the Historical Society of Charles County, the Charles County Museum Restorers, the Society for the Restoration of Port Tobacco, Mt. Carmel Monastery, the Descendants of the Manor Lords of Maryland, the Maryland Genealogical Society, the Daughters of the American Revolution and the National Society of Colonial Dames of Maryland. Mrs. Edelen was also the designer of Charles County's official flag.

The Mary K. Edelen Collection spans 1859 to 1990. In addition to its records on John Hanson, the Hanson family and Mulberry Grove, the collection includes photographs, primary research notes, programs, publications, and information on local history, historic houses and churches, historic preservation, restoration efforts and other compiled resources relating to historical sites in the greater Charles County region.

The collection is contained in thirteen boxed volumes occupying nearly six feet of shelf space.

282. *Southern Maryland Studies Center, College of Southern Mary-*

land, Mary K. Edelen Collection, boxes one through five. This portion of the collection, arranged in alphabetical order by locale, pertains almost entirely to the more prominent colonial era Charles County estates including Mulberry Grove.

283. *Southern Maryland Studies Center, College of Southern Maryland, Mary K. Edelen Collection*, boxes six and seven. These boxes contain miscellany involving various Maryland topics, places and people, some involving Charles County. Box six contains four old maps of Charles County.

284. *Southern Maryland Studies Center, College of Southern Maryland, Mary K. Edelen Collection*, box eight. This box contains several important Historic American Buildings surveys including those on Mulberry Grove, Equality where John Hanson's parents are buried, Durham Church where many nineteenth and twentieth century Hansons are buried, and Poynton Manor. This box also contains nineteenth and twentieth century photographs of Port Tobacco and environs.

285. *Southern Maryland Studies Center, College of Southern Maryland, Mary K. Edelen Collection*, boxes nine through thirteen. These contain miscellany. Box nine contains one John Hanson-related item, box ten contains ten, and box twelve contains eleven items or collections of newspaper clippings pertaining to John Hanson.

General References

286. Bick, Bonnie, "The Wilson Crossing: A Better Vision," *The Sierra Club*, Maryland Chapter, April 26, 1999

287. Bordewich, Fergus, *Bound for Canaan: The Underground Railroad and the War for the Soul of America*, Amistad/Harper Collins, 2005

288. Bordewich, Fergus, *Killing the White Man's Indian,* Anchor Books/Random House, 1996

289. Bordewich, Fergus M.. *Washington, the Making of the American Capital*, Amistad Harper Collins, 2008

290. Briggs, Minnie L., "John Hanson Cherry," *The Washington Star*, December 4, 1938

291. Brock, R. A., editor, *The Official Letters of Alexander Spotswood, Lieutenant-Governor of the Colony of Virginia, 1710-1722*, Virginia Historical Society, Richmond, 1882-1885

292. Brugger, Robert J., *Maryland, A Middle Temperament*, Johns Hopkins University Press, 1988

293. Chapelle, Suzanne, *et al., Maryland: A History of Its People*, Johns Hopkins University Press, 1986

294. von Graffenried, Thomas P., editor and publisher, *History of the von Graffenried Family from 1191 A.D. to 1925*, New York,

1925

295. von Graffenried, Baron Christoph, map of Frederick County, Maryland, and environs, Geography and Map Division, United States Library of Congress, 1712

296. Delaplaine, Hon. Edward S., letter to William N. Morrell, October 31, 1959. John Hanson Society of Maryland papers, Maryland Historical Society

297. Delaplaine, Hon. Edward S., *The Life of Thomas Johnson*, Grafton Press, 1927

298. Dodson, Leonidas, *Alexander Spotswood, Governor of Colonial Virginia, 1710-1722*, University of Pennsylvania Press, 1932

299. Du Lac, J. F., "In the hallowed hall, Md.'s historical heavyweights duke it out," *The Washington Post,* March 6, 2001, page A-1

300. Ellis, Joseph, *His Excellency George Washington*, Alfred A. Knopf, 2008

301. Erickson, Marie Anne, "Local Historian Merits Recognition," *The Frederick News-Post*, Frederick, Maryland, July 31, 2011. The local historian referred to in the article title is Harry Decker.

302. Ferling, John, *The Ascent of George Washington: The Hidden Political Genius of an American Icon*, Bloomsbury Press, 2009

303. Fitzpatrick, John C. editor, *The Writings of George Washington from the Original Manuscript Sources, 1745-1799*, United States Government Printing Office, volume 28

304. Hathorn, Guy B. *et al.*, *Government and Politics in the United States*, Van Nostrand Company, 1961

305. High, Michael, *The C&O Canal Companion,* Johns Hopkins University Press, Baltimore, 2001

306. Hinke, William J., editor and translator, "Report of the Journey of Francis Louis Michel from Berne, Switzerland to Virginia, October 2, 1701-December 1, 1702," *Virginia Magazine of History and Biography*, January 1916 (pp.1-43), April 1916 (pp. 113-141), August, 1916, (pp. 275-303)

307. Irving, Washington, *George Washington: A Biography*, 1856-1859, originally published in five volumes. Reprinted 1994, Charles Neider, editor, Da Capo Press, Cambridge, Massachusetts.

308. Lawson, John, *A New Voyage to North Carolina*, University of North Carolina Press, 1967 (Hugh Talmage Lefler's introduction dealing with the Frederick County explorer Franz Ludwig Michel)

309. Jefferson, Thomas, "Report of a Plan of Government for the Western Territory," archives of the United States in Congress

Assembled, United States Library of Congress

310. Manchester, William, *The Last Lion: Visions of Glory, 1874-1932*, Little, Brown and Company, 1983

311. Marck, John T., *Frederick Calvert, Sixth Lord Baltimore and Henry Harford*, aboutfamouspeople.com/article1022.html

312. Michel, Franz Ludwig, map of Frederick County, Maryland, and environs, Public Records Office, London, United Kingdom, 1707

313. Middleton, Arthur, *Tobacco Coast: A Maritime History of Chesapeake Bay in the Colonial Era*, Johns Hopkins University Press, 1984

314. Peterson, Merrill, editor, *The Portable Thomas Jefferson*, Penguin Books, 1975

315. Schlesinger, Arthur M., *The Colonial Merchants and the American Revolution, 1763-1776*, Facsimile Library, 1939

316. Selig, Robert A., "Wilhelmsburg in the Year 1702: The Account of Franz Ludwig Michel," *Colonial Williamsburg*, the Journal of the Colonial Williamsburg Foundation, Williamsburg, Virginia, Summer, 1998

317. Stein, Mark, *How the States Got Their Shapes*, Harper Collins Smithsonian Books, 2008

318. Stephenson, Richard W. and Marianne M. McKee, editors, *Virginia in Maps: Four Centuries of Settlement, Growth, and Development*, Library of Virginia, Richmond, 2000

319. Todd, Vincent H., editor, *Christoph von Graffenried's Account of the Founding of New Bern*, North Carolina Historical Commission, Raleigh, 1920

320. "Tubman Would Not Have Liked This, "*Underground Railroad Free Press*, March, 2011, at http://www.urrfreepress.com/index_files/Mar_2011.pdf

321. "Expand National Statuary Hall," *Underground Railroad Free Press*, March, 2011, at http://www.urrfreepress.com/index_files/Mar_2011.pdf

322. "Equal Visibility Everywhere's Tubman Bill Amended," *Underground Railroad Free Press*, May, 2011, at http://www.urrfreepress.com/index_files/May_2011.pdf

323. "Survey Takers: 'Move and Expand National Statuary Hall'," *Underground Railroad Free Press*, July, 2011, at http://www.urrfreepress.com/index_files/July_2011.pdf

324. "What We Learned As Young Pages," *The Washington Post*, August 14, 2011, p. C5

325. Whitman, T. Stephen, *Challenging Slavery in the Chesapeake: Black and White Resistance to Human Bondage, 1775-1865*,

Johns Hopkins University Press, 2006

326. Zapotosky, Matt, "Residents Blame National Harbor for Sewage Spills," *The Washington Post*, June 23, 2008

Index

G

H

I

J

Endnotes

1 Taylor, Walter Hanson Stone, letter to George A. Hanson, May 30, 1874, in Hanson, George A., *Old Kent: The Eastern Shore of Maryland*, Baltimore, 1876. Reprinted by Regional Publishing Company, 1967.

2 Smith, Seymour Wemyss, *John Hanson: Our First President*, Brewer, Warren & Putnam, New York, 1932. Reprinted by Invest In America National Council, 1976, p. 102.

3 Hanson, George A., *Old Kent: The Eastern Shore of Maryland*, original publisher unknown but possibly the author, Baltimore, 1876. Reprinted by Regional Publishing Company, 1967.

4 *Ibid.*, p. 113; and Kremer, J. Bruce, *John Hanson of Mulberry Grove*, Albert & Charles Boni, Inc., New York, 1938, pp. 64-65.

5 Newman, Harry Wright, *Charles County Gentry*, published by the author, Washington, DC, 1940. Republished by Clearfield Publishing, Clearfield, Pennsylvania, 1997, p. 221.

6 *Ibid.*, p. 222

7 In 1675, he acquired land with a purchase from Thomas Cosker. The following year, he became heir to the residuary estate of Richard Midgely of whose estate he was co-executor with Midgely's wife. In 1677, he continued his acquisitions with a land purchase from William and Joan Lowday.

8 In eighteenth and nineteenth century documents, one also sees the president sometimes identified as John Hanson, Jr. despite his having been named for his grandfather and not his father. It was his uncle who was actually John Hanson, Jr. However, President John Hanson did occasionally sign his name as John Hanson, Jr. as he did on his will.

9 Governor Stone is the author's seventh-great-grandfather.

10 "The First President's Birthplace," Baltimore *Sun*, April 22, 1951

11 Papenfuse, Edward C., *et al.*, *A Biographical Dictionary of the Maryland Legislature, 1635-1789*, 2 volumes, Johns Hopkins University Press, 1979 and 1985, pp. 407 and 945

12 Lantz, Emily Emerson, "Hanson Lineage and Arms," *The Sun*, Baltimore, Maryland, August 5, 1906

13 Newman, *op. cit.*, p. 237

14 Braun, Anne, "Stone Family Cemetery, Faulkner, Charles County, Maryland," as of November 30, 2010, at http://www.interment.net/data/us/md/charles/stonefam_faulk/index.htm. This graveyard is visible on Google Earth. It is located at coordinates 38ª 26' 34.51" N, 76ª 59' 16.98" W.

15 Newman, *op. cit.*, p. 232.

16 *Ibid.*

[17] Colonial Dames of America, *Ancestral Records and Portraits*, Grafton Press, vol. 1, 1910, pp. 726-727

[18] One also sees this property as Rozer's Refugee and as Roger's Refuge but Rozer's Refuge is correct.

[19] Papenfuse, *op. cit.*, pp. 407 and 945

[20] This term, considered archaic and offensive to many today, is used occasionally here in historical context when wording of historical records is kept.

[21] *Evangelical Lutheran Church Records, 1780-1811*, vol. 4, Evangelical Lutheran Church, Frederick, Maryland

[22] *Maryland Gazette* Collection, MSA SC 2313, Maryland State Archives

[23] John Hanson letters to Philip Thomas of January 29, February 23, March 5, March 10 and April 27, 1782, John Hanson Collection, Maryland Historical Society

[24] Most of the information in this paragraph may be found in "The John Hanson Family Archive & Collection," *The Maryland Sale*, (auction catalogue), Crocker Farm Auctioneers, Sparks, Maryland, August, 2011

[25] Thomas, John Hanson, Jr., letter to Annie Campbell Gordon Thomas, October 16, 1861. Hanson-Thomas Collection, Maryland Historical Society.

[26] One of the first written references to what became known as the Underground Railroad was George Washington's letter of April 12, 1786, to William Morris in Philadelphia recounting Quaker assistance to a freedom seeker escaped from Washington's friend, Mr. Dalby of Alexandria, Virginia. See Fitzpatrick, John C., editor, *The Writings of George Washington from the Original Manuscript Sources, 1745-1799*, United States Government Printing Office, volume 28.

[27] This span runs from 1585 when the first recorded shipment of enslaved people from Africa reached North America at the Spanish colony of Saint Augustine, Florida, to the end of the Civil Wa, though those who aided freedom seekers did not begin to find one another and organize their work until about the 1780s and the enterprise did not take on its name until 1842. For the latter date, see *Underground Railroad Free Press*, vol. 5, no. 23, March, 2010, p.2 at http://www.urrfreepress.com/index_files/Mar_2010.pdf.

[28] Only three to four percent of claimed Underground Railroad sites today can offer conclusive documentary evidence of Underground Railroad involvement, the remainder resting their claims on passed-down oral traditions with occasional circumstantial corroboration. See Fergus Bordewich's *Bound for Canaan*, Amistad Harper Collins, 2005, for the definitive history of the Underground Railroad. Visit urrFreePress.com, website of *Underground Railroad Free Press,* for an introduction to the contemporary international Underground Railroad community.

29 Frost, Karolyn Smardz, *The Life of Josiah Henson: Sources and Documents*, Report for the Ontario Heritage Trust: Uncle Tom's Cabin Historic Site Project, March 2007. Most references including Henson's own account have his birth year as 1789 but Frost shows the virtually certain unlikelihood of this.

30 Henson, Josiah, *The Autobiography of Josiah Henson, Formerly a Slave, Now an Inhabitant of Canada, as Narrated by Himself*, Arthur D. Phelps Publisher, Boston, 1849

31 *Ibid.*

32 Josias Hanson McPherson did not have a Hanson-surnamed uncle.

33 Henson, Josiah, *Uncle Tom's Story of his Life: an Autobiography of the Rev. Josiah Henson, 1789-1876; with a preface by Harriet Beecher Stowe and an Introductory Note by George Sturge and S. Morley; edited by John Lobb*, London: Christian Age Office, 1876

34 In this case, Josiah Henson and the author are fourth cousins, twice removed.

35 Frost, *op. cit.*, p. 7

36 Visit http://www.urrfreepress.com/index_files/Sep_2006.pdf for more on this rediscovery.

37 Much of the historical information on indentured servitude here comes from Coldham, Peter C., *The Complete Book of Immigrants, 1607-1660*, Genealogical Publishing Company, 1987

38 *Ibid.*, p. ix

39 *Ship Good Speed*, Immigrant Ships Transcribers Guild, istg.rootsweb.com, originally compiled August 17, 1999, downloaded June 7, 2003

40 As quoted in Skaggs, David C., *Roots of Maryland Democracy*, Greenwood Press, 1973, p. 59

41 Kremer, *op. cit.*, p. 69

42 Lantz, Emily Emerson, "Hanson Lineage and Arms," *The Sun*, Baltimore, Maryland, August 5, 1906

43 All from John Hanson's *Book of Accounts and Journal, 1730-1737*, in the John Hanson Collection of the Maryland Historical Society

44 The last pages of this journal contain definitions and examples of mathematical operations of the four arithmetic functions, and examples of extractions of roots from square roots up to the ninth root of a number, all, of course, in long hand. These entries are anonymous and from 1831. The journal at the time was almost certainly in the possession of John Hanson's great-grandson, John Hanson Thomas, Jr. (1813-1881), who would have been an eighteen-year-old student at the time. He became a physician.

45 Foster, Joseph, *Alumni Oxonienses, 1715-1886*, University Archives, The Bodleian Library, Oxford University; and Venn, John,

Alumni Cantabrigienses, a biographical list of all known students, graduates and holders of office at the University of Cambridge, from the earliest times to 1751, 4 volumes (1922–27)

[46] Ferling, John, *The Ascent of George Washington: The Hidden Political Genius of an American Icon*, Bloomsbury Press, 2009, pp. 11-12.

[47] Skaggs, *op. cit.*, pp. 18-20

[48] The Calverts' hegemony over the colony was interrupted in 1689 when King James II suspended the Calverts' charter after Charles Calvert, the third Baron Baltimore, publicly withdrew his support of the King in a dispute. The charter was restored to the Calverts upon the death of Charles in 1715 when his younger son and namesake, Charles Calvert, fifth Baron Baltimore, was installed as Proprietor. (Benedict Leonard Calvert, fourth Baron Baltimore, eldest son and heir to his father Charles, died during the interruption.) However, as far as Marylanders were concerned, life didn't change much during the twenty-six-year inter-regnum, as the constraints of the original charter continued to apply.

[49] Newman, *op. cit.*

[50] The other members of this committee were James Hollyday, Edmund Key, John Goldsborough, John Hammond and Daniel Wolstenholme.

[51] Kremer, *op. cit.*, pp.86-87

[52] *Declaration of the Association of the Freemen of Maryland*, Maryland State Archives, Proceedings of the Conventions of the Province of Maryland, 1774-1776, volume 78, page 17

[53] The Ural Range demarcating Europe and Asia is the oldest.

[54] For whatever reason, Franz Ludwig Michel is sometimes mentioned as Francis Louis Michel in American and English writings, as if he had been a French-speaking Swiss.

[55] Selig, Robert A., "Wilhelmsburg in the Year 1702: The Account of Franz Ludwig Michel," *Colonial Williamsburg*, the Journal of the Colonial Williamsburg Foundation, Williamsburg, Virginia, Summer, 1998. For more on Franz Ludwig Michel and his American descendants, see Michael, Peter H., *An American Family of the Underground Railroad*, Author House, 2005.

[56] There is a false account apparently propagated by von Graffenried, with whom Michel had had a falling-out, that Michel was killed by Indians in the western reaches of the Carolinas in 1713, but Swiss civil records show Michel in Bern later than this and that three of his children were born there after 1713. It was von Graffenried's compatriot John Lawson who met his fate at the hands of the Tuscaroras.

[57] The author has often wondered if John Hanson and Andrew Michael knew each other. Did the immigrant Michael stand in the public square quickened by the dignified Hanson's arguments for independence? Did Andrew, son of a Swiss nobleman, and John of

the American gentry ever meet? Of course, the two had no idea that their two families' progeny would join and produce an off-spring to wonder and write about them 250 years later.

58 Visit CoolingSprings.org and urrFreePress.com for more.

59 The City of Baltimore and the County of Baltimore are separate political entities. The city is not part of the county.

60 The Eastern Shore comprises that part of Maryland lying on the Delmarva Peninsula between the Chesapeake Bay and the Atlantic Ocean. For whatever reason, one hears that part of Maryland to the east of the Chesapeake Bay consistently referred to as the Eastern Shore but seldom hears the rest of the state to the west of the bay referred to similarly. The result is that the term Eastern Shore has taken on the status of recognized place name and proper noun, and is thus capitalized. References to the western shore are infrequent enough so that that part of the state has never taken on the term as a firm place name. Thus one sees "western shore" un-capitalized.

61 Morrell, William N., "One Hundred and Fiftieth Anniversary of the Death of John Hanson," *The Maryland Club Woman*, vol. VII, no. 2, October, 1933, p. 3

62 Smith, *op. cit.*, p. 23

63 In addition to the official records and diaries of George Washington and digests of them, the three Washington biographies used most often in preparing *Remembering John Hanson* are Washington Irving's *George Washington: A Biography*, 1856-1859, reprinted 1994, Charles Neider, editor, Da Capo Press, Cambridge, Massachusetts; John Ferling's *The Ascent of George Washington: The Hidden Political Genius of an American Icon*, Bloomsbury Press, 2009; and Joseph Ellis's *His Excellency George Washington*, Alfred A. Knopf, 2008.

64 George Washington and Dr. James Craik had met when they served together on the frontier during the French and Indian War. In that campaign, it was Dr, Craik who had attended to the fatal wounds of General Edward Braddock. At the end of the war, Craik, until then a Virginian, opened his medical office in Port Tobacco. Much later, Washington persuaded Craik to relocate his practice to Alexandria, Virginia, the closest town to Mount Vernon. As president, George Washington appointed James Craik as Physician General of the Army. Craik was one of three physicians summoned by Martha Washington as her husband lay on his death bed. The others were Dr. Gustavus Brown of Port Tobacco and Dr. Elisha Dick.

65 Kremer, *op. cit.*, p. 85

66 Library of Congress, *The Diaries of George Washington*, 51 volumes, 1748-1799. A myth persisting even unto today is that there was a ferry directly between the two estates. However, Hanson's Mulberry Grove is on the Port Tobacco River about a half mile up-stream from its confluence with the Potomac River, and Washing-

ton's Mount Vernon is upstream on the Potomac with about thirty miles of water between the two homes. In their visits, the two would have crossed the Potomac at Mount Vernon and travelled by horseback or carriage between the Maryland side of the river and Mulberry Grove. An alternative was Hooe's Ferry at Port Tobacco and then up the Virginia side of the Potomac to Mount Vernon.

[67] Levering, Ralph, *John Hanson: Public Servant*, monograph as part of the United States Bicentennial observance, Western Maryland College, Westminster, Maryland, 1976, p. 18. Also as "John Hanson: Public Servant," *Maryland Historical Magazine* (Summer 1976).

[68] Papenfuse, Edward C., *et al.*, *A Biographical Dictionary of the Maryland Legislature, 1635-1789*, 2 volumes, Johns Hopkins University Press, 1979 and 1985, p. 405

[69] Papenfuse, Edward C., *Accident, Maryland*, en.wikipedia.org/wiki/Accident,_MD

[70] Charles County land records, deeds of Liber 3, Folio 542 and Liber 3, Folio 685, respectively.

[71] Newman, *op. cit.* Citation at page 244 in the Higginson version.

[72] Andrews, Matthew P., *History of Maryland: Province and State*, Doubleday, Doran & Company, Garden City, New York, 1929. Reprinted by Tradition Press, Hatboro, Pennsylvania, 1965, p. 229.

[73] Weld, Isaac, *Travels through the States of North America and the Provinces of Upper and Lower Canada During the Years 1795, 1796, and 1797*. London, John Stockdale, 1807, pp. 137-139

[74] Frederick County produced one more Maryland governor, Francis Thomas, who served as the twenty-sixth Governor of Maryland from 1842 to1844, and also as a United States Representative from Maryland, representing at separate times the fourth, fifth, sixth, and seventh congressional districts.

[75] George Hanson, *op. cit.*, p. 130.

[76] Most of these land records may be found in Papenfuse, Edward C., *et al.*, *A Biographical Dictionary of the Maryland Legislature, 1635-1789*, 2 volumes, Johns Hopkins University Press, 1979 and 1985, pp. 405-406; and in Frederick County land records.

[77] The author's personal conversation with the 2010 property owner.

[78] Frederick County Deeds, liber P, folio 696, 1773; and Miller, Nancy, "108 West Patrick Street, Frederick," Maryland Historical Trust, January 11, 1972.

[79] Schildknecht, C. E., *Monocacy and Catoctin*, vol. II, 1898, p. 210

[80] Engelbrecht, Jacob, *Property & Almshouse Ledgers*, Eader & Long. Reprinted by Paw Prints Publishing, 1996

[81] The chain of title was John Hanson by will to his widow, Jane Hanson; by will to her son in law, Philip Thomas; by will to his son, John Hanson Thomas, Sr.; by will to the executrix of his estate, Mary Isham Colston Thomas, his wife; to Joseph Talbott.

[82]Levering, *op. cit.*, p. 34; and Williams, T.J.C., *History of Frederick County, Maryland*, L.R. Titsworth & Company, 1910, vol. I, p. 95

[83] *The Diaries of George Washington*, vol. III, 1771-1775, University Press of Virginia, 1976-79; and as quoted in Smith, *op. cit.*, p. 32

[84] Most figures in this paragraph are from Skaggs, David C., *Roots of Maryland Democracy, 1753-1776*, Greenwood Press, 1973, pp. 35-36

[85] These three paragraphs are adapted from Marck, John T., *Frederick Calvert, Sixth Lord Baltimore and Henry Harford*, http://www.aboutfamouspeople.com/article1022.html.

[86] Wellington, United States Senator George L., "Address of Mr. Wellington of Maryland," in *Proceedings in the Senate and House of Representatives Upon the Reception and Acceptance From the State of Maryland of the Statues of Charles Carroll and of John Hanson Erected In the Statuary Hall of the Capitol*, United States Government Printing Office, Washington DC, January 31, 1903

[87] Andrews, *op. cit.*, pp. 303-304

[88] It was at the Raleigh Tavern in 1776 where Phi Beta Kappa, the nation's first scholastic honorary society, was founded.

[89] At that time, Florida was organized into separate Spanish colonies of East Florida and West Florida which were together more or less coterminous to today's Florida excepting the western panhandle which at the time extended to Louisiana.

[90] Schlesinger, Arthur M., *The Colonial Merchants and the American Revolution, 1763-1776*, Facsimile Library, 1939, pp. 288-392

[91] Andrews, *op. cit.*, p. 303

[92] Levering, *op. cit.*, p. 13.

[93] Kremer, *op. cit.*, pp. 101-102

[94] Andrews, *op. cit.*, p. 310

[95] *Ibid.*, p. 310

[96] *Ibid.*, p. 233

[97] "Extension of Remarks of Hon. Richard E. Lankford of Maryland in the House of Representatives," *Congressional Record*, appendix A558, January 29, 1957

[98] Letter from President John Hanson to Dr. Philip Thomas, March 10, 1782, in the Hanson Papers Collection of the Maryland Historical Society, Baltimore.

[99] Edward Delaplaine, long-time Maryland jurist and historian, wrote over a long period on John Hanson, Thomas Johnson, Maryland and Frederick County Revolutionary War-era history. For more on Thomas Johnson, see Delaplaine, Edward S., *The Life of Thomas Johnson*, Grafton Press, 1927, reprinted by Heritage Books, 1998.

[100] Williams, *op. cit.*, pp. 90-93, and Smith, J. F. D., *A Tour of the United States of America*, London, 1784. Smith was one of those

arrested.

[101] Adams, John, *John Adams autobiography, John Adams through 1776, part 1*, Adams Family Papers, Massachusetts Historical Society, p. 2

[102] As quoted in Hakim, Joy, *The New Nation*, Oxford University Press, 2003, p. 97

[103] They were not the only presidents to die on the Fourth of July. James Monroe, fifth president of the second government and fourteenth overall, died at his Oak Hill Plantation near Aldie, Virginia, July 4, 1831.

[104] Adams, John, letter to Samuel Chase, June 14, 1776, *The Works of John Adams*, vol. IX, p. 397, and in Burnett, Edmund C, *Letters of the Members of the Continental Congress, vol. 1, August 29, 1774 to July 4, 1776*, Carnegie Institution of Washington, Washington, DC, 1921, p. 490

[105] Scharf, John Thomas, *Essay on John Hanson*, typescript biographical essay, Miscellaneous Manuscripts Collection, Library of Congress, MSS2184, 1892

[106] Mathias, Senator Charles M., "A Tribute to John Hanson: Maryland Day 1981," *The Congressional Record*, S2645, United States Congress, March 25, 1981

[107] Scharf, John Thomas, *History of Western Maryland*, vol. I, Louis H. Everts Publishing Company, Philadelphia, 1882, p. 555

[108] Skaggs, *op. cit.*, p. vi

[109] Levering, *op. cit.*, p. 18

[110] Jefferson, Thomas, *Autobiography*, draft dated January 6, 1821, The Thomas Jefferson Papers, Library of Congress

[111] Tolzman, Donald Heinrich, *The German-American Experience*, Red Rose Studio, Willow Street, Pennsylvania, 2000

[112] It is useful to delineate among the three members of the prominent Maryland Carroll family who served in important roles during the Second Continental Congress, the United States in Congress Assembled and the second government. Daniel Carroll was a signer of the Articles of Confederation and the Constitution, and served as a delegate to the Second Continental Congress and to the United States in Congress Assembled. Charles Carroll of Carrollton was a signer of the Declaration of Independence and served in the Second Continental Congress from 1776 until 1781, the United States in Congress Assembled throughout its existence, and then in the United States Senate from 1789 until 1792 when he resigned to keep his seat in the Maryland Senate which he preferred. Charles Carroll, Barrister, so called as to distinguished him from the first Charles Carroll, served in the Second Continental Congress from 1776 to 1777. The three are related. It is Charles Carroll of Carrollton whose statue, along with that of John Hanson, is in National Statuary Hall in the United States Capitol.

[113] Adams, John, letter to Abigail Adams, July 3, 1776, Letters of Delegates to Congress: Volume 4, May 16, 1776 - August 15, 1776, Library of Congress

[114] Adams, John, letter to Abigail Adams, July 3, 1776. Original manuscript from the Adams Family Papers, Massachusetts Historical Society

[115] Young, Christopher J., "The Goddard Broadside: Mary Katherine Goddard's Printing of the Declaration of Independence," *Maryland Historical Society News*, Fall, 2011, pp. 26-27

[116] Bowen, Catherine Drinker, *John Adams and the American Revolution*, Little, Brown and Company, 1950, pp. xiii-xiv.

[117] "The John Hanson Family Archive & Collection," *The Maryland Sale*, (auction catalogue), Crocker Farm Auctioneers, Sparks, Maryland, August, 2011

[118] Skaggs, *op. cit.*, pp. 185-186

[119] Not to be confused with the Whig Party two to three generations later.

[120] Skaggs, *op. cit.,* pp. 193-195

[121] Contee, Thomas, *The Original Diary of Thomas Contee Esqr., of Prince George's County, Maryland. In Octr., 1776, to Genl. Washington's Camp near New York, in company with John Hanson, Esq., who married the sister of said Contee*, unpublished diary, 1776. This diary was sold at auction in 2011. It is fully transcribed in *The Maryland Sale* (auction catalogue), Crocker Farm, 15900 York Road, Sparks, Maryland, August, 2011.

[122] *Ibid.*

[123] *Ibid.*

[124] Lantz, Emily Emerson, "The Hanson Family Again," *The Sun*, Baltimore, Maryland, August 12, 1906

[125] Hanson, George, *op. cit.*, p. 127

[126] *Ibid.* and Andrews, *op. cit.*, pp. 339-341

[127] Ferling, John, *The Ascent of George Washington: The Hidden Political Genius of an American Icon*, Bloomsbury Press, 2009, pp. 116-118.

[128] This letter is included in the series in the Maryland Historical Society's John Hanson Collection. The letter was written by the president for his granddaughter who says in her letter that she has just learned to spell her name.

[129] Chirurgical was the term at that time for surgical.

[130] The first public school in Frederick County is credited to Reverend Thomas Bacon, pastor of Frederick's All Saints Episcopal Church, who in 1763 successfully petitioned the Provincial Assembly to establish the school. Rev. Bacon was not the Hanson family's pastor as he died in 1768, the year before the Hansons arrived in Frederick. Andrews, *op. cit.*, pp. 320-321.

[131] Most of what appears here on Dr. Philip Thomas can be found in Scharf, John Thomas, *History of Frederick City, the Districts & Villages of Frederick County From Early Historical Writings*, Louis H. Everts Publishing Company, Philadelphia, 1882.

[132] Gewehr, Wesley, *et al.*, *The United States: A History of a Democracy*, McGraw-Hill, New York, 1960, p. 83

[133] To distinguish this area from the Pacific northwest which in the nineteenth century became of prime interest to the United States, the original Northwest Territory described here became referred to as the Old Northwest and then the Midwest. It is today's Midwest east of the Mississippi River.

[134] Stein, Mark, *How the States Got Their Shapes*, Harper Collins Smithsonian Books, 2008, pp. 48, 73

[135] Smith, *op. cit.*, p. 58

[136] Nelson, Jacob A., *John Hanson and the Inseparable Union,* Meador Publishing Company, Boston, 1939, p. 97

[137] Smith, *op. cit.*, p. 56

[138] *Ibid.*, p. 97

[139] *Ibid.*, p. 71

[140] Stiverson, Gregory A., "Hanson, John," *American National Biography Online*, Oxford University Press, 2000, http://anb.org/articles/01/01-00369.html.

[141] Washington, George, "Letter to Pennsylvania Governor Joseph Reed," *The George Washington Papers*, Manuscript Division, United States Library of Congress, May 28, 1780

[142] *Ibid.*, p. 93

[143] *Maryland Gazette*, March 22, 1781, and Levering, *op. cit,* p. 24

[144] Huntington, Samuel, circular letter of March 2, 1781, *Letter Books of the Presidents of the Second Continental Congress*, National Archives and Records Administration, Washington, DC, central repository

[145] Warfield, Joshua Dorsey, *The Founders of Anne Arundel and Howard Counties, Maryland*, Kohn and Pollock Publishers, Baltimore, 1905

[146] Dorsey, Ella Loraine, letter to the editor of *The Baltimore Sun*, in Letters of Alexander Contee Hanson, Jr., Maryland Historical Society, MS. 408. The letter is undated but would have been written between 1898 when the Hanson statue had been authorized by the Maryland General Assembly and before January 31, 1903, when it was formally donated by Maryland and unveiled in the United States Capitol.

[147] Letter of Samuel Huntington, April 9, 1781, *Letter Books of the Presidents, The Second Continental Congress, February 28 – November 4, 1781*, National Archives

[148] *Ibid.*, Letter of Samuel Huntington, April 16, 1781

[149] *Letter Book of John Hanson*, from *Letter Books of the Presidents of Congress 1781-1787*, National Archives, November 10, 1781.

[150] Papenfuse, Edward C., Archivist of the State of Maryland, private email to the author, October 19, 2010

[151] Smith, *op. cit.*, pp. 101-102

[152] Nelson, *op. cit.*, p. 115

[153] *Proceedings in the Senate and House of Representatives Upon the Reception and Acceptance From the State of Maryland of the Statues of Charles Carroll and of John Hanson Erected In the Statuary Hall of the Capitol*, United States Government Printing Office, Washington DC, January 31, 1903, p. 14 and p. 70

[154] "John Hanson 1st President," *The Sun*, Baltimore, February 21, 1948

[155] The Constitution, deliberately avoiding the fatal unanimity requirement of the Articles of Confederation, stated that the assent of only nine states would be required to ratify the Constitution. New Hampshire became the ninth on June 21, 1788. In quick succession, Virginia on June 25 and New York on July 26 ratified the Constitution. The second government came into being before the last two states, North Carolina on November 21, 1789, and Rhode Island not until May 29, 1790, had ratified.

[156] Smith, *op. cit.*, p. 12

[157] Levering, *op. cit.*, p. 5

[158] Nelson, *op. cit.*, p. 124

[159] Condensed from the definition of government from *Webster's Ninth New Collegiate Dictionary*, Merriam-Webster Publishers, 1990

[160] Garver, Frank Harmon, "The Transition from the Continental Congress to the Congress of the Confederation," *Pacific Historical Review*, vol. 1, no. 2, June, 1932, University of California Press, p. 221

[161] Andrews, *op. cit.*, p. 347.

[162] *The Maryland Gazette*, Annapolis, March 22, 1781.

[163] The Articles of Confederation established the central government as having sole authority for fixing the value of coinage. States and banks continued to print their own scrip until this was prohibited during the Lincoln administration and the federal government required that its currency be used exclusively.

[164] In the Constitution, the title changed to simply President of the United States.

[165] Washington had resigned his seat in Virginia's delegation to the Second Continental Congress when he assumed command of the Continental Army in June 1775.

[166] George Washington, still prosecuting the Revolutionary War as Commander of the Continental Army, did not represent Virginia as a delegate that day.

[167] Weinberg, Aldan, "No Respect," *Frederick* magazine, Frederick, Maryland, February, 2003, p. 47

[168] Nelson, *op. cit.*, p. 134

[169] Schirm, United States Representative Charles R., "Address of Mr. Schirm of Maryland," in *Proceedings in the Senate and House of Representatives Upon the Reception and Acceptance From the State of Maryland of the Statues of Charles Carroll and of John Hanson Erected In the Statuary Hall of the Capitol,* United States Government Printing Office, Washington DC, January 31, 1903, pp. 110-111

[170] Thomson, Charles, Circular letter announcing the election of John Hanson as president, *John Hanson Letter Book from the United States in Congress Assembled,* November 5, 1781, National Archives main collection, Washington DC, (microfilm) cabinet 67A, drawer 3, roll 24, item 16

[171] Both quotations are taken from *Letter Books of the Presidents, The Second Continental Congress, February 28 – November 4, 1781,* National Archives main collection, Washington DC, (microfilm) cabinet 67A, drawer 3, roll 24, item 16

[172] In fact, no accurate source states anything to the contrary that John Hanson was the nation's first president. See the entries in the bibliography here for Andrews, George Hanson, Levering, Michael, Nelson, Newman, Smith, Thomas, Van der Mei, George Washington and Wilstach among others.

[173] "A letter from Baltimore," *The Pennsylvania Gazette,* December 3, 1783. (The *Gazette* wrongly picked up John Hanson's incorrect date of passing of November 15 from the Baltimore paper.)

[174] Though a unified navy operated exclusively by the central government was authorized during the Hanson administration, the United States in Congress Assembled did not order construction of a naval fleet until October 13, 1775, during the administration of Richard Henry Lee.

[175] *John Hanson Letter Books, op. cit.,* November 15, 1781

[176] In a historical quirk of government organization, the Office of the Vice President is, according to the Constitution, within the legislative branch of the United States government as the Vice President serves as the President of the United States Senate. The Framers' intent with this arrangement was to disperse power by having the two highest offices in government head different branches of government. However, the Vice President's role as President of the Senate rapidly devolved into a ceremonial and tie-breaking one and, in their ostensible roles in the executive branch, most vice presidents have had meager if any portfolios delegated to them by their presidents, though some of the most recent vice-presidents have been the exception to this.

[177] This quotation may be found cited in many works through an Internet search. For the original, see *American Archives,* fourth se-

ries, vol. 1019

[178] For a definitive history of the founding of the nation's capital and Morris's role in it, see Fergus M. Bordewich's *Washington, the Making of the American Capital*, Amistad Harper Collins, 2008.

[179] Gewehr *et al.*, *op. cit.*, p. 97

[180] Johnson, Amandus, *Swedish Contributions to American National Life, 1638-1921*, Committee of the Swedish Section of America's Making, New York, 1921, pp. 50-51

[181] Eberlein, H.D. and C.V. Hubbard, *Diary of Independence Hall*, Philadelphia, 1948, as quoted in Levering, *op. cit.*, pp. 25-26.

[182] For an instructive account of the workings of the first cabinet, see the correspondence between Robert Livingston and Robert Morris in Morris, Robert, *The Papers of Robert Morris, 1781-1784*, Elmer J. Ferguson and Elizabeth M. Nuxoll, editors, University of Pittsburgh Press, 1999, p. 69 *et seq.*

[183] Bemis, Samuel F., *The Diplomacy of the American Revolution*, The American Historical Association and Appleton-Century Publishing Company, 1935, p. 256. This assessment has become generally accepted. In his review of this book, James P. Baxter III states of Bemis and the diplomatic achievements of the era, "No previous historian has treated its diplomacy with such fullness of knowledge." Baxter, James, "Review of *The Diplomacy of the American Revolution*", *New England Quarterly*, vol. 8, no. 4, December, 1935, pp. 588-591.

[184] John Hanson letter of August 6, 1782, to Philip Thomas

[185] John Hanson letter of September 24, 1782, to Philip Thomas

[186] The brief account of the establishment and transitions of the United States postal operation here may be found in Andrews, *op. cit.*, pp. 309-310. A full account may be found in Roper, Daniel C., *The United States Post Office*, Funk & Wagnall Company, New York, 1917.

[187] Nelson, *op. cit.*, p. 118

[188] Counting John Hancock who was elected president but did not serve because of illness.

[189] All quotations from John Hanson's letters to Philip Thomas are from the John Hanson Papers, MS1785, the Maryland Historical Society, Baltimore. Dates of individual letters are noted in each case with the text quoted.

[190] Galton Orsborn Co., Auctioneers, "Special Auction Sale of Antiques from the Estate of Annie M. Hanson, Elkridge, Maryland, Great-Great-Granddaughter of John Hanson," *The Sun*, Baltimore, Maryland, October 26, 1943 (auction date)

[191] Roak, John C., letter to Judge Edward Delaplaine of Frederick, Maryland, January, 1959, as quoted in Delaplaine, Judge Edward S., "John Hanson – a study of controversy," *The News*, Frederick, Maryland, August 1, 1981

---

[192] Levering, *op. cit.*, p. 17.

[193] Hathorn, Guy B. *et al.*, *Government and Politics in the United States*, Van Nostrand Company, 1961, p. 22

[194] Briggs, Minnie L., "John Hanson Cherry," *The Washington Star*, December 4, 1938, p. 5. This old tree was still standing in 1938, still bore fruit and by that time had grown enormous for a cherry tree.

[195] *The American* (a Maryland newspaper), February 25, 1812. This date is wrong by four days. For the correct date of February 21, see, George Hanson, *op. cit.*, p. 127; Hughes, Thomas Patrick and Frank Munsell, editors, *American Ancestry: Giving the Name and Descent, in the male line, of Americans Whose Ancestors Settled in the United States Previous to the Declaration of Independence, A. D. 1666,* vol. III, Joel Munsell's Sons, Publishers, Albany, New York, 1892, p. 150; and womenhistoryblog.com/2010/10/jane-contee-hanson.html.

[196] *Ibid.*

[197] Most of the biographical information here on the presidents of the United States in Congress Assembled comes from http://bioguide. congress.gov.

[198] Boudinot, Elias, *Letter to Hannah Boudinot*, November 4, 1782. Statesmen Collection, New Jersey Historical Society and at etext.virginia.edu/toc/modeng/public/DelVol19.html.

[199] For an excellent account of this relationship and of the tragedy of Kilikeena Watie, see Fergus Bordewich's *Killing the White Man's Indian, op. cit.*

[200] Gravestone, Saint Mary's Cemetery, Burlington, New Jersey

[201] Formally, Prince Charles Edward Louis John Casimir Sylvester Maria Stuart

[202] Delaware, New Jersey, New York, Pennsylvania and Virginia

[203] From Thomas Jefferson, "Report of a Plan of Government for the Western Territory," in Merrill Peterson, editor, *The Portable Thomas Jefferson*, Penguin Books, 1975, p. 255; and in Fergus Bordewich, *Bound for Canaan: The Underground Railroad and the War for the Soul of America*, Amistad/Harper Collins, 2005, p. 38.

[204] Virginia law held that the status of the child followed that of the mother.

[205] Gewehr *et al.*, *op. cit.*, p. 81

[206] These letters address eleven of the thirteen state chief executives as governor. The chief executive of Delaware bore the title of President of Delaware and he of New Hampshire, President of the Council.

[207] Ellis, Joseph, *His Excellency George Washington*, Alfred A. Knopf, 2008, p. 169.

[208] A two-thirds majority in each house of Congress and ratification

by three-fourths of the states either by their legislatures or by state conventions are required to amend the Constitution which has been amended seventeen times since the early ratification of the Bill of Rights which comprised the first ten amendments. As of 2010, the most recent amendment was the twenty-seventh restricting when Congress may raise its members' pay. This amendment was ratified on May 7, 1992, after being first proposed September 25, 1789. It was never reintroduced during this 203-year period and took that long to gather the requisite approvals of three-fourths of the states.

209 Robert Hanson Harrison's mother Dorothy Hanson and President John Hanson were first cousins. Dorothy Hanson was the daughter of Robert Hanson, the president's uncle. This is the Robert Hanson from whom the author descends. Robert Hanson Harrison and Alexander Contee Hanson, Sr. were therefore second cousins. Robert Hanson Harrison was of the Harrison family which produced two United States presidents.

210 Ellis, *op. cit.*, pp. xiii-xiv.

211 Ferling, *op. cit.*, p. 151.

212 *Bartgis's Federal Gazette*, vol. VII, no. 381, Frederick, Maryland, Wednesday, August 28, 1799

213 For the researcher, the publication was previously known as *Bartgis's Maryland Gazette* from 1792 until some time later in the 1790s, and as *Bartgis's Republican Gazette* from 1800 until it ceased publication in 1814.

214 Weinberg, Aldan, *op. cit.,*, p. 51

215 Thomas Hawkins Hanson was the son of the president's nephew, Samuel Hanson, Jr.

216 *The Maryland Gazette*, November 21, 1781, and with the identical language except "63" for "sixty–third," *The Maryland Journal*, December, 2, 1783. Both notices incorrectly cite John Hanson's age, the second notice picking up on the first.

217 Newman, *op. cit.*, p. 244.

218 Some in the family spelled the name with a single s, some with a double s.

219 George Hanson, *op. cit.*, p. 127

220 *Ibid.*

221 *Proceedings in the Senate and House of Representatives Upon the Reception and Acceptance From the State of Maryland of the Statues of Charles Carroll and of John Hanson Erected In the Statuary Hall of the Capitol, United States Government Printing Office*, Washington DC, January 31, 1903

222 Morell, William N., form letter to "Dear Associate," November 3, 1933. John Hanson Society of Maryland papers, Maryland Historical Society, Baltimore

223 Smith, *op. cit.*, p. 154

[224] Nelson, *op. cit.*, p. 144

[225] Kremer, *op. cit.*, p. 171

[226] Newman, *op. cit.*, p. 244

[227] Nelson, *op. cit.*, p. 144

[228] "Searchers Hunt Mausoleum For Body Of John Hanson," *The Sun*, Baltimore, Maryland, April 4, 1973

[229] Most of the information regarding the crypt is found in Lanham, Paul, "The Crypt on the Cliff," *News & Notes*, Prince George's County Historical Society, vol. XXVII, no. 5, June, 1998

[230] *The Bangor Daily News*, "First President Was John Hanson," Bangor, Maine, September 9, 1972. Article reprinted from *The Washington Star*, author unattributed, date unknown.

[231] "Searchers Hunt Mausoleum For Body Of John Hanson," *The Sun*, Baltimore, Maryland, April 4, 1973

[232] Pearl, Susan G., "Archeology at Oxon Hill Manor," memorandum, Maryland-National Capital Park and Planning Commission, April 8, 1998

[233] Bick, Bonnie, "The Wilson Crossing: A Better Vision," *The Sierra Club*, Maryland Chapter, April 26, 1999

[234] Zapotosky, Matt, "Residents Blame National Harbor for Sewage Spills," *The Washington Post*, June 23, 2008

[235] Mount Olivet Cemetery burial and financial records.

[236] There was a distant line of Hansons living in Frederick in the mid-nineteenth century and two of these, Alexander Baird Hanson and his wife Susan, are listed among the exhumed in 1913. He was the father of Hanson genealogist and chronicler George Hanson, author of *Old Kent*. Alexander Baird Hanson owned and resided in the mansion at 24 East Church Street now owned by the Historical Society of Frederick County. That Alexander and Susan had headstones and were not buried in the mound of the unknowns indicates that they were not the occupants of the Hanson crypt in the Episcopal graveyard.

[237] "All Bodies Removed From Old Graveyard," *The News*, Frederick, Maryland, November 26, 1913

[238] Scharf, J. Thomas, *History of Western Maryland*, Clearfield Company, 1968 (reprint), p. 288; and Andrews, Mathew, *History of Maryland: Province and State*, Garden City, New York, 1929, p.373. This quotation has been incorrectly attributed to the president himself in the Levering entry of the bibliography.

[239] As reported in Smith, *op. cit.*

[240] *Session Laws, 1972*, vol. 708, page 1910, House Joint Resolution 46, May 5, 1972, Maryland State Archives

[241] Smith was the editor of *The Financial Times* during the Great Depression. His real love was history. He died of pneumonia at thirty-five in January 1932 after finishing his Hanson biography

but before its publication later that year. See his obituary in *Time* at time.com/time/magazine/article/0,9171,742964-1,00.html.

242 George Hanson, *op. cit, passim*

243 Morrell, William N., "One Hundred and Fiftieth Anniversary of the Death of John Hanson," *The Maryland Club Woman*, vol. VII, no. 2, October, 1933, p. 4

244 See the list itself and Morrell, William N., letter to Hon. Nels Johnson, October 1, 1959, John Hanson Society of Maryland papers, Maryland Historical Society, Baltimore

245 The1743 marriage date of Jane and John Hanson is not known. If the marriage occurred in January of 1743, three births not involving twins could not have occurred before the end of 1744 assuming nine-month gestations. Births involving three eight-month gestations would have been possible but very unlikely. Therefore, Anne and Mary are assumed here to be twins.

246 It is recorded that Elizabeth and John were twins. She was named for the president's mother, he for the president's grandfather.

247 This is the second of Jane and John Hanson's children named John.

248 This is the second of Jane and John Hanson's children named Elizabeth. She is the "Kitty" who lived with her parents in Philadelphia during her father's presidency. Pundt's Hanson family genealogy shows Elizabeth Hanson Floweree dying in 1825. However, several sources state that Jane Hanson "outlived all twelve (*sic*) of her children." It is documented that she outlived the first twelve, but there were thirteen. It is accepted here that the second Elizabeth survived her. The error apparently stems from Jane Hanson's obituary in the February 25, 1812, issue of *The American*, a Maryland newspaper.

249 See http://en.wikipedia.org/wiki/John_Hanson and http://en.wikipedia.org/wiki/John_Hanson_(myths)

250 *Ibid.*

251 Marbury, William L., "The High Court of Chancery and the Chancellors of Maryland," address given to the annual meeting of the Maryland State Bar Association, 1905

252 For more, visit the website of the Maryland State Archives and msa.md.gov/megafile/msa/speccol/sc2900/sc2908/html/chancery.html.

253 Ashbury, John W., *And All Our Yesterdays, A Chronicle of Frederick County, Maryland*, Diversions Publications, 1997

254 Much here on Alexander Contee Hanson, Sr. is taken from the Archives of Maryland web site entry on him at http://www.msa.md.gov/megafile/msa/speccol/sc3500/sc3520/000500/000585/html/585bio.html.

255 "Fourteenth Congress: March 4, 1815, to March 3, 1817," web-

site of the United States House of Representatives, http://artandhistory. house. gov/ house_history/bioguide-front/14.pdf.

256 Hanson, Alexander Contee, Jr., letter to Edward Johnson Coale, January 1, 1819. Alexander Contee Hanson, Jr. Collection of the Maryland Historical Society.

257 Much here on Alexander Contee Hanson, Jr. is taken from the Archives of Maryland web site entry on him at http://www.msa.md.gov/megafile/msa/speccol/sc3500/sc3520/002200/002206/html/2206bio.html.

258 Sanner, Patricia, transcript of her talk given to the annual meeting of the John Hanson Society of Maryland, delivered in Frederick, Maryland, April 29, 1973

259 Thomas, Douglas H., *John Hanson, President of the United States in Congress Assembled*, self-published, Baltimore, 1898

260 Most of the information on Douglas Hamilton Thomas and his descendants comes from Mackenzie, George Norberry, *Colonial Families of the United States of America*, (seven volumes), Seaforth Press, Baltimore,1917, pp. 516-518.

261 The information on the relationships between the descendants of President John Hanson, the Marshall family and relationships with other families can be found in George Hanson, *op. cit.*, pp. 132-133; Seymour Wemyss Smith, *John Hanson: Our First President*, Brewer, Warren & Putnam, New York, 1932, throughout; and at various online sources.

262 A short article on Thomas Stone may be found at Ashbury, John W., "Thomas Stone," *Frederick Magazine*, Frederick, Maryland, issue 314, August, 2011, p. 110

263 The line of descent is Jane and John Hanson, Jane and Dr. Philip Thomas, Rebecca and Judge Alexander Contee Magruder, John Hanson Thomas Magruder.

264 "What We Learned As Young Pages," *The Washington Post,* August 14, 2011, p. C5

265 Smith, Scottie Fitzgerald, "The Maryland Ancestors of Zelda Sayre Fitzgerald," *Maryland Historical Magazine*, vol. 78, no. 3, Fall 1983, pp. 217-228

266 A monumental-scale statue is one larger than life-size, usually seven to nine feet tall exclusive of its plinth.

267 The author is publisher of *Underground Railroad Free Press.*

268 The line from President Hanson to Ms. Stevenson is President John Hanson (1715-1783), Jane Contee Hanson the younger (1746-1781) and Dr. Philip Thomas (1747-1815), John Hanson Thomas, Sr. (1779-1815), John Hanson Thomas, Jr., M.D. (1813-1881), Douglas Hamilton Thomas, Sr. (1847-1919), Alice Lee Thomas Stevenson (1903-1972).

269 Weinberg, *op. cit.*, p. 51

270 Morrell, William N., "One Hundred and Fiftieth Anniversary of the Death of John Hanson," *The Maryland Club Woman*, vol. VII, no. 2, October, 1933

271 Except as specifically noted in this appendix, timeline entries come from an extensive date-by-date culling from many of the entries listed in the bibliographies here.

272 According to the newer Gregorian calendar adopted in the colonies in 1752, one hundred seventy years after it had been decreed by Pope Gregory XIII in 1582. John Hanson's birthday was reckoned at April 3 according to the old Julian calendar abandoned by Britain and the colonies in 1752. John Hanson Day in Maryland is celebrated each April 14.

273 Newman, *op. cit.*, p. 243.

274 "Memorial to Patriot Judges, First to Repudiate the British Stamp Act," *New York Times*, November 23, 1904

275 Levering, *op. cit.*, p. 9.

276 *Ibid.*, p. 14.

277 Scharf, J. Thomas, *History of Western Maryland*, vol. I, Clearfield Company, 1968 (reprint), p. 128.

278 Levering, *op. cit.*, p. 16.

279 Scharf, John Thomas, *History of Western Maryland*, vol. I, Louis H. Everts Publishing Company, Philadelphia, 1882, p. 555

280 Adams, Herbert B., *Maryland's Influence upon Land Cessions to the United States*, Baltimore, 1885, p. 39

281 One also sees the date of November 15, 1783, according to the old calendar.

282 Wills, Liber GM no. 2, folio 75, Frederick County, Maryland

283 Newman, *op. cit.*, p. 244. Newman is correct with "85th year" which began when Jane Hanson turned eighty-four.

284 *Proceedings in the Senate and House of Representatives Upon the Reception and Acceptance From the State of Maryland of the Statues of Charles Carroll and of John Hanson Erected In the Statuary Hall of the Capitol*, United States Government Printing Office, Washington DC, January 31, 1903

285 Grover Cleveland served two nonconsecutive terms and is therefore customarily counted twice as the twenty-second and twenty-fourth presidents, Benjamin Harrison serving between the Cleveland terms.

286 If George Hanson and President John Hanson were related in the manner which George Hanson describes, they would have been second cousins four times removed.

287 Hanson, George A., *Old Kent: The Eastern Shore of Maryland*, Baltimore, 1876.

288 Or de Rastrich

[289] From British civil records as cited at http://kristinhall.org /family/Hanson/HansonName.html, George Hanson, *op. cit.*, pp. 110-111, and various other online sources

[290] George Hanson, *op. cit.*, pp. 111-112

[291] Lantz, Emily Emerson, "Hanson Lineage and Arms," *The Sun*, Baltimore, Maryland, July 29, 1906

[292] For example, visit http://kristinhall.org/family/Hanson/HansonName.html. This page was first viewed by the author in 2009.

[293]http://freepages.history.rootsweb.ancestry.com/~calderdalecompanion/h.html. This page was first viewed by the author in 2009.

[294] *Ibid.*

[295] However, the ships' names are at odds with those provided by J. Bruce Kremer in his John Hanson biography. Kremer has the names as the *Kalmar Nyckel* and the *Fogel Grip*, but these are the Swedish names of the ships which carried the New Sweden founders to Tinicum in 1637. Kremer, *op. cit.*, p. 23.

[296] Hanson, *op. cit.*, p. 113

[297] Amandus Johnson (1877-1974), Professor of Scandinavian Languages at the University of Pennsylvania, was founder or cofounder of the American Swedish Historical Museum, the Swedish American Sesquicentennial Association and the American Sons and Daughters of Sweden. He was the author in 1911 of *Swedish Settlements on the Delaware, 1638-1664*, his doctoral dissertation, and many later publications on Swedish-American history.

[298] Program booklet from the dedication ceremony, a copy of which is in the possession of the author.

[299] Dorsey, Anna Hanson McKinney, *Letter to Josephine Ridue*, August 9, 1882, original transcription in the Catholic University Library. Also see http://genforum.genealogy.com/ingram/messages/5116.html.

[300] Anna Hanson McKinney Dorsey's line from the immigrant John Hanson is Judge Samuel Hanson, Samuel Hanson, Jr., Anna Hanson and Nicholas Lingan, Chloe Ann Lingan and William McKinney, to herself.

[301] Kremer, *op. cit.*, two-page table between pp. 40 and 41

[302] Russell, George, "John Hanson of Maryland; A Swedish Origin Disproved," *The American Genealogist*, October, 1988, vol. 63, pp. 211-213

[303] Craig, Peter, personal communication to the author (email), February 2, 3 and 9, 2009

[304] Hanson, *op. cit.*, p. 159

[305] Following is an interesting aside from the Swedish Colonial Society web site. "Gloria Dei traces its roots to the church on Tinicum Island that was dedicated in 1646 by the distinguished missionary,

Johannes Campanius. His translation of Martin Luther's Small Catechism is the first book published in the Algonquin language, and his work among Native Americans was the first attempt by anyone in the original thirteen colonies to spread the Gospel among the native peoples. An existing blockhouse at Wicaco, in south Philadelphia was renovated for worship in 1677 and both sites were used for worship until the present building on the Wicaco site was consecrated on the First Sunday after Trinity, July 2, 1700. It is the oldest church in Pennsylvania and a National Historic site." See http://www. colonialswedes.org/Churches/GloDei.html.

306 Hotten, John Camden, *The Original Lists of Persons of Quality; Emigrants; Religious Exiles; Political Rebels; Serving Men Sold for a Term of Years; Children Stolen; Maidens Pressed; and Others who went from Great Britain to the American Plantations 1600-1700*, Genealogical Publishing Company, Baltimore, 1880. Reprinted 1962.

307 Newman, *op. cit.*, p. 219

308 Proceedings of the Council of Maryland, 1687/8-1693, p. 23, Archives of Maryland Online, http://aomol.net/megafile/msa/speccol/sc2900/sc2908/000001/000008/html/am8--23.html

309 This is the Robert Hanson from whom the author descends.

310 Newman, *op. cit.*, p. 220

311 Internet reference without source noted. From *Trevor Hanson's Genealogy Miscellanea*, btinternet.com

312 Manley, Reverend F. H., "Notes on the History of Great Somerford," *The Wiltshire Archaeological and Natural History Magazine*, volume XXXI, no. XCV, June, 1901, pp. 283-330

313 See http://www.msa.md.gov/msa/speccol/sc2600/sc2685/html/gov06.html for dates of service of these three governors. See Newman, op. cit., p. 220 and p. 224 for the Luke Barber citations.

314 Johnson, Amandus, *Swedish Contributions to American National Life, 1638-1921*, Committee of the Swedish Section of America's Making, New York, 1921, pp. 42-43

315 Newman, *op. cit.*, p. 220

316 Hanson, *op. cit.*, p. 71

317 Newman, *op. cit.*, p. 220

318 Johnson, Amandus, *Swedish Contributions to American National Life, 1638-1921*, Committee of the Swedish Section of America's Making, New York, 1921, p. 46

319 The John Hanson biographies of Smith, Kremer, Nelson and Levering, respectively.

320 http://familytreemaker.genealogy.com/users/h/o/d/Walter-G-Hodge-Cincinnati/

321 Mackenzie *op. cit*, and George Hanson *op. cit.*

322 Hanson, *op. cit.*, pp. 111-112

---

323 Smith, *op. cit.*, pp. 25-26.

324 *Ibid.*, pp. 28-29

325 Kremer, op. cit., p. 64-65.

326 *Council and Burgesses to the King, Bishops and Clergy of the 1600s*

327 Cummings, John, personal communication to the author (email), February 12, 2009.

328 *Ibid.*

329 Craig, *op. cit.*

330 *The News* and *The Post* were Frederick, Maryland, newspapers which during dates cited here were under the same ownership. The two newspapers often published the same articles until merger into the single publication, *The Frederick News-Post,* in 2002. *The Post* was renamed *The Frederick Post* prior to the merger.

Made in the USA
Monee, IL
04 December 2022

19638247R10260